Pascal Programming

Second Edition

B.J.Holmes B.Sc,M.Sc,MBCS,Cert.Ed.

Principal Lecturer in the
Department of Computing and Mathematical Sciences,
Oxford Polytechnic, Headington, Oxford, OX3 0BP

DP PUBLICATIONS LTD
Aldine Place, 142/144 Uxbridge Road,
Shepherds Bush Green, London W12 8AW

1990

In memory of my sister-in-law, Valerie Devereux (June 1954 - October 1989), who took a keen interest in my writing.

Trademark Acknowledgements

Hercules is a registered trademark of Hercules Computer Technology, Inc.
IBM is a registered trademark of the International Business Machines Corporation
Scrabble is a trademark of Spear's games
Sheffield Pascal is a product of Sheffield University.
Turbo Pascal is a trademark of Borland International, Inc.

Disclaimer

The programs presented in this book have been included for their instructional value. They have been computer-tested with considerable care and are not guaranteed for any particular purpose. The author does not offer any warranties or representations, nor does he accept any liabilities with respect to the programs.

A CIP catalogue record for this book is available from the British Library

First Edition 1987
Reprinted 1988
Second Edition 1990
Reprinted 1991, 1992
ISBN 1 870941 65 9

© 1990 B.J. Holmes

Typeset and illustrated by B.J. Holmes

Printed in Great Britain by
The Guernsey Press Co Ltd
Guernsey, Channel Islands

Contents

Preface

The aim of this book is to help the reader acquire and develop the skill of computer programming in a block-structured language and foster an understanding of the related topics of data structures and data processing.

Pascal Programming can be regarded as a complete text on programming and the use of data structures. The contents are sufficient to give confidence to any reader who is studying Computer Studies to GCE Advanced level, BTEC National and Higher National awards, first year undergraduate level and British Computer Society Part One examinations.

The book is also ideally suited to those requiring a knowledge of programming, yet whose major course of study is not computing, for example, engineering students and those requiring a self-study course. The book should also prove useful as a primer for those readers who can already program in other languages, yet wish to learn Pascal in the shortest possible time.

In writing Pascal Programming the author has included the following features.

The material is computer-tested and classroom-tested to guarantee its reliability and use as a teaching text.

No previous knowledge of computer programming or computer concepts is assumed.

The development of the language statements and programs are taken in manageable steps to enable the reader to build a firm foundation of knowledge. The type of programming examples used in both the text and self-test questions are simple enough to give the reader confidence at each stage of learning the language. The text is full of documented worked examples and exercises with answers.

The text contains a comprehensive appraisal of many important topics found in data structures - arrays, records, linked lists, queues, stacks and trees; and in data processing - sorting, searching, merging, file maintenance and data validation.

New trends in software development through the use of data abstraction and object-oriented programming have also been included.

All the programs in this book have been compiled and tested using Turbo Pascal 5.5, on a PC compatible microcomputer. However, throughout the text, the reader is directed to the differences between this dialect and that of Sheffield Pascal, which conforms more to Standard Pascal. The purpose behind this comparison is to enable all of the programs found in the first sixteen chapters to be implemented in other dialects of Pascal that form some resemblance to Standard Pascal.

The book is equally suitable as a course text or a self-instruction text. Questions are provided at the end of most of the chapters for readers to test their knowledge on the topics found in the chapters. The answers to selected self-test questions are given in the first appendix.

Those questions where the answers require original thought and development, and can be used for coursework or homework, have the answers available in a separate Answer Supplement. In addition to the Answer Supplement, all the illustrative programs found in the text, are also supplied on a PC-compatible disc. The immediate availability of these programs saves the time needed to accurately key the programs into the computer, and allows them to be used for demonstrations and development purposes by lecturers and students. Both the Answer Supplement and the disc, are available free of charge, only to lecturers and teachers using this book as a course text.

Every chapter contains a summary section, including a list of keywords. This provides a precis on the contents of each chapter and acts as a check-list of topics that should be understood before the reader progresses to the next chapter.

Within a single book there is enough information to provide a foundation for any reader who wishes to develop and implement a wide variety of software systems in Pascal.

Notes on the Second Edition.
In writing a new edition of Pascal Programming the author has included the following changes.

Every chapter from the first edition has been re-written.

The number of chapters has been increased from fifteen to twenty. There are new chapters on recursion, sorting and searching, dynamic data structures, object-oriented programming and case studies.

Chapters contain computer-generated illustrations to help explain the topics found in the text.

Greater emphasis has been placed on the use of Turbo Pascal.

To demonstrate the use of the Pascal language statements, the text contains seventy-five documented programs.

There are one hundred and twenty questions, to which answers are supplied, either in the appendix or in the Answer Supplement, available free of charge to lecturers adopting the book as a course text.

BJH, Oxford, July 1991.

1

Computer Environment

The purpose of this chapter is to describe a typical computer environment for the development of Pascal programs. The reader will be introduced to equipment and programs that make up a computer system, and the stages in the production of a program.

1.1 Programs, Data and Results.

A computer program is a series of coded instructions for the computer to obey and represents a method of processing the data.

Data is the name given to facts. For example, in a business the number of hours worked by employees or the level of items of stock represent data. Data is input to a computer, processed under the direction of a program into results that are output in the form of say, a payslip, or a report on out of stock items.

1.2 A Digital Computer.

A digital computer is an electronic machine capable of storing and obeying instructions at a very high speed. For example, an instruction can be obeyed in one hundred millionth of one second. The term digital implies that all information is represented by numbers within the computer. The numbers are stored as binary numbers, base 2, since it is convenient to physically represent the binary digits 1 and 0 as two respective voltage levels.

A digital computer is divided into two areas, the main memory and the central processing unit (CPU).

The main memory is used to temporarily store program instructions and data. A computer can only obey program instructions that are stored in the main memory.

The CPU consists of two sub-units, the arithmetic and logic unit (ALU) and the control unit. The ALU performs the processes of arithmetic, logical operations and comparisons on data. Whereas the control unit fetches the instructions from main memory, interprets and obeys them, and coordinates the flow of information about the computer system.

1.3 A Computer Model.

Figure 1.1 illustrates a computer model containing the CPU, main memory and in addition three other units, input, secondary storage and output units, known as peripheral units.

An input unit allows data and computer programs to be input into the computer model.

Since the main memory is only used to temporarily store programs and data, it is necessary to have secondary storage units to provide a permanent storage facility. Programs and data are transferred to and from the secondary storage units to the main memory only when they are required. The information is said to be on-line to the computer. The rate of transfer of information is fast and the speed is dependent upon the type of secondary storage unit being used.

In order to transfer results from the main memory and secondary storage units to the outside world it is necessary to provide an output unit.

1.4 Input and Output Units.

The most popular input unit used in computer systems is a keyboard. The keyboard consists of keys similar to those of a typewriter; both data and programs can be input into the computer by depressing the appropriate keys. A television screen or monitor can be used to simultaneously display the information that is being typed into a computer. Such a display is meant to provide a means of visually checking that the correct information is being entered.

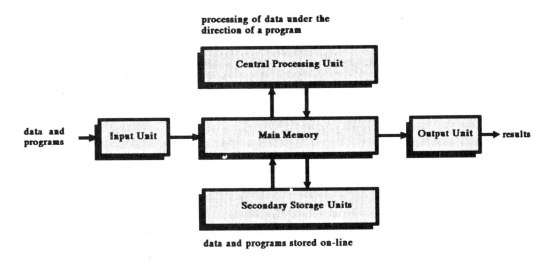

processing of data under the
direction of a program

Central Processing Unit

data and
programs

Input Unit

Main Memory

Output Unit   results

Secondary Storage Units

data and programs stored on-line

Figure 1.1 A Computer Model

A monitor has a dual function, as well as displaying the information that is typed at a keyboard it is also used as an output unit in its own right. Information that has been processed by a computer can also be displayed on a screen. A single input/output device called a visual display unit (VDU) combines both a keyboard and screen.

The major disadvantage of using a monitor as an output unit stems from the inability of the unit to provide a hard copy of the output. Because information on a printed page is so convenient it is necessary to include a printer as another output unit.

There are other types of input units, for example, card and paper tape readers were both common forms of input devices to computers in the 1960's and 70's. Programs and data were encoded by punching holes in paper tape or cards. Bar code readers are used to detect stock codes on supermarket merchandise. Magnetic ink character readers detect bank account numbers and branch codes on bank cheques. Optical character and mark readers are used to detect information written on documents.

Similarly, output units are not only limited to monitors and printers but can include graph and map plotters, synthesised speech units and digital to analogue output for controlling machinery.

1.5 Secondary Storage Units.
These units allow large quantities of information to be stored permanently on some form of magnetic medium such as magnetic tapes or discs. A standard reel of magnetic tape can store up to 40 million characters. A multiple platter magnetic disc pack can store up to 300 million characters. Both magnetic tape and disc units transfer information to, and receive information from, the CPU at speeds of many hundred thousand characters per second.

In recent years floppy disc and hard disc units have become popular secondary storage devices on many microcomputers. As well as varying in size, floppy disc storage capacity can range from approximately 100,000 characters to one million characters. Hard discs are permanently housed in a disc unit, unlike floppy discs that can be transferred between computers. The storage capacity of a hard disc will vary between 10 and 80 million characters, depending on the type of microcomputer system being used. Hard disc storage is also used on mini and mainframe computers with storage capacity in excess of that found on microcomputers. Such discs can be contained in either fixed or exchangeable disc-packs.

1.6 Computer Languages.

A computer language is a set of instructions used for writing computer programs. There are essentially three levels of language, high, low and machine.

Pascal is a high-level language, invented by Niklaus Wirth, a computer scientist at the Institute of Informatics in Zurich. In 1971 he published his language, named after the seventeenth-century French philosopher, Blaise Pascal, who had invented the first automatic adding machine. The language was slightly modified in response to user experience and released in a revised form in 1973. The following segment of code illustrates several statements in a Pascal program.

```
Read(TaxablePay);
IF TaxablePay < 1000 THEN
    tax:=0
ELSE
    tax:=TaxRate*TaxablePay;
{end if}
Write(tax:6:2);
```

As this example illustrates, high-level languages contain statements that are written in English words and symbols. Such languages are not designed specifically for any one brand of computer. A program written in Pascal to run on a PRIME computer that also runs on an IBM PC is said to be portable between the two computers. It must be said now that not all, if any, high-level languages are portable between computers, since computer manufacturers tend to enhance languages with different extra facilities. This enhancement of a language is a departure from the original definition or standard of the language and becomes a dialect of the language. With the more dialects of a language that exist and the difference in architectures between computers, the less portable the language is likely to be.

Low level languages contain statements that are written using mnemonic codes (codes suggesting their meaning and, therefore, easier to remember) to represent operations and addresses that relate to the main memory and storage registers of a computer. Each low level language has instructions which correspond closely to the inbuilt operations of a specific computer. Since different brands of computer use different low level languages a program written for one brand of computer will not run on another brand. Despite the many low level languages in existence they all adhere to the same broad principles of language structure. An example of statements from a typical low level language is:

```
LDA 5000
ADD 6000
STA 5000
```

This program segment adds two numbers and stores the result in a memory location! This type of programming is obviously not as clear as writing sum := sum + number; which is the equivalent operation in Pascal.

Machine level statements are even worse to mentally interpret. They are normally written using one of the number bases 2, 8 or 16. For example the program segment coded in base 2 binary as:

```
11011101 1011011
01001100 1011100
11011100 1011011
```

would require the aid of a reference manual in order to decipher the meaning of each code.

1.7 Language Translation.
A computer stores and uses information in a binary format, therefore, the computer cannot understand programs written in either high or low level languages. Program code written in either a high or low level language must be translated into a binary machine code that the computer recognises. Translation is possible by using a supplied program to translate high or low level language statements into machine code.

Translation to machine code from a high level language is by compiler, and from a low level language by assembler. The translator, compiler or assembler, is resident in the main memory of the computer and uses the high or low level program code as input data. The output from the translator is a program in machine readable code. In addition to translation, a compiler or assembler will report on any grammatical errors made by the programmer in the language statements of the program.

1.8 Operating Environment.
There are two methods of configuring a computer to run programs. However, the choice of method is dictated by the nature of the application the program has been written for.

Interactive processing allows a two-way communication between the user and the computer. If a program is being developed under such a system, changes can be made to the program and the effects immediately noted. This system of processing is common to all microcomputers and time-sharing systems.

Batch processing allows programs to be put into a queue and processed one after another. The programmer cannot intervene during the processing to perform amendments to the program as was possible during interactive processing. In batch processing a program must wait its turn before processing data. This necessarily means that there will be a delay in obtaining results. Consequently batch processing cannot be used when results are needed immediately. A suitable application for batch processing would be running a payroll program, where for example, details of hours worked by employees could be collected one week and processed as a batch to provide payslips the next week.

The reader should be aware that there exists a higher layer of software that controls the computer system above a user's program. Regardless of the mode of processing all computer systems are supplied with an operating system. The role of an operating system covers many areas, however, one important aspect is that of supervising the execution of user written programs. Such supervision includes the premature termination of user programs in the event of attempting to execute illegal operations such as dividing a number by zero or reading from a data file that had not been opened.

1.9 Program Development Environment.
Having given the reader an introduction into the fundamental components of a typical computing environment it is now possible to outline the specific requirements of an environment for the development of Pascal programs.

Hardware
Input: keyboard.
Output: monitor and printer.
Computer: a university or polytechnic environment will probably use a VAX, ICL, IBM or PRIME mini/mainframe configuration that supports a large number of users simultaneously. Alternatively, a desk-top microcomputer such as an IBM PC or Apple Macintosh can be used for a single user. In recent years a third configuration has become possible, where several microcomputers are networked together to share common secondary storage devices.

Secondary Storage: fixed or exchangeable hard discs if using a mini/mainframe system or floppy disc/ hard disc if using a microcomputer system.

Software
Editor: In order to type a Pascal program at the keyboard and save the program on a disc it will be necessary to run a program called an editor. In addition to program entry an editor allows a program to be retrieved from disc and amended as necessary. A Pascal program is stored in a text mode so that the programmer can read the program as it was written. No translation of the Pascal program to a machine recognisable form has been necessary at this stage.

Compiler: This will translate a Pascal program stored in text mode on disc to the program stored in a machine-oriented language on disc. There are several dialects of Pascal available, for example UCSD (developed at the University of California at San Diego), Sheffield Pascal (product of the University of Sheffield - Pascal system for PRIME computers), Turbo Pascal (software product of Borland International, Inc.), etc. Each dialect will have its own compiler for a specific brand of computer. A program written in Pascal for a PRIME computer would require translation using a Sheffield Pascal compiler. However, the same program, in text form, could be transferred to an IBM PC and translated into machine- oriented language using the Turbo Pascal compiler. Note the portability of the language only refers to the language in text mode not machine code.

Within the context of this book, all the programs have been developed using Turbo Pascal version 5.5 on an IBM PC compatible microcomputer. However, the majority of the programs, with the exception of those in the latter part of the book have been transferred to a PRIME minicomputer and compiled and run using a Sheffield Pascal compiler. The development of the programs in one environment and their implementation in another is meant to serve as an illustration of the portability of the version of Pascal being used.

Link/Loader: Before a compiled Pascal program can be run or executed by the computer it must be converted into an executable form. One function of the link/loader is to take the machine-oriented program and combine it with any necessary software (already in machine-oriented form) to enable the program to be run. For example, input and output routines that are supplied by the system will need linking into the program to allow data to be input at a keyboard and results displayed on a monitor. The complete machine code program is then loaded into memory ready for execution.

Throughout the phases of editing, compilation, link/loading and running it is assumed that the reader will be using an interactive processing environment. The four phases illustrated in figure 1.2 summarise the stages necessary in the development of a Pascal program.

1.10 Summary.
A digital computer consists of input, output and secondary storage units that are peripheral to the central processing unit and main memory.

Data is input to the computer and processed under the direction of a program to produce results at an output unit.

There are three levels of computer language, high (Pascal language, etc), low (assembly level language) and machine code (binary patterns).

Programs written in a high-level language such as Pascal, must be compiled and link-loaded into memory before they can be executed on the computer.

The supervision of the running of a program on the computer is one of the tasks of the operating system.

Keywords

Software:

programs, data, results;
high, low and machine level languages;
compiler, assembler, editor, link/loader;
interactive and batch processing, operating systems;
portability.

Hardware:

digital computer, main memory, CPU, ALU;
peripheral units, keyboard, monitor, printer, magnetic tape
and disc units.

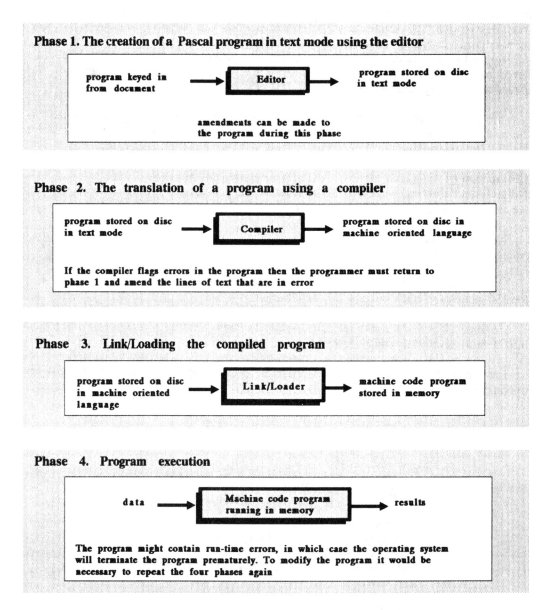

Figure 1.2 The four phases of program development

1.11 Questions.
1. What are the five major hardware units of a digital computer system?

[2]. List three input units and three output units. What are the most common input and output units in a Pascal development environment?

3. Why is it necessary to translate a Pascal program into a machine-oriented language?

4. List the four stages that are necessary before a Pascal program can be executed by a computer.

[5]. What is meant by program portability? Why are low level languages not considered to be portable?

Note. A question number printed within [ ] indicates that the answer is available in a separate Answer Supplement, only available from DP Publications Ltd, to lecturers and teachers using this book as a course text.

2

Data

This chapter serves to introduce the reader to three types of data, integers (whole numbers), reals (numbers with a decimal fraction) and characters. The methods for declaring these types of data and documenting their meaning in a Pascal program is also examined.

2.1 Memory.

The memory of a computer is made up from many thousands of storage cells called bytes. Each byte is capable of storing eight bits (binary digits) and has a unique address in the memory of a computer. Figure 2.1 illustrates a segment of memory showing the contents of bytes and their addresses.

addresses	bytes
9999	01101101
9998	10010010
9997	11011101
9996	01111011
:	:
0000	10011100

Figure 2.1 The representation of addressable bytes in the main memory

When the size of a computer memory is quoted as being, say, 256 Kbytes, this implies that there are 262,144 memory cells. The prefix K is taken to be 1024 and not 1000.

2.2 Integers.

Integers are stored within a fixed number of bytes. A common size for integer storage is two bytes, which gives the range of integers that can be stored as -32768 to +32767. Any integer that lies outside this range cannot be stored in the memory of the computer as an integer. A representation of the integer 1225 in two bytes is shown in figure 2.2.

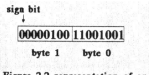

sign bit

```
00000100 11001001
```
byte 1   byte 0

Figure 2.2 representation of an integer in two bytes of memory

This is known as a pure binary representation of the number. Each bit represents a multiple of 2, with the rightmost bit of byte 0 having a value of 1, the next bit a value of 2, the next a value of 4, the next a value of 8, and so on. Summing only those bits that are set at 1, in figure 2.2, results in 1+8+64+128+1024=1225. Notice that the leftmost bit of byte 1 is reserved as the sign bit. A sign bit set at 0 represents a positive number, and set at 1 represents a negative number. Negative numbers are stored using a 2's complement representation. For example the number -1225 will be stored using the following bit pattern.

+1225 = 00000100 11001001
1's complement = 11111011 00110110 interchange 1's and 0's
2's complement = 11111011 00110111 add 1 to rightmost bit

The result of this bit manipulation is a two byte representation of -1225. Notice that the sign bit has been automatically set to 1. Larger integers than those stated, can be stored, provided the number of bytes used to store the integers is increased. Many computers use long integer storage by increasing the number of bytes to four. This gives an effective storage range of -2147483648 to + 2147483647.

Turbo Pascal distinguishes between short integers stored in 1 byte; integers stored in 2 bytes; and long integers stored in 4 bytes.

2.3 Reals.

Real numbers are stored within a fixed number of bytes using a floating point representation of the number. The number of bytes can vary between four, six and eight, however, four is common. Real numbers have two parts, a mantissa (the fractional part) and an exponent (the power to which the base of the number must be raised in order to give the correct value of the number when multiplied by the mantissa). For example 437.875 can be re-written as 0.437875xE3, where 0.437875 is the mantissa, 3 the exponent and E represents the base 10, thus E3 is 10 cubed.

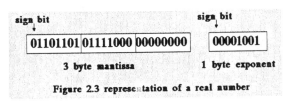

Figure 2.3 representation of a real number

The number +437.875 has a binary equivalent of 110110101.111 and when the binary point is floated to the left and exponent adjusted the number is represented as 0.1101101011111xB9, where B implies the base 2. The organisation of this number in a floating point representation is shown in figure 2.3.

The mantissa (f) must always lie in the ranges $0.5 <= f < 1$ for a positive fraction and $-1 <= f < -0.5$ for a negative fraction. It is then said to be normalised. Negative mantissas and exponents can be represented using the 2'complement technique described in the previous section.

This four byte organisation of a real number would permit real numbers to be stored in the range -1.7xE38 to +1.7xE38 with the smallest real number of 2.9xE-39 and return an accuracy of approximately 6 significant digits. The majority of decimal fractions do not convert exactly into binary fractions, therefore, the representation of a real number is not always accurate. Accuracy of storage can be improved by using a greater number of bytes to represent the mantissa. For example, increasing the mantissa to four bytes gives an 11 significant digit accuracy.

Turbo Pascal distinguishes between real numbers stored in 6 bytes; single precision numbers stored in 4 bytes; double precision numbers stored in 8 bytes and extended precision numbers stored in 10 bytes. When the result of a computation is too large to be represented the number has overflowed storage. Most computers will signal an error if overflow occurs. Conversely, when a result is too small to be represented the number has underflowed storage, and the computer will probably return the result as zero.

2.4 Characters.

Characters are stored in the memory by using 7-bit binary codes. For example, the character A is coded 65, B is coded 66, C is coded 67 etc. The list of ASCII (American Standard Code for Information Interchange) character codes is given in table 2.1.

code	character	code	character	code	character
000	NUL	043	+	086	V
001	SOH	044	,	087	W
002	STX	045	-	088	X
003	ETX	046	.	089	Y
004	EOT	047	/	090	Z
005	ENQ	048	0	091	[
006	ACK	049	1	092	\
007	BEL	050	2	093	]
008	BS	051	3	094	^
009	HT	052	4	095	
010	LF	053	5	096	`
011	VT	054	6	097	a
012	FF	055	7	098	b
013	CR	056	8	099	c
014	SO	057	9	100	d
015	SI	058	:	101	e
016	DLE	059	;	102	f
017	DC1	060	<	103	g
018	DC2	061	=	104	h
019	DC3	062	>	105	i
020	DC4	063	?	106	j
021	NAK	064	@	107	k
022	SYN	065	A	108	l
023	ETB	066	B	109	m
024	AN	067	C	110	n
025	EM	068	D	111	o
026	SUB	069	E	112	p
027	ESC	070	F	113	q
028	FS	071	G	114	r
029	GS	072	H	115	s
030	RS	073	I	116	t
031	US	074	J	117	u
032	space	075	K	118	v
033	!	076	L	119	w
034	"	077	M	120	x
035	#	078	N	121	y
036	$	079	O	122	z
037	%	080	P	123	{
038	&	081	Q	124		
039	'	082	R	125	}
040	(	083	S	126	~
041	)	084	T	127	del
042	*	085	U		

Table 2.1 ASCII codes

The following diagram illustrates the storage of ABC in three bytes of memory using a pure binary representation. The most significant bit (leftmost) in each byte, known as a parity bit, is set at 0 unless the computer system specifically sets this bit to 1.

char	ASCII code	binary representation
A	65	01000001
B	66	01000010
C	67	01000011

Figure 2.4 representation of characters

2.5 Variables.

Data can be thought of as occupying areas of the computer's memory in the same way as people occupy houses in a street. To distinguish different families in different houses we could use either the surname of the family or the number of the house. To distinguish data in different areas of memory we could give the data a name or use the numeric memory address where the data is stored. In the Pascal language it is much easier to refer to data by name and let the computer do the work of finding out where in memory the data is stored. The following diagram illustrates that groups of bytes can be referenced by different data names that represent the stored data.

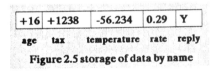

+16	+1238	-56.234	0.29	Y
age	tax	temperature	rate	reply

Figure 2.5 storage of data by name

When a program that uses these data names is executed, the instructions may change the contents of some, if not all, of the groups of bytes. Because of this change or variation in the data the data names are known as variables. A programmer is required to compose many different types of names in a program, of which variables are just one type. The collective name given to all these names is identifiers. Pascal uses the following rules for the composition of identifiers.

An identifier may contain combinations of letters of the alphabet (both upper case A-Z and lower case a-z) and decimal digits, provided the identifier begins with a letter. An identifier must not be the same as those Pascal words found in table 2.2

Identifiers can normally be of any length. The particular implementation of Pascal being used may only recognise up to a certain number of characters. The original Standard for the language specified that only the first eight characters of an identifier would be significant, however, Turbo Pascal recognises up to 63 characters. Although the upper and lower case letters can be used in an identifier, Pascal does not distinguish between the two cases. Turbo Pascal allows embedded underscores _ as part of the identifier. However, for the sake of the portability of the language the underscore will not be used in identifiers in this book.

A programmer should always compose identifiers so they convey the meaning of the data. The variables *age*, *tax*, *temperature*, *rate* and *reply* imply the meaning of the data they represent. When an identifier is constructed from more than one word, each word should begin with an upper case letter so that the identifier can be clearly read and its meaning understood. For example, *HigherRate*, *NormalRate*, *SalesExecutive*, and *EngineSize* are all legal identifiers.

Reserved Words

AND	END	MAXINT	REPEAT
ARRAY	FILE	MOD	SET
BEGIN	FOR	NOT	THEN
CASE	FORWARD	OF	TO
CONST	FUNCTION	OR	TYPE
DIV	GOTO	PACKED	UNTIL
DO	IF	PROCEDURE	VAR
DOWNTO	IN	PROGRAM	WHILE
ELSE	LABEL	RECORD	WITH

Special Identifiers

BOOLEAN	NIL
CHAR	OUTPUT
FALSE	REAL
INPUT	TEXT
INTEGER	TRUE

Predefined Functions

ABS	ARCTAN	CHR	COS
EOF	EOLN	EXP	LN
ODD	ORD	PRED	ROUND
SIN	SQR	SQRT	SUCC
TRUNC			

Predefined Procedures

DISPOSE	GET	NEW	PUT
Read	ReadLn	RESET	Rewrite
Write	WriteLn		

Table 2.2 Words that must not be used as identifiers

2.6 Variable Declaration.

A Pascal program can be classified into two parts, data declarations and instruction sequences. The data declarations must appear before the instruction sequences since they describe the attributes of the data used by the instructions. All the variables that are used by the instructions must be declared. For example:

VAR
      mileage : INTEGER; {distance to travel to work}
      allowance : REAL; {travel allowance per mile}
      reply : CHAR; {answer Y or N}
      CarAllowance : REAL; {gross car allowance}
      expenses : REAL; {monthly travelling expenses}

The abbreviation **VAR** only appears once. Each variable declaration consists of:

variable : data type ; comment

The data types are described as either integer, real or char (character) and conform to their descriptions in the earlier sections of this chapter. Any text contained between {} or (* *) on the same line will be ignored by the compiler and can be used as a comment. The use of comments is optional, however, it is good practice to document the meaning of each variable.

2.7 Constant Declaration.

In many programs there will be data values that do not change, but remain constant during program execution. Examples of items of data that remain constant could be Value Added Tax (15%), mathematical pi (3.14159) and the symbol for percent (%). Such constants would be declared in a Pascal program as:

CONST
      vat = 15; {current rate of Value Added Tax}
      pi = 3.14159; {mathematical pi}
      percent = '%'; {a character is declared between apostrophes}

The abbreviation **CONST** only appears once. Each constant declaration consists of:

variable = literal ; comment

The data type associated with each constant is inherent in the value of the constant, 15 is an integer, 3.14159 is a real and % is a character. Should the rate of vat change in the life of the program the only amendment necessary to the program would be to the line vat = 15; no further changes would be necessary to vat in the instructions. Although the value of pi and percent could be written as the literals 3.14159 and %, respectively, in the instructions, the programmer will, as a matter of convenience, find it easier to use pi and percent as meaningful identifiers in the program.

2.8 Data Declaration.

There is a set order for declaring constants and variables in a Pascal program. The format for data declaration at the beginning of a program is:

```
PROGRAM name (INPUT, OUTPUT);
{begin declarations}
CONST
VAR
{end declarations}
```

where the name given to the program must conform to the rules of composition for identifiers and the function of (INPUT, OUTPUT) is to declare the input of data at the keyboard and output of results to the screen of a monitor or VDU.

In the following example a bicycle shop in Oxford hires bicycles by the day at different rates throughout the year according to the season.

season	code	charge £
Spring Mar-May	A	1.00
Summer June-Aug	B	1.50
Autumn Sept-Nov	C	0.75
Winter Dec-Feb	D	0.50

The proprietor also gives a discount on the number of days a bicycle is hired. If the hire period is greater than 7 days then a reduction of 25% is made. For every bicycle hired a deposit of £5.00 must be paid. Since the charges described are likely to change over a period of years it is wise to code each charge as a constant. The data that is input to the computer will be the season code (A,B,C or D) and the number of days hire. The result that is output will be the complete hire charge taking into account the number of days hire, seasonal charge and deposit. Code a complete data declaration to a Pascal program.

```
PROGRAM hire (INPUT, OUTPUT);

{begin declarations}
CONST
        spring = 1.0; {hire charge Mar-May}
        summer = 1.5; {hire charge June-Aug}
        autumn = 0.75; {hire charge Sept-Nov}
        winter = 0.5; {hire charge Dec-Feb}
        period = 7; {number of days to attract discount}
        discount = 0.25; {25% discount}
        deposit = 5; {£5 deposit paid on hire}

VAR
        season : CHAR; {A-spring, B-summer, C-Autumn, D-Winter}
        days : INTEGER; {number of days hire}
        charge : REAL; {cost of hiring bicycle}
{end declarations}
```

2.9 Summary.

The fundamental data types are integer, real and char.

The ranges of integers and real numbers that can be stored in a computer's memory are dependent upon the number of bytes used to represent the numbers.

The formation of programmer defined names, known as identifiers, must conform to the rules of composition.

The program name, constants and variables must be defined at the beginning of a program.

Keywords

byte, bit;
integer, pure binary representation;
real, mantissa, exponent, floating point;
overflow, underflow;
character, ASCII;
identifier, variable, constant, literal;
data declaration;
INTEGER, REAL, CHAR, CONST, VAR.

2.10 Questions.

[1]. How would the integer +7384 be expressed in a pure binary form using 16 bits? What is the 16 bit representation of -7384?

[2]. If a computer stored real numbers to an accuracy of 9 significant decimal digits and a signed 2 digit exponent in the range 0 to 38, comment upon the representation of the following data.

    a. 3.7948xE16   b. -2.6394782   c. 739.4621348   d. -17694.327xE35
    e. 0.000000471xE-34

3. Using table 2.1 what are the ASCII codes for the following characters?

    A M * a m / ? BEL NUL 9

[4]. Derive the 8-bit binary representation of the three characters * 7 z with the parity bit set to 1.

5. Identify the illegal variable names in the following list. State why you think the names are illegal.

    a. PriceofBricks   b. net-pay   c. X1 d. cost of paper
    e. ReadLn   f. ?X?Y   g. 1856AD

6. Consider the following rules for calculating income tax in a country.

Personal allowances are £1,200 for a single person and £2,300 for a married man. A child allowance is £100 per child. Taxable income is the amount remaining after deducting the personal allowance and total child allowance from the gross salary. Income tax is calculated from taxable income according to the following table.

taxable income on	% tax
first £1,000	no tax
next £1,000	20%
next £2,000	30%
above £4,000	40%

If gross salary, personal status (m-married, s-single) and the number of children are input to the computer, income tax is calculated and output from the computer, code a complete data declaration to a Pascal Program.

3

Instruction Sequence

This chapter contains work on data arithmetic, the input of data at a keyboard and the output of results to a screen. The development of a sequence of instructions is also explained. By the end of the chapter the reader will have enough knowledge to be able to write a Pascal program.

3.1 Assignment.

In section 1.7 it was stated that the Pascal statement *sum := sum + number* was clearer to write and understand than equivalent low level language statements. To a novice the statement may seem a little strange since the variable *sum* appears on both sides of the equation. Following the rules of algebra it would normally be possible to cancel the variable *sum* on both sides, leaving *number* equal to zero. Clearly the assumption that the statement is an equation is wrong. The symbol := is an assignment operator and the statement *sum := sum + number* implies add the current value of *sum* to the current value of *number* and replace *sum* on the left-hand side with the result. The following diagram shows two integers stored in *sum* and *number* before the execution of the assignment statement.

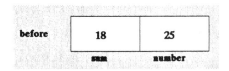

After the statement has been executed the new value of *sum* is 43 and the previous value of *sum* has been overwritten or destroyed.

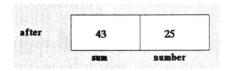

Notice that the original value stored in *number* has not changed.

Similar before and after situations can be applied to other computations to illustrate the use of assignment, where the symbols + - * / represent the operations of addition, subtraction, multiplication and division respectively.

```
A := B + C + D    A  B  C  D
       before    15  2  3  4
       after      9  2  3  4

X := Y - Z        X  Y  Z
       before    21 16  9
       after      7 16  9

wage := hours * rate   wage  hours  rate
          before       250    40    10
          after        400    40    10

mean := sum / count    mean  sum   count
          before       2.5   36.0  10.0
          after        3.6   36.0  10.0

TempStore := alpha    TempStore  alpha
          before          C        A
          after           A        A
```

```
counter := 0        counter
        before        9
        after         0

character := 'X'    character
        before        %
        after         X
```

In this last example the character being assigned must be delimited between two apostrophes.

The destination of a result will always be on the left-hand side of an assignment. Therefore A:=9 implies that A is assigned the value 9. The statement 9:=A has no meaning since 9 is an illegal variable name. However, A:=B would imply that A is assigned the value of B, whereas, B:=A would imply that B is assigned the value of A. In order to exchange the values of the two variables A and B it is necessary to introduce a third, temporary variable T.

T:=A {duplicates the value of A in T}
A:=B {overwrites the value of A with the value of B}
B:=T {overwrites the value of B with the value of T}

Hence the original contents of A and B have been exchanged.

Because the mode of storing integers and reals differs it is necessary to consider the resultant data type of an expression containing both types of variables. The following table summarises these data types.

expression contains	resultant data type
integers only	INTEGER
reals only	REAL
both integer and real	REAL

There are exceptions to this summary. If an expression contains integer division (14/4) the result is real since (3.5) cannot be represented as an integer. However, if a programmer required an answer of 3 remainder 2 then two further operators DIV (quotient) and MOD (remainder) would be necessary. For example, 14 DIV 4 gives the quotient 3 and 14 MOD 4 gives the remainder 2. Both MOD and DIV only have integer operands.

Further, if variables I and R are of type integer and real, respectively, the assignment:

R := I is valid

since this implies a change in the mode of storage. The magnitude of an integer can be represented as a real number, there is no difference in magnitude between the integer (2) and the real (2.0). However, the assignment:

I := R is invalid

since the modes of storing reals and integers are quite different. How would (2.5) be represented as an integer?

When the expression is real and the result needs to be stored as an integer then two functions TRUNC and ROUND can be used to either truncate the result to the next integer towards zero or round the result to the nearest integer. TRUNC(-3.5) = -3, TRUNC(3.5) = 3, ROUND(-3.5) = -4 and ROUND(3.5) = 4.

3.2 Operator Precedence.

If an expression was written as A + B * C - D / E how would it be evaluated? There is a need to introduce a set of rules for the evaluation of such expressions. All operators have an associated hierarchy that determines the order of precedence for evaluating an expression. The following list of operators summarises this hierarchy.

operator	priority
unary - e.g. -1	highest
* / MOD DIV	
+ -	lowest

Expressions are evaluated by taking the operators with the highest priority before those of a lower priority. Where operators are of the same priority the expression is evaluated from left to right. Expressions in parenthesis will be evaluated before non-parenthesised expressions. Parenthesis, although not an operator, can be considered as having an order of precedence after unary minus, for example -b.

The expression A + B * C - D / E can be evaluated by inspecting the operators and grouping operations according to the above rules. The numbers in the diagram indicate the order of evaluation. The equivalent algebraic expression is given at each stage of the evaluation.

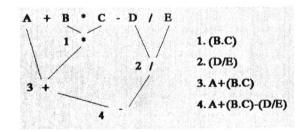

1. (B.C)
2. (D/E)
3. A+(B.C)
4. A+(B.C)-(D/E)

The expression (X * X + Y * Y) / (A + B) can be evaluated in the same way.

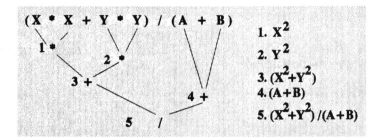

The reader should adopt the habit of using parenthesis in order to make the meaning of an expression as clear as possible. For example, the algebraic expression: U.V / W.X is written in Pascal as U*V/W/X, however, (U*V)/(W*X) is easier to understand. Similary,

$$X^2 + Y^2 + \frac{4.(X + Y)}{Z^2}$$

would be written in Pascal as: (X*X)+(Y*Y)+4*(X+Y)/(Z*Z).

3.3 Input of Data.
The statement ReadLn(input list) allows data, consistent with the type of variables in the input list, to be typed at the keyboard and stored in memory. For example,

    ReadLn(HoursWorked)

would enable the value, say, *38.5 return* to be entered at a keyboard. The end of the line of data is indicated by depressing the *return* or *entry* key on a keyboard. After the execution of this statement HoursWorked would be set at 38.5.

If it was required to input more than one variable on one line then the input list would contain as many variables as necessary, separated by commas. However, the input data are separated by a space or spaces.

    ReadLn(HoursWorked, RateOfPay)

when executed would expect two items of data on one line, such as: 38.5 5.5 *return* After the execution of the statement HoursWorked would be set at 38.5 and RateOfPay at 5.5.

3.4 Output of Results.
The statement WriteLn(output list) allows the values of variables to be displayed on one line of a screen. For example,

    WriteLn(HoursWorked, RateOfPay)

would display *3.85000E+01 5.50000E+00* on one line. E is used to signify the exponent of the number with a base of 10.

It is possible to output messages to a screen by replacing the variable output list by a string of characters. A string is a sequence of ASCII characters enclosed between a pair of apostrophes.

WriteLn('input hours worked = >')

would display the prompt *input hours worked = >* on one line of a screen. WriteLn without an output list would generate a blank line.

A list of variables and strings of characters, separated by commas, can be combined in the output list of a WriteLn statement.

WriteLn('hours = ', HoursWorked, ' rate = ', RateOfPay)

would display *hours = 3.85000E+01 rate = 5.50000E+00* on a screen.

Note: after the execution of a WriteLn statement a new line is automatically generated. If it is necessary to suppress the generation of a new line a Write statement can be used. For example, the following statements:

Write('input number of hours worked = >');
ReadLn(HoursWorked);
Write('input hourly rate of pay = >');
ReadLn(RateOfPay);

would result in the following display on a screen.

input number of hours worked = >38.5
input hourly rate of pay = >5.5

where 38.5 *return* and 5.5 *return* have been typed in response to the prompts.

3.5 Formatted Output.
The format of numeric data on a screen corresponds to the manner in which it is stored. In the example given in the last section real numbers were displayed with mantissas and exponents. This form of notation is not as common as that used to input the two real numbers 38.5 and 5.5. A further refinement can be made to the output list by specifying the field width (maximum number of characters including digits, decimal point and operational sign that are to be displayed) and the number of decimal places to be output. Thus *HoursWorked:4:1* would display a number inside a field width of 4 characters with 1 decimal place. Similarly, *RateOfPay:4:2* would display a number inside a field width of 4 characters with 2 decimal places.

WriteLn('hours = ',HoursWorked :4:1, ' rate = ', RateOfPay :4:2)

would display *hours = 38.5 rate = 5.50*

If the number to be output is of type integer, only the field width need be declared.

3.6 Compound Statement.
A computer will execute one statement after another in a program until instructed to do otherwise. The Pascal language allows program statements to be bracketed by the words *BEGIN* and *END* into a compound statement so that all the statements between these words

will be executed in sequence. Syntactically a compound statement can be regarded as one statement. When a compound statement is used to define the instruction sequence of a Pascal program *END* must be terminated with a full-stop (period). The statements within a compound statement are separated from each other by a semi- colon. However, the use of a semi-colon is optional after the last statement before *END*.

```
{begin sequence}
BEGIN
        {Pascal language statements}
END.
{end sequence}
```

In a problem to calculate the gross wage of an employee a sequence of statements to: input the HoursWorked, input the RateOfPay, calculate the GrossWage and display the result can be coded by the following instructions.

```
{begin sequence}
BEGIN
        Write('input number of hours worked = >');
        ReadLn(HoursWorked);
        Write('input hourly rate of pay = >');
        ReadLn(RateOfPay);
        GrossWage := HoursWorked * RateOfPay;
        WriteLn('gross weekly wage £', GrossWage :6:2);
END.
{end sequence}
```

When data declarations are combined with the last instruction sequence a complete Pascal program will have been written.

```
PROGRAM wages(INPUT, OUTPUT);
{begin declarations}
VAR
        HoursWorked :REAL; {number of hours worked per week}
        RateOfPay :REAL; {hourly rate of pay}
        GrossWage :REAL; {weekly wage before deductions}
{end declarations}
{begin sequence}
BEGIN
        Write('input number of hours worked = >');
        ReadLn(HoursWorked);
        Write('input hourly rate of pay = >');
        ReadLn(RateOfPay);
        GrossWage := HoursWorked * RateOfPay;
        WriteLn('gross weekly wage £', GrossWage :6:2);
END. {wages}
{end sequence}
```

This program was written using an editor, stored on disc, compiled, link/loaded and run as explained in the first chapter.

You are advised to consult the Pascal and Operating System manuals for your computer in order to be able to edit, compile, link/load and run the programs that are given in this book.

```
Results from program being run

input number of hours worked = > 35.0
input hourly rate of pay = > 10.00
gross weekly wage £350.00
```

3.7 Worked Examples.
Problem. Write a program to display the Morse Code for SOS. This program has no input data, therefore, only output to the screen is required, hence, PROGRAM morse(OUTPUT). Since the identifiers *dot* and *dash* do not represent data that change during the lifetime of the program they can both together with the identifier space be represented as constants.

```pascal
PROGRAM morse(OUTPUT);
{begin declarations}
CONST
      dot = '.'; {Morse Code dot}
      dash = '-'; {Morse Code dash}
      space = ' '; {space used to separate groups of Morse Codes}
{end declarations}
{begin sequence}
BEGIN
      WriteLn('Morse Code for SOS'); WriteLn;
      WriteLn(dot,dot,dot,space,dash,dash,dash,space,dot,dot,dot);
END. {morse}
{end sequence}
```

```
Results from program being run

Morse Code for SOS

...   ---   ...
```

Problem. A person buys three newspapers, the Courier, Globe and Mercury. Write a program to input the cost in pence of each newspaper, calculate the total cost in (£) and average cost in (p) and display the result of these two computations.

If the cost of each paper is input in pence then the variable names *Courier, Globe* and *Mercury* can be declared as type INTEGER. The total cost, variable *TotalPounds*, will contain a decimal fraction and therefore be of type REAL. Since the average cost of newspapers is the result of dividing the total cost by 3, the variable *average* must also be of type REAL.

```
PROGRAM newspapers(INPUT, OUTPUT);
{begin declarations}
VAR
        Courier : INTEGER; {price of Courier newspaper}
        Globe : INTEGER; {price of Globe newspaper}
        Mercury : INTEGER; {price of Mercury newspaper}
        TotalPence : INTEGER; {total cost of three newspapers (p)}
        TotalPounds : REAL; {total cost (£)}
        average : REAL; {average cost of newspapers (p)}
{end declarations}
{begin sequence}
BEGIN
        Write('input cost of Courier = >');
        ReadLn(Courier);
        Write('input cost of Globe = >');
        ReadLn(Globe);
        Write('input cost of Mercury = >');
        Readln(Mercury);
        TotalPence := Courier + Globe + Mercury;
        TotalPounds := TotalPence / 100;
        average := TotalPence / 3;
        WriteLn('total cost of papers £', TotalPounds :4:2);
        WriteLn('average cost of papers ', average :4:1, 'p');
END. {newspapers}
{end sequence}
```

> *Results from program being run*
>
> input cost of Courier = > 25
> input cost of Globe = > 30
> input cost of Mercury = > 35
> total cost of papers £0.90
> average cost of papers 30.0 p

Problem. In the final example, write a program to solve the following problem. The dimensions of a living room in a house are 7m long, 5m wide and 2.5m high. The room has a window area of 3 square metres and a door area of 1.5 square metres. Write a program to input the dimensions of the room and calculate the area of available wall space. If 1 litre of emulsion will cover 25 square metres, calculate and display the number of one litre tins required to emulsion the walls of the room.

In this problem the window and door areas, and the area of coverage of a tin of emulsion can be treated as constants. Since the problem requests that the dimensions of the room are to be input at the keyboard, the length, width and height should be treated as variables of type REAL. Before the number of tins of emulsion can be calculated it would be useful, but not necessary, to calculate the area of the walls to be emulsioned. This variable will again be of type REAL. If it is assumed that only 1 litre tins of emulsion can be used then the number of tins will be of type INTEGER. In calculating the number of tins to purchase it will be necessary to adjust the result of dividing the wall area by emulsion coverage to give a whole number of tins, otherwise, the calculation will result in fractional parts of a tin of emulsion. If the smallest amount of paint used is 1mL from a tin, then a constant of 0.999 should be added to the theoretical number of tins before the result is truncated.

```
PROGRAM TinsOfEmulsion(INPUT, OUTPUT);
{begin declarations}
CONST
        EmulsionCover=25.0;
        WindowArea=3.0;
        DoorArea=1.5;
VAR
        length, width, height : REAL;
        WallArea:REAL;
        tins:INTEGER;
{end declarations}
{begin sequence}
BEGIN
        Write('input length = >'); ReadLn(length);
        Write('input width = >'); ReadLn(width);
        Write('input height = >'); ReadLn(height);
        WallArea:=2.0*height*(length+width)-(WindowArea+DoorArea);
        tins:=TRUNC((WallArea/EmulsionCover)+0.999);
        WriteLn('number of tins to purchase =',tins:2);
END. {TinsOfEmulsion}
{end sequence}
```

Results from program being run

input length => 10.0
input width => 10.0
input height => 10.0
number of tins to purchase = 16

3.8 Syntax Diagrams.
A syntax diagram is a pictorial method of representing the format of components in a programming language. The direction of the arrowed lines indicates the order in which the diagram is to be read. In tracing through a diagram it is possible for the lines to branch into several directions. Such a branch shows that there is a choice of components at that particular

point in the diagram. Components on the diagram that are represented in circular or oval symbols are *terminal* components. These components, unlike components represented in square or rectangular symbols, cannot be represented by further syntax diagrams. The diagram that follows depicts the syntax of a program. The words *program, begin* and *end*, and the symbols () , ; . are all terminal symbols. Whereas *identifier, declarations* and *statement* can all be represented by other syntax diagrams.

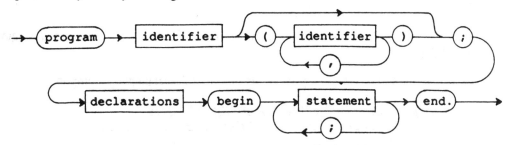

The syntax diagram for an identifier is defined as:

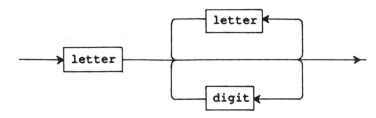

and the syntax diagram for an assignment statement as:

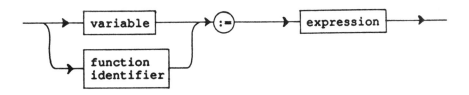

For a complete guide to the syntax diagrams associated with Standard Pascal, the reader should study the syntax diagrams, given in the second appendix, in conjunction with the chapters that describe the semantics of the language statements.

3.9 Summary.
The variable to be assigned a value is the only identifier that appears on the left-hand side of the assignment statement.

The data type on the left-hand side should be the same as the resultant data type on the right-hand side of an assignment statement. However, there are exceptions to this rule, as indicated in the text.

The operands in an arithmetic expression are evaluated according to the rule of priority given to their operators.

In addition to the four operators +, -, * and /, there are the operators MOD, DIV, ROUND, and TRUNC.

Input of data is with the *ReadLn* statement. The output of results and text is with the *Write* and *WriteLn* statements.

Statements can be grouped together between *BEGIN* and *END* to form a single compound statement.

A syntax diagram can be used to represent the format of Pascal language components.

> **Keywords**
>
> *assignment:=, arithmetic expression;*
> *operators (* / MOD DIV + -), ROUND, TRUNC,*
> *operator precedence;*
> *ReadLn, WriteLn, Write, formatted output;*
> *compound statement, BEGIN..END, instruction sequence;*
> *syntax diagrams.*

3.10 Questions.

1. What are the values of the following variables after the execution of the respective assignments?

a.   B := A;   A B C D
     C := A;   36 98 45 29
     D := A;

b.   D := A + B + C + D;   A B C D
                            10 14 29 36

c.   A := B - 2;   A B
                      17 50

d.   Y := X - Y;   X Y
                      19 32

e.   Z := X * Y;   X Y Z
                      18 3 27

f.   B := B / A;   A   B
                      12.5 25.0

g.   X := A DIV B;   A   B   X
                      16   3   25

h. $Y := C \bmod D$;   C D Y
                              18 5 2

i. $K := \text{ROUND}(H)$ K   H
                              18 -36.54

j. $D := \text{TRUNC}(E)$ D   E
                              34 -16.9

[2]. How are the following expressions written in Pascal?

a. $\dfrac{A + B}{C}$ b. $\dfrac{W - X}{Y + Z}$ c. $\dfrac{D - B}{2A}$ d. $\dfrac{1}{2}(A.A + B.B)$

e. $(A - B)(C - D)$ f. $B.B - 4AC$ g. $AXX + BXX + C$

[3]. Find the errors in the following Pascal expressions.

a. AB   b. X*-Y   c. (64+B2)/-6   d. (A-B)(A+B)
e. -2 / A + -6 f. $\dfrac{1*(X-Y)}{2}$

[4]. Re-write the following Pascal expressions as algebraic expressions.

a. $X + 2 / Y + 4$ b. $A * B / (C + 2)$ c. $U / V * W / X$
d. $B * B - 4 * A * C$ e. $A / B + C / D + E / F$

5. In each of the following questions you are expected to write program, constant and data declarations to fit the sequence of instructions given. When you have completed the declarations for each program, file, compile and run the programs on your computer.

   a. The instruction sequence calculates the arithmetic mean of three integers and displays the result to an accuracy of two decimal places.

```
BEGIN
     Write('input three integers separated by spaces e.g. 2 5 7');
     WriteLn('then press the RETURN key');
     ReadLn(x,y,z);
     mean:=(x+y+z)/numbers;
     WriteLn('arithmetic mean of integers = ', mean:10:2);
END. {C3Q5a}
```

   b. The instruction sequence calculates the surface area and volume of a sphere.

```
BEGIN
     Write('input integer value for the radius of the sphere =>');
     ReadLn(radius);
     SurfaceArea:=4*pi*radius*radius;
```

```
        volume:=SurfaceArea*radius/3;
        WriteLn('surface area of sphere =',SurfaceArea:10:2);
        WriteLn('volume of sphere =',volume:10:2);
END. {C3Q5b}
```

c. The instruction sequence prepares a sales invoice.

```
BEGIN
        WriteLn('SALES INVOICE'); WriteLn; WriteLn;
        Write('input cost of item 1');ReadLn(item1);
        Write('input cost of item 2');ReadLn(item2);
        Write('input cost of item 3');ReadLn(item3);
        SubTotal:=item1+item2+item3;
        Tax:=SubTotal*VAT;
        total:=SubTotal+Tax;
        WriteLn('Sub Total',SubTotal:10:2);
        WriteLn('VAT @ 15%', Tax:10:2);
        WriteLn('Total', Total:10:2);
END. {C3Q5c}
```

6. Write a program to input two initials of your name, your height in inches and weight in stones; convert the height to centimetres and weight to kilogrammes and display the following results.

```
        PERSONAL DETAILS
        IDENTIFICATION: BH
        HEIGHT (cm): 180
        WEIGHT (Kg): 75
```

Note: 1 inch = 2.54 cm and 1 stone = 6.364 Kg

7. Write a program to input a temperature in degrees Fahrenheit and display the equivalent temperature in degrees Centigrade. The formula for conversion is: Centigrade = (Fahrenheit-32)*(5/9).

[8]. Write a program to input the length and width of a rectangular-shaped garden, calculate the area of the garden and the cost of turfing a lawn, if a 0.5m border is left around the perimeter of the garden. Assume the cost of turf is £0.75 per square metre. Display the result of these calculations.

[9]. Write a program to input an amount of money as a whole number, for example £157, and display an analysis of the minimum number of £20, £10, £5 notes and £1 coins that make up this amount.

[10]. Write a program to input the length, width and depths at the deepest and shallowest ends of a rectangular swimming pool. Calculate the volume of water required to fill the pool and display this volume.

4

Data Types

This chapter introduces the reader to subrange and enumerated data types. Subrange types enable a programmer to define legal ranges for data, whereas, enumerated types allow a programmer to create new data types that are more meaningful to the nature of the application that the program is written for.

4.1 Integrity of Data.

In writing a computer program it is vital to cater for both good and error data. There is a clear distinction to be made first, between valid and invalid data. Valid data is expected data, a program has been written to process it and the results are predictable. Invalid data is unexpected data, a program has not been written to process it and, therefore, the results are unpredictable.

Good data is regarded as being correct valid data, whereas error data is incorrect valid data.

The programs developed in the last chapter were written on the assumption that good data would be typed at a keyboard. Consider for a moment what would happen if the value 3O had been input in response to the prompt *input cost of Globe* => and the character O had been typed by mistake in place of the digit 0 (zero). The cost of the Globe had been declared as an INTEGER, therefore, the computer was programmed to accept such a data type and not a combination of the digit 3 and the character O. Since the operating system supervises the running of all programs it would terminate this program and display a message *I/O error - program aborted*. This was clearly unexpected data, the program had not been written to cope with it and without the intervention of the operating system the results would have been unpredictable.

However, what if the value of the cost of the Globe had been input as 300 instead of 30? The program would have run correctly, yet the results would have been unreasonable. This value can be regarded as being in error, rather than being invalid, since the program has been written to cater for it but the data is too large to be realistic. Pascal will allow a programmer to specify the legal ranges for two of the data types already encountered - integer and char.

4.2 Subrange Types.

A reasonable range for the price of newspapers might be 15p to 65p. If there exists a variable *CostOfPaper* to replace the variables Courier, Globe and Mercury, then this new variable can be declared of TYPE *price* which is an integer in the subrange 15..65.

```
{type declaration}
TYPE
      price = 15..65; {legal range of prices of newspapers}
{end type declaration}

VAR
      CostOfPaper : price;
```

Since price is an integer by default, there is no need to declare CostOfPaper explicitly as an integer.

If a value for the CostOfPaper is input to the computer using a ReadLn statement, and the value lies outside the range 15 to 65 the operating system will terminate the program. Depending upon the operating system being used this termination of the program may happen as soon as an illegal value is input, or when the data is used in an assignment. Some Pascal systems will allow the user to trap this error and prevent the operating system from intervening.

The program given in section 3.7 to calculate the total and average cost of newspapers is re-written incorporating a sub-range type. The program is run twice. On the second occasion error data is deliberately introduced at the keyboard to illustrate to the reader how the Turbo Pascal PC system copes with the out-of-range data.

```
PROGRAM newspapers(INPUT, OUTPUT);
{program to calculate the total and average cost of newspapers}
TYPE
        price = 15..65; {legal range of prices of newspapers}
VAR
        CostOfPaper : price;
        TotalPence : INTEGER; {total cost of three newspapers (p)}
        TotalPounds : REAL; {total cost (£)}
        average : REAL; {average cost of newspapers (p)}

BEGIN
        Write('input cost of Courier = >');
        ReadLn(CostOfPaper);
        TotalPence := CostOfPaper;
        Write('input cost of Globe = >');
        ReadLn(CostOfPaper);
        TotalPence := TotalPence + CostOfPaper;
        Write('input cost of Mercury = >');
        ReadLn(CostOfPaper);
        TotalPence := TotalPence + CostOfPaper;
        TotalPounds := TotalPence / 100;
        average := TotalPence / 3;
        WriteLn('total cost of papers £', TotalPounds :4:2);
        WriteLn('average cost of papers ', average :4:1, 'p');
END. {newspapers}
```

Results from program being run three times

input cost of Courier = > 3o
Runtime error 201

input cost of Courier = > 30
input cost of Globe = > 70
Runtime error 201

input cost of Courier = > 30
input cost of Globe = > 40
input cost of Mercury = > 50
total cost of papers £1.20
average cost of papers 40.0 p

The word TYPE is used once in a type declaration and must follow any constant declarations and come before variable declarations. The set order for declarations in a Pascal program is:

```
{begin declartions}
CONST
TYPE
VAR
{end declarations}
```

From the last example the general format of the subrange type can be deduced as:

identifier = minval..maxval;

where minval and maxval are scalar values such that the ordinal value of minval must be less than the ordinal value of maxval.

The data types discussed so far, integer, real and char are known as scalar types. This means that their values cannot be sub-divided into further types. All Scalar types in Pascal have the property of being ordered. Given two values it is possible to say whether one value ranks greater than, equal to, or less than the other value. This is obvious for integers and reals since 5 is less then 6, and -1.75 is greater than -4.5. Since characters are coded according to the ASCII table given in chapter 2, A is less than B since the code for A is 65 which is less than the code for B which is 66.

From the sub-range 'A'..'Z'; the ordinal value (position in ASCII table) of A is 65, B is 66 and Z is 90.

From the subrange -10..+10; the ordinal value of the integer -10 is -10, 0 is 0 and +10 is +10.

Pascal has a function ORD that returns the ordinal value of an object in a sub-range. For example, ORD('A') = 65, ORD('B') = 66, ORD(-10) = -10, ORD(+10) = +10, etc.

Reals do not have subranges. Obviously the number of different values between, say, 0.0 and 1.0 is almost infinite. Type real, although a scalar, is not an ordinal type.

In section 2.2 it was stated that the range of integers that could be stored in the memory of a computer varied between computers. Pascal provides a function MAXINT that represents the largest integer that can be stored in the memory of the particular computer being used. Using this function the legal range of positive integers can be expressed as: PosInt = 1..MAXINT

To consolidate the work of this section consider the following worked example.

Problem. A food commodity is graded A,B,C,D and E where grade A represents a superior variety and grade E represents a poor variety. The price of the food reflects the quality of the food. Grade A food attracts the highest price (MaxPrice = 100), grade B food is priced at (MaxPrice/2), grade C at (MaxPrice/3), grade D at (MaxPrice/4) and grade E at (MaxPrice/5).

Write a program to input a grade for food and the quantity of units of food required. Food is only sold in units from 1 to 12 inclusive. Calculate the cost of the purchase.

In calculating the price of the food it is necessary to convert the food grade to a proportion of the MaxPrice. Since ORD('A') is 65, ORD('B') is 66 etc, the expression ORD(FoodGrade)-64 will produce values in the range 1..5 for grades A..E, respectively.

```
PROGRAM FoodPrices(INPUT, OUTPUT);
{program to calculate the cost of food from a food code}
CONST
        MaxPrice = 100;
        MaxQuantity = 12;
TYPE
        grade = 'A'..'E';
        LegalQuantity = 1..MaxQuantity;
VAR
        FoodGrade : grade;
        quantity : LegalQuantity;
        price : REAL;
        CostOfPurchase : REAL;

BEGIN
        Write('input grade of food => ');
        ReadLn(FoodGrade);
        Write('input quantity of food required => ');
        ReadLn(quantity);
        price := MaxPrice / (ORD(FoodGrade)-64);
        CostOfPurchase := quantity * price;
        WriteLn('cost of purchase => £',CostOfPurchase:6:2);
END. {FoodPrices}
```

Results from program being run three times

input grade of food => A
input quantity of food required => 10
cost of purchase => £ 1000.00

input grade of food => x
Runtime error 201

input grade of food => C
input quantity of food required => 100

Runtime error 201

4.3 Enumerated Types.

A programmer is allowed to create new data types. However, the objects associated with these new types cannot be read or written using ReadLn, Write or WriteLn respectively, using a variable of enumerated type.

The purpose of creating enumerated types is to improve the documentation of a program. It is not necessary to invent arbitrary numeric codes to quantify non-numeric values. The associated scalar values can be used directly in a program. For example, in a program that specifies different newspapers the type newspaper could be declared.

```
TYPE
        newspaper = (Times,Telegraph,Today,Mail,Express,Sun,Observer);
```

and an associated variable PaperName could be declared as having type newspaper.

```
VAR
        PaperName : newspaper;
```

Notice from this example that enumerated scalar types are declared using the format:

```
    identifier = (list of scalar values)
```

Within a program it would be legal to assign a scalar to PaperName:

```
    PaperName := Telegraph;
```

Notice also that it is not necessary to enclose the scalar with apostrophes since the value is not a string. Remember, it would be illegal to use ReadLn(PaperName) or WriteLn(PaperName) to input or output objects from the defined type newspaper.

Subranges can also be declared for enumerated types, however, the objects of such ranges cannot be used for input or output. For example:

```
TYPE
        newspaper = (Times,Telegraph,Today,Mail,Express,Sun,Observer);
        tabloid = Today..Sun;
VAR
        PopularPress : tabloid;
```

Within the program the variable PopularPress can be assigned any of the values Today, Mail, Express or Sun. A further example of an enumerated type would be:

```
TYPE
        month = (Mar,Apr,May,Jun,Jul,Aug,Sep,Oct,Nov,Dec,Jan,Feb);
```

with a declaration of the following subranges.

       Spring = Mar..May;
       Summer = Jun..Aug;
       Autumn = Sep..Nov;
       Winter = Dec..Feb;
VAR
       SummerHoliday : Summer;
       WinterHoliday : Winter;

Both variables are of the type month with the subranges specified. The variable WinterHoliday can only be assigned the values Dec, Jan or Feb. Notice that if month had been specified as:

       month = (Jan,Feb,Mar,Apr,May,Jun,Jul,Aug,Sep,Oct,Nov,Dec);

the declaration of the subrange Winter = Dec..Feb would be illegal, since the ordinal value of Dec is greater than the ordinal value for Feb.

Scalar values in one list of an enumerated type cannot be used to form part of another list for a different enumerated type. For example:

TYPE
       DaysOfWeek = (Sun,Mon,Tue,Wed,Thu,Fri,Sat);
       DaysNotWorking = (Sun,Wed,Sat);

would be illegal.

4.4 Scalar List Functions.

The scalar list for type char, although not specifically defined in a program, is implicitly taken to be the list of ASCII codes (see table 2.1). Members of this list will have predecessors and successors. An exception to this statement is the character *null* which has no predecessor and *del* which has no successor. In addition to the ORD function already mentioned, Pascal supports three more functions associated with scalar lists: CHR (inverse of ORD), PRED (predecessor) and SUCC (successor). With reference to table 2.1:

       ORD('J') is 74; CHR(74) is J; PRED('J') is I; SUCC('J') is K.

The scalar list for type integer is all the integers in the range -32768 to +32767 for a 16-bit representation. Within this range of integers:

       PRED(0) is -1; SUCC(0) is +1; ORD(0) is 0; CHR(0) is null.

Notice that the character whose code is zero is the null character from the ASCII character set. In the declaration for month given in the last section:

       month = (Mar,Apr,May,Jun,Jul,Aug,Sep,Oct,Nov,Dec,Jan,Feb);

PRED(May) is Apr; SUCC(Sep) is Oct; ORD(mar) is 0; ORD(Feb) is 11. Both the PRED(Mar) and SUCC(Feb) are illegal and would return an error. CHR(0) would again return the null character and clearly has no meaning with this list of objects.

In the final worked example of this chapter a numerical code for a secret agent is input to the computer and deciphered into the initials of the agent. The numerical code is composed of three numbers, each in the range 0 to 25. Each number is increased by 65 (ASCII code for A), and taken as the ordinal value in the ASCII character set. The character associated with this ordinal value is then found using CHR and output.

```
PROGRAM CodeBreaker(INPUT, OUTPUT);
{program to decipher a numeric code }
CONST
        AsciiConst = 65;
VAR
        code1, code2, code3:INTEGER;
        initial1, initial2, initial3:CHAR;

BEGIN
        Write('input three number code of secret agent ');
        ReadLn(code1, code2, code3);
        initial1:=CHR(code1+AsciiConst);
        initial2:=CHR(code2+AsciiConst);
        initial3:=CHR(code3+AsciiConst);
        WriteLn('the initials of the agent are ', initial1, initial2, initial3);
        WriteLn('his identity is revealed!');
END. {CodeBreaker}
```

Results from program being run

input three number code of secret agent
1 9 7

the initials of the agent are BJH
his identity is revealed !

4.5 Summary.
Data can be classified into subrange and enumerated types.

Data of enumerated type can also have a subrange.

Input data that is outside of permissible ranges will cause the application program to be terminated.

Data of type INTEGER, CHAR and enumerated types are known collectively as ORDINAL types.

The predefined function ORD will return the ordinal position of an object of ordinal type.

The predefined functions PRED and SUCC will return the value of the predecessor or successor, respectively, from a list of objects of ordinal type.

keywords

good, error, valid and invalid data;
subrange type; MAXINT;
scalar, enumerated types;
PRED, SUCC, ORD, CHR.

4.6 Questions.
[1]. Declare an integer variable to have legal values in the range 1 to 31. Write a program to input an integer, compute twice its value, and display the result. Investigate how your computer's operating system copes with computed numbers outside the declared range.

2. Declare subrange types for:

a. decimal digits;
b. a code number representing the week of a year.
c. the range of a compass used for navigation;
d. a three digit identity code that starts at 100;
e. the alphabet.

3. Declare enumerated types for:

a. the operators + - * / ;
b. four playing-card suits;
c. the thirteen cards of a suit;
d. the four points of a navigational compass.

4. Using table 2.1 evaluate the following expressions.

a. PRED(PRED(PRED('A')));
b. SUCC(SUCC(SUCC('Z')));
c. ORD(PRED(SUCC(':')));
d. SUCC(CHR(80)).

5. Write a program to input a single character and print the value of its ASCII code. Also include in the program an input for an integer in the range 0..127 and output the character with the associated ASCII code.

[6]. Write a program to input a character in the range 0 to 9, convert the mode of storage to a decimal digit, multiply the value by pi (3.14159) and output the result.

5

Selection

In chapter 3 the reader was introduced to programs that were based upon the input of data, calculations made using the data and the output of results. Programs written in this manner are fine for solutions to problems that require no more than the computer to follow a sequence of instructions, but are of little use if decisions are to be made within a program. This chapter introduces the reader to coding decisions and branching on the result of a decision to alternative statements in a program.

5.1 If..then.

As a continuation from the work of chapter 3, consider the following problem. A company executive is given a rate of 20p per mile for the use of a car. At the end of each week the executive inputs to a computer his mileage for the week. The computer calculates and displays the travelling expenses that the executive is entitled to receive. In writing a computer program to solve this problem the instruction sequence will most certainly contain statements to:

> input weekly mileage
> calculate allowance
> display allowance

However, what if the management decide that the rate is not enough for those executives with cars whose engines are larger than 1500 cc in capacity? These people should receive an extra 5p per mile. Clearly a decision based on the size of an engine is required in order to calculate the correct travelling expenses. The sequence of statements given above will require modifying to include an extra input statement for the size of a car engine, and a decision as to whether to pay the rate of 20p per mile or allow an extra 5p per mile. The sequence is then modified to:

> input weekly mileage
> calculate travelling expenses at 20p per mile
> input size of car engine
>
> test for engine size and if necessary
> calculate additional allowance
>
> display allowance

The test for the size of the car engine will take the form:

> IF engine size > 1500 THEN
>   calculate additional expenses;
> {end if}

where the symbol > represents greater than. Only if the size of the engine is greater than 1500 cc will the additional allowance be calculated. This statement can be coded into Pascal and incorporated into an instruction sequence to calculate the travelling allowance for an executive.

```
PROGRAM car(INPUT, OUTPUT);
{program to calculate weekly travelling expenses}

CONST
        NormalRate = 0.2;
        ExtraRate = 0.05;
VAR
        mileage : INTEGER; {number of miles travelled per week}
        EngineSize : INTEGER; {size of car engine in cc}
        allowance : REAL; {amount due on travelling expenses}
```

```
BEGIN
        Write('input mileage = >');
        ReadLn(mileage);
        Write('input size of engine = >');
        ReadLn(EngineSize);
        allowance := mileage * NormalRate;

        {selection based on engine size}
        IF EngineSize > 1500 THEN
            allowance := allowance + mileage * ExtraRate;
        {end if}

        WriteLn('weekly travelling expenses due £', allowance:6:2);
END. {car}
```

To test whether a program functions correctly, it is advisable to select appropriate data for testing various parts of the program. In this example the program was run twice, choosing the EngineSize to calculate the allowance at the normal rate and extra rate, respectively.

Results from program being run twice

input mileage => 1000
input size of engine => 1500
weekly travelling expenses due £200.00

input mileage => 1000
input size of engine => 1600
weekly travelling expenses due £250.00

5.2 Boolean Expressions.

In the last example the part of the if..then statement that contained *EngineSize > 1500* is known as a Boolean expression, the value of which is either TRUE or FALSE. If the Boolean expression was true the allowance would be re-calculated to take into account the extra rate and the computer would then execute the next statement to display the weekly travelling expenses. However, if the value was false the computer would by-pass the assignment statement and display the weekly travelling expenses. A list of operators that can be used in Boolean expressions follows.

operator	meaning
>	greater than
<	less than
=	equal to
>=	greater than or equal to
<=	less than or equal to
<>	not equal to

The following examples represent Boolean expressions:

A=6   B>15   X<Y   H>=I+J A+B>C+D

The value of each expression is either true or false depending on the values of the variables in each expression.

Boolean expression	value	A	B	C	D	H	I	J	X	Y
A=6	TRUE	6								
B>15	FALSE		13							
X<Y	FALSE								15	8
H>=I+J	TRUE					5	3	2		
A+B>C+D	TRUE	6	13	5	4					

Boolean is a scalar data type of values false or true and can be declared as:

TYPE
      BOOLEAN = (false,true);
VAR
      SalesExecutive :BOOLEAN;

However, since BOOLEAN is a fundamental data type such as INTEGER, REAL and CHAR there is no need to declare it specifically as a type with objects false and true.

5.3 Boolean Operators.

In the travelling expenses problem what if the management decided that only sales executives with cars whose engines are greater than 1500 cc should receive the additional 5p per mile? There are now two conditions associated with receiving the extra allowance. Both the variable *SalesExecutive* and the expression *EngineSize > 1500* must be true. When a selection is based upon one or more expressions being true or false it is possible to combine the expressions together using Boolean operators and the resultant expression will be true or false. The following truth tables illustrate the outcome of combining two expressions using Boolean operators.

Boolean operator AND

X AND Y is true only if X is true and Y is true.

condition X	condition Y	X AND Y
false	false	false
false	true	false
true	false	false
true	true	true

Boolean operator OR

X OR Y is true if X is true or Y is true or both are true.

condition X	condition Y	X OR Y
false	false	false
false	true	true
true	false	true
true	true	true

Boolean operator NOT

NOT reverses the value of a condition, true becomes false and false becomes true.

condition X	NOT X
false	true
true	false

In the travelling expenses problem if the variable SalesExecutive was of type Boolean, the selection could be re-coded. However, since variables of type Boolean cannot be input to a program it is necessary to insert an extra input statement and selection into the program of the form:

```
SalesExecutive := FALSE;
Write('are you a sales executive, answer y(es) or n(o) = >');
ReadLn(reply);
IF reply = yes THEN
    SalesExecutive := TRUE;
{end if}
```

Notice that it has been necessary to set SalesExecutive to FALSE and only if the reply is 'y', the value of the constant yes, will this be changed to TRUE. The selection for the extra allowance becomes:

```
IF (SalesExecutive) AND (EngineSize > 1500) THEN
    allowance := allowance + mileage * ExtraRate;
{end if}
```

5.4 If..then..else.
The structure of the solution to the travelling expenses problem can be changed. If an executive drove a car with an engine capacity greater than 1500 cc and was a member of the sales department an allowance based on the higher rate would be calculated, otherwise if this condition was false an allowance based on the normal rate would be calculated. The if..then statement has optional code added to cater for the condition being false.

```
IF (SalesExecutive) AND (EngineSize > 1500) THEN
    {calculate allowance at HigherRate}
ELSE
    {calculate allowance at NormalRate};
{end if}
```

This re-structuring implies that the allowance based on the NormalRate will not be calculated prior to the selection being made, as was the case in the earlier example. All the modifications discussed can be incorporated into the following program.

```
PROGRAM car(INPUT, OUTPUT);
{program to calculate weekly travelling expenses}

CONST
      NormalRate = 0.2;
      HigherRate = 0.25;
      yes='y';
VAR
      mileage :INTEGER; {number of miles travelled per week}
      EngineSize :INTEGER; {size of car engine in cc}
      reply :CHAR; {answer Y or N to question}
      SalesExecutive :BOOLEAN;
      allowance :REAL; {amount due on travelling expenses}

BEGIN
      SalesExecutive:=FALSE;
      Write('are you a sales executive? - answer y(es) or n(o) => ');
      ReadLn(reply);

      IF reply = yes THEN
         SalesExecutive:=TRUE;
      {end if}

      Write('input mileage =>');
      ReadLn(mileage);
      Write('input size of engine =>');
      ReadLn(EngineSize);

      {selection based on engine size and executive status}
      IF (SalesExecutive) AND (EngineSize > 1500) THEN
          allowance := mileage * HigherRate
      ELSE
          allowance := mileage * NormalRate;
      {end if}

      WriteLn('weekly travelling expenses due £', allowance:6:2);
END. {car}
```

Since there are two conditions to test in this example in order to calculate the correct allowance it was prudent to run the program four times and use all combinations of data.

> ***Results from program being run four times***
> **are you a sales executive? - answer y(es) or n(o) = > y**
> **input mileage = > 1000**
> **input size of engine = > 1500**
> **weekly travelling expenses due £200.00**
>
> **are you a sales executive? - answer y(es) or n(o) = > n**
> **input mileage = > 1000**
> **input size of engine = > 1500**
> **weekly travelling expenses due £200.00**
>
> **are you a sales executive? - answer y(es) or n(o) = > y**
> **input mileage = > 1000**
> **input size of engine = > 1600**
> **weekly travelling expenses due £250.00**
>
> **are you a sales executive? - answer y(es) or n(o) = > n**
> **input mileage = > 1000**
> **input size of engine = > 1600**
> **weekly travelling expenses due £200.00**

A further modification to this program would be to delete the statement SalesExecutive := FALSE; and extend the statement

```
IF reply = yes THEN
    SalesExecutive := TRUE
ELSE
    SalesExecutive := FALSE;
{end if}
```

Notice from the last two examples of if..then..else that the statement before else is not terminated by a semi-colon. The effect would be to split the if..then..else statement into two statements, which is syntactically incorrect.

5.5 Nested Selections.

In a selection statement what if the statements corresponding to true and false were further selection statements? When if statements are embedded one within another they are said to be nested. It is recommended that each if..then or if..then..else statement is terminated with the comment {end if}, and that if..{end if} or if..else..{end if} are aligned. The following code illustrates that the indentation of respective if statements indicates the level of nesting.

```
IF condition 1 THEN
    statement 1
ELSE
    IF condition 2 THEN
        statement 2
    ELSE
        IF condition 3 THEN
            statement 3
        ELSE
            statement 4
        {end if}
    {end if}
{end if}
```

These statements can be compressed into several lines by grouping else if, however this is only a matter of style. For example:

```
IF condition 1 THEN
    statement 1
ELSE IF condition 2 THEN
    statement 2
ELSE IF condition 3 THEN
    statement 3
ELSE
    statement 4;
{end if}
```

Problem. In the following example a person has established a set of rules for what clothing to wear in order to walk to work comfortably in all weathers in the Spring.

If the barometer indicates storm wear overcoat and hat.
If the barometer indicates rain wear raincoat and takes an umbrella.
If the barometer indicates change behave as for fair if it rained yesterday and as for rain if it did not.
If fair is indicated wear a light over-jacket and takes an umbrella.
If very dry is indicated wear a light over-jacket.

Write a program to input a coded barometer reading, whether it rained yesterday (where necessary) and display the type of clothing to wear.

```
PROGRAM WhatToWear(INPUT, OUTPUT);
{program to inform what to wear in different climatic conditions}

CONST
      yes='y';
TYPE
      BarometerCode = 'A'..'E'; {A-storm, B-rain, C-change, D-fair, E-very dry}
VAR
      reading :BarometerCode;
      reply :CHAR; {answer Y or N to question}

BEGIN
      WriteLn('A-storm, B-rain, C-change, D-fair, E-very dry');
      Write('input barometer code =>');
      ReadLn(reading);

      {start nested selection}
      IF reading = 'A' THEN
          WriteLn('wear overcoat and hat')
      ELSE
         IF reading = 'B' THEN
             WriteLn('wear raincoat and take umbrella')
         ELSE
            IF reading = 'C' THEN
            BEGIN
               Write('did it rain yesterday? answer y(es) or n(o) =>');
               ReadLn(reply);
               IF reply = yes THEN
                   WriteLn('wear over-jacket and take umbrella')
               ELSE
                   WriteLn('wear raincoat and take umbrella')
               {end if}
            END
            ELSE
               IF reading = 'D' THEN
                   WriteLn('wear over-jacket and take umbrella')
               ELSE
                   WriteLn('wear over-jacket')
               {end if}
            {end if}
         {end if}
      {end if}
END. {WhatToWear}
```

> ***Results from program being run six times***
>
> **A-storm, B-rain, C-change, D-fair, E-very dry**
> **input barometer code => A**
> **wear overcoat and hat**
>
> **A-storm, B-rain, C-change, D-fair, E-very dry**
> **input barometer code => B**
> **wear raincoat and take umbrella**
>
> **A-storm, B-rain, C-change, D-fair, E-very dry**
> **input barometer code => C**
> **did it rain yesterday? answer y(es) or n(o) => y**
> **wear over-jacket and take umbrella**
>
> **A-storm, B-rain, C-change, D-fair, E-very dry**
> **input barometer code => C**
> **did it rain yesterday? answer y(es) or n(o) => n**
> **wear raincoat and take umbrella**
>
> **A-storm, B-rain, C-change, D-fair, E-very dry**
> **input barometer code => D**
> **wear over-jacket and take umbrella**
>
> **A-storm, B-rain, C-change, D-fair, E-very dry**
> **input barometer code => E**
> **wear over-jacket**

5.6 Multiple Selection - Case.

In the last example the use of multiple if...then...else statements could have been replaced by a case statement.

```
CASE reading OF
'A' : WriteLn('wear overcoat and hat');
'B' : WriteLn('wear raincoat and take umbrella');
'C' :   BEGIN
            Write('did it rain yesterday? answer Y or N =>'); ReadLn(reply);
            IF reply = 'Y' THEN
                WriteLn('wear over-jacket and take umbrella')
            ELSE
                WriteLn('wear raincoat and take umbrella');
            {end if}
        END;
'D' : WriteLn('wear over-jacket and take umbrella');
'E' : WriteLn('wear over-jacket');
END;
{end case}
```

The identifier *reading* is known as a *selector* and can be a variable or expression. The values 'A', 'B', 'C', 'D' and 'E' are known as *constants* and form a list of one or more possible values of the selector. The type of each value in the list of constants must be consistent with the selector type. The constants must be unique, duplication between lists is not allowed. If the value of the selector is found in the list of constants then the corresponding statement will be executed and the computer will then exit from the case statement to the next executable statement in the sequence. If the selector cannot be matched with a constant the operating system will display an error message and the program will be terminated. A statement can be a single statement or a compound statement. The word end may be followed by the comment {end case} to clearly document the end of the case statement.

Notice from this segment of code that it is permissible to use if..then..else embedded in a case statement. A further modification, to improve the readability of the program, can be made by introducing the variable barometer declared as an enumerated type weather.

```
TYPE
      weather = (Storm,Rain,Change,Fair,VeryDry);
      BarometerCode = 'A'..'E';
VAR
      reading : BarometerCode;
      barometer : weather;
      reply : CHAR;
```

A case statement could then be used to convert reading to an appropriate description of weather.

```
      CASE reading OF
      'A' : barometer:=Storm;
      'B' : barometer:=Rain;
      'C' : barometer:=Change;
      'D' : barometer:=Fair;
      'E' : barometer:=VeryDry;
      END;
      {end case}
```

The value of barometer would be used in the remainder of the program in place of reading.

```
      CASE barometer OF
      Storm :WriteLn('wear overcoat and hat');
      Rain :WriteLn('wear raincoat and take umbrella');
      Change :  BEGIN
                  Write('did it rain yesterday, answer y(es) or n(o) = >'); ReadLn(reply);
                  IF reply = yes THEN
                      WriteLn('wear over-jacket and take umbrella')
                  ELSE
                      WriteLn('wear raincoat and take umbrella')
                  {end if}
              END;
```

```
        Fair :WriteLn('wear over-jacket and take umbrella');
        VeryDry :WriteLn('wear over-jacket');
    END;
    {end case}
```

Problem. Using case statements where appropriate, write a validation routine to determine whether a date input as day, month and year is legal.

```
PROGRAM ValidDate(INPUT, OUTPUT);
{program to validate a date}

TYPE
      MonthDesc = (Jan,Feb,Mar,Apr,May,Jun,Jul,Aug,Sep,Oct,Nov,Dec);
      year = 1986..1999;
      month = 1..12;
      day = 1..31;
VAR
      dd : day;
      mm : month;
      yy : year;
      NumberOfDays : day; {number of days in a month}
      name : MonthDesc; {name of month}

BEGIN
      Write('input date in format DD MM 19YY = >');
      ReadLn(dd, mm, yy); WriteLn;

      {convert month number MM to name of month}
      CASE mm OF
      1 : name := Jan;
      2 : name := Feb;
      3 : name := Mar;
      4 : name := Apr;
      5 : name := May;
      6 : name := Jun;
      7 : name := Jul;
      8 : name := Aug;
      9 : name := Sep;
      10: name := Oct;
      11: name := Nov;
      12: name := Dec;
      END;
      {end case}
```

```
{calculate number of days in month}
CASE name OF
Jan,Mar,May,Jul,Aug,Oct,Dec      : NumberOfDays := 31;
Apr,Jun,Sep,Nov                  : NumberOfDays := 30;
Feb                              :   IF yy mod 4 = 0 THEN
                                         NumberOfDays := 29
                                     ELSE
                                         NumberOfDays := 28;
                                     {end if}

END;
{end case}

{test whether number of days is legal for month}
IF dd > NumberOfDays THEN
    WriteLn('error in date - check day or month')
ELSE
    WriteLn('date checked and is valid')
    {end if}
END. {ValidDate}
```

Results from program being run twice

input date in format DD MM 19YY = >18 03 1987
date checked and is valid

input date in format DD MM 19YY = >30 02 1987
error in date - check day or month

In using the case statement what if the value of the selector is not catered for? If this program is run again and the value for mm is deliberately input as 13 then the operating system will prematurely abandon the running of the program.

Results from program being run

input date in format DD MM 19YY = >18 13 1987
Runtime error 201

In Turbo Pascal it is possible to cater for a selector not being assigned a specific value found in the constants list by including an else clause following the statements that contain constant lists. For example:

```
CASE operator OF
'+' : result := A + B;
'-' : result := A - B;
'*' : result := A * B;
'/' : result := A / B
ELSE
    WriteLn('ERROR - operator not valid');
END;
```

5.7 Summary.

The computer can be directed to obey alternative statements by the use of if..then and if..then..else statements.

The basis of the selection is upon a boolean expression evaluating to either TRUE or FALSE.

Boolean expressions can be grouped together by the operators AND, and OR to form a complex Boolean expression that must evaluate to either TRUE or FALSE.

A Boolean expression can be negated by the use of the operator NOT.

When a variable or expression can take on many values, then such a variable may be used as the basis of a multi-way selection in a case statement.

> **keywords**
>
> *Boolean expression and type, (TRUE, FALSE);*
> *operators (> < = >= <= <> AND, OR, NOT);*
> *IF..THEN; IF..THEN..ELSE; nested IF; ELSE IF;*
> *CASE, selector, constants list.*

5.8 Questions.

1. If A=1, B=-2, C=3, D=4, E='S' and F='J' then state whether the following conditions are true or false.

a. A=B   b. A>B   c. (A<C) AND (B<D) d. (A<C) AND (B>D)
e. (A>B) OR (C<D)   f. E>F
g. ((A+C)>(B-D)) AND ((B+C)<(D-A))

2. How would you code the following conditions in Pascal?

a. X is equal to Y
b. X is not equal to Y
c. A is not less than or equal to B
d. Q is not greater than T

e. X is greater than or equal to Y

f. X is less than or equal to Y and A is not equal to B

g. A is greater than 18 and H is greater than 68 and W is greater than 75

h. G is less than 100 and greater than 50

i. H is less than 50 or greater than 100.

3. Trace through the following segment of code for each new value of A,B and C given in the table, and state the output in each case.

```
IF A>0 THEN
    IF B<0 THEN
        WriteLn('x')
    ELSE
        IF C>20 THEN
            WriteLn('y')
        {end if}
    {end if}
ELSE
    WriteLn('z');
{end if}
```

A	B	C
16	16	32
16	-18	32
-2	-4	16

4. A salesperson earns a commission on the value of sales. The following table shows the scale of the commission. Write a program to input a figure for the value of sales, and calculate and output the commission.

value of sales	% commission
£1-£999	1
£1000-£9999	5
£10000-£99999	10

5. A worker is paid at the hourly rate of £8 per hour for the first 35 hours worked. Thereafter overtime is paid at 1.5 times the hourly rate for the next 25 hours worked and 2 times the hourly rate for further hours worked. Write a program to input the number of hours worked per week, calculate and output the overtime paid.

[6]. A student studying Computer Science at a college is examined by coursework and written examination. Both components of the assessment carry a maximum of 50 marks. The following rules are used by the examiners in order to pass or fail students.

A student must score a total of 40% or more in order to pass.

A total mark of 39% is moderated to 40%.

Each component must be passed with a minimum mark of 15. If a student scores 40% or more but does not achieve the minimum mark in either component he is given a technical fail of 39% (this mark is not moderated to 40%).

Grades are awarded on marks that fall into the following categories.

mark	100-70	69-60	59-50	49-40	39-0
grade	A	B+	B	C	F

Write a program to input the marks for both components, output the final mark and grade after any moderations.

[7]. Write a program to input two real numbers and give the user the choice of adding, subtracting, multiplying or dividing these numbers. Perform the appropriate calculation and display the result. Your program should trap any attempt to divide by zero.

[8]. Return to section 2.8 and from the details given, write a program to calculate the cost of hiring a bicycle.

6

Repetition

In writing computer programs it is often necessary to repeat part of a program a number of times. One way of achieving this would be to write out that part of the program as many times as it was needed. This, however, is a very impractical method since it would produce a very lengthy computer program and the number of times part of the program is to be repeated is not always known in advance. The purpose of this chapter is to introduce the reader to three methods for repetition that overcome the disadvantages mentioned. These methods are based upon the control structures REPEAT..UNTIL, WHILE..DO and FOR..DO. The final part of the chapter explains further methods for inputting both numeric and character data.

6.1 Repeat..Until.

Returning for a moment, to the sequence of instructions given in chapter 3 that processed the gross weekly wage of an employee.

```
BEGIN
      Write('input number of hours worked = >');
      ReadLn(HoursWorked);
      Write('input hourly rate of pay = >');
      ReadLn(RateOfPay);
      GrossWage := HoursWorked * RateOfPay;
      WriteLn('gross weekly wage £', GrossWage :6:2)
END.
```

This sequence of instructions can be repeated to process the gross wages for say, five employees who are all paid at the same hourly rate. If a *counter* is used to keep track of the number of employees who have had their gross wages calculated, then this counter can be used in a condition for stopping the instructions being repeated when the counter becomes equal to 5. A modification to the program segment given above would be:

```
BEGIN
      {initialise counter to zero}
      REPEAT
          {input hours worked}
          {input rate of pay }
          {calculate and output gross wage}
          {increase the value of counter by 1}
      UNTIL counter = 5;
END.
```

All the statements that appear between the REPEAT and UNTIL are executed until the Boolean expression *counter = 5* is true. With this type of loop the statements within the loop must be executed by the computer at least once. Since all employees receive the same rate of pay it would be sensible to re-position the two statements that relate to this input outside the loop, after the initialisation of the counter. The modified program to calculate the gross wages for five employees follows.

```
PROGRAM wages(INPUT, OUTPUT);
{program to calculate the gross weekly wages for five employees}

VAR
        RateOfPay       : REAL; {hourly rate of pay}
        HoursWorked     : REAL; {number of hours worked per week}
        counter         : INTEGER; {count of the number of employees wages processed}
        GrossWage       : REAL; {weekly wage before deductions}
```

```
BEGIN
     counter := 0;
     Write('input hourly rate of pay = >');
     ReadLn(RateOfPay);
     REPEAT
        Write('input number of hours worked = >');
        ReadLn(HoursWorked);
        GrossWage := HoursWorked * RateOfPay;
        WriteLn('gross weekly wage £', GrossWage:6:2);
        counter := counter + 1;
     UNTIL counter = 5;
END. {wages}
```

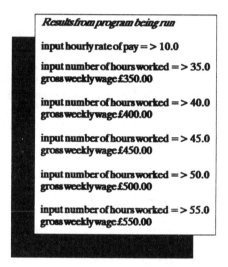

Results from program being run

input hourly rate of pay = > 10.0

input number of hours worked = > 35.0
gross weekly wage £350.00

input number of hours worked = > 40.0
gross weekly wage £400.00

input number of hours worked = > 45.0
gross weekly wage £450.00

input number of hours worked = > 50.0
gross weekly wage £500.00

input number of hours worked = > 55.0
gross weekly wage £550.00

6.2 For..Do.

In the last example the repeat..until loop was controlled by a counter. It is evident that the coding involved.

Initialising a loop counter.

Increasing the value of the counter each time a program segment within the loop had been executed.

Testing the loop counter to determine whether to exit.

The process of coding the loop control in a program can be simplified by the use of the FOR..DO statement. Using this statement the employee wages sequence could be re-coded as:

```
BEGIN
    Write('input hourly rate of pay = >');
    ReadLn(RateOfPay);
    FOR counter := 1 TO 5 DO
    BEGIN
        Write('input number of hours worked = >');
        ReadLn(HoursWorked);
        GrossWage := HoursWorked * RateOfPay;
        WriteLn('gross weekly wage £', GrossWage:6:2);
    END;
    {end for}
END. {wages}
```

The statement that provides the loop control is:

FOR counter := 1 TO 5 DO

When the statement FOR counter := 1 TO 5 DO is executed, counter is initially set to 1. After the initial execution of the code between BEGIN..END; the computer increases the value of the counter by 1 and tests whether the new value of the counter has exceeded the final value of 5. If the value of counter is still within the range 1 to 5 the statements between BEGIN..END; are repeatedly executed. When the counter has been increased beyond the upper limit of 5 the computer will exit from the loop and branch to the next executable statement after the comment {end for}.

If the format of the FOR..DO statement is expressed as:

FOR variable := lower limit TO upper limit DO

then the lower and upper limits can be of any ordinal type, with the lower limit < upper limit. However, if the lower limit > upper limit then the word TO must be replaced by DOWNTO. This is illustrated in the following example.

```
PROGRAM LoopTest(OUTPUT);
{program to demonstrate FOR loops}

CONST
        p=5; q=25; r=3; {lower limit, upper limit, and step value}
TYPE
        COMPASS=(North, South, East, West);
VAR
        {loop variables used in FOR..DO loops}
        i, j, count     :INTEGER;
        letter          :CHAR;
        points          :compass;
```

```
BEGIN
      Write('(a) '); {count down from 10 to 1}
      FOR count:=10 DOWNTO 1 DO write(count:3);
      writeln;

      Write('(b) '); {count first five letters of the alphabet}
      FOR letter:='A' TO 'E' DO write(letter);
      writeln;

      Write('(c) '); {count from p to p+q in steps of r}
      FOR count:=p TO p+q DO
         IF (count-p) MOD r = 0 THEN
             Write(count:3);
         {end if}
      {end for}
      WriteLn;

      Write('(d) ');{count through the positions of the ordinal type COMPASS}
      FOR points:=North TO West DO Write(ORD(points):3);
      WriteLn;

      Write('(e) ');{An example of one loop nested within another loop}
      FOR i:=1 TO 2 DO {outer loop}
      BEGIN
         Write('i=>', i:1, ' j=>');
         FOR j:=1 TO 3 DO {inner loop}
             Write(j:2);
         {end for inner loop}
         WriteLn;
         Write(' ');
      END;
      {end for outer loop}
      WriteLn;
END. {LoopTest}
```

```
  Results from program being run

  (a)  10  9  8  7  6  5  4  3  2  1
  (b)   ABCDE
  (c)   5  8  11 14 17 20 23 26 29
  (d)   0   1   2   3
  (e)   i=>1     j=>1  2  3
        i=>2     j=>1  2  3
```

6.3 While..Do.

In the last example the number of employees was known in advance to be five. How could such a program be written if this figure was not known? The answer is to input data that will act as a trigger to cause the computer to exit from a loop. In the employee wages example if the last item of data was a negative value, this would signify the end of the data to be processed. Such a value is known as a sentinel. The sentinel must not be processed, therefore, it is important that the type of loop that uses a sentinel must test for the end of data before data is processed. This is in contrast to the repeat..until loop that tested for the exit condition after processing data (ie having gone through the loop at least once). The employee wages program can be modified further to allow any number of employees gross wages to be calculated. The instruction sequence is changed to:

```
BEGIN
      {input RateOfPay}
      {input HoursWorked}
      WHILE HoursWorked > = 0 DO
      BEGIN
          {calculate and output GrossWage}
          {input HoursWorked}
      END;
      {end while}
END. {wages}
```

Notice that the syntax does not define clearly the end of the loop. The use of the comment {end while} helps in identifying the limit of the while..do structure. The statement within the loop may be a single or compound statement. Since a negative value is being used as a sentinel it has been necessary to input *HoursWorked* twice, once outside the loop and once at the end of the loop. Failure to include reading *HoursWorked* outside the loop would result in the value of the Boolean expression being indeterminate. A modified program to allow any number of employees wages to be processed follows.

```
PROGRAM wages(INPUT, OUTPUT);
{program to calculate gross weekly wages for any number of employees}
VAR
      HoursWorked :REAL; {number of hours worked per week}
      RateOfPay :REAL; {hourly rate of pay}
      GrossWage :REAL; {weekly wage before deductions}
BEGIN
      Write('input hourly rate of pay = >');
      ReadLn(RateOfPay);
      Write('input number of hours worked = >');
      ReadLn(HoursWorked);
      WHILE HoursWorked > = 0 DO
      BEGIN
          GrossWage := HoursWorked * RateOfPay;
          WriteLn('gross wage £', GrossWage :6:2);
          Write('input number of hours worked = >');
          ReadLn(HoursWorked);
      END;
      {end while}
END. {wages}
```

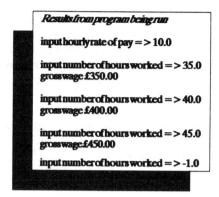

6.4 Worked Example.

A collection of wooden building blocks each have a different pattern. If two bricks are placed side by side they form a pattern combination; change the position of one brick and a different pattern combination is formed. For example:

is different to

Thus the number of patterns that can be formed using two blocks is 2 or 1x2. If three blocks are used the pattern combinations become:

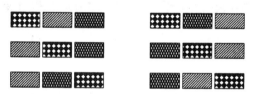

Thus with three blocks the number of pattern combinations is 6 or 1x2x3. Similarly with:

    4 blocks the number of pattern combinations is 1x2x3x4
    5 blocks the number of pattern combinations is 1x2x3x4x5
    6 blocks the number of pattern combinations is 1x2x3x4x5x6
  etc.

From these results the reader should deduce that the number of pattern combinations is always the product of the integers from 1 to the number of blocks (n). In mathematical jargon this is known as the factorial of the number of blocks (n!).

Write a program to output the number of pattern combinations produced as the number of blocks increases from 3 to N. Test the program for different values of N e.g. 10, 20, 30...... How does your computer respond to the different values of N ?

```
PROGRAM patterns(INPUT, OUTPUT);
VAR
      N                 :REAL; {maximum number of bricks}
      bricks            :REAL; {number of bricks used in pattern}
      BrickCounter      :REAL;{accumulative pattern counter}
      pattern           :REAL; {number of patterns}
BEGIN
      {input number of bricks in pattern}
      Write('input the number of different patterned bricks = > ');
      ReadLn(N);
      {terminate the routine if N < = 2}
      WHILE N>2 DO
      BEGIN
         {print heading}
         WriteLn('bricks patterns');
         {outer for loop used for number of bricks in pattern}
         FOR bricks := 2 TO N DO
         BEGIN
            pattern := 1;
            {inner for loop used to calculate patterns}
            FOR BrickCounter := 2 TO bricks DO
               pattern := pattern * BrickCounter;
            {end for}
            WriteLn(bricks :6, pattern:20:0);
         END;
         {end for}
         Write('input the number of different patterned bricks = > ');
         ReadLn(N);
      END;
      {end while}
END. {patterns}
```

```
Results from program being run

input the number of different patterned bricks => 4

bricks              patterns
  2                    2
  3                    6
  4                   24

input the number of different patterned bricks => 13

bricks              patterns
  2                    2
  3                    6
  4                   24
  5                  120
  6                  720
  7                 5040
  8                40320
  9               362880
 10              3628800
 11             39916800
 12            479001600
 13           6227020800

input the number of different patterned bricks => 0
```

Comment: When this program was run on an IBM PC compatible computer using Turbo Pascal a value of N=34 would cause the program to be abandoned owing to machine overflow. The largest real number that could be represented was 1E+38 and the the calculated value for pattern was too large to be represented as a real floating point number. The accuracy to which real numbers are stored on this system was 11 significant digits, therefore, the accuracy of the answers could only be guaranteed for N in the range 3 to 16.

6.5 Input of Numeric Data.
Consider for a moment how the segment of code:

```
REPEAT
    ReadLn(x,y,z);
UNTIL z=0;
```

would read the following data that was input at a keyboard.

```
3  8  4  2  9return
6  2  1  4  3  7return
2  4  0return
```

Note: a line of data is delimited by the return character.

In the first iteration of the loop x=3, y=8 and z=4. The three variables in the input list have been assigned data and the remainder of the data on that line is ignored. The next data to be read will be taken from the second line. In the second iteration x=6, y=2 and z=1. The remainder of the data on the second line is again ignored. Upon the completion of the third iteration x=2, y=4 and z=0. The iteration then terminates since the condition z=0 is now true.

The function of ReadLn, therefore, is to read data corresponding to the variables in the input list and then to skip to the next line, regardless of what data remains on that line.

The ReadLn statement can also be written without an input list. This implies that any data on the line is ignored and subsequent data to be read will be taken from the next line.

The ReadLn statement as the mnemonic suggests reads a line of data. The Pascal language also defines a Read statement, the syntax of which is identical to ReadLn. However, the semantics are quite different. Read has the effect of reading data regardless of how it is divided up into lines. The return becomes a data separator when reading numeric data. The segment of code:

```
REPEAT
    Read(p,q,r);
UNTIL r>10.0;
```

would read the following data that is input at the keyboard. Assume that the variables (p,q,r) are of type real.

```
16.3   7.9    8.1    12.9return
8.7    3.2    9.5    7.4return
11.6return
```

In the first iteration p=16.3, q=7.9 and r=8.1. In the second iteration p=12.9, q=8.7 and r=3.2 (notice the return was used as a separator - its effect as an end of line marker was ignored). In the third iteration p=9.5, q=7.4 and r=11.6. Since the condition r>10.0 is now true, no further iterations of the loop are performed.

6.6 Input of Character Data.

The statements ReadLn and Read can also be used for inputting characters, however, there is no requirement to separate character data by spaces. The following program illustrates how a sentence is input at the keyboard and the number of words in the sentence counted. It is assumed that only one space is used between words and the sentence is terminated by a full-stop.

```
PROGRAM WordCount(INPUT, OUTPUT);
{Program to count the number of words in a sentence}

CONST
        space = ' ';
        FullStop = '.';
VAR
        NextChar : CHAR; {character input from keyboard}
        words          : INTEGER; {number of words in sentence}

BEGIN
        words := 1; {initialise word count to 1}
        WriteLn('input sentence - terminate with full stop');
        Read(NextChar);
        WHILE NextChar < > FullStop DO
        BEGIN
            {count number of spaces between words}
            IF NextChar = space THEN
              words := words + 1;
            {end if}
            Read(NextChar);
        END;
        {endwhile}
        WriteLn;
        WriteLn('number of words in sentence => ', words:3);
END. {WordCount}
```

Results from program being run

input sentence - terminate with full stop
HOW MANY WORDS.

number of words in sentence => 3

In this last example the end of the sentence was detected by using the full-stop as a sentinel. However, it is possible to detect the end of a line of data by using the end of line function EOLN. The boolean function EOLN is true if the next character to be read is a return; otherwise, the value of the function is false.

How, you may ask, can the function be implemented for keyboard input, when clearly there is no way of knowing what the next character to be input will be? The implementation of character input at a keyboard can vary between different dialects of the language. Turbo Pascal and Sheffield Pascal implement character input in two different ways. Consider the following segment of code used to read characters input at the keyboard and write the same characters to the screen.

```
WHILE NOT EOLN DO
BEGIN
    Read(NextChar);
    Write(NextChar);
END;
ReadLn;
```

In running this program the reader might expect to input a character (with the system simultaneously displaying it on the screen) then write the character to the screen. This process is repeated until a return character is input. In running this segment of code on the PRIME computer the output was as forecast:

aabbccddeeffgghh

However, when the same segment of code was run on the IBM compatible microcomputer the output was not the same!

abcdefgh
abcdefgh

Sheffield Pascal immediately passes characters that are typed at the keyboard to the program and the EOLN function only becomes true when the return character has been read. However, the EOLN function for keyboard input in Turbo Pascal utilises a line buffer. As data are typed at the keyboard they are temporarily stored without being passed to the program. Only when the character return has been stored will the contents of the buffer be read, character by character, by the program. Since this is a complete line of data the EOLN function can detect when the next character is a return. By using the concept of the line buffer it becomes clear why the output from the IBM compatible machine appears as it does.

All characters are first input to the line buffer and simultaneously displayed on the screen (thus forming the first row of characters). The return character denotes the end of the line of input.

line buffer containing data typed at a keyboard

When the line of characters is complete (after return has been input) the program segment reads individual characters from the line buffer and writes each character to the screen (thus forming the second row of characters). When the next character to be read is return (character *h* will have just been written to the screen), the EOLN function is set to true and the computer will exit the while..do loop. However, the return character still remains in the line buffer. A further read statement in a later part of the program would pick-up the return as a valid character for processing. Since this would be undesirable, it is necessary to skip to the end of the line by using ReadLn and any further data to be read from the line buffer would be taken from the beginning of the buffer, which is in effect the start of a new line of data.

The last program to count the number of words in a sentence could now be modified using EOLN in place of the full-stop as a sentinal.

```
PROGRAM WordCount(INPUT, OUTPUT);
{program to count the number of words in a phrase}

CONST
        space = ' ';
VAR
        NextChar : CHAR; {character input from keyboard}
        words         : INTEGER; {number of words in sentence}

BEGIN
        words := 1; {initialise word count to 1}
        WriteLn('input phrase - terminate with return');
        WHILE NOT EOLN DO
        BEGIN
           Read(NextChar);
           {count number of spaces between words}
           IF NextChar = space THEN
              words := words + 1;
           {end if}
        END;
        {end while}
        ReadLn; {skip to next new line to by-pass return}
        WriteLn;
        WriteLn('number of words in phrase => ', words:3);
END {WordCount}.
```

```
Results from program being run

input phrase - terminate with return
HOW MANY WORDS IN THIS LINE OF TEXT?

number of words in phrase => 8
```

6.7 Summary.

A repeat..until loop will allow the statements within the loop to be executed at least once.

A for..do loop should be used as a counter in a program.

A while..do loop may never allow the statements within the loop to be executed if the condition for loop entry is false.

All data typed at a terminal in response to a read statement is stored in a temporary memory area known as a line buffer.

The predefined function EOLN is used to detect the end of the line of data that is stored in the line buffer.

keywords

REPEAT..UNTIL, WHILE..DO, sentinel;
FOR .. DO, ReadLn, Read, EOLN, line buffer.

6.8 Questions.

1. Write a program to calculate and output the overtime pay for ten employees. Overtime is paid at £12.00 per hour for every hour worked over 40 hours per week. Assume that employees do not work for fractional parts of an hour.

2. Write a program to output:

a. The odd integers in the range 1 to 29.
b. The squares of even integers in the range 2 to 20.
c. The sum of the squares of odd integers between 1 and 13.
d. The alphabet, both upper and lower case.

3. Write a program to output the first twenty terms of the Fibonacci series (1 1 2 3 5 8 . . .). Note: The next value in the series is the sum of the previous two values.

[4]. Write a program to find the arithmetic mean of a list of positive numbers, and print the arithmetic mean. The number of numbers is not known in advance. Terminate the procedure with zero.

5. Write a program to find the largest number from ten numbers input at the keyboard. Print the largest number.

6. Write a program to output a table of conversion from miles to kilometres. Miles should be integer values in the range 1 to 20.

[7]. Write a program to input a currency symbol of your choice and the exchange rate against Sterling. Output a table showing Sterling amounts from £1 to £20 and the equivalent amount of money in you chosen currency.

[8]. Maximum and minimum temperatures for a 14 day period are input to the computer. Calculate and output the peaks and troughs in both temperatures over this period. You should output the day number and temperature. A peak is a maximum temperature that is greater than the previous day and next day. A trough is a minimum temperature that is less than the previous day and next day.

9. Write a program to input a phrase and display the ASCII code in decimal for each character of the phrase.

[10]. Write a program to generate the values of 2 raised to the power of N, where N is in the range 0 to 15.

[11]. Modify the last program for N in the range -1 to -15. Print a third column in the table displaying the accumulated sum of 2 raised to the power of N for each value of N.

[12]. Write a program to input an unsigned 16-bit binary number and convert the number to a decimal integer.

7

Procedures

The purpose of this chapter is to explain a feature of Pascal that will allow instruction sequences to be divided up into small units that perform specific tasks. This is a preferred method of coding rather than writing one long instruction sequence that incorporates all the tasks to be performed.

7.1 Procedure Format.

The format of a procedure is very similar to that of a program. The following code compares the two formats and illustrates how a procedure is embedded within a program.

PROGRAM NameOfProgram(INPUT, OUTPUT);
{declaration section}

> *PROCEDURE NameOfProcedure(formal parameter list);*
> *{local declaration section}*
> *BEGIN*
> > *{instruction sequence}*
> *END;*
> *{end of procedure}*

{start of program instructions}
BEGIN
> **{instruction sequence containing call to procedure}**
> **NameOfProcedure(actual parameter list);**
END.
{end of program}

Both the program and procedure are given names that conform to the rules for composing identifiers.

A procedure is called or invoked, by specifying the name of the procedure, followed by an actual parameter list, that contains the data to be communicated to or from the procedure.

A procedure uses a formal parameter list to declare data that is to be input or output from a procedure.

Both program and procedure define the data that they use. The data defined at the program level can be referenced throughout by the program and procedures. However, a procedure declaration refers to data that is local to the procedure and is not shared with the rest of the program.

Both formats contain executable instruction sequences.

7.2 Program Structure.

The solution to many programming problems can often be divided into four tasks: initialisation of variables, input of data, calculations on data and the output of results. These tasks can be represented by separate procedures that are called when required from within the program. The following outline program shows how procedures are embedded within the program and the call to each procedure is controlled by the instruction sequence in the final part of the program. This control sequence is often referred to as the main program. The formal parameter list and local declaration section have been deliberately omitted from each procedure in order to clarify the structure of the program.

```
PROGRAM outline(INPUT, OUTPUT);
{declarations section}

     PROCEDURE initialise;
     BEGIN
          {instructions to initialise variables}
     END; {initialise}

     PROCEDURE DataIn;
     BEGIN
          {instructions to input data into program}
     END; {DataIn}

     PROCEDURE calculate;
     BEGIN
          {instructions to calculate results}
     END; {calculate}

     PROCEDURE ResultsOut;
     BEGIN
          {instructions to output results}
     END; {ResultsOut}

{start of main program}
BEGIN
     initialise;
     DataIn;
     WHILE NOT end of data DO
     BEGIN
        calculate;
        DataIn
     END;
     {end while}
     ResultsOut
END. {outline}
{end of main program}
```

The computer will execute the procedures in this program by following the instructions in the main program. This means that the procedure initialise will be called first then executed. The computer then returns to the main program and the next procedure, DataIn, is called. DataIn is executed and the computer returns to the main program. The computer will then test if the sentinel data value has been input. If the end of data has not been reached the computer will enter the while loop and call and execute the procedure calculate followed by the procedure DataIn. These two procedures will continue to be called and executed until the sentinel value has been input. Upon termination of the loop the computer will call and execute the procedure ResultsOut. When this procedure is completed the computer will return to the main program and terminate the program.

The structure of this program is illustrated in the following example. A program is written to input the maximum temperature for each day over a particular season of the year. These temperatures are converted to descriptions of the climate according to the following table.

description	temperature range
very hot	40..30
hot	29..20
mild	19..10
cold	9..0
very cold	-1..-20

The input of data is terminated with a temperature outside the range -20 to +40 degrees. The frequency of different weather conditions over the season is then displayed.

This program falls nicely into the four phases described in the last section. However, the reader's attention should be drawn to the following points.

The declaration of variables in the program has been made at the program level and not at the procedure level. The variables in the program are said to be *global* which implies that they can be referenced within any procedure in the program as well as being referenced in the main program. For this reason the actual and formal parameter lists and local variable declarations can be omitted since they serve no purpose here.

Notice that the procedure DataIn has been called twice, yet the procedure was only written once. Clearly, if program code is to be used at many points within a program it makes sense to write the code as one procedure and call it from these points as many times as necessary.

The main program which is used to control the order in which the procedures are used resembles a skeleton program that has had all the detail taken out of it. This type of code, as will be seen in the next chapter, is the starting point for designing programs using a top-down approach, where an overview of the solution is first documented and the fine detail of much of the coding is postponed to later program development.

```
PROGRAM climate(INPUT, OUTPUT);
{ program to record the frequency of weather conditions }

VAR
        temp : INTEGER; {temperature for one day of season}
        VeryHot, Hot, Mild, Cold, VeryCold : INTEGER;   {frequency of temperatures in
                                                             each category}

{begin procedures}
PROCEDURE initialise;
BEGIN
        VeryHot:=0; Hot:=0; Mild:=0; Cold:=0; VeryCold:=0;
END;{initialise}
```

```
PROCEDURE DataIn;
BEGIN
     Write('input temperature = > ');
     ReadLn(temp);
END;{DataIn}

PROCEDURE calculate;
BEGIN
     IF temp > 29 THEN
        VeryHot:=VeryHot+1
     ELSE IF temp > 19 THEN
        Hot:=Hot+1
     ELSE IF temp > 9 THEN
        Mild:=Mild+1
     ELSE IF temp > -1 THEN
        Cold:=Cold+1
     ELSE
        VeryCold:=VeryCold+1
     {end if}
END;{calculate}

PROCEDURE ResultsOut;
BEGIN
     WriteLn('climate days');
     WriteLn;
     WriteLn('very hot ', VeryHot);
     WriteLn('hot ', Hot);
     WriteLn('mild ', Mild);
     WriteLn('cold ', Cold);
     WriteLn('very cold ', VeryCold);
END;{ResultsOut}
{end procedures}

{start of main program}
BEGIN
     initialise;
     DataIn;
     WHILE (temp > -21) AND (temp < 41) DO
     BEGIN
        calculate;
        DataIn
     END;
     {end while}
     ResultsOut;
END.{climate}
{end of main program}
```

Results from program being run			
input	temperature	=>	20
input	temperature	=>	25
input	temperature	=>	30
input	temperature	=>	35
input	temperature	=>	15
input	temperature	=>	10
input	temperature	=>	5
input	temperature	=>	0
input	temperature	=>	-5
input	temperature	=>	-7
input	temperature	=>	0
input	temperature	=>	10
input	temperature	=>	20
input	temperature	=>	30
input	temperature	=>	40
input	temperature	=>	-21

climate	days
very hot	4
hot	3
mild	3
cold	3
very cold	2

7.3 Local Variables.

A procedure may contain a local declaration section consisting of const,type and var. However, the constants and variables can only be referenced in the procedure in which thay are declared or within another procedure embedded within the declaring procedure. The variables are *local* to the declaring procedures and *non-local* to the embedded procedures. In the following program the variables x,y and z are global, and the variables a,b, and c are local to the procedure alpha. This implies that a,b,c and x,y,z can be used in the procedure alpha, however, only x,y,z can be used outside of this procedure.

```
PROGRAM sum(INPUT, OUTPUT);
{ program to demonstrate the scope of procedure variables }
VAR
      x,y,z:integer;

PROCEDURE alpha;
VAR
      a,b,c:INTEGER;
BEGIN
      Write('input integer values for a and b =>');
      ReadLn(a,b);
      Write('input integer values for x and y =>');
      ReadLn(x,y);
      c:=a+b;
      WriteLn('sum of a and b is ',c)
END;{alpha}

{start of main program}
BEGIN
      alpha;
      z:=x+y;
      WriteLn('sum of x and y is ',z)
END.{sum}
{end of program}
```

```
Results from program being run

input integer values for a and b =>18 12
input integer values for x and y => 3 5
sum of a and b is    30
sum of x and y is     8
```

The function of this program is to call the procedure alpha that requests values for a,b,x and y to be input from a keyboard. The sum of a and b (local to alpha) is calculated and output. The computer returns to the main program and calculates the sum of x and y and outputs the result. This last sum could have been calculated and output in the procedure alpha, since x, y and z are global, however, the value c could not have been calculated and output in the main program since a,b and c are local to alpha. In the next program the variables a,b,c are local to the procedure alpha, however, since procedure beta is embedded within alpha the variables can also be used within this procedure. The variables are referred to as being non-local to beta.

```
PROGRAM reverse(INPUT, OUTPUT);
{ program to demonstrate the scope of non-local variables }

    PROCEDURE alpha;
    VAR
        a,b,c:CHAR;

            PROCEDURE beta;
            BEGIN
                Write('reverse order of characters input ');
                WriteLn(c,b,a)
            END;{beta}

    BEGIN
        Write('input three characters => ');
        ReadLn(a,b,c);
        beta
    END;{alpha}

{start of main program}
BEGIN
        alpha
END.{reverse}
{end of main program}
```

```
Results from program being run

input   three   characters   =>   ABC
reverse   order   of   characters   input   CBA
```

The function of this last program is to call procedure alpha which requests three characters a,b and c to be input; then calls beta that prints out these characters in reverse order. Notice that beta is embedded or nested within alpha, and that beta must be defined before it can be called by the procedure alpha. Within Pascal all data and procedures must be first defined before they can be used.

7.4 Parameters.

It has been stated that a procedure should be used whenever a group of instructions are to be executed from different points within a program. Communication with the procedure is via the procedure name and when specific data is to be passed, via the actual and formal parameter lists. The purpose of the parameter lists is to provide a mechanism for the exchange of data between the main program and procedure or two procedures. This is demonstrated in the following program to print a specific character a number of times. Both the character and the number of repetitions have been defined in the actual parameter list of the procedure call.

```
PROGRAM StarsAndStripes(INPUT, OUTPUT);
{ program to demonstrate the use of literals as parameters }

    PROCEDURE printer(symbol:CHAR; quantity:INTEGER);
    VAR
        counter:INTEGER;
    BEGIN
        WriteLn;
        FOR counter := 1 TO quantity DO
            Write(symbol);
        {end for}
    END;{printer}

BEGIN
    printer('*',10);
    printer('|',20)
END.{StarsAndStripes}
```

```
Results from program being run

* * * * * * * * * *
| | | | | | | | | | | | | | | | | | | |
```

Communication with this procedure is through printer('*',10); where * and 10 are the input values corresponding to symbol and quantity respectively, defined in the procedure. The result of calling procedure printer with symbol assigned * and counter assigned 10 would be a row of ten asterisks. Similarly a call to printer ('|',20) would produce a row of twenty stripes.

The actual parameter list is not restricted to literals, it can also be composed of variables as shown in the next program.

Before studying the next program it is worth mentioning that the control variable used in a for loop cannot be defined as a global variable if the for loop is included within a procedure. In both the last example and the next example the control variable counter is local to the procedure printer.

```
PROGRAM CharacterOutput(INPUT, OUTPUT);
{ program to demonstrate the use of variables in the actual parameter list }

VAR
      rep:INTEGER; {number of times character is output}
      inputchar:CHAR; {character to be displayed}

      PROCEDURE printer(symbol:CHAR; quantity:INTEGER);
      VAR
         counter:INTEGER;
      BEGIN
         WriteLn;
         FOR counter := 1 TO quantity DO
            Write(symbol);
         {end for}
         WriteLn;
      END;{printer}

BEGIN
      Write('input character => ');
      ReadLn(inputchar);
      Write('input repetition => ');
      ReadLn(rep);
      printer(inputchar, rep);
END.{CharacterOutput}
```

Results from program being run

input character => @
input repetition => 20

@@@@@@@@@@@@@@@@@@@@

The variables *inputchar* and *rep* have been defined at the program level and are, therefore, global. However, *symbol* and *quantity* are defined at the procedure level and are local to the procedure printer.

In the last two examples data was provided by the main program and passed across to the procedure. The communication of data was one-way only. There will be many occasions when a procedure is required to communicate data back to the calling program or calling procedure. This is only possible if the name used to identify the data in the formal parameter list is declared explicity as a variable by using VAR. Note also that when this occurs the corresponding parameter in the actual parameter list must also be a variable. To write the parameter as a literal or expression would clearly make no sense, since the parameter must store a data value passed across from the procedure.

A further worked example will be used to try and clarify to the reader the use of procedures and communication with procedures.

It is very common practice to provide account numbers (e.g. bank accounts, building society accounts, etc) with a check-digit. This digit provides a means for the computer to check that the account number has not been incorrectly entered into the computer by transposing digits. A modulus-11 check-digit for a 4 digit account number is calculated in the following way.

Using the account number 9118 as an example: multiply each digit by its associated weight, here we have the weights 5,4,3,2 and calculate the sum of the partial products.

$$(5x9) + (4x1) + (3x1) + (2x8) = 68$$

The sum 68 is then divided by 11 and the remainder 2 is then subtracted from 11, the result 9 is the check digit. The account number, including the check-digit as the last digit, becomes 91189. If the value of the check-digit is computed to be 10 this is replaced by the character X and a check-digit of 11 will be replaced by 0.

To check whether an account number has been entered into the computer correctly a similar calculation is carried out on the account number. The check-digit being given a weight of unity. If having divided the sum by 11 the remainder was non-zero then an error in typing the account number might have been made.

The following program illustrates how a procedure can be used to calculate a modulus-11 check-digit. Notice that a four digit account number *Acc* is passed to the procedure convert which in turn passes back to the main program the modulus-11 check-digit *CD*. Only the identifier *CheckDigit* need be declared as a variable since this variable will be passed back to the calling program, as illustrated below.

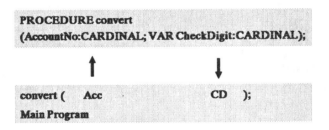

```pascal
PROGRAM Modulus(INPUT, OUTPUT);
VAR
    Acc :INTEGER;{four digit account number}
    CD :INTEGER;{check digit to be calculated}


    PROCEDURE convert(AccountNo:INTEGER; VAR CheckDigit:INTEGER);
    VAR
      d1,d2,d3,d4:INTEGER;{represent each digit of AccountNo}
      sum :INTEGER;{sum of partial products}
    BEGIN
      d1:=AccountNo DIV 1000;
      d2:=(AccountNo MOD 1000) DIV 100;
      d3:=(AccountNo MOD 100) DIV 10;
      d4:=AccountNo MOD 10;
      sum:=(5*d1)+(4*d2)+(3*d3)+(2*d4);
      CheckDigit:=11-sum MOD 11;
    END;{convert}


{start of main program}
BEGIN
    Write('input account number => ');
    ReadLn(Acc);
    convert(Acc, CD);
    Write('modulus 11 check digit is => ');
    IF CD = 10 THEN
        Write('X')
    ELSE
        IF CD = 11 THEN
            Write('0')
        ELSE
            Write(CD);
        {end if}
    {end if}
    WriteLn;
END.{Modulus}
{end of program}
```

```
Results from program being run

input account number => 3456
modulus 11 check digit is =>  8

input account number => 1001
modulus 11 check digit is =>  4

input account number => 1234
modulus 11 check digit is =>  3
```

7.5 Forward References.

If within a procedure, there is a reference to a procedure that has been defined later in a program, the compiler will flag the procedure call as an undefined identifier. In the following program, procedure *beta* is being called from within procedure *alpha* before *beta* has been defined. This is known as a *forward reference*.

```
PROGRAM MutualRecursion(INPUT, OUTPUT);
VAR  A,B:CHAR;

PROCEDURE alpha(VAR a,b:CHAR);
VAR  X,Y:INTEGER;
BEGIN
     beta(X,Y);
END; {alpha)

PROCEDURE beta(VAR x,y:INTEGER);
VAR  A,B:CHAR;
BEGIN
     alpha(A,B);
END; {beta}

BEGIN
     alpha(A,B);
END. {MutualRecursion}
```

A Pascal compiler can only cope with such a forward reference by including the reserved word FORWARD after the procedure name and parameter list of the undefined procedure. The example given above would be modified to include:

```
PROCEDURE beta(VAR x,y:INTEGER); FORWARD;
PROCEDURE alpha(VAR a,b:CHAR);
VAR  X,Y:INTEGER;
BEGIN
     beta(X,Y);
END; {alpha)

PROCEDURE beta;
VAR  A,B:CHAR;
BEGIN
     alpha(A,B);
END; {beta}
```

Notice that the name of the procedure and formal parameter list are followed by the reserved word FORWARD. Only the instructions within the procedure *beta* have been postponed to later. When the contents of the procedure *beta* is defined the formal parameter list does not appear again.

In this example it is clear that procedure *alpha* calls procedure *beta*, then procedure *beta* calls procedure *alpha*, and so on. These procedures are exhibiting *mutual recursion*.

7.6 Summary.

A program should be divided up such that each specific task in a program is coded as a procedure.

Data is communicated between the main program and procedure or between two procedures via parameter lists.

The same number of parameters must appear in both the formal and actual lists.

Each corresponding pair of parameters between the two lists must be of the same data type.

An actual parameter that corresponds to a variable formal parameter must be a variable.

The control variable of a for loop must be defined as being local to the procedure in which it is used.

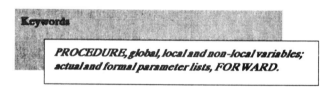

Keywords

PROCEDURE, global, local and non-local variables; actual and formal parameter lists, FORWARD.

7.7 Questions.

1. If the following variables are global:

VAR
        A,B,C:INTEGER;
        X,Y,Z:CHAR;

State the errors, if any, in the following procedure calls and procedure declarations.

	call procedure	declaration
a.	alpha	alpha(d,e,f)
b.	beta(A,B,C)	beta
c.	delta(18,'*')	delta(VAR C:INTEGER;Z:CHAR)
d.	gamma(X,Y)	gamma(i,j,k:INTEGER)

2. Trace through the following programs and determine the output from each program.

a.   PROGRAM alpha(INPUT, OUTPUT);
        VAR
            x:CHAR;
            y:INTEGER;
            PROCEDURE beta(X:CHAR;VAR Y:INTEGER);
            BEGIN
                Y:=ORD(X)
            END;

```
BEGIN
    x:='z';
    beta(x,y);
    WriteLn('ASCII code for ',x,' is ',y)
END.{alpha}
```

b.
```
PROGRAM delta(INPUT, OUTPUT);
VAR
    j:INTEGER;

    PROCEDURE epsilon(symbol:CHAR; n:INTEGER);
    VAR
        i : INTEGER;
    BEGIN
    FOR i:=1 TO n DO
        Write(symbol);
        WriteLn;
    END;{epsilon}

BEGIN
    j:=1;
    WHILE j<11 DO
    BEGIN
        epsilon('.',j);
        j:=j+1;
    END;
    {end while}
END.{delta}
```

[3]. Write a complete program to input a sentence, count the number of words, frequency of each vowel and the number of consonants. Output the result of your analysis. You should write separate procedures for initialisation, data input, calculations and the output of results, and control the use of these procedures through a main program.

4. Write a procedure to calculate the diameter, circumference and area of a circle, when supplied with the radius. Use this procedure in a program that will allow the user to input any number of radii and output the results from the procedure.

5. Examination marks are categorised into the following grades.

mark range	grade
100 - 85	distinction
84 - 65	merit
64 - 40	pass
39 - 0	fail

Write a program to input a sequence of examination marks, and keep a count of the number of marks in each category of grade. At the end of the sequence, output the frequency of the marks in each grade, and the number of examination marks input.

[6]. Write a procedure to convert octal digits (base 8) to words. The input parameter is an octal digit and the output parameter a Boolean variable to denote the success or failure of the translation. Use this procedure in a program that will allow a user to input any number of characters and output either the correct word from the procedure, or an audible warning (bell) to indicate that the character typed was not an octal digit.

[7]. A picture-framer has a supply of picture mouldings of various lengths. He wants to cut from them as many 0.5m lengths as possible and where a 0.5m length cannot be cut he will cut 0.2m lengths. Write a program to input the length of a strip of moulding, calculate the number of 0.5m, 0.2m lengths and the amount of wasted moulding. Repeat the program for different lengths of moulding and keep a running total of the number of 0.5m and 0.2m lengths. At the end of the program output the total number of 0.5m and 0.2m lengths and in addition the total amount of moulding wasted. Use the same procedure twice, to calculate the number of 0.5m lenghts, 0.2m lengths and eventual waste.

8

Program Development

Up to now the type of programming problem that has been used has been very simple to solve. This was to enable the reader to understand the fundamentals of the language without getting entangled with difficult solutions. However, the majority of programming problems are much more complex to solve and it is necessary to be able to design computer programs rather than intuitively composing them at the keyboard. There are numerous methods of designing programs, but only one method known as stepwise refinement will be explained in this chapter. This chapter also explores the stages of developing a program from the initial problem specification through to the final coding and testing of the program.

8.1 Program Design.

The novice programmer may well question why it is necessary to design programs at all. Indeed some programmers produce rough and ready solutions at a keyboard and continue to amend their programs until eventually the program appears to do what was expected. This is not a recommended approach to programming for the following reasons.

The final code is probably not easy to follow since it was no more than cobbled together.

The documentation of variable names and specific items of code are probably non-existent.

The program may not have been broken down into logical tasks and written as separate procedures.

There was probably no plan for testing the program or procedures and indeed the program might easily fail. Remember that such programs are produced by continuous amendments until the program appears to work. This changing or tinkering with code often leads to unforeseen side effects that may not manifest themselves for quite some time.

Lastly, what of the programmer who is asked to maintain (modify) the code at a later date? Without sufficient documentation such a task is normally preceded by tracing through the program in order to gain an insight into how the program functions. Since program maintenance accounts for a substantial proportion of programming budgets, clearly any improvement in programmer productivity must be a saving.

All good development techniques embody some, if not all, of the following stages.

Stage 1: Understand clearly the nature of the problem. Write a narrative on what the program does and how it is meant to achieve this goal. Within this narrative determine what data is to be input and what information is to be output.

Stage 2: Write a rough outline of how to solve the problem. This will be very brief and the first attempt at solving the problem. No detailed coding is expected at this stage. From this outline it is possible to state the initial procedures that can be used in the program.

Stage 3: For each procedure derive an outline of the code required, and refine this code further into other procedures or until it is possible to code the procedure in the chosen language.

Stage 4: Document the purpose and nature of all identifiers and procedures and code each procedure and the main program from the completed design.

Stage 5: Invent simple test data and give all program code a desk check or dry run before typing the program into the computer. This will help to discover many errors before the compilation and execution stages.

Stage 6: Compile and if necessary edit and re-compile the program in order to remove any syntax errors.

Stage 7: Test the program using the same test data that was used for the desk check.

Ensure that the results are consistent with those expected. Apply more stringent tests on the program using data that, where possible, will test the program to its limits.

8.2 Stepwise Refinement.
This technique embodies stages 2 and 3 explained above and is best demonstrated through a worked example.

Problem. Motor-cycle time trials take place over one day only. The course is such that the starting and finishing posts are many miles apart. All motor-cycle entrants are given a unique consecutive number starting at 1 (e.g 1,2,3 etc). This number is used to determine the order in which each entrant will ride. It is assumed in this problem that all the riders will complete the course. The number is also displayed on the motor cycle and rider as a means of identification. The time, based on the 24 hour clock with an accuracy to the nearest minute, is recorded for each entrant at the start and at the finish of the trial. Riders are started at different times and both their start and finish times are recorded for future computer analysis. Write a computer program to input the number of entrants, and the starting and finishing time of each entrant (e.g. start time 12.15 finishing time 13.49). Notice that although the start and finish times are input as real decimal numbers, 12.15 implies 12 hours 15 minutes past midnight. Output the number of the winning rider together with the fastest time in minutes. Also output the mean time for all riders and the slowest time. The model for problem solution given in the last chapter of:

> initialisation of variables
> input of data
> calculations on data
> output of results

can also be applied to this problem. However, since there are many riders in the time trials the input of data and calculations based on this data must be repeated, therefore, the model is refined to:

> initialise
> input number of entrants in trials
> FOR each entrant DO
> > input start and finish times
> > calculate time to complete trial
> > calculate statistics
> {end for}
> output results

With the exception of the for loop each numbered line in this new model can represent a procedure call. In fact the model represents the main program which in essence is the solution to the problem with all the detail removed. Each procedure call can be represented by a further model.

initialise

Set total time for all riders to zero (this is the running total necessary in calculating the mean time);

set the fastest time to a suitable large value (MAXINT) otherwise, items of data may not be less than the initial value;
set the slowest time to complete to zero, otherwise, items of data may not be greater than the initial value.

input number of entrants in trials

```
REPEAT
        input number of entrants
UNTIL number of entrants > 0
```

Notice that by including the input statement in a repeat..until loop only a positive number will be accepted. Any attempt to input a negative or zero value will result in the boolean expression being false and the input statement will be repeated. However, any attempt to input non-integers will be trapped by the operating system and the program would be abandoned.

input start and finish times

```
REPEAT
        input start time
        input finish time
UNTIL finish time > start time
```

Again the use of the repeat..until loop is a valuable aid in ensuring that a finish time is chronologically greater than a start time.

The start and finish times are input in the format of a 24 hour clock, therefore, the calculation of the time to complete the trial is not simply a matter of subtracting the two times. The hour and minute components of the time in the format HH.MM (e.g. 12.15) must be isolated into HH and MM (e.g. 12 and 15 respectively). Program component 4.2 and 4.3 must therefore be refined further. To indicate a lower level of refinement more digits are appended to the steps that are to be refined.

input start time

```
REPEAT
        input start time
        isolate time into hour and minute components
UNTIL no error in input data
```

input finish time

```
REPEAT
        input finish time
        isolate time into hour and minute components
UNTIL no error in input data
```

From these two refinements it is clear that the same code can be used to input the start and finish times and isolate the time into hour and minute components. A new procedure is required to isolate the time into hour and minute components. This routine can also be used to check on the validity of the data that has been input (e.g. -14.20, 26.30, 00.78 are all invalid times and must be rejected). A range check on the hour and minute components can be incorporated into the procedure.

isolate time into hour and minute components
set error flag to true
separate hours
separate minutes
IF hours or minutes not valid THEN
      set error flag to false
{end if}

In calling this procedure the 24 hour-clock time will be an input parameter and hours, minutes and error flag will be output parameters.

calculate time to complete trial
IF finish minutes < start minutes THEN
      calculate difference in minutes using number base 60 and adjust start hours
ELSE
      calculate difference in minutes
{end if}
calculate time of rider

If the start time is 12.15 and the finish time 13.10 then the finish minutes (10) is less than the start minutes (15). The difference in minutes is (60-15+10) and not (15-10). The start hours must then be adjusted to (12+1). If, however, the start time was 12.30 and the finish time was 13.45 then the finish minutes would not be less than the start minutes and the difference in minutes is (45-30) with no adjustment needed to the start hours.

calculate statistics

IF time of rider < fastest time THEN
      set fastest time to time of rider
      set winner to rider number
{end if}
IF time of rider > slowest time THEN
      set slowest time to time of rider
{end if}
add time of rider to total time for all riders
update mean time for riders

Since the calculation of the mean time is only necessary when the total time for all the riders has been calculated it appears very inefficient to have the calculation repeated for each rider. However, the alternative would be to include the calculation of the mean in either the main program or in the procedure to output the results. However, since machine time is of little importance in the execution of this program the author has deliberately kept the calculation within the statistics procedure as a means of preserving the integrity of each procedure.

output results

output winner with fastest time
output mean time
output slowest time

This concludes the step-wise refinement technique for designing the program since it is now possible to translate the pseudo-code into Pascal without the need for further refinement.

8.3 Coding.
Each procedure that was designed using the step-wise refinement technique is now coded into Pascal. During this stage it is far easier to develop a list of variables as each procedure is built rather than anticipating the variables that will be required before coding can take place. Remember at this stage the coding is still a pencil and paper exercise. As an example of how the code is developed consider again the design of the procedure to input start and finish times. Notice how the steps of the design incorporate all the refinements at the lower levels.

input start and finish times

```
REPEAT
      REPEAT
         input start time
         isolate time into hour and minute components
      UNTIL no error in input data
      REPEAT
         input finish time
         isolate time into hour and minute components
      UNTIL no error in input data
UNTIL finish time > start time
```

Coding from this design requires the programmer to write Pascal code and to invent suitable identifiers as follows.

```
PROCEDURE times;
BEGIN
      REPEAT
         REPEAT
            Write('input start time for rider ' ,rider, '= > ');
            ReadLn(StartTime);
            isolate(StartTime,StartHours,StartMinutes,NoError);
         UNTIL NoError;
         REPEAT
            Write('input finish time for rider ' ,rider, '= > ');
            ReadLn(FinishTime);
            isolate(FinishTime,FinishHours,FinishMinutes,NoError);
         UNTIL NoError;
      UNTIL FinishTime>StartTime;
WriteLn;
END; {times}
```

The names of the variables and their data types that had to be invented to produce this code are:

StartTime, FinishTime	: REAL;
StartHours, StartMinutes, FinishHours, FinishMinutes	: INTEGER;
rider	: INTEGER;
NoError	: BOOLEAN;

When all the procedures and the main program have been coded and a list of variable names and their types invented, the procedures and variables can be documented using appropriate comments.

8.4 Comments.

The use of comments was briefly introduced in chapter 2, and up to now little emphasis has been placed on the style of commenting a program. Commenting a program falls into two categories.

(i) Comments can be used to describe the history, version or function of a program, these comments normally appear at the head of the program.

(ii) Comments that are used in the declaration and instructional sequences of the program.

Good comments are those that do not repeat what is already written in the code, they give additional information, clarify the meaning of objects and report on the status of the algorithm at appropriate points.

Each program should contain a comment specifying the author, date, when and by whom the last alteration was carried out and the purpose of the program.

Each procedure of a program should contain a comment which describes the purpose and input and output parameters, if any.

8.5 Complete Program.

In this section all the pseudo-code produced from the stepwise refinement design has been translated into Pascal. In addition the complete program has been commented along the style described in the last section.

PROGRAM TimeTrials(INPUT, OUTPUT);

{Author: B.J.Holmes Date: 10/4/1990
This program requires the number of riders in a time trial scramble to be input, together with the start and finish time for each rider. The number of the winning rider and the fastest time are output, together with the mean time for all riders and the slowest time }

```
VAR
        NumberOfRiders        :INTEGER; {number of entrants in time trials}
        StartTime, FinishTime :REAL; {start and finish time of each rider}

        {start and finish times split into respective hours and minutes
        components e.g. 12.15 split into 12 hours and 15 minutes }
        StartHours,StartMinutes,FinishHours,FinishMinutes:INTEGER;
        TotalTime     :INTEGER; {running total time for all riders}
        TimeOfRider:INTEGER; {time taken to complete course e.g 73 minutes}
        minutes       :INTEGER; {temporary variable used in calculation of time of rider}
        rider         :INTEGER; {number of rider}
        NoError       :BOOLEAN; {flag set at true if no errors detected on input}

        MaxTime       :INTEGER; {time of slowest rider}
        MinTime       :INTEGER; {time of fastest rider}
        MeanTime      :REAL; {average time of all riders}
        winner        :INTEGER; {rider with fastest time}

PROCEDURE initialise;
{initialise all dependent variables}
BEGIN
        TotalTime:=0; MaxTime:=0; MinTime:=MAXINT;
END;{initialise}

PROCEDURE entrants;
{input number of riders}
BEGIN
        REPEAT
           Write('input number of entrants => ');
           ReadLn(NumberOfRiders);
           WriteLn;
        UNTIL NumberOfRiders >0
END;{entrants}

PROCEDURE isolate(var time:real; hours,mins:integer;var flag:boolean);
{split time into hours and minutes
        input time - corresponds to 24 hour clock time
        output hours - hour component of time
        output mins - minute component of time
        output flag - set at false if error found in input data}

BEGIN
        flag:=True;
        hours:=trunc(time);
        mins:=100*(time-hours);
        IF hours < 0 or hours > 23 or mins > 59 THEN
           flag:=False;
        {end if}
END;{isolate}
```

```
PROCEDURE times;
{input start and finish times}
BEGIN
    REPEAT
        REPEAT
            Write('input start time for rider ' ,rider, '= > ');
            ReadLn(StartTime);
            isolate(StartTime,StartHours,StartMinutes,NoError);
        UNTIL NoError;
        REPEAT
            Write('input finish time for rider ' ,rider, '= > ');
            ReadLn(FinishTime);
            isolate(FinishTime,FinishHours,FinishMinutes,NoError);
        UNTIL NoError;
    UNTIL FinishTime > StartTime;
    WriteLn;
END;{times}

PROCEDURE calculate;
{calculate time to complete course}
BEGIN
    IF FinishMinutes < StartMinutes THEN
    BEGIN
        minutes:= (60-StartMinutes) + FinishMinutes;
        StartHours:=StartHours + 1;
    END;
    ELSE
        minutes:=FinishMinutes-StartMinutes;
    {end if}
    TimeOfRider:=60*(FinishHours-StartHours) + minutes;
END;{calculate}

PROCEDURE statistics;
{calculate fastest, slowest and mean time}
BEGIN
    IF TimeOfRider < MinTime THEN
    BEGIN
        MinTime:=TimeOfRider;
        winner:=rider;
    END;
    {end if}
    IF TimeOfRider > MaxTime THEN
        MaxTime:=TimeOfRider;
    {end if}
    TotalTime:=TotalTime + TimeOfRider;
    MeanTime:=TotalTime/NumberOfRiders
END;{statistics}
```

```
PROCEDURE results;
{output information about trials}

BEGIN
     WriteLn;
     WriteLn('winner of time trials is rider number ', winner);
     WriteLn('with the fastest time of', MinTime, ' min');
     WriteLn;
     WriteLn('mean time of riders = ', MeanTime:5:1, ' min');
     WriteLn('slowest time = ', MaxTime, ' min');
END; {results}

{main program}
BEGIN
     initialise;
     entrants;
     FOR rider:=1 TO NumberOfRiders DO
     BEGIN
        times;
        calculate;
        statistics;
     END;
     {end for}
     results;
END. {TimeTrials}
{end of program}
```

8.6 Desk Check.

A programmer, having designed and coded a solution to a problem, must verify that the program is correct before proceeding with typing the program into the computer. In order to verify that the program represents a correct solution to a problem it is necessary to trace through the code using suitable test data. The outcome of such a trace or desk check will be the values of a list of variables, at different stages in a program, summarised in a table. When choosing test data the following points should be kept in mind.

The type and nature of the data is representative of the problem. Numerical data, where applicable, should be chosen for ease of calculation.

Data is meaningful and within well defined ranges. However, this assumes that the program being tested will always use valid data. This is not always the case since some programs will be specifically written to trap bad data. In such circumstances the data must be chosen to cover all eventualities.

To initially test the design of the TimeTrials program the following test data will be used.

comment	test data
number of entrants	3
start time entrant 1	11.00
finish time entrant 1	11.38
start time entrant 2	11.10
finish time entrant 2	12.40
start time entrant 3	11.30
finish time entrant 3	12.10

A table of variables and data values is built as each procedure is systematically traced by hand, in the order dictated by the main program. The reader is advised to build a similar table and compare it with the one that follows to ensure that they understand how to trace the code.

variable	values
NumberOfRiders	3
StartTime	11.00 11.10 11.30
FinishTime	11.38 12.40 12.10
StartHours	11 11 11
StartMinutes	0 10 30
FinishHours	11 12 12
FinishMinutes	38 40 10
TotalTime	0 38 128 168
TimeOfRider	38 90 40
minutes	38 30 40
rider	1 2 3
NoError	T T T T T
MaxTime	0 38 90
MinTime	999 38
MeanTime	12.66* 42.66* 56 *error
winner	1
flag	T T T T T
time	11.00 11.38 11.10 12.40 11.30 12.10
hours	11 11 11 12 11 12
mins	0 38 10 40 30 10

On tracing through the code an anomaly has been uncovered regarding MeanTime. Although the final result of 56 is correct the intermediate results of 12.66 and 42.66 are incorrect. The line of code for calculating the mean should be changed to:

MeanTime:=TotalTime/rider

since the mean time will change as the number of riders increases. Having traced through the code the only error that was discovered was the calculation of MeanTime. On the face of it this code appears to be error-free! After all the final results of :

winner of time trials is rider number 1
with the fastest time of 38 min
mean time of riders = 56.0 min
slowest time = 90 min

agree with the original test data used. With such confidence the programmer can now type the program into the computer and compile the program.

8.7 Syntax Errors.

Syntax errors refer to the grammar of the language not being correctly used. To the beginner these errors can be a nightmare! Not only do they occur in such profusion, but the compiler messages that are generated appear to have little or no meaning. If the program TimeTrials is input to a Turbo Pascal compiler the following error messages would be output.

Error 44: Type Mismatch and referred to the line of the procedure isolate mins:=100*(time-hours).

Since the right-hand side of the assignment is stored as a real value the left-hand side must also be of the same data type. As mins is declared as an integer there is clearly a mismatch of data types. One solution is to convert the right-hand side to integer storage, by using the TRUNC function. The line is then edited to:

mins:=TRUNC(100*(time-hours));

Error 17: THEN expected and referred to the line of the procedure isolate IF hours < 0 OR hours > 23 OR mins > 59 THEN.

The syntax demands that each boolean expression is enclosed in parenthesis. The line must be edited to:

IF (hours < 0) OR (hours > 23) OR (mins > 59) THEN

Error 41: Unknown identifier or syntax error and referred to the line of the procedure calculate else. Upon inspection of the code surrounding the offending else the true cause of the error can be detected.

```
        StartHours:=StartHours+1;
    END;
    ELSE
        minutes:=FinishMinutes-StartMinutes;
```

There is no requirement to terminate the END with a semi-colon since an ELSE follows. Edit the line END; by removing the semi- colon.

Having performed the necessary edits to the code the program is re-compiled. This time the compiler does not notify of any errors and it is reasonable to assume that the program can be link loaded and executed.

8.8 Run-time Errors.

If the program was run the following results would appear on the screen of the terminal.

winner of time trials is rider number 1
with the fastest time of 0 min
mean time of riders = 0.0 min
slowest time = 0 min

These are clearly not the results that were expected from the desk check. Despite there being no syntax errors, there are errors in the program that have appeared at run-time. The only way of detecting these errors is to desk check the code again and if this does not prove to be successful then introduce a trace into the code.

An initial trace can be incorporated into the main program. This involves displaying the values of variables at different points in the code. The additional code used for the trace has been emphasised in bold type in the main program.

```
{main program}
BEGIN
        initialise;
        entrants;
        FOR rider:=1 TO NumberOfRiders DO
        BEGIN
            times;
            WriteLn('rider number=',rider);
            WriteLn('StartTime=',StartTime);
            WriteLn('StartHours=',StartHours);
            WriteLn('StartMinutes=',StartMinutes);
            WriteLn('FinishTime=',FinishTime);
            WriteLn('FinishHours=',FinishHours);
            WriteLn('FinishMinutes=',FinishMinutes);
            calculate;
            WriteLn('TimeOfRider=',TimeOfRider);
            statistics;
            WriteLn('MinTime=',MinTime);
            WriteLn('winner=',winner);
            WriteLn('MaxTime=',MaxTime);
            WriteLn('TotalTime=',TotalTime);
            WriteLn('MeanTime=',MeanTime);
            WriteLn;
        END;
        results
END.{TimeTrials}
{end of program}
```

The results from running this program, using the trace with the original test data, are as follows.

```
input number of entrants => 3
input start time for rider 1 => 11.00
input finish time for rider 1 => 11.38
rider number=1
StartTime=1.1E+01
StartHours=0
StartMinutes=0
FinishTime=1.138E+01
FinishHours=0
```

FinishMinutes=0
TimeOfRider=0
MinTime=0
winner=1
MaxTime=0
TotalTime=0
MeanTime=0E+00

input start time for rider 2 => 11.10
input finish time for rider 2 => 12.40
rider number=2
StartTime=1.11E+01
StartHours=0
StartMinutes=0
FinishTime=1.24E+01
FinishHours=0
FinishMinutes=0
TimeOfRider=0
MinTime=0
winner=1
MaxTime=0
TotalTime=0
MeanTime=0E+00

input start time for rider 3 => 11.30
input finish time for rider 3 => 12.10
rider number=3
StartTime=1.13E+01
StartHours=0
StartMinutes=0
FinishTime=1.21E+01
FinishHours=0
FinishMinutes=0
TimeOfRider=0
MinTime=0
winner=1
MaxTime=0
TotalTime=0
MeanTime=0E+00
winner of time trials is rider number 1
with the fastest time of 0 min
mean time of riders = 0.0 min
slowest time = 0 min

Upon analysing the trace it is clear that the time is being returned from procedure isolate as 0 hours and 0 minutes. There could be two possible causes of this. Either the calculations for hours and minutes are incorrect or the declaration of the parameters is incorrect. Well, can you spot the mistake?

The declaration of the local variables in the formal parameter list contains an error. It has been incorrectly written as:

isolate(VAR time:REAL;hours,mins:INTEGER;VAR flag:BOOLEAN)

which implies that only time and flag have values that may be passed back to the calling routine. Hence StartHours, StartMinutes, FinishHours and FinishMinutes remain at zero since hours and minutes, although local to isolate, have not been defined as output parameters. The correct declaration is:

isolate(time:REAL; VAR hours, mins:INTEGER; VAR flag:BOOLEAN)

When this edit has been made and the program re-compiled the following trace is output.

```
input number of entrants = > 3
input start time for rider 1 = > 11.00
input finish time for rider 1 = > 11.38
rider number=1
StartTime=1.1E+01
StartHours=11
StartMinutes=0
FinishTime=1.138E+01
FinishHours=11
FinishMinutes=37
TimeOfRider=37  ·
MinTime=37
winner=1
MaxTime=37
TotalTime=37
MeanTime=3.7E+01

input start time for rider 2 = > 11.10
input finish time for rider 2 = > 12.40
rider number=2
StartTime=1.11E+01
StartHours=11
StartMinutes=9
FinishTime=1.24E+01
FinishHours=12
FinishMinutes=39
TimeOfRider=90
MinTime=37
winner=1
MaxTime=90
TotalTime=127
MeanTime=6.35E+01

input start time for rider 3 = > 11.30
input finish time for rider 3 = > 12.10
```

rider number=3
StartTime=1.13E+01
StartHours=11
StartMinutes=29
FinishTime=1.21E+01
FinishHours=12
FinishMinutes=9
TimeOfRider=40
MinTime=37
winner=1
MaxTime=90
TotalTime=167
MeanTime=5.56E+01
winner of time trials is rider number 1
with the fastest time of 37 min
mean time of riders = 55.7 min
slowest time = 90 min

If these results are checked against the expected results from the original desk check it is clear that they are still not quite correct. The fastest time is out by one minute and the mean time is out by 0.3. If the print out from the trace is examined, the reader may notice that StartMinutes and FinishMinutes are not always consistently correct.

StartTime	StartMinutes	FinishTime	FinishMinutes
11.00	0	11.38	37
11.10	9	12.40	39
11.30	29	12.10	9

The error must lie in the calculation of mins in the procedure isolate. If the assignment mins:=TRUNC(100*(time-hours)) is applied to the time 11.38 the result is:

$$TRUNC(100*(11.38-11)) = TRUNC(100*0.38)$$

Now you might be tempted to think that the TRUNC(38) is 38. But stop and think for a moment how the argument is stored inside the computer. The result of multiplying an integer(100) by a real(0.38) is a real. However, the representation of 38 as a real number may be 3.79999999E+01, in which case TRUNC(3.79999999E+01) becomes 37. The remedy is simple ! Do not use the function to truncate the number but to round it up to the nearest integer. A final edit is made on the procedure isolate such that:

$$mins:=ROUND(100*(time-hours))$$

The program is again re-compiled, link loaded and run, and this time produces the same results as the desk check. Finally, the extra lines of code needed to trace the values of the variables should be edited out of the main program. The program will then require a final compilation so that the object code is consistent with the finally edited program.

A more comprehensive set of test data is now invented to test the validity of the code, especially the data validation routines. It is left to the reader to type the program into their computer, with the suggested amendments, and after compilation invent further data to provide a stringent test on the validity of the program. However, the reader should be aware of two points.

The program in its present form cannot accurately cope with many riders who return the same minimum time to complete the course. Therefore, if there is a tie for first place the rider whose statistics were calculated first would retain the title of winner.

Remember the maximum size for a positive integer is 32,767 in Turbo Pascal running on an IBM compatible machine. What if this program was used on time trials with more than 500 riders and the average time to complete the course was 75 minutes. Would the program cope ? A simple calculation of 500*75 gives a TotalTime of 37,500 minutes which overflows the memory for the variable TotalTime. The answer is of course to change the type of variable from integer to real and inspect the code for any possible errors as a result. In the procedure initialise TotalTime:=0 would need to be changed to TotalTime:=0.0.

8.9 Summary.

Write a rough outline of how to solve the problem. This will form the basis of the main program by recognising which procedures will be needed.

Write a rough outline of how to solve each procedure, and keep refining the solution to each procedure until each procedure can be coded into Pascal.

Document the meaning of all identifiers and the purpose of each procedure and the main program.

Invent suitable test data and desk check each procedure, as necessary, and the entire program. This will help to minimise both logical and syntax errors.

Compile the program and if error free run it using the test data for the desk check. The results of the desk check and run-time check should be compared for accuracy.

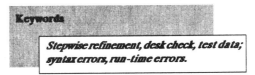

Keywords

Stepwise refinement, desk check, test data; syntax errors, run-time errors.

8.10 Questions.

Design and write computer programs to solve the following problems. Your answers should include: a complete design using step-wise refinement; a comprehensive fully documented program; test data and a desk check of the design with specimen results and the results from the program being run using the same test data as in the desk check.

[1]. A diamond merchant has recently received a consignment of stones. The diamonds are to be categorised into the weight classes given in the table. At the end of the weighings the merchant requires a print out of the total number of stones in each category and the percentage weight of each category. Assume that the electric balance the merchant uses is calibrated in milligrammes. Complete a program to input the weights of the diamonds and output the required statistics. Note: 200 mg is equivalent to 1 carat (SI).

class	carats
A	>100
B	>65
C	>35
D	>15
E	>5
F	<=5

[2]. The following rules enable an insurance company to determine the type of motor-insurance to issue, and the cost of the premium with any excesses to its clients. If the age of the driver is 25 years or more, the car is manufactured in the U.K. and the accident record is good, the premium charged is 6% of the declared value of the car and a comprehensive policy is issued. If the accident record is bad, the premium is raised to 7% and the policy holder pays the first £10 of a claim and a comprehensive policy is issued.

If the age of the driver is 25 years or more, the car is not of U.K. manufacture and the accident record is good, the policy holder pays the first £10 of any claim and a comprehensive policy of 6% is issued. If the above conditions apply, except that the accident record is bad, the premium is raised to 7% and a third party policy only is issued.

If the age of the driver is less than 25 years, the car is manufactured in the U.K. and the accident record is good the premium charged is 6% and a comprehensive policy is issued with the holder paying the first £10 of a claim. If the accident record is bad and the other conditions apply then the risk is declined.

If the age of the driver is less than 25 years, the car is not manufactured in the U.K. and the accident record is good, the premium charged is 8%, the policy holder pays the first £10 of any claim and a comprehensive policy is issued. If the accident record is bad and the other conditions apply then the risk is declined.

Assume that if a person has not had an accident within the last three years then the accident record is good.

Complete a computer program to output the type of motor insurance policy, the amount of the premium and excess payable on any claim, if applicable, when the following information is input to the computer. The age of the driver, U.K. or foreign car, number of years since last accident and the insured value of the car.

[3]. Consider the following rules for calculating income tax in a country.

Personal allowances are £1,200 for a single person and £2,300 for a married man. A child allowance is £100 per child. Taxable income is the amount remaining after deducting the personal allowance and the total child allowance from the gross income. Income tax is calculated from taxable income according to the table at the end of this question.

If gross salary, personal status (married or single) and the number of children are input to a computer, complete a program to calculate and print the income tax to be paid. Assume that married women are classified as single for tax purposes.

taxable income on		tax on taxable income
first	£1000	no tax
next	£1000	20%
next	£2000	30%
above	£4000	40%

[4]. A simple method for finding the area under a curve y=f(x) by computer is to find the area between the plotted function y=f(x), the x-axis and the limits x=a, x=b, using Simpson's rule. An approximation to the area becomes 1/3h(Y0 + 4Y1 +Y2)

If the area under the curve is divided into strips and Simpson's rule is applied to each strip between the limits x=a and x=b then clearly the more strips there are the more accurate will be the estimation of the area. Also the more strips there are the smaller h becomes.

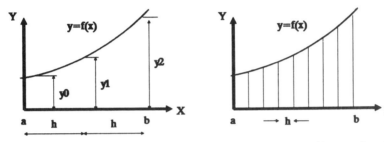

Complete a program to evaluate the area under the curve using Simpson's rule, and apply the program to find the area under the curve y=x*x, the x-axis and the limits x=1 to x=4.

[5]. Convert numbers represented in Roman numerals to decimal numbers. For example MDCLXIV = 1664. The following table indicates the size of each Roman numeral.

Roman	Arabic
M	1000
D	500
C	100
L	50
X	10
V	5
I	1

[6]. Develop a procedure for a bank cheque writing program, in which an amount of money in Sterling, up to £999,999.99 is input and converted into words. Only convert the £'s into words and not the pence. For example £123.45 would be converted to one hundred twenty three pounds 45p. You may omit the £ sign in the data.

9

Mathematics

This chapter is designed to inform the reader of topics in Pascal that relate to mathematics yet does not delve into mathematical theory. The chapter should not be omitted by the non-mathematical programmer since it brings to light several interesting features of the language.

The chapter contains a section on implicit functions, of which the reader will already be familiar through the use of ROUND, TRUNC, MOD, DIV, PRED, SUCC, ORD and CHR; a section on explicit programmer defined functions through the use of FUNCTION, which is similar in format to PROCEDURE. Finally a section on mathematical sets is included. This is a feature that is not common to programming languages yet can provide a valuable aid towards data validation.

9.1 Implicit Functions.

The following mathematical functions are available in the Pascal language and are in addition to those covered in earlier chapters.

Name	Description	Argument	Result
ABS	absolute value of argument	real/integer	same as argument
ARCTAN	the arc tangent of the argument (radians)	real/integer	real
COS	the cosine of the argument (radians)	real/integer	real
EXP	the value of e (2.71828) raised to the power of the argument	real/integer	real
LN	the logarithm to the base e of the argument	real/integer	real
ODD	true if argument is odd	integer	boolean
SIN	the sine of the argument (radians)	real/integer	real
SQR	the square of the argument	real/integer	same as argument
SQRT	the positive square root of the argument (positive)	real/integer	real

The following examples represent an interpretation of the meaning of those functions that are listed above.

ABS(X) returns the absolute value or modulus of X. e.g. ABS(-3.7) = 3.7
ARCTAN(X) returns the arc tangent of X in radians - i.e. the angle whose tangent is X. e.g. ATN(1) = 0.7854... since the tangent of 45 degrees (0.7854..radians) = 1.
COS(X) returns the cosine of X where X is in radians. e.g. COS(1.0472) = 0.5 note: 60 degrees = 1.0472 radians.
EXP(X) returns the exponential of X. e.g. EXP(1) = 2.71828 note: e = 2.71828...
LN(X) returns the natural logarithm of X where X > 0. e.g. LOG(2.71828) = 1; LOG(1) = 0
ODD(X) returns the boolean value true if X is odd, otherwise false if X is even. X must be an integer. e.g. ODD(3) is true, ODD(4) is false
SIN(X) returns the sine of X where X is in radians. e.g. SIN(0.5236) = 0.5 note: 30 degrees = 0.5236 radians.
SQR(X) returns the square of the argument. e.g. SQR(-10) = 100.
SQRT(X) returns the positive square root of the argument. e.g. SQRT(10) = 3.162277...

9.2 Explicit Functions.

Clearly it is impossible to provide all the functions (mathematical and non-mathematical) that a programmer may require in an application program. Therefore, incorporated into the Pascal language is a feature that allows a programmer to define explicitly any function. The syntax of a function definition is almost the same as that of a procedure. However, instead of supplying output parameters from a procedure the name of the function is the output variable. For this reason it is necessary to declare the data type of the function. The format of a function is given as:

```
FUNCTION NameOfFunction(formal parameter list): type declaration;
       local declaration section
BEGIN
       function body
END;
```

To define a function for the tangent of an angle the following code would be necessary. The formal parameter list will consist of input parameters only. For this reason the word VAR can be omitted. The name of the function is assigned a value within the function body. It is for this reason that the first line of the function declaration must also include a type declaration for the name of the function.

```
FUNCTION tan(angle:INTEGER):REAL;
CONST
       PI = 3.14159;
VAR
       radians:REAL; {angle in radians}
BEGIN
       radians := (angle * PI)/180;
       tan := sin(radians)/cos(radians); {value assigned to function tan}
END;{tan}
```

The following program prints the tangents of angles between 0 degrees and 20 degrees in steps of 1 degree. The function is called in exactly the same manner as any other function i.e. function name followed by argument(s). In this example the function has been called by tan(degrees). This function call has been deliberately written into the WriteLn statement to save introducing an extra variable and assignment statement.

```
PROGRAM TrigTable(OUTPUT);
VAR
       degrees:INTEGER; {angle in degrees}

FUNCTION tan(angle:INTEGER):REAL;
CONST
       PI = 3.14159;
VAR
       radians:REAL;
BEGIN
       radians:=(angle*PI)/180;
       tan:=sin(radians)/cos(radians);
END; {tan}

BEGIN
       WriteLn('degrees            tangent');
       WriteLn;
       FOR degrees:=0 TO 20 DO
          WriteLn(degrees:2,'      ',tan(degrees):10:4)
          {end for}
END. {TrigTable}
```

Results from program being run	
degrees	**tangent**
0	0.0000
1	0.0175
2	0.0349
3	0.0524
4	0.0699
5	0.0875
6	0.1051
7	0.1228
8	0.1405
9	0.1584
10	0.1763
11	0.1944
12	0.2126
13	0.2309
14	0.2493
15	0.2679
16	0.2867
17	0.3057
18	0.3249
19	0.3443
20	0.3640

9.3 Graphical Output.

Often it is required to output a graphical display. The next example illustrates how this is achieved for both the sine and cosine functions. Since the average size of a V.D.U. screen is approximately 80 characters wide and the absolute maximum value for both functions is 1, it is necessary to introduce factors that increase the width of the sine and cosine waves and centralise the position of the waves on the screen.

If a sine wave is to be output vertically the central axis should be positioned approximately 40 characters from the left hand edge of the screen. The width of the sine wave must also be increased by a factor of, say, 30 characters. Figure 9.1 illustrates the positioning of such a wave on the screen.

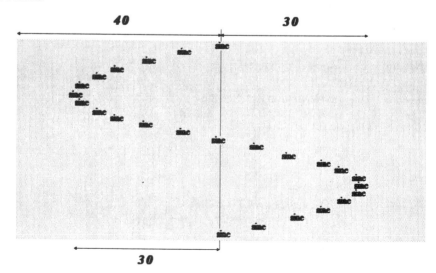

Figure 9.1 Position of Sine wave on a screen

In the following example a plot for the sine wave is given every 15 degrees over a continuous cycles. Once this program is running it will not terminate naturally! The reader is advised to investigate a method for the termination of a program on their computer system before attempting to execute this program. As an illustration, a BREAK key is provided on the IBM compatible computer and CTRL P is used on the PRIME system to abort a program that is being executed.

```pascal
PROGRAM graph1 (OUTPUT);
{program to output a sine curve}
CONST
        scale = 30;
        centre = 40;
        increment = 15;
        PI = 3.14159;
VAR
        i:INTEGER; {counter used in plotting distance from left-hand edge of screen}
        angle:INTEGER; {angle in degrees}

FUNCTION SineTrace:INTEGER;
{evaluate position on the screen for plotting sine wave}
BEGIN
        SineTrace:=TRUNC(centre-scale*sin(angle*PI/180));
END; {SineTrace}

BEGIN
        angle:=0;
        WHILE angle > = 0 DO
        BEGIN
           FOR i:=1 TO SineTrace DO
               Write(' ');
           {end for}
           WriteLn('sine');
           angle:=angle+increment;
        END;
{end while}
END. {graph1}
```

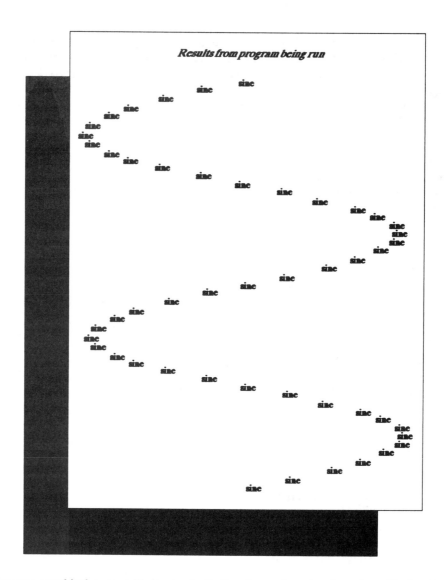

Results from program being run

The next graphical output illustrates both the sine and cosine functions displayed on the same screen. This program, as with the last, must be terminated by the user.

```
PROGRAM graph2(OUTPUT);
{program to output sine and cosine curves}
CONST
        scale = 30;
        centre = 40;
        increment = 15;
        PI = 3.14159;
VAR
        i:INTEGER; {counter used in plotting distance from left-hand edge of screen}
        angle:INTEGER; {angle in degrees}
```

```
FUNCTION SineTrace:INTEGER;
{evaluate position on screen for plotting sine wave}
BEGIN
     SineTrace:=TRUNC(centre-scale*sin(angle*PI/180));
END; {SineTrace}

FUNCTION CosTrace:INTEGER;
{evaluate position on screen for plotting cosine wave}
BEGIN
     CosTrace:=TRUNC(centre-scale*cos(angle*PI/180));
END; {CosTrace}

BEGIN
     angle:=0;
     WHILE angle > = 0 DO
     BEGIN
     {determine which wave point to plot first on the same line}
        IF CosTrace < SineTrace THEN
        BEGIN
           FOR i:=1 TO CosTrace DO
              Write(' ');
           {end for}
           Write('cos');
           FOR i:=CosTrace+1 to SineTrace DO
              Write(' ');
           {end for}
           Write('sine');
        END
        ELSE
        BEGIN
           FOR i:=1 TO SineTrace DO
              Write(' ');
           {end for}
           Write('sine');
           FOR i:=SineTrace+1 TO CosTrace DO
              Write(' ');
           {end for}
           Write('cos');
        END;
        {end if}
        WriteLn;
        angle:=angle+increment;
     END;
     {end while}
END. {graph2}
```

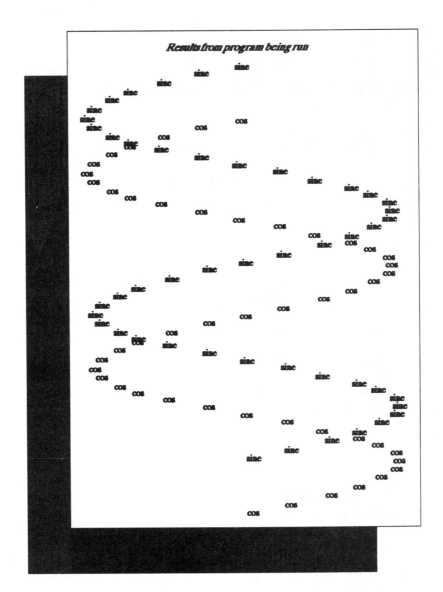

Results from program being run

9.4 Random Numbers.

Computers are frequently used to simulate or model real-world events, such as the frequency of traffic on road systems, queues of shoppers in a supermarket, etc. The heart of any simulation is a source of random numbers to reproduce the random effects of the real world. For a series of values to be random they must exhibit at least two qualities.

The numbers must be unbiased. There can be no digit or number which is found more or less frequently than others.

The values must be non-predictive. A zero cannot foretell the appearance of another zero, or some other particular value. This also applies to the size of the values, the production of a small or large value should not give any clue about the size of subsequent values.

Rolling a die will generate random numbers with the values 1,2,3,4,5 and 6. If after numerous rollings all six numbers did not appear to occur with equal frequency then the numbers would not be random. Similarly if there was some pattern in their order which allowed predictions of future values then they would not be classed as being random. This illustrates the concept of randomness. The values must appear an equal number of times (unbiased), and sequences should not be repeated frequently (non-predictive).

Both of these attributes are intended to be observed over, say, a few million values.

In computer simulations it is often necessary to use the same set of random numbers over many trials. This repetition of the same random numbers implies that they are not truely random and they are therefore termed pseudo-random numbers. The repetition of the same random numbers allows the model to be tested under exactly the same conditions each time.

Both Turbo Pascal and Sheffield Pascal support a pseudo-random number function. The format of the Turbo Pascal function is either:

RANDOM or RANDOM(argument)

If the argument is absent the function returns the random number X in the range $0 <= X < 1$. However, if the argument is present it must be of type integer and will return a random number Y, of type integer, in the range $0 <= Y <$ argument.

The Sheffield function RANDOM(argument), where the argument is of the type integer, will return a random number X of type real in the range $0 <= X < 1$. The function is controlled by the value of the argument thus:

argument < 0 : initialise the seed of the random number sequence to the time of day in centiseconds and return the first random number;

argument $= 0$: return the next random number in the sequence;

argument > 0 : initialise the seed of the random number sequence to the value of the argument and return the first random number.

Clearly there is an incompatibility between the implementaion of the function in the two dialects. Although the function will compile in both dialects it will not always give the same results. For this reason the function may be regarded as not being truely portable. The presence of a random number function in Pascal is non-standard, therefore, will not be used in this book.

A method that is frequently used in practice for generating pseudo-random numbers on a computer is a congruence method. This method will produce pseudo-random numbers with long cycles (long stream of values before the stream repeats itself) that have a sufficiently uniform distribution (unbiased). The formula for achieving such a set of values is: $X_{n+1} = a\ X_n\ (MOD\ b)$

For example, if $a = 2$, $b = 19$ and the initial value or seed $X_0 = 15$ then the following stream of values would result.

n	Xn	Xn+1
0	15	11
1	11	3
2	3	6
3	6	12
4	12	5
5	5	10
6	10	1
7	1	2
8	2	4
9	4	8
10	8	16
11	16	13
12	13	7
13	7	14
14	14	9
15	9	18
16	18	17
17	17	15
18	15	11
19	11	3
20	..	..
21	..	..

Figure 9.2 Random numbers produced by the congruence method

In choosing the values of a, b and X_0 the following points should be considered.

The maximum cycle length is never greater than b, so the value $b = 19$ in the example was too small. A suitable choice for b is :

$b = 10^w$ where w is the number of significant figures used.

The constant a should be chosen such that $a = 8p + (-)3$ where p is a positive integer. This will improve the cycle length. The value of a should be close to:

$$2^{w/2}$$

in order to prevent successive values being too closely related. The initial seed Xo is relatively prime to b (only common factor is 1).

These rules can be incorporated into the following function, written in Turbo Pascal, that when invoked will produce a random number (RN) in the range $0.1 <= RN < 1$.

```
FUNCTION RND:DOUBLE;
CONST
     a=LONGINT(19);
     b=LONGINT(100000000);
VAR
     RN:DOUBLE; {random number 0.1<=RN<1}
     y :LONGINT;
BEGIN
     y:=(a*seed) MOD b;
     seed:=y;
     RN:=ABS(y);
     REPEAT
        RN:=RN/10.0;
     UNTIL RN < 1.0;
     RND:=RN
END;{RND}
```

The function RND can be used in an expression to compute a random number in the range 1 to 6 for the simulation of rolling a die a set number of times. Since $0.1 <= RND < 1$ the expression: (TRUNC(1000.0*RND)MOD 6)+1 will generate random numbers in the range 1 to 6 with reasonable uniformity. The following program uses the function RND to generate random integers in the range 1 to 6, as a simulation of rolling a die. The number of trials refers to the number of times the die is rolled.

In the following program the directives {$N+}, and {$N-} respectively turn on and off two different models of floating-point code generation. {$N+} enables DOUBLE precision real representation to be used. Notice also the use of LONGINT as a type declaration for the constants a and b. This ensures that both constants will be represented using a four-byte mode of storage.

```
{$N+}
PROGRAM random(INPUT,OUTPUT);
{program to generate random numbers in the range 1 to 6 on an IBM PC compatible}
VAR
     seed:LONGINT; {seed value}
     trials:INTEGER; {number of times die is rolled}
     number:INTEGER; {random numbers to a line}
```

```
FUNCTION RND:DOUBLE;
CONST
     a=LONGINT(19);
     b=LONGINT(100000000);
VAR
     RN:DOUBLE; {random number 0.1 < = RN < 1}
     y :LONGINT;
BEGIN
     y:=(a*seed) MOD b;
     seed:=y;
     RN:=ABS(y);
     REPEAT
         RN:=RN/10.0;
     UNTIL RN < 1.0;
     RND:=RN
END;{RND}

BEGIN
     seed:=19;
     Write('input number of trials = > ');
     ReadLn(trials);
     FOR number:=1 TO trials DO
     BEGIN
         IF (number-1) MOD 10 = 0 THEN
             WriteLn;
         {end if}
         Write(((TRUNC(1000.0*RND)MOD 6) +1):2);
     END;
END.{random}
{$N-}
```

> **Results from program being run**
>
> **input number of trials = > 100**
>
> ```
> 2 2 5 2 3 3 2 1 3 1
> 5 5 1 4 2 3 2 4 4 6
> 6 3 5 1 6 5 2 2 3 2
> 4 1 6 6 6 5 4 3 3 6
> 6 4 2 4 6 5 1 2 3 5
> 4 2 3 1 3 3 1 5 4 6
> 6 6 3 1 6 2 4 3 3 3
> 6 6 3 1 4 1 6 3 6 1
> 1 5 3 4 6 5 5 4 6 1
> 3 3 4 4 2 1 6 3 2 6
> ```

9.5 Sets.

A set is a collection of objects of the same data type. For example, [1,3,5,7,9] represents a set of odd integers; [2,4,6,8,10] represents a set of even integers and [1..10] represents a set of both odd and even integers. A set that contains no objects is said to be empty and is represented as [ ]. These sets can be declared in Pascal as follows.

```
TYPE
      numbers = SET OF 1..10;
VAR
      odds, evens: numbers;
BEGIN
      odds:=[1,3,5,7,9];
      evens:=[2,4,6,8,10];
END.
```

Although set of INTEGER and set of CHAR (both scalar types) are syntactically correct, many implementations of Pascal restrict the size of the set and will reject this declaration. The set [-32768..32767] and the set of characters making up the ASCII set will be beyond the limits of most Pascal compilers. Reduced sets, however, are quite acceptable e.g. [A..Z], [0..99] etc.

A further example of set declaration follows.

```
TYPE
      colours = (red, orange, yellow, green, blue, indigo, violet);
      ColourSet = SET OF colours;
VAR
      rainbow: colours;
      paint: ColourSet;
```

The assignments

paint:= [ ] defines the empty set;

paint:= [red, blue, violet] defines three objects in the set;

paint:= [red..yellow, blue..violet] defines six objects in the set;

paint:= [orange, rainbow] is legal since rainbow will contain an object from colours;

paint:= orange is illegal since paint is of type ColourSet, and not colours, however,

paint:= [orange] is legal;

rainbow:= [blue] is illegal since rainbow is of type colours and is not a set, however,

rainbow:= blue is legal.

There are three processing operations, union, intersection and difference that can be performed on sets.

The union + of two sets is the set that contains all the objects from both sets.

e.g. [1,3,5,7,9] + [2,4,6,8,10] = [1,2,3,4,5,6,7,8,9,10]

The intersection * of two sets is the set containing only objects which are present in both sets.

e.g. [1,3,5,7,9] * [1,2,3,4,5] = [1,3,5]

The difference - of two sets is the set containing all the elements of the first set which are not members of the second set.

e.g. [1,3,4,6,7,8] - [1,3,7] = [4,6,8]

Sets may be compared using the following set relational operators

equality	set1 = set2
inequality	set1 < > set2
subset	set1 < = set2
proper subset	set1 < set2
superset	set1 > = set2
proper superset	set 1 > set2
set membership	object IN set

Set1 and set2 can be set variables or set values. The value of a set relation is either true or false corresponding to mathematical set theory. In the following examples if

alpha: = [a..z], vowel: = [a,e,i,o,u], omega: = [a,b,c,d,e]

then vowel = omega is false, since the two sets do not contain identical objects, however, vowel omega would be true;

vowel < alpha is true since the five vowels form a proper subset of the alphabet;

alpha > = omega is true since all the objects of omega can be found in alpha;

vowel > omega is false since three of the objects in omega do not appear in vowel;

'd' IN omega is true since the object is a member of the set omega;

'd' IN vowel is false since the object does not belong to the set vowel.

Problem. A small photographic society has a membership of fifteen people. The names of the members are:

Jack, Fred, Bill, Sybil, Basil, Jane, Barry, Colin, Audrey, John, Margaret, Joan, Stuart, Maud and Eve.

Groups of members specialise in different aspects of photography as follows.

Landscapes: Jack, Bill, Audrey, Maud;
Portrait: Jane, Colin, Jack, Stuart;
Macro: Barry, Basil;
Still-life: Fred, Bill, Margaret;
Glamour: Jack, Fred, Bill, John, Stuart, Margaret
Nature: Basil, Jane, Audrey.

Write a computer program to print a list of names of members who specialise in the following categories.

(i)   Landscapes and/or Nature.
(ii)   Portrait and Glamour.
(iii)   Nature and either Macro or Still-life.
(iv)   No specialities at all.

Before you scan through the following program to see how the author has solved the problem it is important for the reader to realise that you cannot output the contents of a set directly. It is necessary to compare the name of a member with the contents of a set using the IN operator. If the relationship is true the name of the member (enumerated type) must be selected using a CASE statement, then printed.

```
PROGRAM sets(OUTPUT);
{program to illustrate the use of sets}

TYPE
        members = (Jack,Fred,Bill,Sybil,Basil,Jane,Barry,Colin,
                    Audrey,John,Margaret,Joan,Stuart,Maud,Eve);
        membership = SET OF members;

VAR
        Groupmembers : membership; {specialists in category sets}
        landscapes, portrait, macro, StillLife, glamour, nature : membership;
        name : members; {name of member}
        TotalMembership : membership; {names of all the members}
```

```
PROCEDURE PrintName;
BEGIN
     CASE name OF
         Jack :Write('Jack ');
         Fred :Write('Fred ');
         Bill :Write('Bill ');
         Sybil :Write('Sybil ');
         Basil :Write('Basil ');
         Jane :Write('Jane ');
         Barry :Write('Barry ');
         Colin :Write('Colin ');
         Audrey :Write('Audrey ');
         John :Write('John ');
         Margaret:Write('Margaret');
         Joan :Write('Joan ');
         Stuart :Write('Stuart ');
         Maud :Write('Maud ');
         Eve :Write('Eve ')
     END
     {end case}
END;{PrintName}

PROCEDURE SelectName;
BEGIN
     name:=Jack;
     IF name IN Groupmembers THEN
         PrintName;
     {end if}
     REPEAT
         name:=SUCC(name);
         IF name IN Groupmembers THEN
             PrintName;
         {end if}
     UNTIL name=Eve;
     WriteLn; WriteLn;
END; {SelectName}

BEGIN
     landscapes:= [Jack,Bill,Audrey,Maud];
     portrait:= [Jane,Colin,Jack,Stuart];
     macro:= [Barry,Basil];
     StillLife:= [Fred,Bill,Margaret];
     glamour:= [Jack,Fred,Bill,John,Stuart,Margaret];
     nature:= [Basil,Jane,Audrey];
     TotalMembership:= [Jack..Eve];
```

```
Groupmembers:=landscapes + nature;
WriteLn('specialists in either landscapes or nature or both');
SelectName;

Groupmembers:=portrait*glamour;
WriteLn('specialists in both portrait and glamour');
SelectName;

Groupmembers:= (macro + StillLife) * nature;
WriteLn('specialists in nature and macro or still life or both');
SelectName;

Groupmembers:=TotalMembership- (landscapes+portrait+macro
                             +StillLife+glamour+nature);
WriteLn('members who do not specialise in any category');
SelectName;
END. {sets}
```

Results from program being run

specialists in either landscapes or nature or both
Jack Bill Basil Jane Audrey Maud

specialists in both portrait and glamour
Jack Stuart

specialists in nature and macro or still life or both
Basil

members who do not specialise in any category
Sybil Joan Eve

9.6 Set Theory in Data Validation.

The use of set theory can be a valuable aid to coding data validation routines. Traditional tests for digits and upper case letters of the alphabet would require the following coding:

```
IF ((NextChar >= '0') AND (NextChar <= '9'))
OR ((NextChar >= 'A') AND (NextChar <= 'Z')) THEN ...
```

However, by using set theory this can be reduced to:

```
IF NextChar IN ['0'..'9', 'A'..'Z'] THEN ...
```
Similary, in testing whether a character is a vowel the statement

```
IF (NextChar = 'a') OR (NextChar = 'e') OR (NextChar = 'i')
            OR (NextChar = 'o') OR (NextChar = 'u') THEN ...
```

could be replaced by IF NextChar IN ['a','e','i','o','u'] THEN ...

The validation of characters as being alphabetic or signed numeric integers can be incorporated into the following explicit functions.

```
FUNCTION AlphaTest(NextChar : CHAR):BOOLEAN;
{returns false if character not upper or lower case alphabetic}
BEGIN
     AlphaTest := FALSE;
     IF NextChar IN ['A'..'Z', 'a'..'z'] THEN
        AlphaTest := TRUE;
     {end if}
END; {AlphaTest}

FUNCTION DigitTest(NextChar : CHAR):BOOLEAN;
{returns false if character not a digit, + or - sign}
BEGIN
     DigitTest := FALSE;
     IF NextChar IN ['0'..'9', '+', '-'] THEN
        DigitTest := TRUE;
     {end if}
END; {DigitTest}
```

9.7 Summary.
Pascal provides mathematical functions that are implicitly defined in the language.

A programmer can explicitly define new functions that may include predefined functions that are either explicit, implicit or both.

Since a function always has a value associated with its name, the function must be defined as being of a specific data type.

Data can be classified into mathematical sets, with operations and comparisons being made upon the sets.

The elements of a set cannot be input or output using the Read or Write statements.

Keywords

ABS, ARCTAN, COS, EXP, LN, ODD, SIN, SQR, SQRT;
FUNCTION;
graphs, random numbers, pseudo-random numbers,
congruence method;
sets, union, intersection and difference;
IN, set comparison

9.8 Questions.

[1]. If LOGb(X) = LOGa(X) / LOGa(b) then derive a function to calculate the logarithm of a number of any valid given base. Use this function in writing a computer program to find the logarithms of the numbers from 2 to 10 in steps of 0.5 to the bases 2 to 10 in steps of 2. Your output should be in the form of a table having the numbers down the page and the bases across the page.

[2]. Write a program to calculate the roots of a quadratic equation $ax^2 + bx + c$

from the formula $x = \dfrac{-b \pm \sqrt{b^2 - 4ac}}{2a}$ The values of a,b and c should be input at the

beginning of the program. Consider the implications within your program of $b^2 < 4ac$

3. Write a program to output a graph of the function EXP(-X)*SIN(2*PI*X) over continuous cycles. What happens to the graph after a short period of time?

[4]. Write a program to test the accuracy of your computer by evaluating the following expressions.

a. $(x^{0.5})^2 - x$ where $0 <= x <= 1$ increment of 0.05

b. elog(x) - x where $1 <= x <= 10$ increment of 1

c. tan(arctan(x)) - x where $-100 <= x <= 100$ increment of 10.

5. Write a program to simulate the rolling of two dice and determine the number of doubles that appear for the digits 1 to 6 inclusive, when the dice are rolled:

a. 10 times b. 100 times c. 1000 times.

Use either the random number function given in the chapter or one supplied with your dialect of Pascal.

6. A pack of cards is coded into suit and value using the convention C-Club, D-Diamond, H-Heart, S-Spade and 2,3,4,5,6,7,8,9,T-10, J-Jack, Q-Queen, K-King, A-Ace. Then the code C3 would represent the three of Clubs, HK King of Hearts, etc. Write a program to input a hand of thirteen coded cards. Validate each code and report on any errors. Display the description of each card in the hand.

7. In determining what to bid in Bridge the following system of card evaluation can be used; Ace - 4 points, King - 3 points, Queen - 2 points and Jack - 1 point. Therefore, a hand containing two Aces, three Kings and two Jacks would score 19 points. Extend the last program to output the number of points in a hand of thirteen cards.

[8]. The following list of students are registered on a Computer Studies course.

Adams, Betts, Collins, Evans, Hill, Jones, Long, Nutt, Osborne Pritchard, Quayle, Robbins, Stevens, Thomas, Wills.

The following subjects are taken by the students specified:

Programming: Adams, Collins, Evans, Long, Quayle, Thomas.
Architecture: Betts, Hill, Thomas.
Data Processing: Betts, Collins, Hill, Pritchard.
Systems Analysis: Long, Osborne, Quayle, Robbins.
Data Structures: Betts, Evans, Hill, Jones, Stevens, Thomas.
Data Base Studies: Collins, Hill, Long, Quayle, Stevens.

Write a program to determine the following results. You should list the names of those students in each of the required groups.

a. Students who study both Programming and Systems Analysis.
b. Students who combine Programming with either Data Processing or Data Structures.
c. Those students who do not study Architecture.
d. Those students who have registered yet do not study any subjects.

10

Arrays

Up to now little importance has been attached to the organisation of data in the memory of a computer. All variables have been associated with discrete items of data only. Within the remainder of this book the reader's attention will be focused upon appropriate methods for structuring data. This chapter introduces the topic of data structures by examining the commonest of the data structures known as an array. A justification for the use of data structures over no structure is explained together with the semantics and syntax of arrays in Pascal.

10.1 Advantages of Structured Data.

To highlight some of the advantages of using structured data over non-structured data consider the following example. In the last chapter the use of random numbers was discussed in the simulation of rolling a die. If the frequency of occurrences of each face of the die was to be calculated and output the program would be coded as follows. The italic typeface is used to indicate areas of code that are clumsy when using no data structures.

```
{$N+}
PROGRAM dice(INPUT, OUTPUT);
{program to count the number of times 1,2,3,4,5 and 6 appear when a die is rolled a
fixed number of times}

VAR
       trials: INTEGER;{number of times die is rolled}
       seed: LONGINT;{seed value for random number generator}
       face: INTEGER;{face value 1 to 6}
       roll: INTEGER;{counter for each roll of die}
       one, two, three, four, five, six: INTEGER;

{random number generator}
FUNCTION RND:DOUBLE;
CONST
       a=LONGINT(19);
       b=LONGINT(100000000);
VAR
       RN:DOUBLE; {random number 0.1 < =rn < 1}
       y:LONGINT;
BEGIN
       y:= (a*seed) MOD b;
       seed:=y;
       RN:=ABS(y);
       REPEAT
           RN:=RN/10.0;
       UNTIL RN < 1.0;
       RND:=RN
END;{RND}

BEGIN
       seed:=19;
       Write('input number of trials => ');
       ReadLn(trials);
       WHILE trials < > 0 DO
       BEGIN
           {initialise frequencies}
           one:=0; two:=0; three:=0; four:=0; five:=0; six:=0;
```

```
                {simulate rolling die}
                FOR roll:=1 TO trials DO
                BEGIN
                    face:= (TRUNC(1000.0*RND) MOD 6) +1;
                    {increase frequency by 1}
                    CASE face OF
                    1: one:=one+1;
                    2: two:=two+1;
                    3: three:=three+1;
                    4: four:=four+1;
                    5: five:=five+1;
                    6: six:=six+1
                    END;
                    {end case}
                END;
                {end for}

                {output frequencies}
                WriteLn('face frequency');
                WriteLn('1',one:12);
                WriteLn('2',two:12);
                WriteLn('3',three:12);
                WriteLn('4',four:12);
                WriteLn('5',five:12);
                WriteLn('6',six:12);
                WriteLn;

                Write('input number of trials => ');
                ReadLn(trials);
            END;
            {end while}
    END.{dice}
    {$N-}
```

The solution to this problem is unnecessarily lengthy owing to the way in which the data has been stored. The frequency of occurrence of each face of the die is stored as a single variable with no relationship between the six variables (*one, two, three, four, five* and *six*). If the frequencies were stored in a structure having the same variable name and the different frequencies were distinguishable from each other by their position in the structure then the coding of the program could be considerably reduced. The type of data structure described is a one-dimensional array with the name frequency and can be visualised as depicted in figure 10.1.

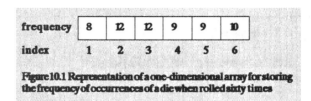

Figure 10.1 Representation of a one-dimensional array for storing the frequency of occurrences of a die when rolled sixty times

To access any frequency stored in the array the array name *frequency* followed by the position of the frequency is used. For example, frequency[4] contains the value 9, therefore, the statement WriteLn(frequency[4]); would output the value 9 on the screen of a terminal.

The same reference is used to change the contents of any cell in the array. If the contents of cell 3 was to be increased by 1, say, the following code would be used: frequency[3]:=frequency[3]+1; and after execution the contents of the third cell frequency[3] would be 13.

The procedural coding represented in italic typeface in the last program can be replaced by using the following statements.

```
{initialise frequencies}
FOR face:=1 TO 6 DO
     frequency[face]:=0;
{end for}
```

As the loop variable face changes from 1 to 6 so frequency[1]:=0, frequency[2]:=0 .....frequency[6]:=0.

```
{increase frequency by 1}
frequency[face]:=frequency[face]+1;
```

If a pseudo-random number for face was calculated to be 3 then the current value of frequency[3] is increased by 1.

```
{output frequencies}
FOR face:=1 TO 6 DO
     WriteLn(face,frequency[face]:10);
{end for}
```

As the loop variable face changes from 1 to 6 so the values of frequency[1] through to frequency[6] are displayed on the screen of the terminal.

To summarise, the following advantages have been gained in introducing an array data structure in this example. The homogeneous nature of the data can be classified under the one name *frequency*, instead of *one, two, three, four, five* and *six*. Clearly this is useful if many hundreds of items of data are to be stored.

Direct access to a single item of data is possible: frequency[3] will give the contents of the third cell in the array.

The amount of coding in the program has been reduced quite significantly by using a one-dimensional array. This is evident if the reader compares the size of the program in this section, with that of the same program in the next section.

10.2 One-dimensional Array.
The one-dimensional array depicted in figure 10.1 must be declared as a variable before it can be used. The data declaration *one, two, three, four, five, six : INTEGER;* in the previous program is replaced by:

CONST
      MaxValue = 6;
VAR
      frequency: ARRAY[1..MaxValue] OF INTEGER;

This informs the compiler of an array structure named *frequency* that contains six data cells numbered 1 through 6 [1..MaxValue]. The contents of each cell is an item of data of type integer.

When referencing the contents of the array *frequency* the reader should note that only the indices 1,2,3,4,5 and 6 are legal in denoting the position of a cell. Whatever calculations are performed on the contents of the array they must be consistent with the data type that has been declared i.e. integer. With the one-dimensional array *frequency* the statements frequency[7]:=17 and frequency[3]:=16.7 are both illegal.

The die frequency program has been listed again in its modified form. The reader should be confident about the changes made to the program before proceeding with the rest of this chapter.

```
{$N+}
PROGRAM dice(INPUT, OUTPUT);
CONST
      MaxValue = 6;
VAR
      trials : INTEGER;
      seed : LONGINT;
      roll, face : INTEGER; {indices to the array frequency}
      frequency : ARRAY[1..MaxValue] OF INTEGER;

FUNCTION RND:DOUBLE;
CONST
      a=LONGINT(19);
      b=LONGINT(100000000);
VAR
      RN:DOUBLE; {random number 0.1 < =rn<1}
      y:LONGINT;
```

```
BEGIN
      y:=(a*seed) MOD b;
      seed:=y;
      RN:=ABS(y);
      REPEAT
          RN:=RN/10.0;
      UNTIL RN < 1.0;
      RND:=RN
END;{RND}

BEGIN
      seed:=19;
      Write('input number of trials => ');
      ReadLn(trials);
      WHILE trials < > 0 DO
      BEGIN
          {initialise cells of array to zero}
          FOR face:=1 TO MaxValue DO
              frequency[face]:=0;
          {end for}

          {simulate rolling die}
          FOR roll:=1 TO trials DO
          BEGIN
              face:=(TRUNC(1000.0*RND) MOD 6)+1;
              frequency[face]:=frequency[face]+1;
          END;
          {end for}

          {output frequencies}
          WriteLn('face frequency');
          FOR face:=1 TO MaxValue DO
              WriteLn(face:4,frequency[face]:10);
          {end for}
          WriteLn;

          Write('input number of trials => ');
          ReadLn(trials);
      END;
      {end while}
END.{dice}
{$N-}
```

```
┌─────────────────────────────────────────────────────┐
│  Results from program being run                      │
│                                                      │
│  input  number  of  trials  (0  to  exit)  => 1000  │
│  face        frequency                               │
│  1           176                                     │
│  2           167                                     │
│  3           161                                     │
│  4           155                                     │
│  5           179                                     │
│  6           162                                     │
│  input  number  of  trials  (0  to  exit)  =>  0     │
└─────────────────────────────────────────────────────┘
```

10.3 Packed Arrays.

The size of a computer word differs between machines, however, 16, 24 and 32 bit words are common. If the amount of computer memory is to be conserved then it makes sense to pack as many characters or numbers into a word as possible. To conserve storage space arrays may be prefixed by the word PACKED, which is a directive to the compiler to re-arrange the storage of elements in an array in the interest of economy of space. The effect of packed should not be obvious to the programmer since the meaning of the program should remain the same whether packed is used or not. The declarations:

TYPE

name = ARRAY[1..20] OF CHAR;

packname = PACKED ARRAY[1..20] OF CHAR;

are equivalent, except that the latter would require less storage space and possibly take longer to access owing to the extra overhead of unpacking the contents of the array.

Sheffield Pascal will only allow the contents of two character arrays of the same size to be compared, if both are packed arrays. This restriction does not apply to Turbo Pascal. Furthermore, since Turbo Pascal is designed to run on machines with 8-bit words (bytes), the concept of a packed array has no meaning. The word packed can, however, be used to facilitate the portability of the language between computers.

10.4 Text Input.

Consider the problem of inputting a line of text from a keyboard to the computer and preserving that line of text for future reference. Without the use of arrays the only method available has been to declare a number of variables of type char and using a statement of the form ReadLn(a,b,c,d.....). However, it is now possible to declare a one-dimensional array *buffer* that will hold a line of text:

```
CONST
      MaxChar = 80;
VAR
      buffer: PACKED ARRAY[1..MaxChar] OF CHAR;
```

Since most terminals have screens that represent 80 characters on one line (MaxChar) the position of each character has been declared as being in the range [1..MaxChar]. A further declaration of the position of a character is also necessary in order to access the array:

VAR index: INTEGER;

Such an array can be represented pictorially as shown in figure 10.2.

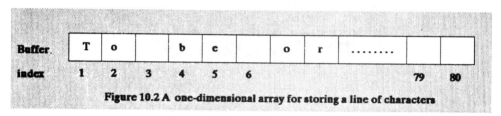

Figure 10.2 A one-dimensional array for storing a line of characters

The following program demonstrates how text can be input, stored and output using this array. Note the declaration of the constant *null=CHR(0)* is not compatible in Sheffield Pascal. In this dialect all character constants must be delimited by apostrophes. This incompatibilty will be found throughout the rest of the book.

```
PROGRAM InText(INPUT, OUTPUT);
{program to input a line of text}

CONST
        null = CHR(0);
        MaxChar = 80;
VAR
        buffer: PACKED ARRAY[1..MaxChar] OF CHAR;
        index: INTEGER; {indicates the position of character in array}
BEGIN
        WriteLn('input a line of text from keyboard');
        FOR index:=1 TO MaxChar DO
          IF EOLN THEN
             buffer[index]:=null
          ELSE
             Read(buffer[index]);
          {end if}
        {end for}
        ReadLn;
        WriteLn('contents of buffer is');
        WriteLn(buffer)
END.{intext}
```

The desk check in figure 10.3, illustrates how this program functions. The text input at the keyboard is the phrase *"To be or not to be"* *return*.

To output the contents of an array containing text there is no need to access each cell of the array, instead the name of the array only need be written WriteLn(buffer). However, in Sheffield Pascal the array must be declared as being PACKED.

index	input	EOLN	buffer[index]
1	T	*FALSE*	T
2	o	*FALSE*	o
3	*space*	*FALSE*	*space*
4	b	*FALSE*	b
5	e	*FALSE*	e
6	*space*	*FALSE*	*space*
7	o	*FALSE*	o
8	r	*FALSE*	r
9	*space*	*FALSE*	*space*
10	n	*FALSE*	n
11	o	*FALSE*	o
12	t	*FALSE*	t
13	*space*	*FALSE*	*space*
14	t	*FALSE*	t
15	o	*FALSE*	o
16	*space*	*FALSE*	*space*
17	b	*FALSE*	b
18	e	*FALSE*	e
19	*return*	*TRUE*	*null*
20		*TRUE*	*null*
.			
.			
79		*TRUE*	*null*
80		*TRUE*	*null*

Figure 10.3 Desk check of text stored in buffer

The position of an element within an array is not confined to an index of type integer. For example, if a frequency count was to be kept on the number of vowels in a sentence, the vowel could indicate the position of the respective frequency, as illustrated in figure 10.4.

Vowelcount	2	5	4	2	0
vowel	a	e	i	o	u

Figure 10.4 The index to an array can be objects of enumerated type

If vowel is declared as an enumerated type:

TYPE
     vowel = (a,e,i,o,u);

then the declaration of the array becomes:

VAR
     VowelCount: ARRAY[vowel] OF INTEGER;

The following program demonstrates the use of two arrays. The first array is used to store the characters of a sentence, input at the keyboard. The second array is used to record a frequency count on the number of vowels in the sentence. When the vowel analysis is complete the frequency of the vowels is output to the screen of a terminal.

When passing an array type to a function or procedure, it is advisable to declare it as a VAR parameter, otherwise, time and space will be wasted in copying the array as a local item within the function or procedure. For example:

TYPE line = PACKED ARRAY[1..MaxChar] OF CHAR;

PROCEDURE TextInput(VAR buffer:line);

```
PROGRAM Vowels(INPUT, OUTPUT);
{program to count and report on the number of vowels in a sentence or phrase}

CONST
      null = CHR(0);
      MaxChar = 80;
TYPE
      vowel = (a,e,i,o,u);
      line = PACKED ARRAY[1..MaxChar] OF CHAR;
VAR
      buffer: line; {stores sentence}
      VowelCount:ARRAY[vowel] OF INTEGER; {frequency of vowels}

PROCEDURE initialise;
{set frequency of each vowel to zero}
VAR
      ch:vowel;
BEGIN
      FOR ch:=a TO u DO
          VowelCount[ch]:=0;
      {end for}
END;{initialise}
```

```
PROCEDURE TextInput(VAR buffer:line);
{input a one-line sentence}
VAR
     index:INTEGER;
BEGIN
     WriteLn('input a sentence');
     FOR index:=1 TO MaxChar DO
        IF EOLN THEN
           buffer[index]:=null
        ELSE
           Read(buffer[index]);
        {end if}
     {end for}
     ReadLn;
END; {TextInput}


PROCEDURE analysis(buffer:line);
{inspect each character of the sentence and increase frequency of vowels only}
VAR
     index:INTEGER;
     ch:vowel;
BEGIN
     index:=1;
     WHILE buffer[index] <> null DO
     BEGIN
        IF buffer[index] IN ['a','e','i','o','u'] THEN
        BEGIN
           CASE buffer[index] OF
           'a':ch:=a;
           'e':ch:=e;
           'i':ch:=i;
           'o':ch:=o;
           'u':ch:=u;
           END;
           {end case}
           VowelCount[ch]:=VowelCount[ch]+1;
        END;
        {end if}
        index:=index+1;
     END;
     {end while}
END; {analysis}
```

```
PROCEDURE VowelOut;
{output the frequency of vowels in the sentence}
VAR
      ch:vowel;
BEGIN
      WriteLn;
      WriteLn('a   e   i   o   u');
      FOR ch:=a TO u DO
          Write(VowelCount[ch]:4);
      {end for}
      WriteLn;
END; {VowelCount}


BEGIN
      initialise;
      TextInput(buffer);
      analysis(buffer);
      VowelOut
END.{Vowels}
```

```
Results from program being run

input a sentence
How many vowels in this sentence?
   a    e    i    o    u
   1    4    2    2    0
```

If you think that you understood the last program then try and answer these questions.

How does *FOR ch:='a' to 'u' DO* differ from *FOR ch:=a to u DO* and is it legal ?

Why has *buffer[index]* not been compared with the set [a,e,i,o,u]?

Why hasn't the author written:

VowelCount[buffer[index]]:=VowelCount[buffer[index]]+1 ?

Taking the questions in the order presented, ch:='a' to 'u' do would cause ch to take on the values a,b,c,d,e,f......u and since the allowable indices for VowelCount are a,e,i,o,u an error will occur.

Buffer[index] contains data of type char and not the enumerated type vowel, therefore, buffer[index] in [a,e,i,o,u] would be a mismatch of data types.

This point also applies to the last question VowelCount can only have indices of type vowel, hence VowelCount[buffer[index]] is a data type mismatch. For this reason it has been necessary to convert the data of buffer[index] to data of an enumerated type.

10.5 Two-dimensional Arrays.

An array is not confined to one dimension (i.e. one index) but can be extended to two-dimensions and beyond in order to provide a necessary flexible data structure for the solution to a problem.

A two-dimensional array is a repetition of a one-diemsional array. The structure can be thought of as a matrix or grid structure. As a simple example of such a structure, the word game of Scrabble uses a board with 15 rows and 15 columns, as depicted in figure 10.5.

columns

rows	1	2	3	4	5	6	7	8	9	10	11	12	13	14	15
1	J	U	I	C	E										
2	A				L	A	U	N	C	H					
3	M	O	D	E	M			A							
4								U							
5								G							
6								H							
7								T							
8								Y	A	C	H	T			
9															
10															
11															
12															
13															
14															
15															

Figure 10.5 Scrabble board showing 15 rows and 15 columns

Figure 10.5 illustrates a Scrabble board that can be thought of as a grid or matrix. The two-dimensional array that is formed can be seen as a repetition of a one-dimensional array that contains 15 cells.

The board can be defined as an array in Pascal by making the following declaration.

```
CONST
      MaxRow = 15;
      MaxColumn = 15;
TYPE
      line = PACKED ARRAY[1..MaxColumn] OF CHAR;
VAR
      ScrabbleBoard : ARRAY[1..MaxRow] OF line;
```

However, a much preferred declaration would be:

```
VAR
      ScrabbleBoard:PACKED ARRAY[1..MaxRow, 1..MaxColumn] OF CHAR;
```

This clearly indicates that the two-dimensional array is composed from 15 rows and each row is composed of 15 columns of the type char. The contents of the array is accessed through two indices, one for the row and one for the column, in that order, e.g ScrabbleBoard[row, column]. Using the illustration given in figure 10.4 it should be clear to the reader that:

ScrabbleBoard[3,1] contains the character M,
ScrabbleBoard[2,8] contains the character N,
ScrabbleBoard[1,5] contains the character E

and so on.

To build a new word ACE downwards from row 1 of column 9 the following assignment statements would be necessary.

ScrabbleBoard[1,9]:='A';
ScrabbleBoard[3,9]:='E';

If a program was required to allow the user to input words and display them on the board then the following routines would be necessary. The declaration of variables should then be extended to cater for the two indices.

```
VAR
      ScrabbleBoard: PACKED ARRAY[1..MaxRow, 1..MaxColumn] OF CHAR;
      row, column: INTEGER;
```

The reader must never assume that because an array has not been used that it will empty. Therefore, the first segment of code should initialise each square of the Scrabble board to a blank space. This can be simply achieved by using two for loops, one to control the row index and the other to control the column index.

```
FOR row:=1 TO MaxRow DO
BEGIN
      FOR column:=1 TO MaxColumn DO
          ScrabbleBoard[row, column]:=space;
      {end for}
END;
{end for}
```

This assumes that the constant space has already been declared *CONST space =CHR(32);*

If the start (Srow,Scol) and finish (Frow,Fcol) row and column coordinates of a word to be input to the board are known, and the word has already been input from a keyboard and stored in a one-dimensional array called buffer then the letters of the word can be transferred to the array ScrabbleBoard using the following segment of code. In this code i and j are local loop variables used as indices to the array ScrabbleBoard with the purpose of denoting the position of characters of the word on the same column or same line respectively.

```
index:=1;
IF Srow=Frow THEN {horizontal word i.e. same row}
       FOR j:=Scol TO Fcol DO
       BEGIN
           ScrabbleBoard[Srow,j]:=buffer[index];
           index:=index+1;
       END
       {end for}
ELSE {vertical word i.e. same column}
       FOR i:=Srow TO Frow DO
       BEGIN
           ScrabbleBoard[i,Scol]:=buffer[index];
           index:=index+1;
       END;
       {end for}
{end if}
```

Having stored characters in the array ScrabbleBoard it is useful if the contents of the board can be displayed on the screen of a terminal so that new words can be invented and input to the computer. The output of the array is again controlled by two loop variables row and column.

```
FOR row:=1 TO MaxRow DO
BEGIN
       FOR column:=1 TO MaxColumn DO
           Write(ScrabbleBoard[row,column]);
       {end for}
       WriteLn;
END;
{end for}
```

These segments of code have been included in the following program that will allow the user to build words on the scrabble board.

```
PROGRAM scrabble(INPUT, OUTPUT);
{program to insert words on to a Scrabble board}
CONST
       null=CHR(0);
       space=CHR(32);
       no='N'; {reply to question}
       MaxChar = 80; {number of characters in input buffer}
       MaxRow = 15;
       MaxColumn = 15;
TYPE
       line = PACKED ARRAY[1..MaxChar] OF CHAR;
VAR
       Srow,Scol,Frow,Fcol:INTEGER; {start and finish coordinates}
       answer:CHAR; {reply to question}
```

```
      {2-D array representing Scrabble board}
      ScrabbleBoard : PACKED ARRAY[1..MaxRow,1..MaxColumn] OF CHAR;
      row,column:INTEGER;
      {1-D array used to store characters from keyboard}
      buffer:line;

PROCEDURE TextInput(VAR buffer:line);
{input a word}
VAR
      index:INTEGER;
BEGIN
      Write('input word => ');
      FOR index:=1 TO MaxChar DO
         IF EOLN THEN
             buffer[index]:=null
         ELSE
             Read(buffer[index]);
         {end if}
      {end for}
      ReadLn;
END; {TextInput}

PROCEDURE PrintOut;
{output contents of scrabble board}
VAR
      row, column: INTEGER;
BEGIN
      WriteLn('1 2 3 4 5 6 7 8 9 10 11 12 13 14 15');
      FOR row:=1 TO MaxRow DO
      BEGIN
         Write(row:2);
         FOR column:=1 TO MaxColumn DO
            Write('   ',ScrabbleBoard[row, column]);
         {end for}
         WriteLn;
      END;
      {end for}
END;{PrintOut}

PROCEDURE ClearArray;
{clear all letters from scrabble board by substituting spaces}
VAR
      row, column:INTEGER;
BEGIN
      FOR row:=1 TO MaxRow DO
      BEGIN
         FOR column:=1 TO MaxColumn DO
             ScrabbleBoard[row, column]:=space;
         {end for}
      END;
      {end for}
END;{ClearArray}
```

```
PROCEDURE Inword;
{input coordinates of new word and store the word in the array representing the scrabble
board}
VAR
      index, i, j:INTEGER; {indices}
BEGIN
      Write('input starting coordinates of word => ');
      ReadLn(Srow,Scol);
      Write('input ending coordinates of word => ');
      ReadLn(Frow,Fcol);
      TextInput(buffer);
      index:=1;
      IF Srow=Frow THEN {same row}
         FOR j:=Scol TO Fcol DO
         BEGIN
            ScrabbleBoard[Srow,j]:=buffer[index];
            index:=index+1;
         END
         {end for}
      ELSE {same column}
         FOR i:=Srow TO Frow DO
         BEGIN
            ScrabbleBoard[i,Scol]:=buffer[index];
            index:=index+1;
         END;
         {end for}
      {end if}
END;{InWord}


BEGIN
      ClearArray;
      REPEAT
         Inword;
         PrintOut;
         Write('do you want to input another word - answer Y /N ?');
         ReadLn(answer);
      UNTIL answer=no;
END.{scrabble}
```

Results from program being run after the fourth word has been input

do you want another word - answer Y/N ? Y
input starting coordinates of word => 2 8
input ending coordinates of word => 8 8
input word => NAUGHTY

	1	2	3	4	5	6	7	8	9	10	11	12	13	14	15
1	J	U	I	C	E										
2	A				L	A	U	N	C	H					
3	M	O	D	E	M			A							
4								U							
5								G							
6								H							
7								T							
8								Y							
9															
10															
11															
12															
13															
14															
15															

do you want another word - answer Y/N ? Y
input starting coordinates of word => 8 8
input ending coordinates of word => 8 12
input word => YACHT

	1	2	3	4	5	6	7	8	9	10	11	12	13	14	15
1	J	U	I	C	E										
2	A				L	A	U	N	C	H					
3	M	O	D	E	M			A							
4								U							
5								G							
6								H							
7								T							
8								Y	A	C	H	T			
9															
10															
11															
12															
13															
14															
15															

do you want another word - answer Y/N ? N

10.6 Multi-dimensional Arrays.

As was hinted at the beginning of the last section, it is possible to have an array of more than two-dimensions. This simply means that an array can have more than two indices. Although it was relatively easy to imagine that a two-dimensional array could be pictured as a matrix, grid or board used for Chess, Draughts, Scrabble etc, do not fall into the trap of trying to visualise multi-dimensional arrays as solid objects. You might be tempted to think of a three-dimensional array as a cuboid, but how would you visualise arrays with 4, 5, 6 or more dimensions?

A three-dimensional array is a repetition of two-dimensional arrays, a four-dimensional array is a repetition of three-dimensional arrays and so on. The declaration of a three-dimensional array *ThreeD* could be coded as:

```
TYPE
      TwoD=ARRAY[1..10, 1..5] OF INTEGER;
VAR
      ThreeD: ARRAY[1..4] OF TwoD;
```

implying maximum dimensions of ThreeD[4,10,5]. Similarly, a four-dimensional array *FourD* could be coded as:

```
TYPE
      ThreeD=ARRAY[1..4, 1..10, 1..5] OF INTEGER;
VAR
      FourD: ARRAY[1..3] OF ThreeD;
```

implying maximum dimensions of FourD[3,4,10,5].

However, although these declarations fit nicely into the definition just given of multi-dimensional arrays the reader might prefer to declare the two arrays in the following alternative format.

```
VAR
      ThreeD: ARRAY[1..4, 1..10, 1..5] OF INTEGER;
      FourD: ARRAY[1..3, 1..4, 1..10, 1..5] OF INTEGER;
```

The method of access to the arrays will be through their respective indices. For example the following statements are all legal.

```
ThreeD[2,9,4]:=26;
ReadLn(ThreeD[1,8,3]);
WriteLn(ThreeD[plane, row, column]);
FourD[a,b,c,d]:=48;
ReadLn(FourD[3,2,8,3]);
WriteLn(FourD[w,x,y,z]);
```

The next example illustrates how to manipulate data in a three-dimensional array.

Problem. A national union of workers is divided into four regions designated North, South, East and West. Within each region there are two divisions known as rural and urban. In a national ballot to elect a union president every member is allowed to vote for only one of four candidates. The names of the candidates are Bloggs, Davies, Jones and Smith. Write a program to execute the following procedures.

Input all the votes cast for each candidate by division and region and calculate and output the total number of votes cast for all candidates.

Calculate and output the total number of votes cast for each candidate in each of the four regions.

Calculate and output the percentage number of votes cast for each candidate and output the winner of the election.

Figure 10.6 illustrates the components of the three-dimensional array used to store the votes cast. Notice that this diagram depicts four two-dimensional arrays, one for each of the four regions. The rows in each two-dimensional array represents the two divisions and the columns the four candidates. The numbers in the array represent a sample of the votes.

    votes[North, Rural, Bloggs] = 86
    votes[North, Rural, Davies] = 91
    votes[North, Urban, Jones] = 92

Using the illustration in figure 10.6 can you correctly identify the three other votes ?

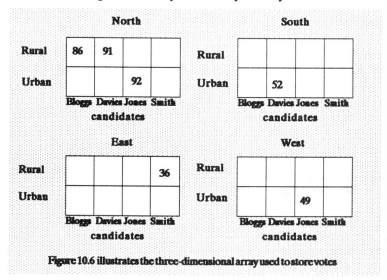

Figure 10.6 illustrates the three-dimensional array used to store votes

The answer to the last question is: votes[South, Urban, Davies] = 52; votes[East, Rural, Smith] = 36; votes[West, Urban, Jones] = 49.

The solution to the voting problem follows. It is left to the reader to trace through the program to find out how it functions.

```
PROGRAM election(INPUT, OUTPUT);
{program to
(i) input votes for all candidates, over divisions and regions
(ii) calculate the total number of votes cast
(iii) calculate the number of votes cast for each candidate in each region
(iv) calculate the % votes cast for each candidate
(v) output the winner }

TYPE
        regions = (North, South, East, West);
        divisions = (Rural, Urban);
        candidates = (Bloggs, Davies, Jones, Smith);
VAR
        {3-D array used to store votes by region, branch and candidate}
        votes: ARRAY[regions, divisions, candidates] OF INTEGER;
        {1-D array used to store the total votes for each candidate}
        CandidateVote: ARRAY[candidates] OF INTEGER;
        TotalVotes:INTEGER; {total number of votes cast for all candidates}
        PartialVotes:INTEGER; {partial sum of votes cast}
        NextRegion : regions;
        NextCandidate : candidates;
        winner: candidates; {new president of union}

PROCEDURE PrintRegion(NextRegion : regions);
{output the name of a region}
BEGIN
        Write('region ');
        CASE NextRegion OF
        North: WriteLn('North');
        South: WriteLn('South');
        East : WriteLn('East');
        West : WriteLn('West');
        END;
        {end case}
END;{PrintRegion}

PROCEDURE PrintCandidate(NextCandidate : candidates);
{output the name of a candidate}
BEGIN
        CASE NextCandidate OF
        Bloggs : Write('Bloggs ');
        Davies : Write('Davies ');
        Jones : Write('Jones ');
        Smith : Write('Smith ');
        END;
        {end case}
END;{PrintCandidate}
```

```
PROCEDURE initialise;
{read data from keyboard and store in a three-dimensional array; calculate total votes cast
for all candidates}
VAR
        region: regions;
        division: divisions;
        candidate: candidates;
BEGIN
        TotalVotes:=0;
        FOR region:=North TO West DO
        BEGIN
           NextRegion:= region;
           PrintRegion(NextRegion);
           FOR division:= Rural TO Urban DO
           BEGIN
              Write(' branch ');
              IF division = Rural THEN
                 WriteLn('Rural')
              ELSE
                 WriteLn('Urban');
              {end if}
              Write(' input all candidates votes => ');
              FOR candidate:=Bloggs TO Smith DO
              BEGIN
                 Read(votes[region, division, candidate]);
                 Write(' ');
                 TotalVotes:=TotalVotes +votes[region, division, candidate];
              END;
              {end for}
              WriteLn;
           END;
           {end for}
           WriteLn;
        END;
        {end for}
END;{initialise}


PROCEDURE RegionVotes;
{calculate and output the number of votes cast for each candidate in each region}
VAR
        region: regions;
        division:divisions;
        candidate: candidates;
BEGIN
        FOR region:=North TO West DO
        BEGIN
           NextRegion:= region;
           PrintRegion(NextRegion);
           WriteLn('candidate votes');
```

```
        FOR candidate:=Bloggs TO Smith DO
        BEGIN
            PartialVotes:=0;
            FOR division:=Rural TO Urban DO
                PartialVotes:=PartialVotes +votes[region,division,candidate];
            {end for}
            NextCandidate := candidate;
            PrintCandidate(NextCandidate);
            WriteLn(PartialVotes);
        END;
        {end for}
        WriteLn;
    END;
    {end for}
END;{RegionVotes}


PROCEDURE PercentageVote;
{calculate the % vote cast for each candidate}
VAR
        region: regions;
        division: divisions;
        candidate: candidates;
BEGIN
        WriteLn('candidate % vote');
        FOR candidate:=Bloggs TO Smith DO
        BEGIN
            NextCandidate := candidate;
            PrintCandidate(NextCandidate);
            PartialVotes:=0;
            FOR region:=North TO West DO
            BEGIN
                FOR division:=Rural TO Urban DO
                    PartialVotes:=PartialVotes +votes[region,division,candidate];
                {end for}
            END;
            {end for}
            CandidateVote[candidate]:=PartialVotes;
            WriteLn(round(PartialVotes/TotalVotes*100):3);
        END;
        {end for}
END;{PercentageVote}


PROCEDURE win;
{from the one-dimensional table created in the last procedure output the winner of the
election}
VAR
        candidate:candidates;
BEGIN
        winner:=Bloggs;
```

```
        FOR candidate:=Davies TO Smith DO
            IF CandidateVote[winner] < CandidateVote[candidate] THEN
                winner:=candidate;
            {end if}
        {end for}
        Write('winner of election is President ');
        PrintCandidate(winner);
END;{win}

BEGIN
        initialise;
        RegionVotes;
        PercentageVote;
        win;
END. {election}
```

Results from this program being run are shown on the next page.

Note: in Standard Pascal a for loop variable cannot be passed as a parameter to another procedure. Therefore, in the last example it has been necessary to assign the variables region and candidate to temporary variables NextRegion and NextCandidate respectively, in order to print the names of the regions and candidates.

10.7 Summary.
Data that is common in nature can be classified under the name of an array.

Access to the contents of the array is direct by using the name of the array and an index or indices.

The number of indices required to access a cell of an array gives the dimension of an array. For example Buffer[I] - one dimension; ScrabbleBoard[I,J] - two dimensions; votes[I,J,K] - three dimensions, etc.

The use of suitable arrays, and other data structures, often reduces the amount of coding in a program.

Text input at the keyboard can be stored in an array. Such text is often referred to as a string, however, Standard Pascal does not support the data type string.

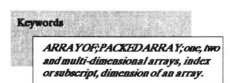

Keywords

ARRAY OF; PACKED ARRAY; one, two and multi-dimensional arrays, index or subscript, dimension of an array.

Results from program being run

region North
  branch Rural
    input all candidates votes => 86 91 82 70
    branch Urban
    input all candidates votes => 101 67 92 35
region South
  branch Rural
    input all candidates votes => 40 70 53 18
    branch Urban
    input all candidates votes => 21 52 34 21
region East
  branch Rural
    input all candidates votes => 53 37 48 36
    branch Urban
    input all candidates votes => 86 97 84 98
region West
  branch Rural
    input all candidates votes => 84 31 66 23
  branch Urban
    input all candidates votes => 98 21 49 36

region North

candidate	votes
Bloggs	189
Davies	158
Jones	174
Smith	105

region South

candidate	votes
Bloggs	61
Davies	122
Jones	87
Smith	39

region East

candidate	votes
Bloggs	139
Davies	134
Jones	132
Smith	134

region West

candidate	votes
Bloggs	182
Davies	52
Jones	115
Smith	59

candidate	% vote
Bloggs	30
Davies	25
Jones	27
Smith	18

winner of election is President Bloggs

10.8 Questions.

1. Write a program to store the alphabet as characters in an array. The program should output:
(a) the entire alphabet; (b) the first six characters of the alphabet; (c) the last ten characters of
the alphabet; (d) the tenth character of the alphabet.

2. A one-dimensional array X contains eight integers, sorted into ascending order. Devise a
routine which moves the items of X to another one-dimensional array Y, so that Y contains the

eight numbers sorted into descending order. The numbers in X can be input in ascending order.

3. Write a program to play noughts and crosses against the computer. Use a two-dimensional array to store the noughts and crosses. Let the computer be the cross and the position of play by the computer is created using a random number generator. Display the board on the screen and the final result of a game.

4. A palindrome is a word that is spelt the same backwards as forwards e.g. RADAR, POOP etc. Write a routine to input a word and analyse whether it is a palindrome or not.

5. A computerised minefield is divided into a 10x10 matrix. Write a game program to generate the random position of mines in the field. The number of mines is also a random number in the range 1 to 10. Invite a player to input pairs of coordinates of a path through the minefield. The computer generates the starting position in the South, and the only legal move a player can make is to any adjacent position in the matrix. The object of the game is to trace a path through the field, without stepping on a mine, and to finish at the Northern perimeter. Only at the end of the game should the computer reveal the position of the mines.

[6]. Write a program to store two twenty digit integers as characters of a string and perform the operations of addition and subtraction on the two integers. Output the answer as a string of digits.

[7]. The following string processing procedures and functions can be found in some dialects of Pascal. Design and code explicit functions and procedures that will serve the same purpose.

DELETE(S,I,N) - procedure changes the value of string S by deleting N characters starting at the Ith character of S.

INSERT(S1,S2,I) - procedure changes the value of the string S2 by inserting the string S1 at the Ith position of S2.

COPY(S,I,N) - procedure that returns the substring of S which is the N characters starting at the Ith position. The result overwrites S.

CONCAT(S1,S2) - procedure that returns the result of the concatenation (joining together) of the strings S1 and S2. The result is stored in S2.

COMPARE(S1,S2) - Boolean function that compares two strings for equality.

LENGTH(S) - function that returns the length of string S.

POS(S1,S2) - function that scans through the string S2 to find the first occurence of the substring S1 within S2. The value returned is the index within S2 of the first character of the matched substring. If no match is found the value is zero.

Hint. Simulate a string as a packed array of characters of maximum size 80. Store the length of the string in cell 0 as an ASCII character.

11

Sorting and Searching

The purpose of this chapter is to provide an insight into methods used to organise information. Such methods must provide for a means of sorting information using a defined key or keys, and a means of searching through the information efficiently using a particular key, such that the access time to information is fast.

11.1 Introduction.

The reader should be well aware of the need to present information in a usable form. Consider the organisation of a telephone directory, entries are ordered into strict alphabetical sequence by name. To find a telephone number, knowing the name of the person you wish to call, is simply a matter of locating the appropriate section of the directory from the first few letters of the surname, and then searching several pages until a match is found for the surname. The address and telephone number of the person will be listed against the surname.

Another example of the organisation of information is that of a bus timetable from a central station. The destinations of buses are ordered alphabetically by town or village, and for each destination a chronological listing of bus departure times from the central station, with arrival times at places on route are given. If the time of departure of a bus from the station is to be found, the page containing the destination can be quickly found because of the alphabetical ordering of towns on respective pages of the timetable. Departure times are listed chronologically, making reference to a specific part of the day simple. Bus departure and arrival times can then be selected from that part of the timetable. In both these examples the information is required to be ordered or sorted on a part of the information. Telephone directories are sorted on names, bus timetables on destinations and times of day. Such information is said to have been sorted on a *key*. Names of people, town or village destination names and times of the day all being examples of keys to information.

Computers are capable of storing very large amounts of information, and it is of paramount importance that the information is kept in an ordered format for the following reasons.

To provide fast access to the information given an appropriate key.

To allow an orderly presentation of information when producing reports.

To simplify changes, insertions, amendments and deletions to the information, without destroying the key order of the remaining information.

11.2 Sorting.

Sorting methods used in computing can be classified into two areas, internal and external sorting. Internal sorting involves the storage in main memory of all the data to be sorted. However, when the amount of data is too large to be stored and sorted in the main memory, it is stored on an external secondary storage medium, such as tape or disc, and successive parts of the data are sorted in the main memory. Such a technique is known as external sorting. The type of sorting method that is used will depend upon at least one of the following factors.

The amount of information to be sorted. Clearly it would be very time consuming to use a relatively inefficient sorting method on a large quantity of data.

The computer configuration being used - the size of the main memory and the number of tape/disc units.

The nature of the application and the urgency of the results.

In this section one internal sorting method, known as the insertion sort, will be explained. Figure 11.1 illustrates how pseudo-random numbers stored in a one-dimensional array are ordered within the array, using this method. Notice that the author has chosen the lowest index value in the array to be 0 and not 1. This is simply a matter of preference.

The second number (7) in the array, is compared with the first (18) and ordered into ascending sequence (7,18). The next number (15) in the array, is then inserted into the correct position (7,15,18) in relation to the previously ordered numbers. The next number (8) in the array, is inserted into the correct position (7,8,15,18) in relation to the previously ordered numbers. Finally, the last number (13) in the array, is inserted into the correct position (7,8,13,15,18) in relation to the previously ordered numbers. Since this was the last number in the array, the numbers are now stored in ascending order.

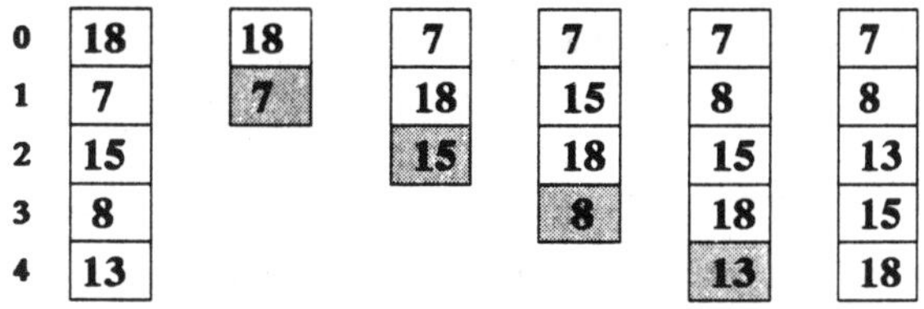

Figure 11.1 An illustration of consecutive keys being inserted into their correct position in the array

The algorithm used to order the numbers can be represented by the following Pascal code, in which the array A is used to store the five numbers.

```
FOR index:=1 TO size-1 DO
BEGIN
    current:=A[index];
    location:=index;
    WHILE (location > 0) AND (A[location-1] > current) DO
    BEGIN
        A[location]:=A[location-1];
        location:=location-1;
    END;
    {end while}
    A[location]:=current;
END;
{end for}
```

This code is given a desk check, with the aid of figures 11.1 and 11.2, as a means of showing how the algorithm orders the five numbers.

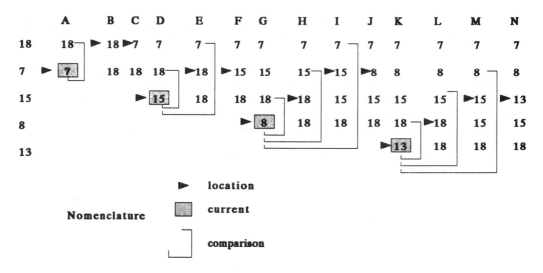

Figure 11.2 The movement of keys in an insertion sort

column in figure 11.2	index	current	location	A[location-1]	A[location]	A[location-1] > current
A	1	7	1	18	7	TRUE
B			0		18	
C			0		7	
D	2	15	2	18	15	TRUE
E			1	7	18	FALSE
F			1		15	
G	3	8	3	18	8	TRUE
H			2	15	18	TRUE
I			1	7	15	FALSE
J			1		8	
K	4	13	4	18	13	TRUE
L			3	15	18	TRUE
M			2	8	15	FALSE
N			2		13	

Desk Check of algorithm for Insertion Sort in conjunction with figure 11.2

In the program that follows, an array A, is filled with 50 random numbers in the range 0 to 100, using the procedure FillArray. These numbers are then sorted into ascending order, using the insertion sort procedure SortInteger. The contents of the ordered array is then displayed on the screen of a VDU using the procedure DisplayArray.

```
{$N+}
PROGRAM demo1(INPUT, OUTPUT);
{program to sort an array of pseudo-random numbers}

CONST
     size=50;
TYPE
     RandomNumbers = ARRAY[0..size-1] OF INTEGER;
VAR
     A:RandomNumbers;
     seed:LONGINT;

FUNCTION RND:DOUBLE;
CONST
     a=LONGINT(19);
     b=LONGINT(100000000);
VAR
     RN:DOUBLE;
     y:LONGINT;
BEGIN
     y:=(a*seed) MOD b;
     seed:=y;
     RN:=ABS(y);
     REPEAT
         RN:=RN/10.0;
     UNTIL RN < 1.0;
     RND:=RN;
END; {RND}

PROCEDURE FillArray(VAR A:RandomNumbers; limit:INTEGER; size:INTEGER);
{procedure to fill an array with random numbers in the range 0 to limit; size represents the
number of integers in the array}

VAR
     index:INTEGER;
BEGIN
     FOR index:=0 TO size-1 DO
         A[index]:=TRUNC(1000.0*RND) MOD (limit+1);
     {end for}
END;{FillArray}

PROCEDURE DisplayArray(A:RandomNumbers; size:INTEGER;
                            NumbersPerLine:INTEGER; FieldWidth:INTEGER);
{procedure to display an array containing integers; size represents the number of integers in
the array; NumbersPerLine represents the number of integers that will be displayed on one
line and FieldWidth is the total allowable width for displaying an integer}

VAR
     index:INTEGER;
```

```pascal
BEGIN
     FOR index:=0 TO size-1 DO
     BEGIN
        Write(A[index]:FieldWidth);
        IF (index+1) MOD NumbersPerLine = 0 THEN
           WriteLn;
        {end if}
     END;
     {end for}
     WriteLn;
END;{DisplayArray}

PROCEDURE SortInteger(VAR A:RandomNumbers; size:INTEGER);
VAR
     current, location, index:INTEGER;
BEGIN
     FOR index:=1 TO size-1 DO
     BEGIN
        current:=A[index];
        location:=index;
        WHILE (location > 0) AND (A[location-1] > current) DO
        BEGIN
           A[location]:=A[location-1];
           location:=location-1;
        END;
        {end while}
        A[location]:=current;
     END;
     {end for}
END; {SortInteger}

BEGIN
     seed:=19;
     FillArray(A,100,size);
     DisplayArray(A,size,10,6);
     SortInteger(A, size);
     DisplayArray(A, size, 10, 6);
END.{demo1}
{$N-}
```

Results from program being run

58	79	29	45	66	29	27	68	56	83
89	16	20	40	9	16	11	83	24	30
36	58	43	1	44	11	38	43	29	22
88	89	91	64	7	86	24	28	77	31
33	0	62	21	8	32	98	8	91	37
0	1	7	8	8	9	11	11	16	16
20	21	22	24	24	27	28	29	29	29
30	31	32	33	36	37	38	40	43	43
44	45	56	58	58	62	64	66	68	77
79	83	83	86	88	89	89	91	91	98

11.3 Records.

In the introduction to this chapter, it was explained that information should be ordered on keys. The last example, of ordering cardinal numbers, has been used only to illustrate the insertion sort algorithm. Before the reader can use the algorithm to sort information on particular keys, it is necessary to introduce a new data structure known as a record.

A record is a collection of values, possibly of different types, whose components are accessed by name.

Figure 11.3 illustrates how an address can be divided into the components *street, town* and *postcode*. Address is depicted as a record data type, that contains the *fields* street, town and postcode, each of type TextString.

121 Bridge St	Abingdon	OX16 6TY

street   town   postcode

```
TYPE   address  =   RECORD
                    street    :  string;
                    town      :  string;
                    postcode  :  string;
            END;
```

Figure 11.3 An illustration of three fields in a record

It is possible for a field of a record to be of type record. For instance, in figure 11.4, the record data type *friend* has three fields, *surname, FirstName* and *abode*. However, abode has the data type *address*, but address has been previously defined as a record type. As figure 11.4 illustrates, a single field *abode* of the record, can itself be a record containing the fields *street, town* and *postcode*.

		street	town	postcode
Thompson	Stephen	121 Bridge St	Abingdon	OX16 6TY

surname   FirstName   abode

```
TYPE  friend  =  RECORD
                 surname      : string;
                 FirstName    : string;
                 abode        : address;
            END;
```

Figure 11.4 Composition of a record showing a field that has already been defined in a previous record description

Up to now, when using arrays, their contents have been single items of data, for example, numbers of different data types, characters or text strings. Pascal allows records to be used in arrays. An array of friends' names and addresses is possible, as illustrated in figure 11.5.

0	Rankin	Robert	23 Sea View	Southampton	SO2 9QT
1	Fielding	Michael	80 Baker St	Bournemouth	BH7 6GH
2	Evans	Florence	17 High Court	Witney	OX8 4DF
3	Adams	Rachel	414 Long St	London	EC1 7GH
4	Davies	John	1 Short Drive	Oxford	OX5 3ER
5	Farthing	Penelope	76 Grange View	Poole	BH15 6GH
99	Jones	Martyn	62 Bedford Rise	Hull	H78 9UH

```
VAR    AddressBook  :  ARRAY[0..99]  OF  friend;
```

Figure 11.5 Records can be stored in an array and accessed using the name of the array, index and field name

If this array is given the variable name *AddressBook*, then it can be declared as

```
VAR
    AddressBook : ARRAY[0..99] OF friend;
```

Where the type declaration of friend is coded as:

```
TYPE
    TextString = PACKED ARRAY[0..29] OF CHAR;
```

```
address = RECORD
                street : TextString;
                town : TextString;
                postcode : TextString;
            END;

friend =    RECORD
                surname : TextString;
                FirstName : TextString;
                abode : address;
            END;
```

The respective fields of a record can be accessed by using the position of the record in the array, qualified by the name of the field. Therefore, with reference to figure 11.5

AddressBook[0].surname is *Rankin*
AddressBook[0].FirstName is *Robert*
AddressBook[0].abode.street is *23 Sea View*
AddressBook[0].abode.town is *Southampton*
AddressBook[0].abode.postcode is *S02 9QT*

This is obviously a very cumbersome way in which to access the fields of a record in the array. Pascal offers a shorthand approach to referencing fields in records, by using the WITH statement. For example, the contents of the array *AddressBook*, illustrated in figure 11.5 could be displayed on the screen of a VDU using the following code. The procedure *TextOut* is used to output the contents of the appropriate array of type *TextString*.

```
FOR index:=0 TO size-1 DO
BEGIN
    WITH AddressBook[index] DO
    BEGIN
        TextOut(surname); Write(space); TextOut(FirstName);
        WriteLn;
        WITH abode DO
        BEGIN
            TextOut(street); Write(space); TextOut(town);
            Write(space); TextOut(postcode); WriteLn;
        END;
    END;
END;
```

Further use of the WITH statement illustrates that:

```
WITH AddressBook[0] DO
BEGIN
    TextOut(surname); Write(space); TextOut(FirstName);

END;
```

is the same as:

```
TextOut(AddressBook[0].surname); Write(space);
TextOut(AddressBook[0].Firstname);
```

and

```
WITH AddressBook[0] DO
BEGIN
    WITH abode DO
        TextOut(street); Write(space); TextOut(town);

    END

END;
```

is the same as:

```
TextOut(AddressBook[0].abode.street); Write(space);
TextOut(AddressBook[0].abode.town);
```

The following program illustrates how the array AddressBook is filled with data, and the contents of the array is displayed on the screen of a VDU.

```
PROGRAM demo2(INPUT, OUTPUT);
{program to input records into an array, then output the contents of the array}
CONST
    MaxSize=99; {maximum number of records in the array}
    SizeOfString=30; {maximum number of characters in a text string}
    space = CHR(32);
    null=CHR(0); {character used to fill text strings}
TYPE
    TextString=PACKED ARRAY[0..SizeOfString-1] OF CHAR;
    address= RECORD
                street:TextString;
                town :TextString;
                postcode:TextString;
            END;
    friend=  RECORD
                surname:TextString;
                Firstname:TextString;
                abode:address;
            END;
    LineInBook = ARRAY[0..MaxSize-1] OF friend;{an array of records}
VAR
    AddressBook: LineInBook;
    size:INTEGER; {number of records to be stored in array}
```

```
PROCEDURE TextInput(VAR buffer:TextString);
{procedure for inputting a line of text}
VAR
      index:INTEGER;
BEGIN
      FOR index:=0 TO SizeOfString-1 DO
         IF EOLN THEN
            buffer[index]:=null
         ELSE
            Read(buffer[index]);
         {end if}
      {end for}
      ReadLn;
END; {TextInput}


PROCEDURE TextOut(buffer:TextString);
{procedure to display a line of text up to but not including the delimiters}
VAR
      index:INTEGER;
BEGIN
      FOR index:=0 TO SizeOfString-1 DO
         IF buffer[index] < > null THEN
            Write(buffer[index]);
         {end if}
      {end for}
END; {TextOut}


PROCEDURE CreateRecord(VAR AddressBook:LineInBook; VAR size:INTEGER);
{procedure to build a record}
VAR
      index:INTEGER;
BEGIN
      WriteLn('input the following details '); WriteLn; WriteLn;
      FOR index:=0 TO size-1 DO
      BEGIN
         WITH AddressBook[index] DO
         BEGIN
            Write('surname = > '); TextInput(surname);
            Write('first name = > '); TextInput(Firstname);
            Write('address street = > '); TextInput(abode.street);
            Write(' town = > '); TextInput(abode.town);
            Write(' postcode = > '); TextInput(abode.postcode);
            WriteLn;
         END;
         {end with}
      END;
      {end for}
END; {CreateRecord}
```

```
PROCEDURE DisplayRecord(AddressBook:LineInBook; size:INTEGER);
{procedure to output the contents of a record on the screen of a vdu}

VAR
      index:INTEGER;
BEGIN
      FOR index:=0 TO size-1 DO
      BEGIN
         WITH AddressBook[index] DO
         BEGIN
            TextOut(surname); Write(space); TextOut(FirstName);
            WriteLn;
            WITH abode DO
            BEGIN
               TextOut(street); Write(space); TextOut(town);
               Write(space); TextOut(postcode); WriteLn;
            END;
            {end with}
         END;
         {end with}
      END;
      {end for}
END; {DisplayRecord}

BEGIN
      Write('how many records to enter? '); ReadLn(size);
      CreateRecord(AddressBook, size);
      DisplayRecord(AddressBook, size);
END.{demo2}
```

The results from this program being run are given on the next page.

11.4 Sorting an array of records.

The insertion sort described in section 11.2, and used to sort pseudo-random numbers, can be adapted to sort an array of records on a specific field, known as a primary key. The array of records illustrated in figure 11.5 could be sorted into ascending order on the *surname* field as the primary key. The lines of bold text in the following code, show the lines of code that must be adapted to sorting the array of records.

```
FOR index:=1 TO size-1 DO
BEGIN
   current:=A[index];
   location:=index;
   WHILE (location > 0) AND (A[location-1] > current) DO
   BEGIN
      A[location]:=A[location-1];
      location:=location-1;
   END;
   A[location]:=current;
END;
```

Results from program being run

```
how many records to enter? 6
input the following details
surname     =>Rankin
first name  =>Robert
address     street =>23 Sea View
            town =>Southampton
            postcode =>SO2 9QT

surname     =>Fielding
first name  =>Michael
address     street =>80 Baker St
            town =>Bournemouth
            postcode =>BH7 6GH

surname     =>Evans
first name  =>Florence
address     street =>17 High Court
            town =>Witney
            postcode =>OX8 4DF

surname     =>Adams
first name  =>Rachel
address     street =>414 Long St
            town =>London
            postcode =>EC1 7GH

surname     =>Davies
first name  =>John
address     street =>1 Short Drive
            town =>Oxford
            postcode =>OX5 3ER

surname     =>Farthing
first name  =>Penelope
address     street =>76 Grange View
            town =>Poole
            postcode =>BH15 6GH


Rankin   Robert
23 Sea View  Southampton  SO2 9QT

Fielding   Michael
80 Baker St  Bournemouth  BH7 6GH

Evans  Florence
17 High Court  Witney  OX8 4DF

Adams   Rachel
414 Long St   London  EC1 7GH

Davies  John
1  Short Drive  Oxford  OX5 3ER

Farthing  Penelope
76 Grange View  Poole   BH15 6GH
```

The only change to current:=A[index] is a change of type; current is now a record of type *friend*, the same data type as the contents of array A.

The natural re-coding of the statement (A[locataion-1] > current) would be (A[location-1].surname > current.surname).

In the following program the array AddressBook is created, displayed, sorted into ascending order using the surname field as primary key, and the contents of the sorted array displayed again. Those procedures that have been listed in other programs in this chapter have only their procedure headings printed in italics. This is to save repeating the same code many times in the same chapter. For those readers who want to try the program on their computer, they must code the procedures in full and not just its italicised headings.

```
PROGRAM demo3(INPUT, OUTPUT);
{program to sort an array of records, into ascending order on the surname field as primary
key}

CONST
        MaxSize=99; {maximum number of records in the array}
        SizeOfString=30; {maximum number of characters in a text string}
        space = CHR(32);
        null=CHR(0);{character used to delimit all text strings}

TYPE
        TextString=PACKED ARRAY[0..SizeOfString-1] OF CHAR;
        address = RECORD
                        street:TextString;
                        town :TextString;
                        postcode:TextString;
                   END;

        friend=   RECORD
                        surname:TextString;
                        Firstname:TextString;
                        abode:address;
                   END;

        LineInBook = ARRAY[0..MaxSize-1] OF friend;{an array of records}

VAR
        AddressBook: LineInBook;
        size:INTEGER; {number of records to be stored in array}

PROCEDURE TextInput(VAR buffer:TextString);

PROCEDURE TextOut(buffer:TextString);
```

```
PROCEDURE CreateRecord(VAR AddressBook:LineInBook; VAR size:INTEGER);

PROCEDURE DisplayRecord(AddressBook:LineInBook; size:INTEGER);

PROCEDURE SortRecord(VAR A:LineInBook; size:INTEGER);
{procedure to sort an array of records on the primary key surname, using an
Insertion Sorting algorithm}

VAR
      location, index:INTEGER;
      current:friend;
BEGIN
      FOR index:=1 TO size-1 DO
      BEGIN
         current:=A[index];
         location:=index;
         WHILE (location > 0) AND (A[location-1].surname > current.surname) DO
         BEGIN
            A[location]:=A[location-1];
            location:=location-1;
         END;
         {end while}
         A[location]:=current;
      END;
      {end for}
END;{SortRecord}

BEGIN
      Write('how many records to enter? '); ReadLn(size);
      CreateRecord(AddressBook, size);
      DisplayRecord(AddressBook, size);
      SortRecord(AddressBook, size);
      DisplayRecord(AddressBook, size);
END.{demo3}
```

The results from this program being run are given on the next page.

11.5 Searching.

In addition to obtaining a list of the entire contents of an array, it is possible to obtain information about single records in the array. To find the address of a friend whose surname is already known, is simply a matter of comparing each surname of each record in the array, until either a match is found and the address of the friend can then be output, or the end of the array is reached, in which case the surname of the friend cannot be found in the array.

Results from program being run

how many records to enter? 6
input the following details
surname   =>Rankin
first name   =>Robert
address   street =>23 Sea View
                    town =>Southampton
              postcode =>SO2 9QT

surname   =>Fielding
first name   =>Michael
address   street =>80 Baker St
              town =>Bournemouth
              postcode =>BH7 6GH

(remainder of input as before)

Rankin   Robert
23 Sea View   Southampton   SO2 9QT

Fielding   Michael
80 Baker St   Bournemouth   BH7 6GH

Evans   Florence
17 High Court   Witney   OX8 4DF

Adams   Rachel
414 Long St   London   EC1 7GH

Davies   John
1   Short Drive   Oxford   OX5 3ER

Farthing   Penelope
76 Grange View   Poole   BH15 6GH

Adams   Rachel
414 Long St   London   EC1 7GH

Davies   John
1   Short Drive   Oxford   OX5 3ER

Evans   Florence
17 High Court   Witney   OX8 4DF

Farthing   Penelope
76 Grange View   Poole   BH15 6GH

Fielding   Michael
80 Baker St   Bournemouth   BH7 6GH

Rankin   Robert
23 Sea View   Southampton   SO2 9QT

The code required to carry out this search would be:

```
FOR index:=0 TO size-1 DO
    IF key = A[index].surname THEN
    BEGIN
        found:=TRUE;
        location:=index;
        (* exit from code *)
    END;
    {end if}
END;
{end for}
found:=FALSE;
```

In this coded example, if the key, the supplied surname of a friend, matches a surname of a record, then the Boolean variable *found* is set to TRUE indicating that the surname has been found. The variable, *location*, is assigned the value of the index so that the position of the required record in the array, is known. Having matched the surname, there is no further need to continue searching through the array, and it is therefore necessary to exit from the code. However, if the search for the surname is not successful, then the entire array would have been examined. The variable *found* is therefore set at FALSE outside of the FOR loop used to control access to each record.

One important point about the contents of the array has been overlooked. The array has been sorted on the surname field as primary key. Upon comparing the supplied key with the surname field for a record, if the supplied key is alphabetically less than the surname field, then the record to match the supplied key does not exist in the array and the search can be discontinued. This point is illustrated in figure 11.6

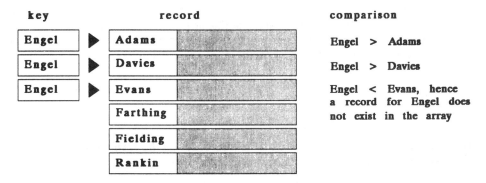

Figure 11.6 Sequential search on an array of sorted records

The code used to search the array can be modified to take this last point into account. Remember the contents of the array must be ordered if the following sequential search is used.

```
FOR index:=0 TO size-1 DO
BEGIN
   IF key = A[index].surname THEN
   BEGIN
      found:=TRUE;
      location:=index;
      (* exit from code *)
   END;
   {end if}
   IF key < A[index].surname THEN
   BEGIN
      found:=FALSE;
      (* exit from code *)
   END;
   {end if}
END;
{end for}
found:=FALSE;
```

Before a procedure is coded to represent the sequential search algorithm, one problem must be resolved. How does the computer exit from a procedure, when the computer has just executed a statement that is not at the end of the procedure? The answer, reluctantly, is to use a GOTO *label* statement. I say reluctantly because an over use of GOTO statements can lead to poorly structured code.

The GOTO statement provides the computer with a means of unconditionally branching out of a block of code, if there are no further requirements to execute that code. But where does the computer branch to? It is necessary to define an *unsigned integer label* at the beginning of the program or procedure to indicate where the computer must branch to. The label is then used in the program or procedure to mark the point of re-entry into the code.

The following program illustrates how the sequential search can be used to retrieve the address of a friend.

PROGRAM demo4(INPUT, OUTPUT);
{Program to sort an array of records, into ascending order on the surname field as primary key, then search the array using the primary key to find an address.}

CONST
   MaxSize=99; {maximum number of records in the array}
   SizeOfString=30; {maximum number of characters in a text string}
   space=CHR(32);
   null=CHR(0);{character used to fill text strings}
   no='n';

```
TYPE
    TextString=PACKED ARRAY[0..SizeOfString-1] OF CHAR;
    address = RECORD
                street:TextString;
                town:TextString;
                postcode:TextString;
            END;
    friend=  RECORD
                surname:TextString;
                Firstname:TextString;
                abode:address;
            END;
    LineInBook = ARRAY[0..MaxSize-1] OF friend;{an array of records}
VAR
    AddressBook: LineInBook;
    size:INTEGER; {number of records to be stored in array}
    key:TextString; {surname used to search array}
    found:BOOLEAN; {TRUE if surname found otherwise FALSE}
    location:INTEGER; {index where surname match was found}
    reply:CHAR;

PROCEDURE TextInput(VAR buffer:TextString);

PROCEDURE TextOut(buffer:TextString);

PROCEDURE CreateRecord(VAR AddressBook:LineInBook; VAR size:INTEGER);

PROCEDURE DisplayRecord(AddressBook:LineInBook; size:INTEGER);

PROCEDURE SortRecord(VAR A:LineInBook; size:INTEGER);

PROCEDURE search( A:LineInBook;size:INTEGER;key:TextString;
                    VAR found:BOOLEAN; VAR location:INTEGER);
{procedure to perform a sequential search on an array of records}

LABEL 1;

VAR
    index:INTEGER;
BEGIN
    FOR index:=0 TO size-1 DO
    BEGIN
      IF key = A[index].surname THEN
      BEGIN
        found:=TRUE;
        location:=index;
        GOTO 1;
      END;
      {end if}
```

```
            IF key < A[index].surname THEN
            BEGIN
                found:=FALSE;
                GOTO 1;
            END;
            {end if}
        END;
        {end for}
        found:=FALSE;
1: {exit procedure}
END; {search}

BEGIN
    Write('how many records to enter? '); ReadLn(size);
    CreateRecord(AddressBook, size);
    SortRecord(AddressBook, size);
    REPEAT
        Write('input surname of friend => '); TextInput(key);
        search(AddressBook, size, key, found, location);
        IF found THEN
        BEGIN
            TextOut(AddressBook[location].surname); Write(space);
            TextOut(AddressBook[location].FirstName); WriteLn;
            WITH AddressBook[location].abode DO
            BEGIN
                TextOut(street); Write(space); TextOut(town);
                Write(space); TextOut(postcode); WriteLn;
            END;
            {end with}
        END
        ELSE
            WriteLn('friend not listed in the address book');
        {end if}
        Write('continue input y(es) or n(o)'); ReadLn(reply);
    UNTIL reply=no;
END. {demo4}
```

The results from this program are given on the next page.

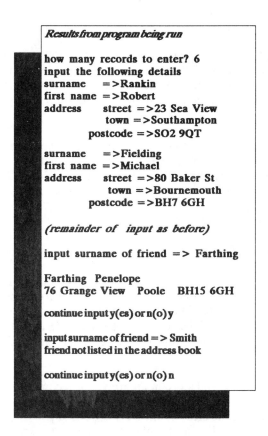

```
Results from program being run

how many records to enter? 6
input the following details
surname    =>Rankin
first name =>Robert
address      street =>23 Sea View
              town =>Southampton
          postcode =>SO2 9QT

surname    =>Fielding
first name =>Michael
address      street =>80 Baker St
              town =>Bournemouth
          postcode =>BH7 6GH

(remainder of  input as before)

input surname of friend => Farthing

Farthing  Penelope
76 Grange View   Poole   BH15 6GH

continue input y(es) or n(o) y

input surname of friend => Smith
friend not listed in the address book

continue input y(es) or n(o) n
```

11.6 Summary.

Information should be kept in an ordered format so that it is easy to display the information in a meaningful way and to enable the information to be searched with relative speed and ease of use.

An array can be used to hold information in an ordered format.

Information can be held in a record structure which consists of fields clustered together to represent different entities of information.

Records stored in an array can be sorted on a key field into some form of order. An efficient, yet simple, sorting algorithm for this purpose is the Insertion Sort, but there are many other algorithms.

Records stored in an array, that have been ordered upon a key, will allow for a speedy search for information. However, there is a more efficient algorithm for searching an array that will be explained in the next chapter.

Keywords

> *Insertion Sort, key;*
> *field, record;*
> *serial search, sequential search;*
> *RECORD, WITH, GOTO.*

11.7 Questions.

1. A list of ten different positive integers in the range 1 to 100 are input at the keyboard and stored in a one-dimensional array. The numbers are not input in any order, however, the value of the number is used as an index to its position in the array. Without using a sorting algorithm, write a program to input this data and display the data on a screen, sorted into ascending order.

2. The median of a set of numbers is that number which has the same number of values above and below it. For example, in the set [0,3,9,18,7,5,4] the median is 5 since three numbers are larger [7,9,18] and three numbers are smaller [0,3,4] than 5. Write a program to compute the median of a set of non-zero integer numbers input to the computer.

    (a) for an odd number of values;

    (b) for an even number of values.

    Note: clearly for an odd number of values the median will be the central value of the ordered set of numbers. An even number of values will not have one central value, but two central values. The median is taken to be the average of the two central values. There exists a standard BOOLEAN function ODD, that can be used to test whether a number is odd or even. For example ODD(3) would return the value TRUE, and ODD(2) would return the value FALSE.

[3]. Write a program to input and store in an array, ten records that contain the names of telephone exchanges and their corresonding STD codes. For example Oxford 0865 might be one record in the array. Sort the array on the STD code as key. Write a routine to search for the exchange when given the STD code. Display the results of the search.

[4]. Figure 11.7 illustrates the movement of keys in a one-dimensional array, when a selection sort algorithm is used to place the keys into ascending order. As can be seen from this diagram, in pass 1 the largest key (18) is found and swapped with the key (13) in cell 4; in pass 2 the next largest key (15) is found and swapped with the key (8) in cell 3; in pass 3 the next largest key (13) is found and swapped with the key (8) in cell 2, and finally in pass 4 the next largest key (8) is found and swapped with the key (7) in cell 1. Notice that only one swap is made for each pass through the array. Write a procedure to implement the selection sort for any number of numeric keys.

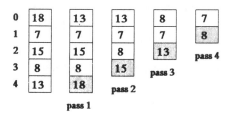

Figure 11.7 An illustration of a Selection Sort

12

Recursion

Procedures and functions have been used by calling them in either the main program or from within another procedure. By now this method of access to such units of code should be familiar to the reader. The calling of one procedure from within another procedure is quite acceptable. But what if the procedure being called is the same procedure that is doing the calling? The procedure or function is in effect calling itself.

The reason for allowing a procedure or function to call itself is, in many instances, to simplify the programming of a solution. Within this chapter the meaning of recursion will be explained, together with examples of how it can be used, and specifically applied to sorting and searching algorithms.

12.1 Definition.

One might be tempted to offer a simple definition of recursion as a procedure or function that calls itself. However, this would be incomplete, since there is no mention of how the called procedure gets closer to the solution or how to stop the procedure repeatedly calling itself.

Recursion can be regarded as a technique for performing task T, by performing a similar task T_i. The task T_i is exactly the same in nature as the original task T, however, it represents a solution to a smaller problem than T.

Thus task T recursively calls task T_1; task T_1 recursively calls task T_2; task T_{n-1} recursively calls task T_n. Where T_n is a solution to a smaller problem than T_{n-1}; T_2 is a solution to a smaller problem than T_1; T_1 is a solution to a smaller problem than T. Eventually the recursive calls must lead to a solution T_n, which cannot allow for further recursive calls, since a terminating criterion has been reached.

With these facts in mind, the reader should always address the following three questions before constructing a recursive solution.

How can we define the solution in terms of a smaller solution of the same type?

How is the size of the solution being diminished at each recursive call?

What instance or level of the solution, can serve as the degenerate case, and does the manner in which the solution size is diminished ensure that this degenerate case will always be reached?

12.2 Worked Examples.

In this section three worked examples will be fully explained with the aid of diagrams. The reader is advised to spend some time on this section in order to understand the technique of recursion.

The following program contains a procedure to output the value of variable i, in the range from 1 to 5 inclusive. Rather than constructing a FOR i:=1 TO 5 DO loop, the value of i is updated and output in a procedure, the procedure is then called again recursively, to repeat updating i and to output the value of i. The procedure is recursively called until i becomes equal to 5.

```
PROGRAM demo1 (OUTPUT);
{program to demonstrate recursive calls and returns}
VAR
        i:INTEGER;
```

```
PROCEDURE NumberOut(i:INTEGER);
LABEL 1;
BEGIN
     i:=i+1;
     WriteLn('recursive call to level ',i:2);
     IF i<5 THEN
          NumberOut(i)
     ELSE
          GOTO 1;
     {end if}
     WriteLn('returning through level',i:2);
1: {return}
END; {NumberOut}

BEGIN
     i:=0;
     NumberOut(i);
END. {demo1}
```

```
Result from program being run

recursive  call  to  level  1
recursive  call  to  level  2
recursive  call  to  level  3
recursive  call  to  level  4
recursive  call  to  level  5
returning  through  level  4
returning  through  level  3
returning  through  level  2
returning  through  level  1
```

In the context of this solution, consider the three questions about constructing recursive algorithms, given in the last section.

A smaller solution has been defined since only one value of i is output by the procedure, and not all five values.

Since i is being increased by 1, after each recursive call, the size of the solution is being diminished since i will eventually become equal to 5.

The degenerate case is when i is equal to 5. No further recursion is then possible, and all values in the range 1..5 have been output.

In figure 12.1 on the next page, a recursive call produces another instance or level of the procedure, depicted by the code being superimposed upon the calling code.

The remaining code after NumberOut(i), has been blacked-out in the recursive calls to

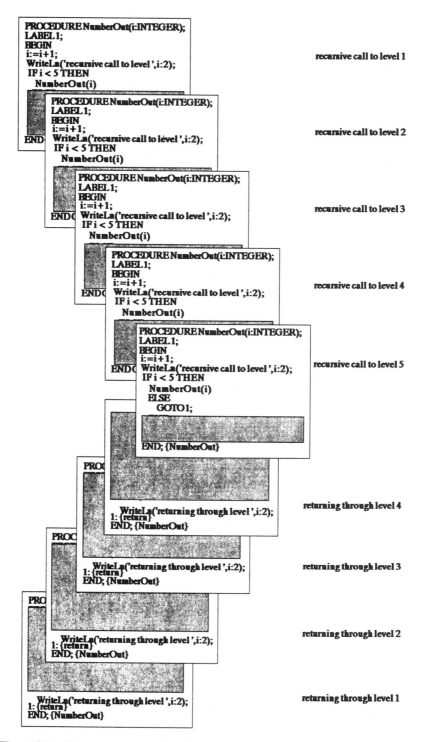

Figure 12.1 An illustration of recursive calls to procedure NumberOut, and the eventual return back through the layers of recursion.

levels 1,2,3 and 4, since this code has not yet been executed.

Level 5 serves as the degenerate case in which i=5. No further recursion is possible and the code

```
IF i < 5 THEN
    NumberOut(i);
ELSE
    GOTO 1;
{end if}
```

will cause GOTO 1 to be executed. The computer must return through each level or instance of the code, before the program can finish.

Since the computer is returning to the procedure that envoked the call, the next statement after the call, NumberOut(i), will be executed. However, NumberOut(i), was in one branch of a selection, therefore, the next statement to be executed will be after the selection statement.

For this reason all the code that had been executed is now blacked-out, since it will not be used as the computer returns back through the levels, or instances, of the procedure.

Notice also, that within each level the value of *i* has remained the same as it was when the level was originally invoked. Hence, in returning through the levels *i* is output as 4,3,2 and 1 respectively.

The second program in this section illustrates how a procedure can be called recursively to output the contents of a string backwards.

```
PROGRAM demo2(OUTPUT);
{program to print a string backwards}
CONST
        alphabet='abcdefghijklmnopqrstuvwxyz';
TYPE
        TextString=ARRAY[1..26] OF CHAR;

PROCEDURE WriteBackward(alpha:TextString; size:INTEGER);
BEGIN
        IF size > 0 THEN
        BEGIN
            Write(alpha[size]);
            WriteBackward(alpha, size-1);
        END;
        {end if}
END; {WriteBackward}

BEGIN
        WriteBackward(alphabet, 26);
END. {demo2}
```

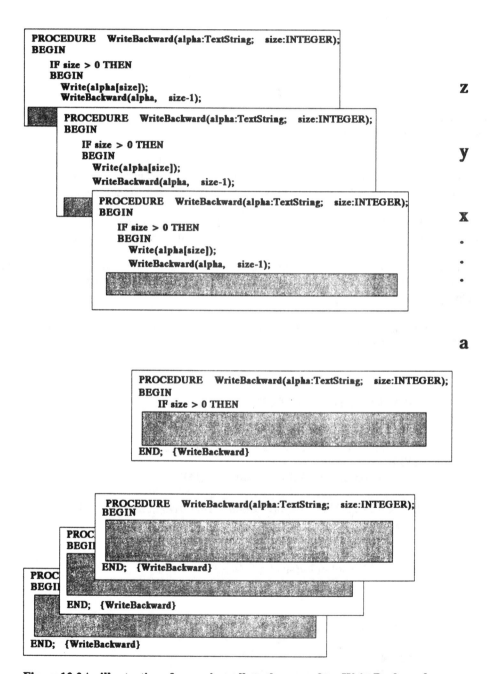

Figure 12.2 An illustration of recursive calls to the procedure WriteBackward

There are two observations to make from the program and figure 12.2 on the previous page. The index *size* is set at the last cell of the array and the contents, z, output; size is then reduced by 1 and a recursive call to WriteBackward outputs y; size is then reduced by 1 and WriteBackward is recursively called again. The output of characters continues until size is zero. Since the recursive call WriteBackward(alpha,size-1) is the last executable statement of the procedure WriteBackward, and the computer must return through each instance of the procedure, no further output is possible.

The last program in this section illustrates how a function can be called recursively to calculate the factorial value of a number.

```
PROGRAM demo3(INPUT, OUTPUT);
{program to calculate the factorial value of a number}
VAR
      n:REAL;

FUNCTION factorial(n:REAL):REAL;
BEGIN
      IF n < =0.0 THEN
          factorial:=1.0
      ELSE
          factorial:=n*factorial(n-1.0);
      {end if}
END; {factorial}


BEGIN
      Write('input number whose factorial is required (0 to exit) = > ');
      ReadLn(n);
      WHILE n > 0 DO
      BEGIN
          WriteLn('n ',n:6:0,' n! ',factorial(n):10:0);
          Write('input number whose factorial is required (0 to exit) = > ');
          ReadLn(n);
      END;
      {end while}
END. {demo3}
```

Result from program being run

```
input number whose factorial is required (0 to exit) = > 3
n  3   n!    6
input number whose factorial is required (0 to exit) = > 4
n  4   n!    24
input number whose factorial is required (0 to exit) = > 5
n  5   n!    120
input number whose factorial is required (0 to exit) = > 6
n  6   n!    720
input number whose factorial is required (0 to exit) = > 0
```

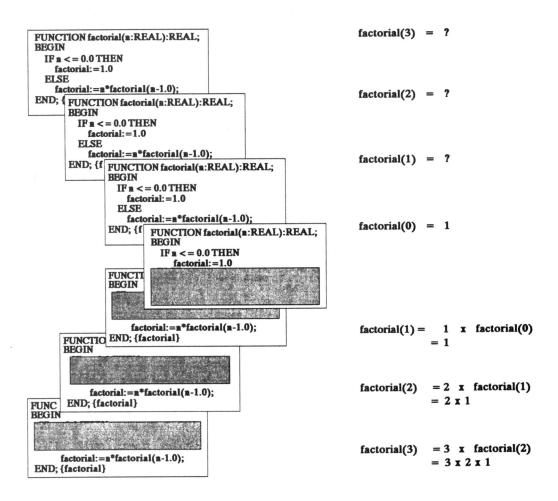

Figure 12.3 An illustration of recursive calls to function factorial

In this example the value of the factorial of a number cannot be calculated until the procedure has recursively reached factorial(0). Upon returning to the next instance of factorial(1), the value 1*factorial(0) can then be calculated. Returning to the instance of factorial(2), the value 2*factorial(1) can then be calculated. Finally returning to the instance of factorial(3), the value 3*factorial(2) can be calculated.

12.3 Binary Search.

This method requires that the keys are sorted into ascending or descending order prior to the search. In this example the key is a field in a record and the records are stored in a one-dimensional array. The array is divided into two parts and the relative position of the key with regard to one of the two parts is found. This sub-array is again divided into two parts and the relative position of the key with regard to one of the two new parts is found. The method continues until either a key match is found or the size of the sub-array is reduced to two keys and neither key matches. Figure 12.4 illustrates the sub-dividing of an array until a key match is found. When a sub-array contains an even number of keys the mid-point is taken to be the next lowest key from the centre. The key to be matched in this illustration is Quayle. Notice that only three comparisons are necessary compared with ten comparisons if a serial or sequential search had been performed.

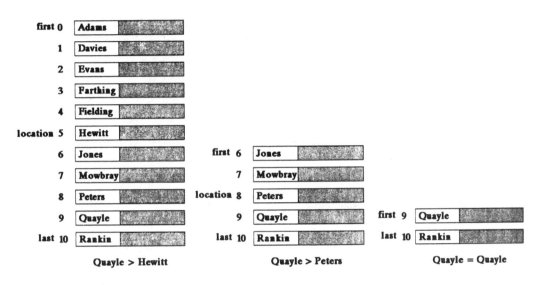

Figure 12.4 Binary Search for the surname Quayle in an array of records

```
PROGRAM demo4(INPUT, OUTPUT);
{program to test a binary search of an array of records}
CONST
        MaxSize=99; {maximum number of records in the array}
        SizeOfString=30; {maximum number of characters in a text string}
        space = CHR(32);
        null=CHR(0);{character used to delimit all text strings}
        no='n';
TYPE
        TextString=PACKED ARRAY[0..SizeOfString-1] OF CHAR;
        address= RECORD
                        street:TextString;
                        town :TextString;
                        postcode:TextString;
                    END;
        friend=  RECORD
                        surname:TextString;
                        Firstname:TextString;
                        abode:address;
                    END;
        LineInBook = ARRAY[0..MaxSize-1] OF friend;{an array of records}
```

VAR
> AddressBook: LineInBook;
> size :INTEGER; {number of records to be stored in array}
> key :TextString; {surname used to search array}
> found :BOOLEAN; {TRUE if surname found otherwise FALSE}
> location :INTEGER; {index where surname match was found}
> reply :CHAR;

{The procedures TextInput, TextOut, CreateRecord, DisplayRecord and SortRecord are identical to those found in the last chapter. For this reason only the italicised procedure headings have been listed here}

PROCEDURE TextInput(VAR buffer:TextString);

PROCEDURE TextOut(buffer:TextString);

PROCEDURE CreateRecord(VAR AddressBook:LineInBook; VAR size:INTEGER);

PROCEDURE DisplayRecord(AddressBook:LineInBook; size:INTEGER);

PROCEDURE SortRecord(VAR A:LineInBook; size:INTEGER);

PROCEDURE BinarySearch(VAR A:LineInBook; key:TextString; first, last : INTEGER;
> VAR found:BOOLEAN; VAR location:INTEGER);
{procedure to perform a binary search on an array of records}

```
BEGIN
    IF first > last THEN
        found:=FALSE
    ELSE
    BEGIN
        location:= (first+last) DIV 2;
        IF key = A[location].surname THEN
            found:=TRUE
        ELSE
            IF key < A[location].surname THEN
                BinarySearch(A,key,first,location-1,found,location)
            ELSE
                BinarySearch(A,key,location+1,last,found,location);
            {end if}
        {end if}
    END;
    {end if}
END; {BinarySearch}
```

```
BEGIN
      Write('how many records to enter? '); ReadLn(size);
      CreateRecord(AddressBook, size);
      SortRecord(AddressBook, size);
      DisplayRecord(AddressBook, size);
      REPEAT
         Write('input surname of friend = > '); TextInput(key);
         BinarySearch(AddressBook, key, 0, size-1, found, location);
         IF found THEN
         BEGIN
            TextOut(AddressBook[location].surname); Write(space);
            TextOut(AddressBook[location].FirstName); WriteLn;
            WITH AddressBook[location].abode DO
            BEGIN
               TextOut(street); Write(space); TextOut(town);
               Write(space); TextOut(postcode); WriteLn;
            END;
            {end with}
         END
         ELSE
            WriteLn('friend not listed in the address book');
         {end if}
         Write('continue input y(es) or n(o)'); ReadLn(reply);
      UNTIL reply = no;
END. {demo4}
```

The results are identical to those found on page 177, only the method of searching for a record is different. The recursive nature of the binary search is indicated in figure 12.5 on the next page.

12.4 Quicksort.

In this method an array is divided into two partitions. The dividing point is chosen to be the mid-point position in the array. Starting at the lowest position in the array a comparison is made between a datum at this position and the datum at the mid-point position. If the datum is less than the datum at the mid-point position a comparison is made with the next datum in the partition. Comparisons continue until a datum is found to be larger or equal in size to the datum at the mid-point position. Starting at the highest position in the array the process is repeated until a datum is found that is smaller or equal in size to the datum at the mid-point position. The data in each partition that prevented further comparisons from being made is then swapped over. Further comparisons and swapping of data will continue until each datum in each partition has been compared. All keys above the mid-point or pivot will be less than the pivot key and all keys below the pivot will be greater than the pivot key. The contents of the partitions are not yet ordered, so the method is then applied to each partition recursively until the subpartitions contain only one item of data. Figure 12.6 illustrates the ordering of the keys about the pivot point before the technique is applied to the subpartitions recursively.

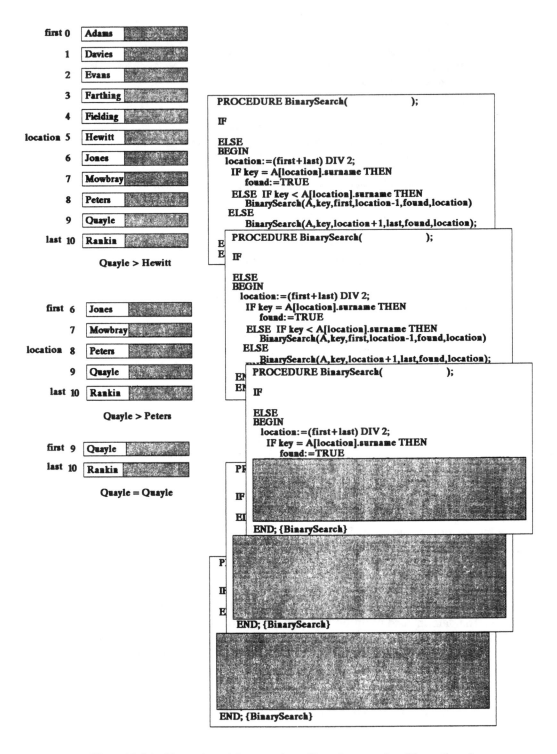

Figure 12.5 An illustration of the recursive calls to the procedure Binary Search

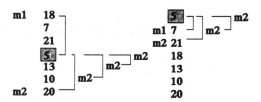

Nomenclature:

m1 - marker1
m2 - marker2

▓▓ mid point or pivot key

☐ comparison of two keys

Figure 12.6 An illustration of the ordering about a pivot key
in the Quicksort

```
{$N+}
PROGRAM demo5(INPUT, OUTPUT);
{program to sort an array of pseudo-random numbers}

CONST
      size=50;
TYPE
      RandomNumbers = ARRAY[0..size-1] OF INTEGER;
VAR
      A:RandomNumbers;
      seed:LONGINT;
      LowerLimit, UpperLimit : INTEGER;
```

{The function RND and procedures FillArray and DisplayArray are identical to those found in the last chapter. For this reason only the italicised function/ procedure headings have been listed here}

FUNCTION RND:DOUBLE;

PROCEDURE FillArray(VAR A:RandomNumbers; limit:INTEGER; size:INTEGER);

PROCEDURE DisplayArray(A:RandomNumbers; size:INTEGER;
                NumbersPerLine:INTEGER; FieldWidth:INTEGER);

```
       PROCEDURE QuickSort(VAR A:RandomNumbers;
                           VAR LowerLimit, UpperLimit:INTEGER);
VAR
       marker1, marker2:INTEGER;
       MidPoint, temp:INTEGER;
BEGIN
       marker1:=LowerLimit; marker2:=UpperLimit;
       MidPoint:=A[(LowerLimit+UpperLimit) DIV 2];
       WHILE marker1 <= marker2 DO
       BEGIN
          WHILE A[marker1] < MidPoint DO
             marker1:=marker1+1;
          {end while}
          WHILE MidPoint < A[marker2] DO
             marker2:=marker2-1;
          {end while}
          IF marker1 <= marker2 THEN
          BEGIN
             temp:=A[marker1];
             A[marker1]:=A[marker2];
             A[marker2]:=temp;
             marker1:=marker1+1;
             marker2:=marker2-1;
          END;
          {end if}
       END;
       {end while}
       IF LowerLimit < marker2 THEN
          QuickSort(A, LowerLimit, marker2);
       {end if}
       IF marker1 < UpperLimit THEN
          QuickSort(A, marker1, UpperLimit);
       {end if}
END; {QuickSort}

BEGIN
       seed:=19;
       FillArray(A,100,size);
       WriteLn('unsorted data');
       DisplayArray(A,size,10,6);
       LowerLimit:=0; UpperLimit:=size-1;
       QuickSort(A, LowerLimit, UpperLimit);
       WriteLn('sorted data');
       DisplayArray(A, size, 10, 6);
END.{demo5}
{$N-}
```

The results are similar to those found on page 163, only the method of sorting the numbers has changed. Figure 12.7 illustrates the recursive nature of the Quicksort algorithm.

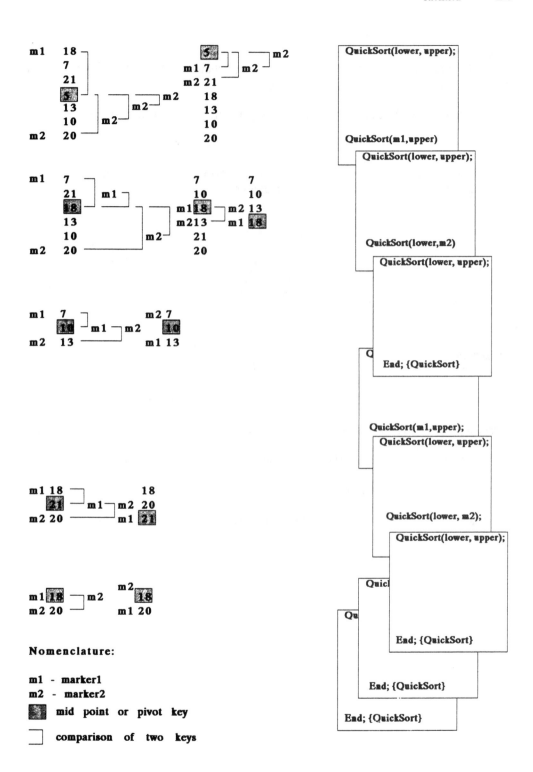

Nomenclature:

m1 - marker1
m2 - marker2

▓ mid point or pivot key

⌐ comparison of two keys

Figure 12.7 An illustration of the recursive nature of Quicksort

12.5 Summary.

A recursive procedure or function is a program unit that is capable of calling itself until a terminating condition, the degenerate case, is met.

Every time a procedure or function is called it generates an instance of that program unit.

Every instance of the program unit will have its own set of local variables.

Communication between different instances or levels of recursive program units is achieved through passing data through the actual parameter list.

Keywords

Recursion, degenerate case, instances or levels; Binary Search; Quicksort.

12.6 Questions.

Write recursive procedures in the answers to the following questions.

1. Write a program to sum a one-dimensional array containing non-negative integers.

2. Write a program to raise a number to a power, for example $X^n = X * X^{n-1}$ if $n > 0$.

[3]. Write a program to generate the first fifteen terms in a Fibonacci series.

4. Write a program to find the largest element in an array.

[5]. Implement the selection sort, from the last chapter, as a recursive procedure.

13

Text Files

Within this chapter the reader's attention will be focused upon Pascal statements that allow input and output of data streams from secondary storage media, as an alternative to the keyboard and screen.

13.1 Why use files?

The only method described up to now for inputting data to a computer has been through a keyboard in conjunction with either a Read or ReadLn statement. This form of input, although useful, is not adequate for coping with large volumes of data and suffers from the following disadvantages.

In using a keyboard for the input of data the advantage of using a high-speed computer to process work becomes irrelevant since the speed of the computer system becomes dependent upon the typing speed of the user.

Data that is input via a keyboard to the main memory of a computer is not permanently stored. Switch the power off from the computer and the data stored in the main memory is destroyed. Switch the power on again and the user must re-load and run the program before entering the data again!

To avoid these disadvantages data should be stored on magnetic tape or disc in the form of a data file. Such storage has the following advantages.

Peripheral devices such as magnetic tape and disc units can transfer data from the medium on which it is stored to the main memory of the computer at hundreds of thousands of characters per second. Thus the speed of data input/output becomes more realistic in terms of the power of the computer.

Data can be stored permanently on both magnetic tape and disc. Switch the power off and the data remains on the magnetic medium. Magnetic tapes and disc packs are portable, so not only can data be moved from one computer to another but libraries of data can also be kept. Data stored on magnetic tape or disc can be duplicated for security.

Changes to data held on peripheral media (tape or disc) will not involve changes to the program that use the data. In fact a program can and will bring about changes to the data and not the reverse.

13.2 Text Files.

A stream of characters input via a keyboard and output to the screen of a monitor can be thought of as the contents of text files being read from a keyboard or written to a screen. Indeed the heading, PROGRAM identifier(INPUT, OUTPUT); essentially defines two system text files, INPUT and OUTPUT. Text files, however, are not confined to keyboard input and screen output, they can be read from or written to secondary storage media.

The method of re-directing the input and output is through the program heading. The INPUT and OUTPUT system file declarations are replaced by the explicit names of the text files being used. For example, PROGRAM insured(data, results); specifies two files *data* and *results* that are used in place of INPUT and OUTPUT. These two files must be declared as variables of type TEXT, for example, VAR data, results :TEXT;

The inclusion of text files does not prohibit the use of the system files INPUT and OUTPUT. For a program that reads data from both the keyboard and file *data*, and writes information to both the screen and file *results*, the program heading would be modified to: PROGRAM identifier(INPUT, data, OUTPUT, results). However, only the data and results files are declared as variables of type TEXT.

There are two ways in which a text file may be created. The first is from within a program by using Write and WriteLn statements to direct output to a magnetic disc or tape instead of the screen. The second is by using the system editor in the same way as a program is created (via keyboard entry) and stored on magnetic tape or disc. A text file is a stream of ASCII characters, divided into lines, each with an end of line marker, and the end of the file is appended, by the system, with an end of file marker. A text data file is stored in the same format as a source program file.

13.3 File Processing Activities.
Opening a file.
Before a file can be used it must be opened. Two predefined procedurers in Pascal allow a file to be opened for reading and writing. These procedures are RESET and REWRITE respectively, and cause a file pointer to be positioned at the beginning of the file. RESET(data) opens the file *data* ready for reading the first line; REWRITE(report) opens the file *report* ready for writing (or overwriting existing lines), which in effect initialises the file to containing zero records.

Warning. Both RESET and REWRITE must not be used in conjunction with the system files INPUT and OUTPUT that are used for keyboard input and screen output.

The name of the file to be created (written) or inspected (read) must be present in the parameter list of the program heading. With Sheffield Pascal on a PRIME computer this filename must appear in the user's disc directory when a file is to be read. All reference to the file either at the program level or PRIMOS (operating system) level will be through the same filename. However, in Turbo Pascal it is necessary to assign the filename in the program to a filename in the directory of one of the disc drives on the PC. For example the statement ASSIGN(data,'A:data'); will associate the text file *data* with the ASCII file data held on disc drive A of a PC. All disc-based text files in Turbo Pascal must be assigned to a disc drive before RESET or REWRITE, for those files, can be used. Since ASSIGN is not part of Standard Pascal the reader is recommended to erase these statements from the programs that follow, if the programs are to be run in a Standard Pascal environment, such as Sheffield Pascal.

Reading a text file.
The lines of a text file can be read by using Read and ReadLn. However, the statements are modified by including the name of the file to be read. For example Read(data, value); would read a numeric value from one line of a text file that might contain the data depicted in figure 13.1. The statement Read(data, article[index]); would be embedded within a loop to read the text string on the same line. Having read the value and article the line would be terminated by using a ReadLn(data) statement.

Detecting the end of line.
Whenever there are sufficient Read statements to consume all the data on one line of a text file, there is little need to detect explicitly the end of a line in the file. However, if the number of items appearing on a line is not known in advance, as with a string of text, the end of line function can be used for a specific file. For example: IF EOLN(data) THEN ..

Detecting the end of a file.
The repeated execution of Read statements will cause all the data in the file to be read and an attempt will be made to read beyond the end of the file. This will result in a run-time error and the program being terminated by the operating system. Therefore, it is important that a method should exist for detecting the end of a file. The boolean function end of file EOF, is TRUE when the file pointer is beyond the last record (at the end of the file), otherwise it returns a value of FALSE. Since the file pointer is positioned at the first record to be read, if an attempt was made to open an empty file, it will in effect be pointing at the end of file. The value of the function EOF will therefore be TRUE.

In the Pascal language there is no need to read the file before testing for the end of file. This is not the case in other high-level languages such as COBOL and some dialects of BASIC.

Writing to a file.
Information is written to a file by the use of Write and WriteLn. However, the statements are modified by including the name of the file. For example the statement WriteLn(results, value:6, article); would append the information for value and article to the file called *results* and advance the file pointer to the next line of the file.

Closing a File.
There is no predefined procedure in Standard Pascal to close a file. The mode of use of a file is changed by opening the file again (even though it is in effect still open). A file opened for writing by REWRITE is changed to reading by RESET. When records are written to a file, the last few records although created, do not always get transferred from the system output buffer to the file. In order to flush the records from the buffer and append them to the file being created a RESET statement should be used in effect to close the file.

13.4 Single Input/Output Files.

Problem. A text file contains the following lines of data that relate to the insured values of several domestic appliances. For example a television is insured for £450, a music centre for £300, etc.

450	television
300	music centre
750	desk-top computer
200	microwave oven
350	washing machine
180	freezer

Figure 13.1 The contents of the data file

If inflation is 6.5% per annum, then write a program to read, line-by-line, the contents of the text file, increase the amount each appliance is insured for, by the rate of inflation, and write the new value together with the name of the appliance to a results file.

```
PROGRAM insured(data, results);
{program to increase the insured value of domestic items by the rate of inflation}
CONST
      inflation=0.065;
      MaxChar=20;
TYPE
      TextString=PACKED ARRAY[0..MaxChar-1] OF CHAR;
VAR
      value : INTEGER;
      article : TextString;
      data, results : TEXT; {text file type}

PROCEDURE ReadLine( VAR FileName:TEXT; VAR value:INTEGER;
                          VAR article:TextString);
{procedure to read the items of data that appear in any one line of the text file}
CONST
      space=CHR(32);
VAR
      index:INTEGER;
BEGIN
      Read(FileName, value);
      FOR index:=0 TO MaxChar-1 DO
         IF EOLN(FileName) THEN
            article[index]:=space
         ELSE
            Read(FileName, article[index]);
         {end if}
      {end for}
      ReadLn(FileName);
END; {ReadLine}

BEGIN
      {ASSIGN statements apply to TURBO Pascal only}
      ASSIGN(data,'a:data'); ASSIGN(results,'a:results');
      {open data file for input and results file for output}
      RESET(data); REWRITE(results);

      {read data file, increase insured value and write the details to the results file}
      WHILE NOT EOF(data) DO
      BEGIN
         ReadLine(data, value, article);
         value:=ROUND(value*(1+inflation));
         WriteLn(results, value:6, article);
      END;
      {end while}

      {force the contents of the buffer to be written to results file}
      RESET(results);
END. {insured}
```

Figure 13.2 illustrates the contents of the *results* file after the program has been executed. The contents of the *data* file will remain as depicted in figure 13.1.

479   television
320   music centre
799   desk-top computer
213   microwave oven
373   washing machine
192   freezer

Figure 13.2 The contents of the results file after the program was run

13.5 Multiple File Processing.

Problem. A text file contains information about members of a swimming club. Each line of the file contains information on the name, sex, age and competition results for each member of the club. For example the contents of the text file *members* might include:

Jones	M	17	1 2 3
Holmes	M	18	1 1 1
Evans	F	15	1 0 1
Peters	F	14	1 1 0
Nichols	M	18	1 2 2
Adams	F	15	1 1 2
Betts	M	17	3 1 1
Jenkins	M	16	1 0 1
Patel	F	15	2 0 1
Morgan	F	15	1 0 3
Phillips	M	17	1 2 1
Smith	F	16	1 1 3

Figure 13.3 The contents of the members file

The last entry, competition results, shows the placing (1) first, (2) second, (3) third and (0) not placed or absent from the competition of a member in three previous competitions.

This file of members is to be used to create two new files of swimmers. A file of male swimmers in the age range (16 < age <=18) and a file of female swimmers in the age range (14 < age <=16). The files will contain the names of the eligible members and the total number of points scored by each member over three competition. A points system is used to signify how well each swimmer did in the last three competition. Three points are awarded for first place, two points for second place and one point for third place. No points are awarded for not being placed or being absent from a competition. A member with two first places and one second place would be awarded eight points.

The contents of the files may contain the following information.

File of male members

Jones	6
Holmes	9
Nichols	7
Betts	7
Phillips	8

File of female members

Evans	6
Adams	8
Patel	5
Morgan	4
Smith	7

Figure 13.4 Male and female files showing the points awarded to each member

From these two files of eligible members it is required to select two swimming teams. Both teams are single sex, having members with the highest points over the last three competitions.

The problem can be solved as follows.

Each entry in the members file is read, and for those members that match the criteria of age and sex, the name of the member and total number of points awarded, is written to the appropriate male or female file.

Each male and female file is then analysed for the three swimmers with the highest number of points. Each file is read, perhaps several times, until three swimmers have been chosen.

```
PROGRAM swimmers(members, males, females, OUTPUT);
{program to produce two text files of swimmers from one text data file and select two teams
of three swimmers with the best record from each file}
CONST
      MaxChar=20;
TYPE
      TextString=PACKED ARRAY[0..MaxChar-1] OF CHAR;
      results=ARRAY[1..3] OF INTEGER;
VAR
      name:Textstring;
      sex :CHAR;
      age :INTEGER;
      competitions: results;
      members, males, females : TEXT;
```

```
PROCEDURE ReadLine(VAR FileName:TEXT; VAR name: TextString; VAR sex :
                        CHAR; VAR age : INTEGER; VAR competitions:results);
{procedure to read all the data on any one line of the text file}
VAR
      CompNumber:INTEGER;
      index:INTEGER;
BEGIN
      FOR index:=0 TO MaxChar-1 DO
          Read(Filename, name[index]);
      {end for}
      Read(Filename, sex, age);
      FOR CompNumber:=1 TO 3 DO
          Read(FileName, competitions[CompNumber]);
      {end for}
      ReadLn(FileName);
END; {ReadLine}


FUNCTION score(competitions:results):INTEGER;
{function to calculate the score obtained in the competitions first place = 3 points,
second place = 2 points and third place = 1 point}
VAR
      CompNumber:INTEGER;
      points :INTEGER;
BEGIN
      points:=0;
      FOR CompNumber:=1 TO 3 DO
          IF competitions[CompNumber] < > 0 THEN
              points:=points+4-competitions[CompNumber];
          {end if}
      {end for}
      score:=points;
END; {score}


PROCEDURE MakeFiles(name:TextString; sex:CHAR; age:INTEGER;
                        competitions:results);
{procedure to create two files of swimmers on the criteria of sex and age}
CONST
      male='M'; female='F';
BEGIN
      IF (sex=male) AND ((age > 16) AND (age <=18)) THEN
          WriteLn(males, name, score(competitions))
      ELSE IF (sex=female) AND ((age > 14) AND (age <= 16)) THEN
          WriteLn(females, name, score(competitions));
      {end if}
END; {MakeFiles}
```

```
PROCEDURE SelectScores(VAR FileName:TEXT);
{procedure to select three swimmers with the highest number of points}
VAR
      points:INTEGER;
      count:INTEGER;
      MaxScore:INTEGER;
      name:TextString;
      index:INTEGER;
BEGIN
      count:=0;
      MaxScore:=9;
      REPEAT
         RESET(FileName);
         WHILE NOT EOF(FileName) AND (count < > 3) DO
         BEGIN
            FOR index:=0 TO MaxChar-1 DO
               Read(FileName, name[index]);
            {end for}
            ReadLn(Filename,points);
            IF points=MaxScore THEN
            BEGIN
               Write(name); WriteLn(points:6);
               count:=count+1;
            END;
            {end if}
         END;
         {end while}
         MaxScore:=Maxscore-1;
      UNTIL (count=3) OR (MaxScore < 0);
END; {SelectScores}


PROCEDURE ProcessTeams;
{output each team chosen from the swimmers with the highest points}
BEGIN
      WriteLn('Male swimming team 16-18 years'); WriteLn;
      SelectScores(males); WriteLn;
      WriteLn('Female swimming team 14-16 years'); WriteLn;
      SelectScores(females); WriteLn;
END; {ProcessTeams}


BEGIN
      {ASSIGN used in TURBO Pascal only}
      ASSIGN(members,'a:members');
      ASSIGN(males,'a:males');
      ASSIGN(females,'a:females');

      {open members for input and males and females for output}
      RESET(members); REWRITE(males); REWRITE(females);
```

```
        WHILE NOT EOF(members) DO
        BEGIN
            ReadLine(members, name, sex, age, competitions);
            MakeFiles(name, sex, age, competitions);
        END;
        {end while}
        {force contents of buffers to be written to the ends of the output files}
        RESET(males); RESET(females);
        ProcessTeams;
    END.{swimmers}
```

Results from program being run

Male swimming team 16-18 years

Holmes	9
Phillips	8
Nichols	7

Female swimming team 14-16 years

Adams	8
Smith	7
Evans	6

13.6 Report Writing.

Directing output to a screen is fine for a small amount of data, however, since the output scrolls off the screen, it is of little use if the file contains a considerable number of records. A printed output, on paper, of the contents of a file is usually more acceptable. With Pascal it is possible to direct the output that normally appears on a screen to a text file stored on magnetic tape or disc. The contents of the text file can, at the users request, then be printed on paper.

Problem. A bookshop keeps a stock file of all the books in the shop. A small sample of this file is shown in figure 13.5.

The format of the file is such that the first item on each line is the title of a book, the second item is the price code for the book and the final item is the number of copies of the book in stock.

The price code is A=£3.75; B=£5.20; C=£5.95; D=£7.50; E=£8.95

Art in Athens	E 1
Birds of prey	A 2
Down on the farm	A 1
Eagles of Scotland	D 1
Gone with the wind	B 3
Hate, lust and love	A 2
Maths for adults	C 3
Raiders of planet X	B 3
Splitting the atom	E 1
The invisible man	A 1
The Otter	A 2
The Tempest	C 4
The Trojan Wars	C 2
The Vampire bat	D 2
Under the oceans	A 2

Figure 13.5 The contents of the stock file

A report on the contents of the stock file is required. The report should contain an entry for every book in stock showing the price of the book, and not its code, the stock level for each title and whether a new book is to be ordered if only one copy of the book remains in stock. Finally a summary of the total number of books in stock and the value of the stock held should be printed. The format of the report is illustrated in figure 13.6.

STOCK REPORT ON BOOKS

Title	quantity	price
Art in Athens	1	8.95 RE-ORDER BOOK
Birds of prey	2	3.75
Down on the farm	1	3.75 RE-ORDER BOOK
Eagles of Scotland	1	7.50 RE-ORDER BOOK
Gone with the wind	3	5.20
Hate, lust and love	2	3.75
Maths for adults	3	5.95
Raiders of planet X	3	5.20
Splitting the atom	1	8.95 RE-ORDER BOOK
The invisible man	1	3.75 RE-ORDER BOOK
The Otter	2	3.75
The Tempest	4	5.95
The Trojan Wars	2	5.95
The Vampire bat	2	7.50
Under the oceans	2	3.75

SUMMARY

Total amount of stock 30 books
Total value of stock £162.65

Figure 13.6 The layout of the stock report

```
PROGRAM books(stock, report);
{program to read a book file and produce a report on the price of the books, the total number
of books, the total value of books in stock and the books to re-order}

CONST
        MaxChar=20;
        ReorderLevel=1;
TYPE
        Price=ARRAY['A'..'E'] OF REAL;
        TextString=PACKED ARRAY[0..MaxChar-1] OF CHAR;
VAR
        title:TextString;
        PriceCode:CHAR;
        level :INTEGER;
        stock, report : TEXT;
        TotalStock : INTEGER; { number of books in the shop}
        TotalValue : REAL; {value of the stock in the shop}
        PriceTable : Price; {look-up table for holding the prices of the books}


PROCEDURE initialise;
{procedure to build look-up table for the price of the books, and set the total number of books
and total value to zero}
BEGIN
        PriceTable['A']:=3.75; PriceTable['B']:=5.2; PriceTable['C']:=5.95;
        PriceTable['D']:=7.50; PriceTable['E']:=8.95;
        TotalStock:=0;
        TotalValue:=0;
END; {initialise}


PROCEDURE ReadLine(VAR FileName:TEXT; VAR title:TextString; VAR
                        PriceCode:CHAR; VAR level:INTEGER);
{procedure to read a single line of the stock file}
CONST
        space=CHR(32);
VAR
        index:INTEGER;
BEGIN
        FOR index:=0 TO MaxChar-1 DO
            IF EOLN(FileName) THEN
                title[index]:=space
            ELSE
                Read(FileName, title[index]);
            {end if}
        {end for}
        ReadLn(FileName, PriceCode, level);
END; {ReadLine}
```

```
BEGIN
     initialise;
     {open the stock file for reading and report file for writing}
     ASSIGN(stock,'a:stock'); ASSIGN(report,'a:report');
     RESET(stock); REWRITE(report);

     {write information to the report file}
     WriteLn(report,' STOCK REPORT ON BOOKS'); WriteLn(report);
     WriteLn(report,'Title quantity price');WriteLn(report);
     WHILE NOT EOF(stock) DO
     BEGIN
          ReadLine(stock, title, PriceCode, level);
          Write(report, title, level:6, PriceTable[PriceCode]:12:2);
          IF level < = ReorderLevel THEN
               WriteLn(report,' RE-ORDER BOOK')
          ELSE
               WriteLn(report);
          {end if}
          TotalStock:=TotalStock+level;
          TotalValue:=TotalValue+ (level*PriceTable[PriceCode]);
     END;
     {end while}

     WriteLn(report); WriteLn(report);
     WriteLn(report,'SUMMARY'); WriteLn(report);
     WriteLn(report,'Total amount of stock ',TotalStock:4,' books');
     WriteLn(report,'Total value of stock £',TotalValue:6:2);
     WriteLn(report);
     {force the contents of the buffer to be written to the end of the output file}
     RESET(report);
END. {books}
```

To obtain a print-out of the report in a PC based environment the following commands should be given.

> Ctrl P *return* direct output to the printer that is currently on-line.
> TYPE A:report *return*
> Ctrl P *return* re-direct output to the screen

13.7 Summary.
A text file is a data stream of ASCII characters.

The input of data to a program can come from a text file in secondary storage, as well as being input at a keyboard.

A text file can be created using an editor or from the output produced by a program.

The input and output statements that have been used for keyboard and screen I/O are applicable to text file I/O.

Text files must be declared in the program heading.

Text files must be declared as variables of type TEXT.

Text files are opened for input using RESET and output using REWRITE.

There are no statements for closing a text file, however, it is recommended to use RESET to flush the output buffer.

Functions EOLN and EOF are used to detect the position of access to a text file.

Keywords

Text File, RESET, REWRITE;
EOLN, EOF;
Report Writing.

13.8 Questions.

1. Create a serial file that contains the details of items of stock in a brewery. Lines are of fixed length and contain the following details.

    stock number 5 characters;
    description 25 characters;
    stock quantity INTEGER;
    unit price REAL;

Assume that the lines are not in stock number order when they are input into the computer. Limit the number of test data lines to ten in this question. Using an editor, input and store the test data on a text file. Using an external sorting package, such as SORT in MSDOS, order the contents of the file on the stock number as primary key.

2. Using the ordered text file created in the last question, write a program to output the following report.

STOCK REPORT

STOCK NUMBER	DESCRIPTION	UNIT COST	LEVEL	VALUE
91189	Best Bitter Brls	25.50	100	2550.00
92258	Master Brew Mild Brls	20.00	200	4000.00
9236X	Stock Ale Brls	15.00	100	1500.00
.	.	.	.	.
.	.	.	.	.
			TOTAL VALUE	12450.00

[3]. A serial file is to be created containing the details of telephone subscribers. Lines are of fixed length and contain the following details.

> surname and initials 20 characters;
> telephone number 20 characters;
> previous meter reading INTEGER;
> current meter reading INTEGER;

Invent a minimum of ten test data lines containing the data described. Using an editor, input and store the lines into a text file. Using an external package, such as SORT in MSDOS, order the file on surname and initials as primary key.

[4]. Using the ordered text file created in the last question, write a program to output the following report.

TELEPHONE SUBSCRIBERS		
NAME	NUMBER	UNITS USED
Allen P	Abingdon 41937	2719
Brown J	Oxford 2245643	645
Carter F	Banbury 212	1768
.	.	.
.	.	.

[5]. Write a program to invite a user to replace any existing item of text within a text file by a new item of text. For example, if the text file contained the following poem 'I watched a blackbird' by Thomas Hardy 1840-1928:

> *I watched a blackbird on a budding sycamore*
> *One Easter Day, when sap was stirring twigs to the core;*
> *I saw his tongue, and crocus-coloured bill*
> *Parting and closing as he turned his trill;*
> *Then he flew down, seized on a stem of hay,*
> *And upped to where his building scheme was under way,*
> *As if so sure a nest were never shaped on spray.*

it is possible to replace any of the words or phrases by new words and phrases. There are three occurrences of the word *his* that could be replaced by the word *her* and two occurrences of the word *he* that could be replaced by *she*. The last line could also be changed to ...*were built on which to lay* !

The mechanics of such a program are as follows. Since Standard Pascal does not have the data type *string* it is necessary to store the words or phrases, that are to be found and replaced, in packed arrays of data type char. Since the usual width of the screen of a monitor is 80 characters, the size of the packed array has also been chosen to be 80 characters. Both the text to be replaced and the text used for replacement are stored in arrays of this dimension. For example:

> **never shaped on spray.**
> 123...   80

array *InString* stores the text to be replaced

> **builtonwhich to lay!**
> 123...   80

array *OutString* stores the new text to be inserted

A third array of characters is formed from the characters in the text file. This array will hold the same number of characters as are stored in the array InString.

> **I watched a blackbird**
> 123...   80

array *Hold* stores a frame of text to be inspected

The contents of array InString is compared with the contents of array Hold, if they match the contents of array OutString is written to the new output text file. The contents of Hold is then replenished with the same number of characters from the text file. If the contents of the two arrays do not match only the first character of the array Hold is written to the new output text file. The contents of array Hold is then shifted one character to the left and a new character is read from the text file to replace the last shifted character in array Hold.

> **watched a blackbird o**
> 123...   80

array *Hold* with contents shifted one place to left

The contents of array InString is repeatedly compared with the contents of array Hold until the end of file is encountered.

14

Pointers

Within this chapter a new data type will be introduced, the pointer. Since pointers are the basis of data structures such as linked lists, queues, trees and graphs, these structures will be explained to the reader in this and the next chapter.

14.1 Introduction.

The only internal static data structure that has been explained so far, is the array. The term internal refers to the entire structure being stored in the main memory of the computer. The array is described as being static since its size must be declared before it can be used in a program. For example in the following declaration:

```
CONST
    MaxChar = 80;
TYPE
    TextString = PACKED ARRAY [0..MaxChar-1] OF CHAR;
```

the size of the array will always be a maximum 80 characters, irrespective of whether it is completely or partially filled.

A file structure does have the advantage that the number of records it contains does not have to be declared in advance. Files will vary in their sizes according to the amount of data available and the processing requirements of the program. Files are not stored in the main memory of the computer, therefore, to access file-based records tends to be slower than to access records stored in an array. The data structures to be introduced in this chapter have the following advantages over arrays and files.

The maximum size of the structures does not need to be declared in advance.

The structures can grow or shrink in size, depending upon how large or small the volume of data, that is being processed.

The structures are stored in the main memory of the computer, therefore, access to the data tends to be faster than using files.

14.2 Pointers.

The fundamental scalar data types used within this book have been integer, real and char. Declarations such as:

```
VAR
    X : INTEGER;
    Y : REAL;
    Z : CHAR;
```

imply that X, Y and Z are identifiers of memory addresses that store data of the type integer, real and char, respectively, as depicted in figure 14.1.

A pointer is an identifier that does not store a scalar data value, but stores an address of where to find the data in memory. This address literally points to where the data is stored. The

X   **Y**   **Z**

Figure 14.1 Identifiers used to represent storage of different data types

following declarations:

VAR
        X : POINTER TO INTEGER;
        Y : POINTER TO REAL;
        Z : POINTER TO CHAR;

correspond to the diagramatic representation given in figure 14.2.

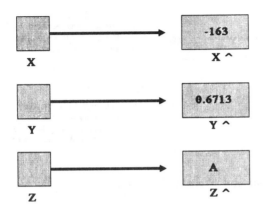

Figure 14.2 Pointers used to represent the storage of different data types

The declaration of a pointer is given as $^\wedge$ *identifier*, whereas the contents of the memory location that is being pointed at is given as *identifier* $^\wedge$. Therefore, $X^\wedge$, $Y^\wedge$ and $Z^\wedge$ are the values -163, 0.6713 and A respectively.

Pointers are assigned an address by the procedure NEW, and the address is removed by the procedure DISPOSE. The data associated with pointers is stored in an area of memory known as the *heap*. In the following example, P has been declared as a pointer to an address in the heap containing an integer.

The pointer can be declared as:

        TYPE
            pointer = $^\wedge$ INTEGER;
        VAR
            P : pointer;
or as:

        VAR
            P : $^\wedge$ INTEGER;

Figure 14.3 illustrates typical operations for the creation, use and disposal of a pointer.

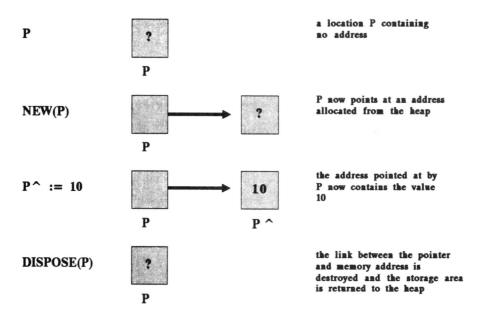

Figure 14.3 The creation and disposal of a pointer

Other pointers can be assigned to existing pointers. This implies that they both point at the same address. For example the statements NEW(p); q:=p implies that both p and q point at the same address. The first program demonstrates the facts that have been presented in this section.

```
PROGRAM demo1 (INPUT, OUTPUT);
{program to reference an integer via a pointer}
TYPE
      pointer= ^ INTEGER;
VAR
      p,q : pointer;
BEGIN
      NEW(p);
      Write('input a single integer = > '); ReadLn(p ^ );
      q:=p;
      WriteLn('value of integer being pointed at is ', q ^ :5);
      DISPOSE(p);
END. {demo1}
```

Results from program being run

input a single integer => 12345
value of integer being pointed at is 12345

14.3 Linked Lists.

In the last section the concept of a pointer was introduced. It was implied from the examples that pointers could point to memory locations containing either of the three scalar types - integer, real or char. It is common practice for pointers to point to records. For example, a pointer *head* could point to a record, called *node*, containing two fields, *word* and *link*. The declaration for this structure would be:

```
TYPE
    pointer = ^node;
    node =    RECORD;
                word : PACKED ARRAY [1..3] OF CHAR;
                link : pointer;
              END;
VAR
    head : pointer;
```

Diagramatically this structure can be represented as shown in figure 14.4.

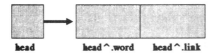

head   head^.word   head^.link

Figure 14.4 A pointer can point at a record

According to the declaration of the record the contents of head^.link is a pointer. If this pointer points at a second node then the two nodes have been linked together and formed a linked list as illustrated in figure 14.5.

head   first node   second node

Figure 14.5 Records can be linked together to form the nodes of a linked list

The next program in this chapter is a summary of the segments of code that have been illustrated in this section. The program builds the three-node linked list, that is illustrated in figure 14.6, and displays the contents of the nodes on the screen of a monitor.

The beginning of the linked list is indicated by the pointer head and the end of the list by the NIL (/) pointer. A NIL pointer implies there are no further nodes to be pointed at. The contents of nodes are output by making reference to the identifiers head^.word, pointer1^.word and pointer2^.word respectively.

```
PROGRAM demo2(INPUT, OUTPUT);
{program to build and display a linked list}
CONST
        space=CHR(32);
TYPE
        pointer= ^ node;
        node=RECORD
                    word:PACKED ARRAY[1..3] OF CHAR;
                    link:pointer;
                 END;
VAR
        head, pointer1, pointer2 : pointer;
BEGIN
        NEW(head);
        head ^ .word:='THE';
        NEW(pointer1);
        head ^ .link:=pointer1;
        pointer1 ^ .word:='CAT';
        NEW(pointer2);
        pointer1 ^ .link:=pointer2;
        pointer2 ^ .word:='SAT';
        pointer2 ^ .link:=NIL;
        WriteLn(head ^ .word, space, pointer1 ^ .word, space, pointer2 ^ .word);
        DISPOSE(head); DISPOSE(pointer1); DISPOSE(pointer2);
END. {demo2}
```

```
Results from program being run
THE CAT SAT
```

Although this program illustrates a method of building a linked list, it is not a desirable method. Apart from the pointer head, for every new node introduced into the list a new pointer variable must be introduced. Clearly a linked list containing, say twenty nodes, would require nineteen pointers (pointer1, pointer2 .. pointer19), in addition to the pointer head. Having to declare a fixed number of pointers in advance defeats the idea of constructing a dynamic linked-list.

The next program illustrates how to create and display a linked list of any size containing words of up to twenty-five characters in length.

In this program the first node is built by calling the procedure CreateNode using the parameter head. This creates a node as illustrated in figure 14.7.

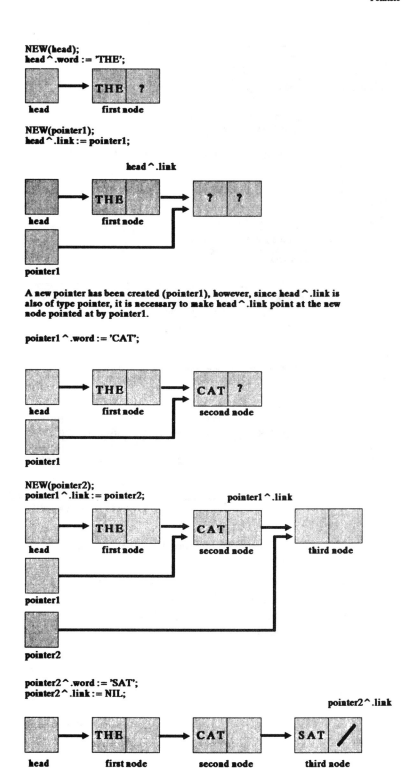

```
NEW(head);
head^.word := 'THE';
```

```
NEW(pointer1);
head^.link := pointer1;
```

A new pointer has been created (pointer1), however, since head^.link is also of type pointer, it is necessary to make head^.link point at the new node pointed at by pointer1.

```
pointer1^.word := 'CAT';
```

```
NEW(pointer2);
pointer1^.link := pointer2;
```

```
pointer2^.word := 'SAT';
pointer2^.link := NIL;
```

Figure 14.6 The formation of a linked list containing three nodes

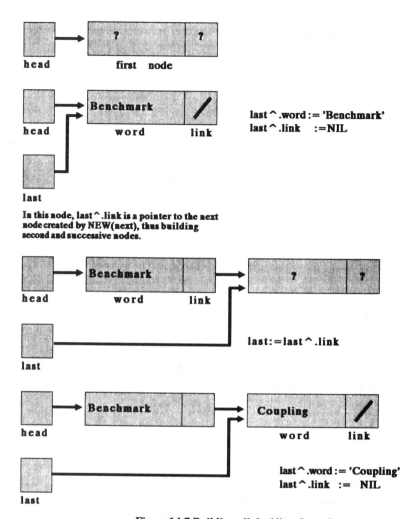

last^.word := 'Benchmark'
last^.link   :=NIL

In this node, last^.link is a pointer to the next
node created by NEW(next), thus building
second and successive nodes.

last:=last^.link

last^.word := 'Coupling'
last^.link := NIL

Figure 14.7 Building a linked list of any size

To traverse this linked list in order to display its contents, as shown in figure 14.8, requires writing the contents of current^.word, then replacing the contents of the pointer **current** by current^.link which is a pointer to the next node. When the value of current^.link is NIL, the end of the list will have been reached.

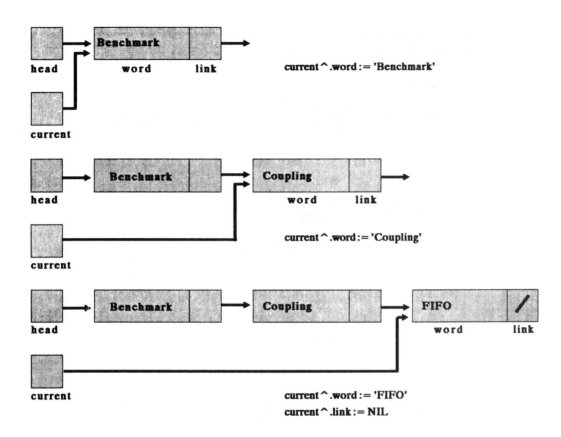

Figure 14.8 Traversing a linked list to output the contents of each node

```
PROGRAM demo3(INPUT, OUTPUT);
{program to build a linked list, of any size, containing words and display the contents of the
linked list after it has been completed}

CONST
    MaxChar=25;
    space=CHR(32);
    sentinel=CHR(46); {full stop as an input terminator}

TYPE
    TextString=PACKED ARRAY[0..MaxChar-1] OF CHAR;
    pointer = ^ node;
    node=RECORD
            word:TextString;
            link:pointer;
        END;

VAR
    head:pointer;
```

```
PROCEDURE CreateList(VAR head:pointer);
{build a linked list of words that are input at the keyboard}
VAR
      last:pointer;

      PROCEDURE CreateNode(VAR next:pointer);
      {create a single node containing the input word and a NIL pointer}
      VAR
         index:INTEGER;
      BEGIN
         NEW(next);
         Write('input word into list = > ');
         FOR index:=0 TO MaxChar-1 DO
            IF EOLN THEN
               next ^ .word[index]:=space
            ELSE
               Read(next ^ .word[index]);
            {end if}
         {end for}
         ReadLn;
         next ^ .link:=NIL;
      END; {CreateNode}

BEGIN
      WriteLn('terminate input with period/full stop');
      CreateNode(head);
      last:=head;
      WHILE last ^ .word[0] < > sentinel DO
      BEGIN
         CreateNode(last ^ .link);
         last:=last ^ .link;
      END;
      {end while}
END; {CreateList}

PROCEDURE ListOut(head:pointer);
{display the contents of a linked list}
VAR
      current:pointer;
BEGIN
      current:=head;
      WHILE current < > NIL DO
      BEGIN
         WriteLn(current ^ .word);
         current:=current ^ .link;
      END;
      {end while}
END; {ListOut}
```

```
BEGIN
      CreateList(head);
      ListOut(head);
END. {demo3}
```

```
Results from program being run
terminate with  period/ full  stop
input  word  into  list  =>    Benchmark
input  word  into  list  =>    Coupling
input  word  into  list  =>    FIFO
input  word  into  list  =>    Clock
input  word  into  list  =>    Ada
input  word  into  list  =>    Monitor
input  word  into  list  =>
Benchmark
Coupling
FIFO
Clock
Ada
Monitor
.
```

14.4 Linked-List Maintenance.

In order to maintain a linked list it will be necessary to insert new nodes into the list and delete redundant nodes from the list. The method of insertion and deletion of nodes is straightforward. Consider a linked list in which the records are ordered on the key field *word*. In traversing such a linked list of words, the words would appear in an alphabetical sequence. In the following example a new node is to be created containing the word GRAPE. The linked list will be traversed until the position for insertion into the list is located. In figure 14.9 the position is between the nodes containing the words FIG and MELON. To insert a new node it is necessary to introduce a new pointer *temp*, that will be used to point at the new node. The sequence of statements that are required to insert the node are as follows.

```
NEW(temp); { create a new node }
temp^.word:=TempWord; { store the word to be inserted in the new node }
temp^.link:=current; { the new node points to the next node in the list }
last^.link:=temp; { the last node points to the inserted node }
```

If the last node is the same as the current node then the new node must be inserted at the head of the list, therefore, the statement last^.link:=temp should be changed to:

```
IF last = current THEN
   head := temp;
ELSE
   last^.link:=temp;
{end if}
```

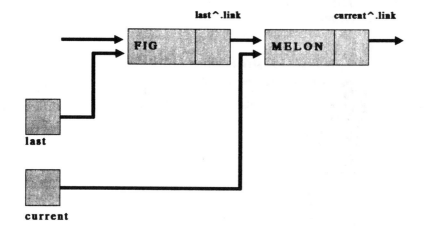

If temporary pointers, last and current, are used to denote the
positions of the preceding and following nodes then the insertion
of a new node can be drawn as:

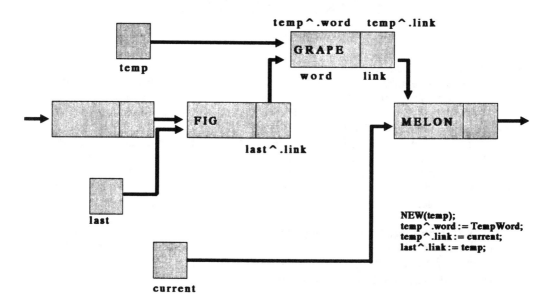

```
NEW(temp);
temp^.word := TempWord;
temp^.link := current;
last^.link := temp;
```

Figure 14.9 The insertion of a node into a linked list

The deletion of a node from a linked list is even easier. Figure 14.10 illustrates four nodes within a linked list. If the third node in the diagram is to be deleted the link field of the second note must be altered to point at the fourth node. The pointer to the third node can then be disposed. The code that performs this deletion of a node is:

```
last ^ .link:=current ^ .link
DISPOSE(current)
```

the link between LEMON and ORANGE is broken and a new link formed between LEMON and PLUM. Since current is pointing to ORANGE the effect of disposing ofcurrent is to remove ORANGE.

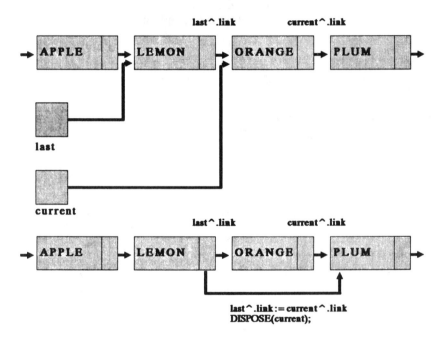

Figure 14.10 Deletion of a node from a linked list

If a node is to be deleted from the head of a linked list then the code must be modified to:

```
IF last = current THEN
BEGIN
    temp:=head;
    head:=head ^ .link;
    DISPOSE(temp);
END
ELSE
BEGIN
    last ^ .link:=current ^ .link;
    DISPOSE(current);
END;
{end if}
```

In both these examples it is necessary to search the linked list for the position of the node to be inserted or the position of the node to be deleted. When the list is being searched for the insertion of a new word it is possible that the word may already exist in the list. Similarly, when the list is being searched prior to the deletion of a word, it is possible that the word may not exist in the list. Both exceptions must be catered for in the algorithm.

The procedure that follows performs a sequential search on the contents of an ordered linked list. The reader is advised to study and desk-check this code, since it will appear again in the final program.

```
PROCEDURE search(VAR head, last, current:pointer; key:TextString;
                 VAR NotFound:BOOLEAN);
{procedure to search for the position of a key in the linked list}
LABEL 1;
BEGIN
    NotFound:=TRUE;
    current:=head;{point at head of list with variables current and head}
    last:=current;
    WHILE (current < > NIL) AND NotFound DO
    BEGIN
        IF key < current^.word THEN
            GOTO 1;
        {end if}
        IF key = current^.word THEN
        BEGIN
            NotFound:=FALSE;
            GOTO 1;
        END
        ELSE
        BEGIN
            last:=current; {move to next node in list and continue search}
            current:=current^.link;
        END;
        {end if}
    END;
    {end while}
1: {exit}
END; {search}
```

In the final program, nodes of a linked list contain a glossary of computer jargon. The linked list is created by reading a text file containing a sequence of word and definition pairs. The user of the program is invited to view the complete glossary, insert new words and definitions into the glossary or delete words from the glossary. The purpose of the program is to demonstrate the creation, insertion and deletion of nodes in a linked list. The format of a record stored in a node of the linked list is:

```
word : TextString;
definition : TextString;
link : pointer;
```

When the modification of the linked list is complete the list is written back to the original text file ready for future maintenance at a later date.

Prior to this program being run for the first time, the data file *list* had been created and was initially empty. The contents of this file was built using the program and not an editor.

```
PROGRAM demo4(INPUT, OUTPUT, DataFile);
{program to allow a user to inspect, insert and delete information found in a glossary of
computing terms}
CONST
      return=0;
      space=CHR(32);
      MaxChar=80;
      no='N';
TYPE
      TextString=PACKED ARRAY[0..MaxChar-1] OF CHAR;
      pointer= ^ node;
      node=RECORD
                word:TextString;
                definition:TextString;
                link:pointer;
            END;
VAR
      head, last, current : pointer;
      code:CHAR;
      DataFile:TEXT;
      key, definition:TextString;
      NotFound:BOOLEAN;


PROCEDURE CreateList(VAR head:pointer);
{build a linked list by reading successive lines from a text file that has already been created}
VAR
      last:pointer;

      PROCEDURE ReadText(VAR FileName:TEXT; VAR item:TextString);
      {procedure to read an item from the text file}
      VAR
         index:INTEGER;
      BEGIN
         FOR index:=0 TO MaxChar-1 DO
            IF EOLN(FileName) THEN
               item[index]:=space
            ELSE
               Read(FileName, item[index]);
            {end if}
         {end for}
         ReadLn(FileName);
      END; {ReadText}
```

```
      PROCEDURE CreateNode(VAR next:pointer);
      {build a single node in a linked list}
      BEGIN
         NEW(next);
         ReadText(DataFile, next^.word);
         ReadText(DataFile, next^.definition);
         next^.link:=NIL;
      END; {CreateNode}

BEGIN
      ASSIGN(DataFile,'A:DataFile');
      RESET(DataFile);
      CreateNode(head);
      last:=head;
      WHILE NOT EOF(DataFile) DO
      BEGIN
         CreateNode(last^.link);
         last:=last^.link;
      END;
      {end while}
END; {CreateList}

PROCEDURE ListOut(head:pointer);
{display the contents of the linked list}
VAR
      current:pointer;
BEGIN
      WriteLn('               ----------------------');
      WriteLn('               | G L O S S A R Y |');
      WriteLn('               ----------------------');
      current:=head;
      WHILE current < > NIL DO
      BEGIN
         Write(current^.word);
         Write(current^.definition); WriteLn;
         current:=current^.link;
      END;
      {end while}
END; {ListOut}

PROCEDURE search(VAR head, last, current:pointer; key:TextString;
                     VAR NotFound:BOOLEAN);
{procedure to search for the position of a key in the linked list}
LABEL 1;
BEGIN
      NotFound:=TRUE;
      current:=head; {point at head of list with variables current and head}
      last:=current;
```

```
        WHILE (current < >NIL) AND NotFound DO
        BEGIN
           IF key < current ^ .word THEN
              GOTO 1;
           {end if}
           IF key = current ^ .word THEN
           BEGIN
              NotFound: = FALSE;
              GOTO 1;
           END
           ELSE
           BEGIN
              last: = current; {move to next node in list and continue search}
              current: = current ^ .link;
           END;
           {end if}
        END;
        {end while}
1: {exit}
END; {search}


PROCEDURE insert(VAR head, last, current:pointer; key, definition:TextString);
{procedure to insert a new node into the linked list}
VAR
      temp:pointer;
BEGIN
      NEW(temp);
      temp ^ .word: = key;
      temp ^ .definition: = definition;
      temp ^ .link: = current;
      IF last = current THEN
         head: = temp
      ELSE
         last ^ .link: = temp;
      {end if}
END; {insert}


PROCEDURE delete(VAR head, last, current:pointer);
{procedure to delete an existing node from the linked list}
VAR
      temp:pointer;
BEGIN
      IF last = current THEN
      BEGIN
         temp: = head;
         head: = head ^ .link;
         DISPOSE(temp);
      END
      ELSE
```

```
        BEGIN
            last ^ .link:= current ^ .link;
            DISPOSE(current);
        END;
        {end if}
    END; {delete}

    PROCEDURE copy(head:pointer);
    {procedure to copy the contents of the linked list back to DataFile}
    VAR
        current:pointer;
    BEGIN
        REWRITE(DataFile);
        current:=head;
        WHILE current < > NIL DO
        BEGIN
            WriteLn(DataFile, current ^ .word);
            WriteLn(DataFile, current ^ .definition);
            current:=current ^ .link;
        END;
        RESET(DataFile); {flush output buffer}
    END; {copy}

    PROCEDURE menu(VAR reply:CHAR);
    BEGIN
        WriteLn('do you want to:');
        WriteLn('A - insert new entry into glossary?');
        WriteLn('B - delete existing entry?');
        WriteLn('C - inspect the glossary?');
        Write('input one letter A,B or C = > ');
        ReadLn(reply);
    END; {menu}

    PROCEDURE ReadString(VAR item:TextString);
    {procedure to read a string of characters}
    VAR
        index:INTEGER;
    BEGIN
        FOR index:=0 TO MaxChar-1 DO
            IF EOLN THEN
                item[index]:=space
            ELSE
                Read(item[index]);
            {end if}
        {end for}
        ReadLn;
    END; {ReadString}
```

```
PROCEDURE InputKey(VAR key:TextString);
{input a search key from the keyboard}
VAR
        index:INTEGER;
BEGIN
        Write('input word = > ');
        ReadString(key);
END; {InputKey}

BEGIN
        CreateList(head);
        REPEAT
          menu(code);
          CASE code OF
          'A': BEGIN
                  InputKey(key);
                  search(head, last, current, key, NotFound);
                  IF NotFound THEN
                  BEGIN
                      Write('input definition = > ');
                      ReadString(definition);
                      insert(head, last, current, key, definition);
                  END
                  ELSE
                      WriteLn('*** warning word already in list ***');
                  {end if}
              END;
          'B': BEGIN
                  InputKey(key);
                  search(head, last, current, key, NotFound);
                  IF NotFound THEN
                      WriteLn('*** warning word not found in list ***')
                  ELSE
                      delete(head, last, current);
                  {end if}
              END;
          'C': ListOut(head);
          END;
          {end case}
          WriteLn; Write('continue? Y(es) or N(o) ');
          ReadLn(code);
        UNTIL code = no;
        copy(head);
END. {demo4}
```

Results from program being run

```
do you want to:
A-insert new entry into glossary?
B-delete existing entry?
C-inspect the glossary?
input one letter A,B or C => C
```

|GLOSSARY|

Clock
a hardware device that generates an interrupt at regular intervals

FIFO
first in first out queue

Monitor
a collection of routines that control and protect a particular resource

```
continue? Y(es) N(o) Y  .

do you want to:
A-insert new entry into glossary?
B-delete existing entry?
C-inspect the glossary?
input one letter A,B or C => =>A

input word => Ada
input definition => a high-level language suitable for embedded systems

continue? Y(es) N(o) Y

do you want to:
A-insert new entry into glossary?
B-delete existing entry?
C-inspect the glossary?
input one letter A,B or C => =>B

input word => LIFO
 *** warning word not found in list ***

continue? Y(es) N(o) Y

do you want to:
A-insert new entry into glossary?
B-delete existing entry?
C-inspect the glossary?
input one letter A,B or C => =>B
input word => FIFO

continue? Y(es) N(o) Y

do you want to:
A-insert new entry into glossary?
B-delete existing entry?
C-inspect the glossary?
input one letter A,B or C => C
```

|GLOSSARY|

Ada
a high-level language suitable for embedded systems

Clock
a hardware device that generates an interrupt at regular intervals

Monitor
a collection of routines that control and protect a particular resource

```
continue? Y(es) N(o) N
```

14.5 Summary.

A pointer is an address in the main memory of a computer. It points to an area of memory that has been allocated from the heap.

Allocation of data storage from the heap is through the statement NEW, and freeing the storage area back to the heap is through the statement DISPOSE.

Since the allocation of addresses happens when the program is running, the structures built are said to be dynamic. Dynamic structures grow and shrink, during running of a program, according to the amount of data to be stored.

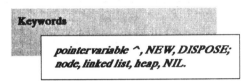

Keywords

pointer variable ^, NEW, DISPOSE; node, linked list, heap, NIL.

14.6 Questions.

1. Illustrate how to explicitly insert a node at the head and end of a linked list. Repeat the exercise for the deletion of a node at either end of the linked list.

2. From your illustrations in question 1, derive code to insert and delete the nodes.

3. Write a program to create a linked list of integers stored in key disorder. Build a second linked list that contains the integers from the first linked list sorted into key order. As each integer is used from the first linked list, delete it from the first linked list. When all the integers are sorted display the contents of the second linked list.

[4]. A circular linked list is defined when the last node of the list points to the first node of the list. Illustrate what you understand by this statement and write procedures to:

(a) Store and display numbers held in the circular list.
(b) Reverse the links in the circular list and re-display the information.

[5]. Modify the worked example in section 14.4 by writing recursive procedures to:

(a) Output the contents of a linked list.
(b) Search for a key in an ordered linked list.

[6]. The 'Early Bird' organisation specialises in a computer-aided telephone call 'wake-up' service. Customers telephone the company and state at what time of the day or night they want an alarm call. The data taken from each customer is:

time of alarm call;
telephone number;
name of customer;
special messages.

Write a program to store the data for each customer in the node of a linked list. Organise the list into chronological order based on a 24-hour clock. Assume that calls are only stored for a 24-hour period from noon of one day to noon the next day. The program should be menu driven and allow for the insertion, deletion and amendment of data. The next telephone alarm call to be made should be displayed on the screen, as a reminder to the operator.

15

Dynamic Structures

This chapter continues the use of pointers in data structures, and describes how queues, stacks and binary trees are represented and used.

15.1 Queues.

Queues are a familiar aspect of everyday life. People queue in orderly lines to wait for buses, wait to be served in a post office or bank. The general concept of a queue is a line of objects that has a front and a rear. The first object in the queue is said to be at the front of the queue, whereas the last object in the queue is said to be at the rear of the queue. In a *First In First Out (FIFO)* queue, an object can only join the queue at the rear and leave the queue at the front. There are many examples in Computer Studies of the use of queues. In a real-time system queues of processes waiting to use a processor or queues of jobs waiting to use a resource such as a printer, are quite common.

Queues can be built out of linked lists. The rear of a queue is depicted in figure 15.1. Notice that a pointer (rear) is used to indicate the last node in the queue.

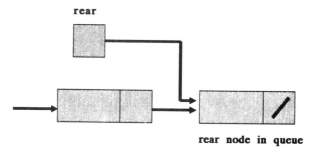

Figure 15.1 Showing the rear of the First In First Out (FIFO) queue

To allow another node to join the queue requires a new node temp, to be introduced. This node will contain the details of the latest member to join the queue. The code required to insert a new node at the rear of the queue follows. This code should be read in conjunction with the illustration in figure 15.2.

```
NEW(temp);
rear^.link := temp;
```

will allocate a new node, *temp*, and point the old rear node in the queue to this new node;

```
temp^.contents:=data;
temp^.link:=NIL;
```

will store the new data in the new node and set the pointer of this node to NIL since it is the new rear node;

```
rear:=temp
```

will force the rear pointer to point at the last node in the queue i.e. the node that has just been inserted into the rear of the queue.

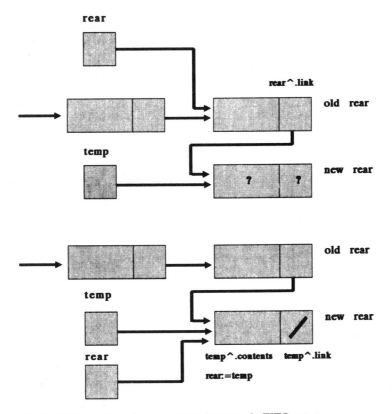

Figure 15.2 Inserting a new node into the rear of a FIFO queue
    Members of the queue can only leave from the front. The coding required to remove a
member from the front of a queue follows, and should be read in conjunction with figure 15.3.

temp := front;

will assign a temporary pointer to also point at the front of the queue

front := front ^ .link;

will change the front of the queue to point at the second node in the queue and has the effect of
by-passing the first item in the queue;

DISPOSE(temp);

since temp was pointing at the original first node in the queue this node is no longer required
and can be disposed.

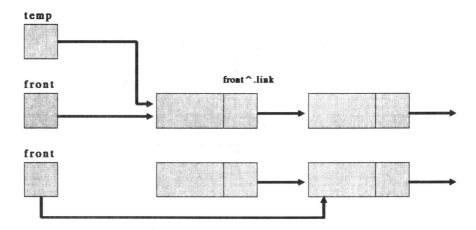

Figure 15.3 Removing a node from the front of a FIFO queue

15.2 Stacks.

A stack is a form of queue in which members of the queue can join and leave at one end only. The queue is known as a *LIFO* queue - *Last In First Out*. The entry/ exit point of the stack is known as the stack top and the position of this stack top is controlled by a stack pointer. An item that joins the queue is said to be pushed on to the stack. An item that leaves the queue is said to be popped from the stack. The methods for pushing and popping items from a stack are illustrated in figures 15.4 and 15.5 respectively, and should be used in conjunction with the code that follows.

To push a new node on the stack requires the following code.

```
NEW(temp);
temp^.contents:=item;
temp^.link:=StackTop;
```

will assign a new node, *temp,* store the new item in this node and force the new node to point to the original top of the stack;

```
StackTop:=temp;
```

will force the pointer StackTop to point at the same node as the pointer (temp), this will now point to the new node inserted into the top of the stack.

To pop an item from the top of a stack, is exactly the same process as removing an item from the front of a FIFO queue.

```
temp:=StackTop;
```

use temporary pointer to point at the top of the stack;

```
item:=StackTop^.contents;
StackTop:=StackTop^.link;
```

will store data from top node in stack and force StackTop pointer to point at next node in stack;

   DISPOSE(temp);

will remove node pointed at by *temp* - this will be the original first node in the stack.

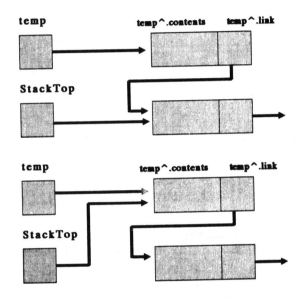

Figure 15.4 Pushing a new node on a stack

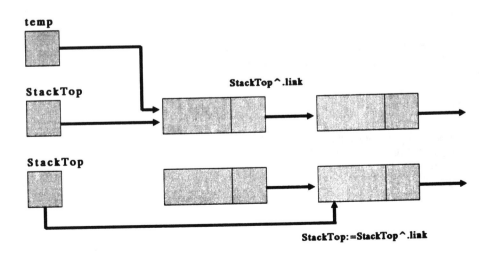

Figure 15.5 Popping a node from a stack

The first worked example of this chapter builds a stack of characters, copies the characters in the reverse order of input, to a second stack then pops and displays the characters from this second stack.

```
PROGRAM StackDemo(INPUT, OUTPUT);
{program to demonstrate how characters can be pushed and popped from a stack}
CONST
        terminator = CHR(32); {use space return to exit}
TYPE
        stack =  ^ node;
        node = RECORD
                        data:CHAR;
                        link:stack;
                    END;
VAR
        stack1, stack2 : stack;
        character:CHAR;

PROCEDURE initialise(VAR s:stack);
{set the stack pointer to NIL}
BEGIN
        s:=NIL;
END; {initialise}

FUNCTION empty(s:stack):BOOLEAN;
{function is TRUE when the stack is empty, otherwise FALSE}
BEGIN
        IF s=NIL THEN
            empty:=TRUE
        ELSE
            empty:=FALSE;
        {end if}
END; {empty}

PROCEDURE push(VAR s:stack; character:CHAR);
{insert a single character on top of the stack}
VAR
        temp:stack;
BEGIN
        NEW(temp);
        temp ^ .data:=character;
        temp ^ .link:=s;
        s:=temp;
END; {push}
```

```
PROCEDURE pop(VAR s:stack; VAR character:CHAR);
{remove a character from the top of the stack}
VAR
      temp:stack;
BEGIN
      IF NOT empty(s) THEN
      BEGIN
          temp:=s;
          character:=s^.data;
          s:=s^.link;
          DISPOSE(temp);
      END;
END; {pop}

BEGIN
      initialise(stack1); initialise(stack2);
      WriteLn('enter single characters on to a stack SPACE RETURN to exit');
      {characters input at the keyboard are pushed on to the stack}
      ReadLn(character);
      WHILE character < > terminator DO
      BEGIN
          push(stack1, character);
          ReadLn(character);
      END;
      {end while}
      {characters are popped from one stack and pushed on to another stack.
      The contents of the second stack is then popped and displayed on the screen.
      This outputs characters in the same order as they were input}
      WriteLn;
      WriteLn('characters input at the keyboard');
      WHILE NOT empty(stack1) DO
      BEGIN
          pop(stack1, character);
          push(stack2, character);
      END;
      {end while}
      WHILE NOT empty(stack2) DO
      BEGIN
          pop(stack2, character);
          WriteLn(character);
      END;
      {end while}
END. {StackDemo}
```

Results from program being run

enter single characters on to a stack SPACE RETURN to exit
a
b
c
d

Characters input at the keyboard
a
b
c
d

15.3 Reverse Polish Notation.

In compiler writing it is more convenient to evaluate arithmetic expressions written in Reverse Polish notation than it is to evaluate arithmetic expressions written in infix notation. The following algorithm can be used to convert infix notations to reverse polish notations. For example, the expression a*(b+c/d) in infix notation is written as abcd/+* in Reverse Polish notation. The algorithm uses operator priorities as defined in figure 15.6. The operators [and] are used to delimit the infix expression. For example the expression a*(b+c/d) will be coded as [a*(b+c/d)].

operator	priority
^	4
*	3
/	3
+	2
-	2
(	1
[	0

Figure 15.6 Operator Priorities

Using figure 15.7, if brackets [or (are encountered, each is pushed on to a stack. All operands that are encountered, for example a,b and c, are displayed on the screen. When an operator is encountered its priority is compared with that of the operator priority at the top of the stack. If when comparing priorities the operator encountered is not greater than the operator on the stack, the stack operator is popped and displayed. This process is repeated until the encountered operator has a higher priority than the stack top operator. The encountered operator is then pushed on to the stack. When a) is encountered all the operators up to, but not including (, are popped from the stack one at a time and displayed. The operator (is then deleted from the stack. When the operator] is encountered all the remaining operators, up to but not including [, are popped from the stack one at a time and displayed. The string of characters that is displayed will be in Reverse Polish notation.

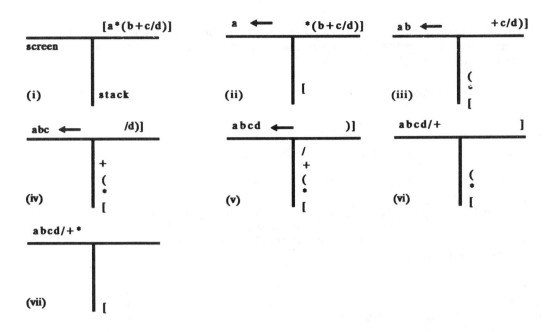

Figure 15.7 An illustration of the algorithm used to convert infix expressions to reverse polish expressions

The program that follows reads infix arithmetic expressions from a text file, converts each expression to Reverse Polish notation and displays the results on the screen of a monitor.

```
PROGRAM ReversePolish(DataIn, OUTPUT);
{program to demonstrate how characters can be pushed and popped from a stack}
CONST
      OpConst='^*/+-([';
      null=CHR(0);
TYPE
      stack = ^node;
      node=RECORD
                  data:CHAR;
                  link:stack;
             END;
      symbol=  RECORD
                  operator:CHAR;
                  priority:INTEGER;
              END;
VAR
      OperatorList:ARRAY[1..7] OF symbol;
      DataIn:TEXT;
      OpData:ARRAY[1..7] OF CHAR;
      OperatorStack:stack;
      NextCharacter, item :CHAR;
```

{The function empty and procedures initialise, push and pop were given in detail in the last program. To avoid repeating the same procedures only the italicised function/procedure headings are listed here}

PROCEDURE initialise(VAR s:stack);

FUNCTION empty(s:stack):BOOLEAN;

PROCEDURE push(VAR s:stack; character:CHAR);

PROCEDURE pop(VAR s:stack; VAR character:CHAR);

```
PROCEDURE initialisation;
{Open the DataFile containing the infix expressions.
Store the operators and their associated priorities in the array operators.
Create an empty stack}
VAR
     index:INTEGER;
BEGIN
     ASSIGN(DataIn,'A:DataIn');
     RESET(DataIn);
     OpData:=OpConst;
     FOR index:=1 TO 7 DO
     BEGIN
        OperatorList[index].operator:=OpData[index];
        OperatorList[index].priority:=7-index;
     END;
     initialise(OperatorStack);
END; {initialisation}


FUNCTION PriorityOp(character:CHAR):INTEGER;
{function to return the priority of an operator}
VAR
     index:INTEGER;
BEGIN
     FOR index:=1 TO 7 DO
        IF character = OperatorList[index].operator THEN
           PriorityOp:=OperatorList[index].priority;
        {end if}
     {end for}
END; {PriorityOp}
```

```
FUNCTION PriorityStack:INTEGER;
{find the priority of the operator at the top of the stack}
VAR
      index:INTEGER;
      character:CHAR;
BEGIN
      pop(OperatorStack, character);
      push(OperatorStack, character);
      PriorityStack:=PriorityOp(character);
END; {PriorityStack}

PROCEDURE analysis(NextCharacter:CHAR);
{perform the algorithm as described in the text}
VAR
      character:CHAR;
BEGIN
      IF NextCharacter=')' THEN
      BEGIN
         pop(OperatorStack, character);
         WHILE character < > '(' DO
         BEGIN
            Write(character);
            pop(OperatorStack, character);
         END;
         {end while}
      END
      ELSE IF NextCharacter = ']' THEN
      BEGIN
         pop(OperatorStack, character);
         WHILE character < > '[' DO
         BEGIN
            Write(character);
            pop(OperatorStack, character);
         END;
         {end while}
      END
      ELSE IF (NextCharacter = '(') OR (NextCharacter = '[') THEN
         push(OperatorStack, NextCharacter)
      ELSE IF NextCharacter IN ['^','*','/','+','-'] THEN
      BEGIN
         WHILE PriorityOp(NextCharacter) < = PriorityStack DO
         BEGIN
            pop(OperatorStack, character);
            Write(character);
         END;
         {end while}
         push(OperatorStack, NextCharacter);
      END
      ELSE
```

Figure 15.8 A single node with two pointer fields

If it is required to insert a second node, containing the fruit BANANA, such that the data is kept in an alphabetical order, then the reasoning would be:

    IF BANANA < LEMON THEN
        branch to left
    ELSE
        branch to right
    END

The new node would be inserted as follows shown in figure 15.9.

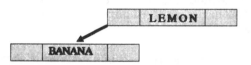

Figure 15.9 Attaching a node to the left branch since

BANANA < LEMON

A third node containing ORANGE could be inserted using the same reasoning, as depicted in figure 15.10.

Figure 15.10 Attaching a node to the right branch since
ORANGE > LEMON

The data structure that is being formed is the basis of a binary tree. The term binary is used since there is the possibility of two paths at each node, pointing at the next node. If the following fruits are inserted into the binary tree the data structure will appear as depicted in figure 15.11.

LEMON, BANANA, FIG, ORANGE, QUINCE, APPLE, PEAR, GRAPE, MELON.

Those nodes that do not point to other nodes and have both pointers set at nil are known as leaf nodes. The pointer at the top of the structure from which all nodes are descended is known as the root. The node containing LEMON is the parent to the nodes containing BANANA and ORANGE. Similarly, the node containing BANANA is the parent to the nodes containing APPLE and FIG. BANANA and ORANGE are children of the parent LEMON, and APPLE and FIG are children of the parent BANANA. Similar observations can be made about the relationships between other nodes.

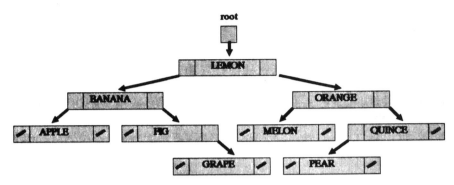

Figure 15.11 An illustration of a binary tree

To obtain a balanced tree, the value of the item pointed at by the root, should represent a mid-value for all the data stored in the tree. If the first item had been an APPLE, the shape of the tree would have been quite different, since no branches would appear to the left of the node containing APPLE. If the names of the fruits had been sorted, then the binary tree would degenerate into a linked list.

A binary tree has operations performed on it to initialise the tree, attach and remove nodes from the tree and display the contents of the tree.

A node of the tree that is depicted can be described in Pascal as:

```
TYPE
     TextString=ARRAY[0..MaxChar-1] OF CHAR;
     tree= ^ node;
     node=RECORD
             left:tree;
             word:TextString;
             right:tree;
          END;
```

The following procedures are used to manipulate data in a binary tree.

```
PROCEDURE initialise(VAR parent:tree);
{assign a NIL pointer to the root of a binary tree}
BEGIN
     parent:=NIL;
END; {initialise}
```

The purpose behind the initialise procedure is to set the root pointer of a tree to NIL.

The next procedure will allow a new node to be attached to a tree. The following code should be examined in conjunction with the illustration in figure 15.12, of attaching a new node containing the fruit 'DATE' to the binary tree depicted in figure 15.11.

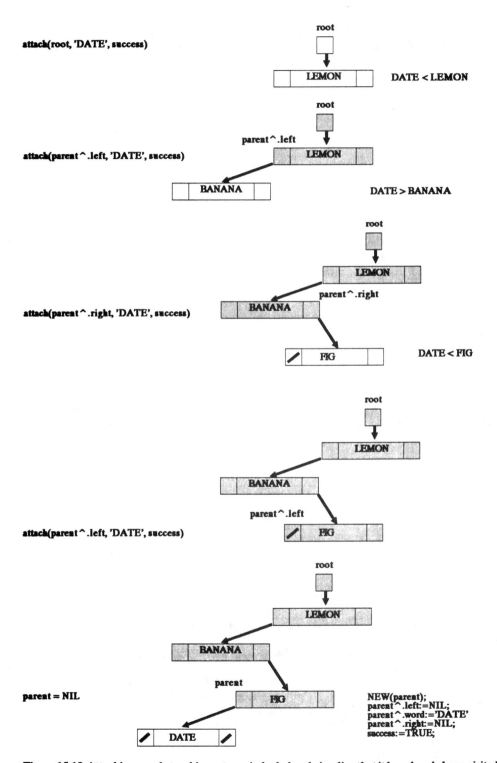

attach(root, 'DATE', success)

root

LEMON   DATE < LEMON

attach(parent^.left, 'DATE', success)

root

parent^.left

LEMON

BANANA   DATE > BANANA

attach(parent^.right, 'DATE', success)

root

LEMON

BANANA   parent^.right

FIG   DATE < FIG

attach(parent^.left, 'DATE', success)

root

LEMON

BANANA

parent^.left

FIG

parent = NIL

root

LEMON

BANANA

parent

FIG

DATE

```
NEW(parent);
parent^.left:=NIL;
parent^.word:='DATE'
parent^.right:=NIL;
success:=TRUE;
```

Figure 15.12 Attaching a node to a binary tree. A shaded node implies that it has already been visited.

```
PROCEDURE attach(VAR parent:tree; NewWord:TextString; VAR success:BOOLEAN);
{insert a new word into the tree - success is TRUE if no duplicate word was found, otherwise
success is FALSE and NewWord is not inserted}
BEGIN
      IF parent = NIL THEN
      BEGIN
         NEW(parent);
         parent^.left:=NIL;
         parent^.word:=NewWord;
         parent^.right:=NIL;
         success:=TRUE;
      END
      ELSE IF NewWord < parent^.word THEN
         attach(parent^.left, NewWord, success)
      ELSE IF NewWord > parent^.word THEN
         attach(parent^.right, NewWord, success)
      ELSE
      BEGIN
         Write('*** WARNING ***',NewWord);
         WriteLn(' already exists in the tree');
         success:=FALSE;
      END;
END; {attach}
```

When a node is to be removed from a tree it is necessary to search the tree for that node. Figure 15.13 illustrates how the word 'GRAPE' is found prior to removing the node. The method of seraching through the tree is similar to that depicted in figure 15.12, when it was necessary to search for the correct place to insert the new node.

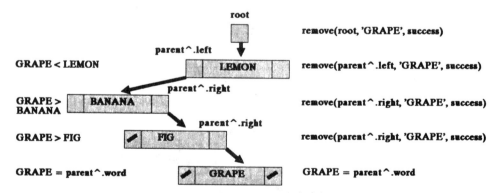

Figure 15.13 Recursive search for the contents of a node in a binary tree

The removal of a node from a tree is not such a simple matter as attaching a new node to the tree. When the node to be removed has been located it might be a leaf node (no children), a node with either the left or right branch pointers NIL (one child) or a node with both the left and right pointers pointing at two respective sub-trees (two children). Figure 15.14 illustrates how to delete the node in each of the three circumstances described. Both figures 15.13 and 15.14 should be viewed in conjunction with the code for the procedure tu remove a node from the tree.

```
PROCEDURE remove(VAR parent:tree; OldWord:TextString; VAR success:BOOLEAN);
{delete the node containing OldWord from the tree - success is TRUE if the OldWord was
found, otherwise success is FALSE if the OldWord does not exist in the tree}
VAR
      temp:tree;
      NextWord:Textstring;
BEGIN
      IF parent < > NIL THEN
      BEGIN
        IF OldWord = parent ^ .word THEN
        BEGIN
            success:=TRUE;
            IF (parent ^ .left=NIL) AND (parent ^ .right=NIL) THEN
            BEGIN
                temp:=parent;
                parent:=NIL;
                DISPOSE(temp);
            END
            ELSE IF parent ^ .left = NIL THEN
            BEGIN
                temp:=parent;
                parent:=parent ^ .right;
                DISPOSE(temp);
            END
            ELSE IF parent ^ .right = NIL THEN
            BEGIN
                temp:=parent;
                parent:=parent ^ .left;
                DISPOSE(temp);
            END
            ELSE
            BEGIN
                successor(parent ^ .right, NextWord);
                parent ^ .word:=NextWord;
            END
        END
        ELSE IF OldWord < parent ^ .word THEN
            remove(parent ^ .left, OldWord, success)
        ELSE
            remove(parent ^ .right, OldWord, success);
        {end if}
      END
      ELSE
      BEGIN
        Write('*** WARNING ***', OldWord);
        WriteLn(' not found in the tree');
        success:=FALSE;
      END;
      {end if}
END; {remove}
```

The procedure successor is necessary in finding the contents of a node that is the next in sequence to the node to be removed. The procedure searches through the right sub-tree of the node to be removed until the left-most element in this sub-tree is found.

```
PROCEDURE successor(VAR parent:tree; VAR NextWord:TextString);
{The procedure successor is necessary in finding the contents of a node that is the next in
sequence to the node to be removed. The procedure searches through the right sub-tree of the
node to be removed until the left-most element in this sub-tree is found}
VAR
      temp:tree;
BEGIN
      IF parent < > NIL THEN
         IF parent ^ .left = NIL THEN
         BEGIN
            NextWord:=parent ^ .word;
            temp:=parent;
            parent:=parent ^ .right;
            DISPOSE(temp);
         END
         ELSE
            successor(parent ^ .left, NextWord);
         {end if}
      {end if}
END; {successor}
```

Finally the method of displaying the contents in sequential order, of the tree, uses as an inorder tree traversal. During an inorder traversal, the contents each node is displayed after all nodes in its left sub-tree, but before any node in its right subtree. Figure 15.15 illustrates the recursive execution of the procedure display, used to output the binary tree containing three nodes depicted in figure 15.10.

```
PROCEDURE display(VAR parent:tree);
{display the contents of a tree on the screen of a terminal - the order of traversing the tree is
inorder, therefore, each node is output after all nodes in its left sub-tree but before any node
in the right sub-tree}
BEGIN
      IF parent < > NIL THEN
      BEGIN
         display(parent ^ .left);
         WriteLn(parent ^ .word);
         display(parent ^ .right);
      END;
END; {display}
```

There are two other methods for traversing a binary tree - *preorder* and *postorder* traversals. In a preorder traversal a node is processed before the computer traverses either of the node's subtrees, however, with a postorder traversal both the subtrees of a node are traversed before processing the node. Figure 15.16 shows a binary tree containing numerical data and the results of performing preorder and postorder traversals to output the data.

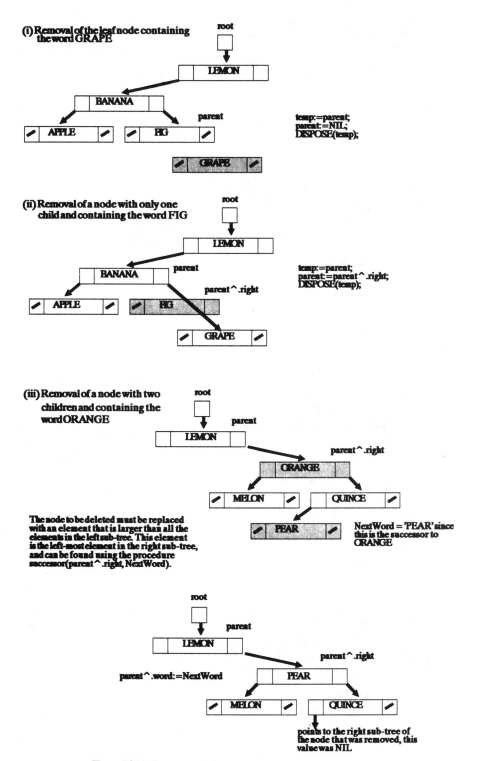

Figure 15.14 The removal of nodes from a binary tree

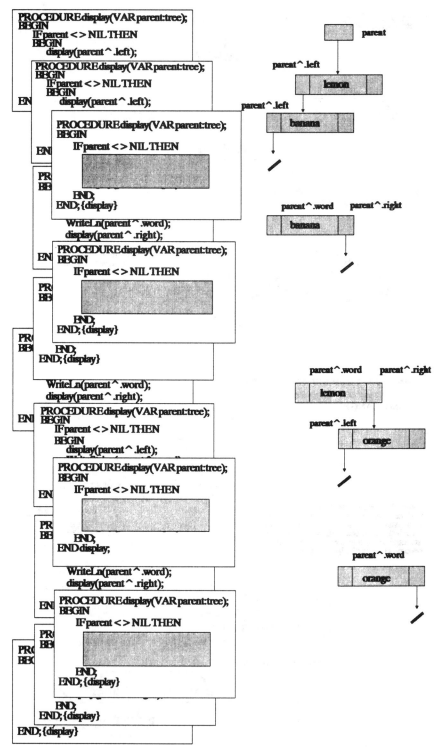

Figure 15.15 Recursive inorder traversal of a binary tree to output the contents of each node

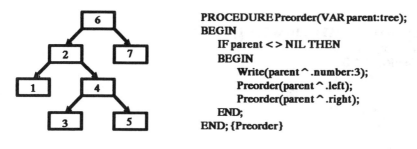

```
PROCEDURE Preorder(VAR parent:tree);
BEGIN
    IF parent < > NIL THEN
    BEGIN
        Write(parent ^ .number:3);
        Preorder(parent ^ .left);
        Preorder(parent ^ .right);
    END;
END; {Preorder}
```

Output from a Preorder traversal would be: 6 2 1 4 3 5 7

```
PROCEDURE Postorder(VAR parent:tree);
BEGIN
    IF parent < > NIL THEN
    BEGIN
        Postorder(parent ^ .left);
        Postorder(parent ^ .right);
        Write(parent ^ .number:3);
    END;
END; {Postorder}
```

Output from a Postorder traversal would be 1 3 5 4 2 7 6

Figure 15.16 Preorder and Postorder tree traversal

15.5 Binary Tree Maintenance.

In the final program of this chapter, the list of fruits given in the last section, are each read from a text file and stored in a binary tree. Before each fruit is stored it is first examined to see whether it already exists in the tree. If it does exist it is not inserted again. When the tree is completely built it is recursively searched and the contents of each node is output in the correct order. Notice that the data is now sorted into alphabetical sequence. The user is then given the opportunity of inserting new nodes or deleting existing nodes from the tree. At the end of the session the contents of the binary tree is written back to the text file using a preorder traversal of the tree. If a preorder traversal was not performed then the balance of the tree would not be maintained.

The procedures that have already been coded in this chapter, have only their italicised procedure headings displayed in this program. For the reader who wishes to run the program it will be necessary to expand the code to its fullest by making reference to the code for the procedures given in the text.

```
PROGRAM TreeMaintenance(INPUT, DataFile, OUTPUT);
{program to read a list of words from a data file and insert them, in order, into a binary tree.
When the end of the data file is reached the contents of the tree is output in alphabetical
sequence. The user is then invited to insert new nodes or delete nodes in the binary tree}
CONST
    quit='Q';
    MaxChar=20;
```

```
TYPE
     TextString=ARRAY[0..MaxChar-1] OF CHAR;
     tree= ^ node;
     node=RECORD
               left:tree;
               word:TextString;
               right:tree;
           END;
VAR
     DataFile : TEXT;
     BinTree : tree;
     fruit : TextString;
     success : BOOLEAN;
     reply : CHAR;
```

PROCEDURE initialise(VAR parent:tree);

PROCEDURE attach(VAR parent:tree; NewWord:TextString; VAR success:BOOLEAN);

PROCEDURE successor(VAR parent:tree; VAR NextWord:TextString);

PROCEDURE remove(VAR parent:tree; OldWord:TextString; VAR success:BOOLEAN);

PROCEDURE display(VAR parent:tree);

```
PROCEDURE ReadLine(VAR FileName:TEXT; VAR item:TextString);
{read a line of the text data file}
CONST    space=CHR(32);
VAR      index:INTEGER;
BEGIN
     FOR index:=0 TO MaxChar-1 DO
         IF EOLN(FileName) THEN
             item[index]:=space
         ELSE
             Read(FileName, item[index]);
         {end if}
     {end for}
     ReadLn(FileName);
END; {ReadLine}

PROCEDURE PreorderWrite(VAR FileName:TEXT; VAR parent:tree);
BEGIN
     IF parent < > NIL THEN
     BEGIN
         WriteLn(FileName, parent ^ .word);
         PreorderWrite(FileName, parent ^ .left);
         PreorderWrite(FileName, parent ^ .right);
     END;
END; {PreorderWrite}
```

```
BEGIN
      initialise(BinTree);
      {build the binary tree from the data file}
      ASSIGN(DataFile,'A:DataFile'); RESET(DataFile);
      WHILE NOT EOF(DataFile) DO
      BEGIN
         ReadLine(DataFile, fruit);
         attach(BinTree, fruit, success);
      END;
      {invite the user to insert or delete nodes in the binary tree}
      REPEAT
         WriteLn('the binary tree contains the following data');
         display(BinTree); WriteLn;
         WriteLn('Do you want to:');
         WriteLn('(I)nsert'); WriteLn('(D)elete'); WriteLn('(Q)uit');
         WriteLn('input code I, D, or Q => ');
         ReadLn(reply);
         IF reply = 'I' THEN
            REPEAT
               Write('input word for insertion => ');
               ReadLine(INPUT,fruit);
               attach(BinTree, fruit, success);
            UNTIL success
         ELSE IF reply = 'D' THEN
            REPEAT
               Write('input word for removal => ');
               ReadLine(INPUT,fruit);
               remove(BinTree, fruit, success);
            UNTIL (success) OR (BinTree=NIL);
         {end if}
      UNTIL reply = quit;
      {copy contents of binary tree back to the data file}
      REWRITE(DataFile);
      PreorderWrite(DataFile, BinTree);
      RESET(DataFile);
END. {TreeMaintenance}
```

The results from this program being run are on the next page.

15.6 Summary.

In a First In First Out (FIFO) queue entry to the queue is at the back, whereas to exit from the queue is at the front. In a Last In First Out (LIFO) queue entry and exit are both at the head of the queue. This type of queue is also known as a stack. Items of data are pushed on to a stack (inserted) or popped from the stack (deleted).

The representation of queues has been through a linked list structure having one pointer per node.

A structure in which the node has two pointers, one left and one right, forms the basis of a

Results from program being run

the binary tree contains the following data

apple
banana
fig
grape

Do you want to
(I)nsert
(D)elete
(Q)uit
input code I, D or Q = > I
input word for insertion = > banana
*** WARNING *** banana already exists in the tree
input word for insertion = > date

the binary tree contains the following data

apple
banana
date
fig
grape

Do you want to
(I)nsert
(D)elete
(Q)uit
input code I, D or Q = > D
input word for removal = > peach
*** WARNING *** peach not found in the tree
input word for removal = > fig

the binary tree contains the following data

apple
banana
date
grape

Do you want to
(I)nsert
(D)elete
(Q)uit
input code I, D or Q = > Q

binary tree. The advantage of storing data in a binary tree over a linked list is that, provided the tree is balanced, the time it takes to search for an item of data is much quicker. Data in a binary tree accessed by using an in-order tree traversal has the advantage of processing data in an ordered sequence (i.e. alphabetically ordered). To access the contents of each node in order, the contents is accessed after all nodes in its left sub-tree have been accessed and before any nodes in its right sub-tree.

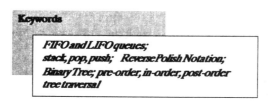

Keywords

FIFO and LIFO queues;
stack, pop, push;   Reverse Polish Notation;
Binary Tree; pre-order, in-order, post-order
tree traversal

15.7 Questions.

1. Write a function that will return the size of a stack. Use this new function to modify procedure push, so that a test on the maximum size of the stack can be made before inserting a new record.

[2]. Write the following procedures and functions to operate on a FIFO queue.

```
{initialise head of queue to NIL pointer}
PROCEDURE initialise(VAR q:FIFO);
{test for empty queue}
FUNCTION empty(q:FIFO):BOOLEAN;
{insert a customer into the queue}
PROCEDURE PlaceInQueue(   VAR q:FIFO; customer, arrival, service : INTEGER;
                          VAR NumberInQueue : INTEGER);
{remove a customer from the queue}
PROCEDURE RemoveFromQueue(VAR q:FIFO; VAR arrival, departure, service,
                          NumberInQueue : INTEGER; LastDeparture : INTEGER);
{display the details of the customers who are waiting in the queue}
PROCEDURE QueueDetails(VAR q:FIFO; NumberInQueue:INTEGER);
```

This structure will be used in the next question. The format of the record structure for the node from the data required in the question is:

```
FIFO = ^node;
node =    RECORD
              CustomerNumber : INTEGER;
              TimeOfArrival : INTEGER;
              ServiceTime : INTEGER;
              link : FIFO;
          END;
```

[3]. Write a program to simulate the arrival of customers at a single check-out in a supermarket. Your model should cater for the arrival of at least twenty customers. Use a

random number generator to produce a number in the range 1-100, to represent a cumulative percentage. The appropriate time interval for the inter-arrival times and service times can then be obtained from the following tables.

Inter-arrival time distribution. (time between customers arriving)

time interval	cumulative %
0.1-1.0	8
1.1-2.0	25
2.1-3.0	50
3.1-4.0	70
4.1-5.0	85
5.1-6.0	89
6.1-7.0	93
7.1-8.0	95
8.1-9.0	97
9.1-10.0	100

Thus given a random number of, say, 33 would yield an inter-arrival time of between 2.1 and 3.0 minutes. The mean value in this range can be taken giving an inter-arrival time of 2.55 minutes.

Service time distribution. (time spent at the check-out not in the queue)

time interval	cumulative %
1.0-1.5	15
1.5-2.0	40
2.0-2.5	60
2.5-3.0	75
3.0-3.5	85
3.5-4.0	90
4.0-4.5	95
4.5-5.0	100

The same method of generating a service time is used as for generating an inter-arrival time, a random number of 84 would yield a service-time of between 3.0 - 3.5 minutes. The mean value being 3.25 minutes. Use a FIFO queue to simulate the customers waiting to be served. In each node store the customer number, time of arrival and the time to be spent at the check-out. Each time a customer has completed a transaction at the check-out display the time elapsed since the customer joined the queue and the present size of the queue.

4. Modify the binary tree routines to store integers. Generate a set of integer random numbers and store them in a binary tree. Output the numbers sorted into ascending order.

5. If the values of operands are stored in a linked list then using the following procedure evaluate a reverse polish string. Traverse the string from left to right and continue to push operands on the stack until an operator is encountered. For a unary operator pop an operand from the stack, evaluate it and push the result back on the stack. For a binary operator pop two operands from the stack, evaluate the result and push the answer back on the stack. Continue

traversing the reverse polish string until the end of the string, then pop the contents of the stack and display this value. You will need to modify the stack routines to cater for storing real numbers. Introduce a new set of routines for the data type link, which represents a linked list and its associated operations.

[6]. A graph consists of nodes and edges. A node is a basic component, which usually contains some information. An edge connects two nodes. A directed graph, often called a *digraph*, is a graph whose edges have direction. Thus an edge not only relates two nodes, it also specifies a predecessor - successor relationship. Figure 15.17 illustrates a directed graph. The direction of each edge is denoted by an arrow. The predecessor - successor relationship between the nodes can be represented as characters in a file as follows.

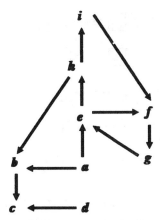

Figure 15.17 An example of a directed graph

abe (implying that if a is the predecessor then b and e are its respective successors)
bc
c (implying that c has no successor)
dc
efh
fg
ge
hbi
if

This information can be stored in an array of linked lists as depicted by the array, direction, in figure 15.18. The array, visit, in the same diagram, is used to tag with TRUE or FALSE the nodes that have already been visited.

Write a procedure BuildGraph that reads the file of directed edges and places each direction in the node of a linked list as illustrated in figure 15.18. The head of each linked list is stored in the array named direction. Output the contents of this structure to verify that your program is correct.

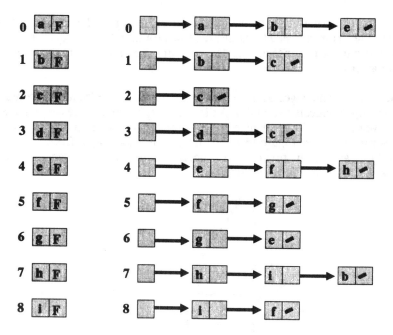

Array visit is used to tag a point when it has been visited

Array direction stores pointers to linked lists. Each linked list represents the points on the graph that can be visited from one starting point

Figure 15.18 Method of representing a graph as an array of linked lists

[7]. Using the representation of the directed graph created in the last question, write a program to input start and finish nodes, then compute the series of nodes that must be visited to complete the journey. Alternatively, specify if the journey is not possible. For example, given the start node as (f) and the finish node as (b), the series of nodes that must be visited to travel from (f) to (b) is (fgehb). If the start node was (f) and the finish node was (a) then the journey is not possible since there is no connection in the direction (e) to (a) or (b) to (a). Pay particular attention to (i) backtracking from a dead-end, and (ii) not going around part of the graph in circles.

Hints. For every node visited push its value on to a stack. This will simplify re-tracing your steps, since backtracking would involve popping nodes from the stack. Whenever a node in the linked list is visited, delete it from the list. Thus the head of each linked list will always point to the next possible node to visit. The structure depicted in figure 15.18 can always be rebuilt by reading the contents of the data file again. Keep the contents of the array named visit up-to-date since this contains the information about those nodes that have already been visited.

16
Record Files

A file composed from records is a more common form of representing a data file. Within this chapter record file creation and inspection, the activities of appending records to the end of a file, sorting files, merging data files and updating a master file from a transaction file will be explored.

The reader is recommended to study chapter 11 again, before commencing this chapter.

16.1 File Creation and Inspection.

A text file was created by either using an editor or the output, directed to secondary storage, from a program. A file of records can only be created by a program.

The file processing statements used for text files can also be used for record files. Therefore, statements such as RESET, REWRITE, and EOF are used in the same context as text files. Records in a file are read using a Read statement and written using a Write statement.

In the first worked example of this section a file is to be created containing records with details of the name, department and telephone extension number of staff who work in a college.

The format of a record in the file is:

```
StaffDetails =   RECORD
                    name : TextString;
                    department : TextString;
                    extension : INTEGER;
                 END;
```

where TextString is an array of characters.

When using text files the name of the file was described as being of type TEXT. This type description is not possible with a file of records and a new data type must be introduced. The record described above would be used to describe the data type of the file as:

StaffFile = FILE OF StaffDetails;

(Note - a TEXT file is a FILE OF CHAR)

Having described a data type for a record (StaffDetails) and a data type for a file (StaffFile), it is then possible to define two variables

```
VAR
    StaffRecord : StaffDetails;
    staff : StaffFile;
```

The statements REWRITE, RESET and EOF would refer directly to the name of the file - REWRITE(staff), RESET(staff), EOF(staff). Records to this file would be written using

Write(staff, StaffRecord) and read using Read(staff, StaffRecord).

Notice that the entire record is either read or written and no reference is made to the individual fields within the Read or Write statements.

```
PROGRAM build(INPUT, staff);
{program to create a file of records from data input via a keyboard}
CONST
      MaxChar=20;
TYPE
      TextString=PACKED ARRAY[0..MaxChar-1] OF CHAR;
      StaffDetails=    RECORD
                          name:TextString;
                          department:TextString;
                          extension:INTEGER;
                       END;
      StaffFile = FILE OF StaffDetails;
VAR

      StaffRecord:StaffDetails;
      staff:StaffFile;

PROCEDURE TextInput(VAR item : TextString);
CONST
      space=CHR(32);
VAR
      index:INTEGER;
BEGIN
      FOR index:=0 TO MaxChar-1 DO
         IF EOLN THEN
            item[index]:=space
         ELSE
            Read(item[index]);
         {end if}
      {end for}
      ReadLn;
END; {TextInput}

PROCEDURE FieldInput(VAR staff:StaffFile);
{procedure to build individual fields in the record}
CONST
      No='N';
VAR
      reply:CHAR;
BEGIN
      WriteLn('input the following details'); WriteLn;
      WITH StaffRecord DO
      BEGIN
         REPEAT
            Write('name = > '); TextInput(name);
            Write('department = > '); TextInput(department);
            Write('extension = > '); ReadLn(extension);
            Write(staff, StaffRecord);
            Write('continue? Y(es) or N(o) '); ReadLn(reply);
         UNTIL reply=No;
```

```
        END; {with}
END; {FieldInput}

BEGIN
        ASSIGN(staff,'A:staff');
        REWRITE(staff);
        FieldInput(staff);
        RESET(staff); {flush output buffer}
END. {build}
```

Results from program being run

input the following details

```
name            => Jones, F
department      =>  Maths
extension       => 456
continue? Y(es) or N(o) Y
name            => Holmes, B
department      =>  Computing
extension       => 123
continue? Y(es) or N(o) Y
name            => Evans, M
department      =>  Biology
extension       => 768
continue? Y(es) or N(o) N
```

Having created a file of records it may be necessary to inspect the contents of the file. With a text file the contents could be inspected using an editor or an operating system command to list the contents of the file. With a record file such methods cannot be used and it is necessary to write a program to read the contents of the file and either write each field of each record to the screen or direct the output to a text file. In the second example of this section a program has been written to read and display the contents of the staff file.

```
PROGRAM inspect(OUTPUT, staff);
{program to inspect the file of staff records}
CONST
        MaxChar=20;
TYPE
        TextString=PACKED ARRAY[0..MaxChar-1] OF CHAR;
        StaffDetails=   RECORD
                        name:TextString;
                        department:TextString;
                        extension:INTEGER;
                     END;
        StaffFile = FILE OF StaffDetails;
```

```
VAR
        StaffRecord:StaffDetails;
        staff:StaffFile;
BEGIN
        WriteLn(' Contents of Staff File'); WriteLn;
        WriteLn('Name Department Extension');
        ASSIGN(staff, 'A:staff');
        RESET(staff);
        WHILE NOT EOF(staff) DO
        BEGIN
           WITH StaffRecord DO
           BEGIN
              Read(staff, StaffRecord);
              WriteLn(name, department, extension:3);
           END;
           {end with}
        END;
        {end while}
        WriteLn;
END. {inspect}
```

Results from program being run

Contents of Staff File

Name	Department	Extension
Jones, F	Maths	456
Holmes, B	Computing	123
Evans, M	Biology	768

16.2 Appending Records.

Often it is necessary to attach records to the end of an existing file. The activity of appending records allows records to be written to a file starting at the position after the last record on the file.

An algorithm to append records to a file consists of copying the contents of the original file to a new file, then writing new records into the new file after the position of the last original record to be copied. Finally the contents of the new file is copied back to the original file, overwriting the original records. Such an algorithm might contain the following sequence of operations.

{open files}
open original file for reading
open new file for writing

{copy contents of original file to new file}
WHILE NOT EOF(original file) DO
    read record from the original file
    write record to the new file
END

{continue to copy new records to the new file}
REPEAT
    input new record
    write new record to new file
UNTIL no more data

{re-open files}
open new file for reading
open original file for writing

{copy contents of new file to original file overwriting the contents of the original file}
WHILE NOT EOF(new file) DO
    read record from new file
    write record to original file
END
flush output buffer of original file

In the next worked example, the contents of the staff file created in section 16.1, will have extra records appended to it.

```
PROGRAM AppendRecords(INPUT, staff, temporary);
{program to append records to the end of the staff file}
CONST
      MaxChar=20;
TYPE
      TextString=PACKED ARRAY[0..MaxChar-1] OF CHAR;
      StaffDetails=    RECORD
                          name:TextString;
                          department:TextString;
                          extension:INTEGER;
                       END;
      StaffFile = FILE OF StaffDetails;
VAR
      StaffRecord:StaffDetails;
      staff, temporary : StaffFile;
```

```
PROCEDURE TextInput(VAR item : TextString);
CONST
      space=CHR(32);
VAR
      index:INTEGER;
BEGIN
      FOR index:=0 TO MaxChar-1 DO
          IF EOLN THEN
              item[index]:=space
          ELSE
              Read(item[index]);
          {end if}
          {end for}
          ReadLn;
END; {TextInput}

PROCEDURE FieldInput(VAR staff:StaffFile);
CONST
      No='N';
VAR
      reply:CHAR;
BEGIN
      WriteLn('input the following details'); WriteLn;
      WITH StaffRecord DO
      BEGIN
          REPEAT
              Write('name = > '); TextInput(name);
              Write('department = > '); TextInput(department);
              Write('extension = > '); ReadLn(extension);
              Write(staff, StaffRecord);
              Write('continue? Y(es) or N(o) '); ReadLn(reply);
          UNTIL reply=No;
      END; {with}
END; {FieldInput}

BEGIN
      ASSIGN(staff,'A:staff');
      ASSIGN(temporary,'A:temporary');
      RESET(staff); {open staff file for reading}
      REWRITE(temporary); {open temporary file for writing}

      {copy contents of staff file to temporary file}
      WHILE NOT EOF(staff) DO
      BEGIN
          Read(staff, StaffRecord);
          Write(temporary, StaffRecord);
      END;
      {end while}
      FieldInput(temporary);
```

```
            RESET(temporary); {open file for reading}
            REWRITE(staff); {overwrite staff file}
            WHILE NOT EOF(temporary) DO
            BEGIN
                Read(temporary, StaffRecord);
                Write(staff, StaffRecord);
            END;
            {end while}
            RESET(staff); {flush output buffer}
        END. {AppendRecords}
```

Results from program being run

input the following details

```
name            => Franks, J
department    =>  Engineering
extension      => 285
continue? Y(es) or N(o) Y
name            => Adams, P
department    =>  Computing
extension      => 190
continue? Y(es) or N(o) Y
name            => Long, M
department    =>  Art
extension      => 870
continue? Y(es) or N(o) N
```

The contents of the staff file can be inspected to ensure that the records have been appended correctly by running the second program in section 16.1.

Results from program being run

Contents of Staff File

Name	Department	Extension
Jones, F	Maths	456
Holmes, B	Computing	123
Evans, M	Biology	768
Franks, J	Engineering	285
Adams, P	Computing	190
Long, M	Art	870

16.3 Sorting a File of Records.

A file of records can be organised in either a serial or sequential manner. Serial organisation implies that the position of each record in the file is not ordered on any particular key. Access to records can only be achieved by reading one record after another until either the end of the file has been reached, in which case all the records will have been read, or a key match was found for the record that was required.

A sequential organisation of records in a file involves sorting the records of a serial file into key order. Such ordering offers the advantages of searching an ordered set of records as explained in chapter 11, and the orderly presentation of the contents of a file when it is output.

Sequential files may be organised on many keys. For example, a file of records of staff in a college may be sorted on department as the primary key, and within each department sorted on name as the secondary key. The output from such a file would be an alphabetical listing of departments and within each department of staff names.

The effect of appending records, in the last section, was to change the order of the records in the original staff file. For the purpose of report writing, merging and updating files, the organisation of files should be sequential and not serial. This calls for the contents of the file to be ordered on a chosen key or keys. There are several methods available for sorting records in a file.

Many operating systems provide a sorting utility to order the contents of a file. If such a utility is available to the reader then it should be used when needed.

Alternatively, the sorting techniques that were discussed in chapter 11 could be applied to ordering records in a file, provided the entire contents of the file is first copied into an array of a suitable size. Obviously the size of the array limits the amount of data that can be sorted. If file sizes are so large that all the data cannot be accommodated into the array then the reader must use an external sorting algorithm if a sorting utility is not available.

External sorting algorithms will not be discussed further in this text.

The program that follows uses the insertion sort that was developed in chapter 11. The contents of the file created in the last section is copied into an array, the records in the array are then sorted on the primary key name, and the sorted records from the array are then written to a new file called temporary.

```
PROGRAM Sortfile(staff, temporary);
{program to read the contents of the staff file into an array, sort the records on the key, using
the insertion sort, and copy the contents of the sorted array to a new file named temporary}
CONST
        MaxChar=20; MaxSize=100; {maximum number of records that can be sorted}
TYPE
        TextString=PACKED ARRAY[0..MaxChar-1] OF CHAR;
        StaffDetails=    RECORD
                        name:TextString;
                        department:TextString;
                        extension:INTEGER;
                    END;
```

```
      StaffFile = FILE OF StaffDetails;
      ArrayRecord = PACKED ARRAY[0..MaxSize-1] OF StaffDetails;
VAR
      StaffRecord:StaffDetails;
      staff, temporary : StaffFile;
      HoldingArray : ArrayRecord;
      size:INTEGER; {size of the holding array}


PROCEDURE SortRecord(VAR A:ArrayRecord; size:INTEGER);
{procedure to sort an array of records on the primary key name, using the
Insertion Sorting algorithm}
VAR
      location, index : INTEGER;
      current:StaffDetails;
BEGIN
      FOR index:=1 TO size-1 DO
      BEGIN
         current:=A[index];
         location:=index;
         WHILE (location > 0) AND (A[location-1].name > current.name) DO
         BEGIN
            A[location]:=A[location-1];
            location:=location-1;
         END;
         {end while}
         A[location]:=current;
      END;
      {end for}
END; {SortRecord}


PROCEDURE FillArray(VAR FileName:StaffFile; VAR A:ArrayRecord;
                        VAR size:INTEGER);
VAR
      index:INTEGER;
BEGIN
      size:=0;
      WHILE NOT EOF(FileName) DO
      BEGIN
         Read(FileName,A[size]);
         size:=size+1;
      END;
      {end while}
END; {FillArray}
```

```
PROCEDURE CopyArray(VAR FileName:StaffFile; A:ArrayRecord; size:INTEGER);
{procedure to transfer, record by record, the contents of the array to a temporary binary file}
VAR
      index:INTEGER;
BEGIN
      FOR index:=0 TO size-1 DO
          Write(FileName,A[index]);
      {end for}
END; {CopyArray}

BEGIN
      ASSIGN(staff,'A:staff');
      RESET(staff);
      FillArray(staff, HoldingArray, size);
      SortRecord(HoldingArray, size);
      ASSIGN(temporary,'A:temporary');
      REWRITE(temporary);
      CopyArray(temporary, HoldingArray, size);
END. {Sortfile}
```

Results from program being run

Contents of temporary file

Name	Department	Extension
Adams, P	Computing	190
Evans, M	Biology	768
Franks, J	Engineering	285
Holmes, B	Computing	123
Jones, F	Maths	456
Long, M	Art	870

16.4 The Read Ahead Problem.

If it is required to read ahead in a file, in order to compare the same fields of two adjacent records, the EOF function will eventually return the value TRUE when the end of file has been reached. This will inevitably result in the last record not being processed. Consider the following example.

A file of records described as:

```
            RECORD
                  DwellingCode : CHAR;
                  Address : TextString;
            END;
```

may contain the data:

```
D 23 Spring Gardens, Oxford
D 87 The Yews, Great Tew
S The Willows, Shipton-on-Stour
S 34 Tower Street, Witney
```

If a report is required on the contents of the file, giving the number of dwellings in each code group. The report might appear as:

```
DETACHED
23 Spring Gardens, Oxford
87 The Yews, Great Tew
Number of properties = 2

SEMI-DETACHED
The Willows, Shipton-on-Stour
34 Tower Street, Witney
Number of properties = 2
```

The following segment of code uses the read ahead feature to compare the change of DwellingCode from 'D' to 'S' in order to output the total number of properties in the detached category.

```
RESET(DataFile);
Read(DataFile, DataRecord);
WHILE NOT EOF(DataFile) DO
BEGIN
    code:=DataRecord.DwellingCode;
    PropertyTotal:=0;
    CASE code OF
    'D': WriteLn('DETACHED');
    'S': WriteLn('SEMI-DETACHED');
    END;
    WriteLn;
    WHILE NOT EOF(DataFile) AND (code=DataRecord.DwellingCode) DO
    BEGIN
        WriteLn(DataRecord.address);
        PropertyTotal:=PropertyTotal+1;
        Read(DataFile, DataRecord); {inner read statement}
    END;
    {end while}
    WriteLn;
    WriteLn('Total number of properties = ', PropertyTotal:2);
END;
{end while}
```

Consider the following implication. Prior to the last record in the file being read the EOF function is FALSE. The last record is read by the inner read statement Read(DataFile,

DataRecord). The file pointer is now positioned at the end of the file and the EOF function is TRUE. However, the last record has not yet been processed, the address has not been displayed and the total number of properties not increased. The inner loop is terminated, the number of properties is output with a total one less than it should be, and the outer loop is terminated.

There are three methods of overcoming the problem of not processing the last record. The first method is to introduce a dummy record at the end of the file knowing that it will never be processed. This is not a recommended approach. Amending a data file in order for it to be processed correctly is a poor solution.

The second method introduces a new boolean variable EndOfFile that is only set to TRUE when attempting to read the file after the end of file has been reached. The EOF function used in the WHILE loop terminating statements in the last segment of code would be replaced by an EndOfFile variable and the Read statements would be replaced by a call to the following ReadFile procedure.

This method is to be prefered in a Pascal environment that does not support the feature described in the next section, the file buffer variable. The Turbo Pascal environment is one where the file buffer variable is not supported.

```
PROCEDURE ReadFile(VAR FileName : PropertyFile;
                   VAR RecordName : PropertyDetails;
                   VAR EndOfFile : BOOLEAN);
{procedure to read a record in a file and set EndOfFile TRUE only when attempting to read
past the end of the file. This procedure is suitable when read-ahead is necessary in a program}
BEGIN
     EndOfFile:=FALSE;
     IF EOF(FileName) THEN
         EndOfFile := TRUE
     ELSE
         Read(FileName, RecordName);
     {end if}
END; {ReadFile}
```

The third method uses the concept of a file buffer variable, that will be explained in the next section.

16.5 File Buffer Variable.
Having explored the idea of a pointer in the chapter 14, the concept of a file buffer variable for the input and output of records in a file can now be discussed.

Associated with a file is a file position pointer that simply points at the next record in the file to be processed. The identifier FileName in effect points to a file variable buffer denoted by FileName ^ . The contents of this buffer is the same data that is being pointed at in the file by the file position pointer.

The file buffer variable acts like a window on any record in the file

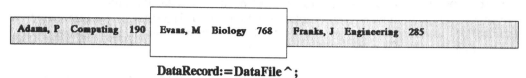

DataRecord:=DataFile ^ ;

GET(DataFile) moves the file position pointer along to the next record

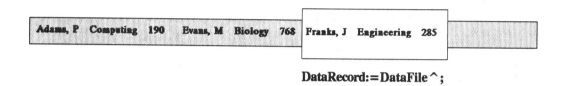

DataRecord:=DataFile ^ ;

Figure 16.1 An illustration of the File Buffer Variable

Without explicitly reading the file it is possible to examine the contents of the file buffer. Thus the assignment DataRecord:=DataFile ^ ; will assign the contents of the buffer to the variable DataRecord.

There exists a procedure GET(FileName) to advance the position of the file pointer to the next component of the file. The result of using a GET statement at the end of a file is undefined.

Thus the statement Read(FileName, DataRecord); is equivalent to:

```
BEGIN
    DataRecord:=DataFile ^ ;
    GET(FileName);
END;
```

Another procedure PUT(FileName) appends the contents of the buffer variable FileName ^ ; to the file. The manipulation of the file position pointer is implicit in the action of PUT. Therefore, the statement Write(FileName, DataRecord); is equivalent to:

```
BEGIN
    DataFile ^ :=DataRecord;
    PUT(Filename);
END
```

Using the concept of a file buffer variable, the segment of code used to illustrate the disastrous consequences of using Read in a read ahead situation, can be modified to permit the read ahead to work perfectly well.

```
    RESET(DataFile);
    {read the first record without moving the file position pointer}
    IF NOT EOF(DataFile) THEN DataRecord:=DataFile^ ;
    WHILE NOT EOF(DataFile) DO
    BEGIN
        code:=DataRecord.DwellingCode;
        PropertyTotal:=0;
        CASE code OF
        'D': WriteLn('DETACHED');
        'S': WriteLn('SEMI-DETACHED');
        END;
        WriteLn;
        WHILE NOT EOF(DataFile) AND (code=DataRecord.DwellingCode) DO
        BEGIN
            WriteLn(DataRecord.address);
            PropertyTotal:=PropertyTotal+1;
            {move the file position pointer to the next record}
            GET(FileName);
            {if not end of file read buffer without moving pointer}
            IF NOT EOF(DataFile) THEN DataRecord:=DataFile^ ;
        END;
        {end while}
        WriteLn;
        WriteLn('Total number of properties = ', PropertyTotal:2);
    END;
    {end while}
```

16.6 Two-way File Merge.

The technique of merging two sequential files involves the interleaving of records from both files to form a new sequential file. The keys of the two files to be merged are compared, if the keys are in ascending order, the record with the lower key value is written to the new file. The file that supplied the record is then read again and processing containues until the end of both files is encountered.

In the following algorithm to merge two files, it is necessary to compare the key of file1 with the key of file2. However, when the end of either file is reached it is necessary to set the key field, of the file that has ended, to a higher value than all the other keys in the two files. The purpose of this practice is to force the remainder of the records in the remaining file to be copied to file3. The first character in the keyfield, RecordName.name[0], is substituted with CHR(127), thus setting the key to *high-value*.

The action of reading a record must be followed by testing for the end of the file, and if this condition is true, then setting the key field to high-value.

The procedure ReadFile, given in the section on reading ahead, can be modified to accommodate setting the key field to a high value at the end of the file.

```
PROCEDURE ReadFile(VAR FileName : DataFile;
                   VAR RecordName : DataDetails;
                   VAR EndOfFile : BOOLEAN);
{procedure to read a record in a file and set EndOfFile TRUE only when attempting to read
past the end of the file. This procedure is suitable when read-ahead is necessary in a program}
BEGIN
      EndOfFile:=FALSE;
      IF EOF(FileName) THEN
      BEGIN
         EndOfFile := TRUE;
         RecordName.key[0]:=CHR(127); {set key high}
      END
      ELSE
         Read(FileName, RecordName);
      {end if}
END; {ReadFile}
```

The algorithm for merging the two files relies on the fact that both files are already sorted on the primary key *name*.

```
    open file1 and file2 for reading {the two files to be merged}
    open file3 for writing {the file containing the records from file1 and file2 interleaved in
                           key order}
    read file1 and at end of file set key to high value
    read file2 and at end of file set key to high value
    WHILE NOT end of both files DO
        IF key file1 < key file2 THEN
            write file1 record to file3
            read file1 and at end of file set key to high value
        ELSE
            write file2 record to file3
            read file2 and at end of file set key to high value
        END
    END
    flush output buffer of file3
```

Imagine that a college has two sites, and that two staff files *staff1* and *staff2* exist, one for each site. In other words there are two files having the same format as the file described in section 16.1. Assume that the two files have been sorted into ascending order on the primary key name.

The following program illustrates how to merge *staff1* and *staff2* to produce a third sequential file *staff3*.

```
PROGRAM merge(staff1, staff2, staff3);
{program to perform a two-way merge on staff1 and staff2, writing the result
of the merger to staff3}
CONST
      MaxChar=20;
TYPE
      TextString=PACKED ARRAY[0..MaxChar-1] OF CHAR;
      StaffDetails=    RECORD
                              name:TextString;
                              department:TextString;
                              extension:INTEGER;
                         END;
      StaffFile = FILE OF StaffDetails;
VAR
      StaffRecord1, StaffRecord2, StaffRecord3 : StaffDetails;
      staff1, staff2, staff3 : StaffFile;
      EndOfFile1, EndOfFile2 : BOOLEAN;


PROCEDURE ReadFile(VAR FileName : StaffFile;
                          VAR RecordName : StaffDetails;
                          VAR EndOfFile : BOOLEAN);
{procedure to read a record in a file and set EndOfFile TRUE only when attempting to read
past the end of the file. This procedure is suitable when read-ahead is necessary in a
program}
BEGIN
      EndOfFile:=FALSE;
      IF EOF(FileName) THEN
      BEGIN
          EndOfFile := TRUE;
          RecordName.name[0]:=CHR(127); {set key high}
      END
      ELSE
          Read(FileName, RecordName);
      {end if}
END; {ReadFile}


BEGIN
      ASSIGN(staff1, 'A:staff1');
      ASSIGN(staff2, 'A:staff2');
      ASSIGN(staff3, 'A:staff3');
      RESET(staff1);
      RESET(staff2);
      REWRITE(staff3);
      ReadFile(staff1, StaffRecord1, EndOfFile1);
      ReadFile(staff2, StaffRecord2, EndOfFile2);
```

```
    WHILE (NOT EndOfFile1) OR (NOT EndOfFile2) DO
    BEGIN
       IF StaffRecord1.name < StaffRecord2.name THEN
       BEGIN
          Write(staff3, StaffRecord1);
          ReadFile(staff1, StaffRecord1, EndOfFile1);
       END
       ELSE
       BEGIN
          Write(staff3, StaffRecord2);
          ReadFile(staff2, StaffRecord2, EndOfFile2);
       END;
       {end if}
    END;
    {end while}
    RESET(staff3); {flush output buffer}
END. {merge}
```

contents of staff1

Adams	Maths	123
Davies	Computing	345
Evans	Geography	876

contents of staff2

| Bates | Science | 438 |
| Holmes | Computing | 111 |

contents of staff3 after two-way merge

Adams	Maths	123
Bates	Science	438
Davies	Computing	345
Evans	Geography	876
Holmes	Computing	111

16.7 Variant Records.

In the definition of the record type it has been assumed that all records in a file will conform to the type definition. However, it is possible that some records can have two parts - a fixed part and a variant part. Consider for a moment a record containing personal details of employees. If a person is married the details of their spouse is also included.

```
TYPE
    personnel = RECORD
                    {fixed part}
                    name : NameString;
                    address : AddressString;
                    telephone : TelephoneString;
                    DateOfBirth : DateString;
                    Department : TextString;
                    post : TextString;
                    {variant part}
                    CASE married : BOOLEAN OF
                    TRUE : (SpouseName : NameString;
                            DateOfMarriage : DateString;
                            NumberOfChildren : INTEGER)
                    FALSE : ()
                END;
```

From this example it can be seen that the case statement is used to represent the variant part of the record. The case selector, in this example *married* is regarded as another field of the record structure, whose type is defined as boolean. The selector can be of any previously defined ordinal type. The type boolean has been used here, but any user defined type is possible. The labels of the case statement, here true or false, indicate the alternative variant record field components. In this example if an employee is married, three additional fields are appended to the record:

        SpouseName
        DateOfMarriage
        NumberOfChildren

However, if an employee is not married these fields do not exist, as indicated by empty parenthesis (). The following diagram serves to illustrate the two types of record.

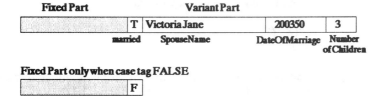

Figure 16.2 An illustration of a variant record

16.8 File Update.

Information that is contained in data files is not always static, it can be subject to changes. Such changes to the information will come about through the insertion, amendment and deletion of records. The process of changing the information held on data files is known as updating.

The most common types of files used in an updating situation are the master file and the transaction file.

Master files are files of a fairly permanent nature. For example a stock file, personnel file, a customer file. A feature of these files is that they are regularly updated to show a current situation. For example, when orders are processed the amount of stock should be decreased in a stock file. It is seen, therefore, that master records will contain both data of a static nature, for example, a stock-number, description of a level of stock and a minimum re-order level, and data which by its nature will change each time a transaction occurs, for example the depletion of a stock level.

A transaction file is made up from the various transactions created from source documents, for example, sales invoices. In a stock control application the transaction file will contain a list of stock items that have been sold. This file will be used to update the master file. As soon as it has been used for this purpose it is no longer required. It will, therefore, have a very short life because it will be replaced by another transaction file containing the next list of stock items that have been sold.

The file containing details about staff in a college is suitable for updating. The staff file may require records to be deleted when staff leave, amended when staff change office or department or both and inserted when new staff are appointed.

A transaction file will be used to record all the changes to the staff master file. A code can be used in each transaction record that denotes (A)mend, (D)elete or (I)nsert a record. When a record is to be deleted on the master file these is no need to incorporate the department and extension fields. These fields should only be present in a transaction record when a record is to be amended or inserted. The format of records on the transaction file can, therefore, be variant and described as:

```
TransDetails=    RECORD
                    name:TextString;
                    CASE TransCode:CHAR OF
                    'A','I': (department:TextString;
                                extension:INTEGER);
                    'D' : ()
                 END;
```

An algorithm for the update of a sequential master file from a sequential transaction file, creating a new updated master file follows.

open transaction file and master files for reading
open new master file for writing
read transaction file at end set transaction key to high value

read master file at end set master key to high value
WHILE not end of both files DO
      IF transaction key < master key and transaction code is (I)nsert THEN
         write transaction record to new master file
         read transaction file at end set transaction key to high value
      ELSE
         IF transaction key = master key THEN
            IF transaction code is (A)mend THEN
               write transaction record to new master
               read transaction file at end set transaction key to high value
               read master file at end set master key to high value
            ELSE
               read transaction file at end set transaction key to high value
               read master file at end set master key to high value
            END
         ELSE
            write master record to new master file
            read master file at end set master key to high value
         END
      END
END
flush output buffer for new master file

This algorithm is used in the final program of the chapter to update a staff master file from a transaction file. The contents of the three files are shown at the end of the program listing.

```
PROGRAM update(transaction, master, NewMaster);
{program to update a master file from a transaction file}
CONST
        MaxChar=20;
        Amend='A'; Delete='D'; Insert='I';
TYPE
        TextString=PACKED ARRAY[0..MaxChar-1] OF CHAR;
        TransDetails=   RECORD
                        name:TextString;
                        CASE TransCode:CHAR OF
                        'A','I': (department:TextString;
                                        extension:INTEGER);
                        'D' : ()
                        END;
        TransFile = FILE OF TransDetails;
        StaffDetails=   RECORD
                        name:TextString;
                        department:TextString;
                        extension:INTEGER;
                        END;
```

```
                StaffFile = FILE OF StaffDetails;
        VAR
                TransRecord : TransDetails;
                StaffRecord : StaffDetails;
                transaction : TransFile;
                master, NewMaster : StaffFile;
                EndOfTrans, EndOfMaster : BOOLEAN;

        PROCEDURE ReadTrans(    VAR FileName : TransFile;
                                VAR RecordName : TransDetails;
                                VAR EndOfFile : BOOLEAN);
        BEGIN
                EndOfFile:=FALSE;
                IF EOF(FileName) THEN
                BEGIN
                    EndOfFile:=TRUE;
                    RecordName.name[0]:=CHR(127);
                END
                ELSE
                    Read(FileName, RecordName);
                {end if}
        END; {ReadTrans}

        PROCEDURE ReadMaster(VAR FileName : StaffFile;
                                VAR RecordName : StaffDetails;
                                VAR EndOfFile : BOOLEAN);
        BEGIN
                EndOfFile:=FALSE;
                IF EOF(FileName) THEN
                BEGIN
                    EndOfFile:=TRUE;
                    RecordName.name[0]:=CHR(127);
                END
                ELSE
                    Read(FileName, RecordName);
                {end if}
        END; {ReadMaster}

        PROCEDURE WriteRecord(VAR FileName:StaffFile;
                                TransRecord:TransDetails;
                                StaffRecord:StaffDetails);
        BEGIN
                StaffRecord.name:=TransRecord.name;
                StaffRecord.department:=TransRecord.department;
                StaffRecord.extension:=TransRecord.extension;
                Write(FileName, StaffRecord);
        END; {WriteRecord}
```

```
BEGIN
     ASSIGN(transaction,'A:transaction');
     ASSIGN(master,'A:master');
     ASSIGN(NewMaster,'A:NewMaster');
     RESET(transaction);
     RESET(master);
     REWRITE(NewMaster);

     ReadTrans(transaction, TransRecord, EndOfTrans);
     ReadMaster(master, StaffRecord, EndOfMaster);

     WHILE (NOT EndOfTrans) OR (NOT EndOfMaster) DO
     BEGIN
       IF (TransRecord.name < StaffRecord.name) AND
       (TransRecord.TransCode = Insert) THEN
       BEGIN
          WriteRecord(NewMaster, TransRecord, StaffRecord);
          ReadTrans(transaction, TransRecord, EndOfTrans);
       END
       ELSE IF (TransRecord.name = StaffRecord.name) THEN
          IF TransRecord.TransCode = Amend THEN
          BEGIN
             WriteRecord(NewMaster, TransRecord, StaffRecord);
             ReadTrans(transaction, TransRecord, EndOfTrans);
             ReadMaster(master, StaffRecord, EndOfMaster);
          END
          ELSE
          BEGIN
             ReadTrans(transaction, TransRecord, EndOfTrans);
             ReadMaster(master, Staffrecord, EndOfMaster);
          END
       ELSE
       BEGIN
          Write(NewMaster, StaffRecord);
          ReadMaster(master, StaffRecord, EndOfMaster);
       END;
       {end if}
     END;
     {end while}

     RESET(NewMaster);
END.{update}
```

contents of transaction file

Berry	I	English	682
Collins	D		
Edwards	A	Art	275
Jenkins	I	History	711
Quayle	I	Maths	240
Williams	D		

contents of master file

Adams	Maths	314
Collins	Geography	428
Davies	Computing	121
Edwards	Art	273
Holmes	Computing	122
Jones	Maths	521
Peters	Physics	295
Smith	History	710
Williams	English	683

contents of master file after file update

Adams	Maths	314
Berry	English	682
Davies	Computing	121
Edwards	Art	275
Holmes	Computing	122
Jenkins	History	711
Jones	Maths	521
Peters	Physics	295
Quayle	Maths	240
Smith	History	710

16.9 Summary

A file may contain records in place of a data stream of characters.

The statements used to access a record file are the same as those used to access a text file. RESET, REWRITE, Read, Write and EOF having the same meaning for both types of files.

Instead of components of a line of text being read or written, the Read and Write statements refer specifically to complete records and not individual fields.

Record files are created from a user program and not by using the system editor.

Similarly a record file must be accessed via a program to have its contents displayed and not by using the system editor or a system command.

Serial files have no relationship between the key of a record and the position of a record with respect to neighbouring records.

Sequential files are sorted on a key or keys. The relationship between neighbouring records is one of order.

Record files can be sorted by one of the methods already explored, provided the contents of the file is stored in an array prior to sorting. Alternative file sorting methods range from system utilities, such as MSDOS SORT, to external sorting algorithms that can be programmed.

Two or more files can only be merged if they are all sorted on the same key or keys. Similarly a master file can only be updated from a transaction file if both files are sorted on the same key or keys.

The read ahead problem can often lead to the last record in a file not being processed. The remedy is to either use a dummy record, or introduce a new EndOfFile variable that is TRUE only when an attempt is made to read beyond the last record in the file.

A file buffer variable allows an alternative means of accessing a record in a file, without having to move the file position pointer after inspecting the record.

A record can be divided into two parts, a fixed part and a variant part. The variant part will be present depending upon the value of one of the fields within the fixed part. A record may have more than one variant part.

> ### Keywords
>
> *Record, RESET, REWRITE, Read, Write, EOF;*
> *appending records, sorting files, Two-way Merge;*
> *Read Ahead, file buffer variable, GET, PUT;*
> *variant records, file update, master file, transaction file.*

16.10 Questions

1. A small building society keeps on file details of its customers holding ordinary share accounts. Records are of fixed length and contain the following fields.

> branch code (6 characters);
> account number (6 characters);
> number of £1 shares (integer).

Assume that the file is already sorted on branch code as primary key in ascending order and account number as secondary key in ascending order. Write a program, using the algorithm given, to read the file and display the following report on a screen. This question assumes that you have already created a test data file in the format given.

```
        THE HAPPY HOMES BUILDING SOCIETY
     DETAILS OF ORDINARY SHARE ACCOUNT CUSTOMERS

BRANCH CODE: Brad02

ACCOUNT NUMBER                              £1 SHARES
114345                                      1000
141456                                      550

      •                                        •

                              TOTAL   23456


BRANCH CODE: Hali07

ACCOUNT NUMBER                              £1 SHARES
101456                                      2578

      •                                        •
```

Algorithm to read the shares file and display the report on a screen.

> *open share file for reading*
> *display first two headings*
> *read a record from the share file*
> *WHILE NOT EOF(share file) DO*
>   *store branch code*
>   *display branch code and display sub-heading*
>   *initialise total number of £1 shares to zero*
>   *WHILE NOT EOF(share file) and same branch code DO*
>   *display account number and number of £1 shares*
>   *increase total by number of £1 shares*
>   *read record from the share file*
>   *END*
>   *display total number of £1 shares in the branch*
> *END*

[2]. An estate agent wants to keep on file the following details about properties.

> vendor's name (20 characters);
> address of property (20 characters);
> price of property (real);
> type of dwelling (1 character); coded   A detached
>   B semi-detached
>   C terraced
>   D bungalow
>   E flat
> number of bedrooms (integer);
> tenure (1 character); coded   F freehold
>   L leasehold.

The file contains fixed length records already sorted on type of dwelling as primary key in ascending order and price of property as secondary key in descending order. Write a program, using the algorithm given, to read the file and write the following report as a text file. The question assumes that you have already created a test data file in the format given.

```
QUICK & FIDDLE ESTATE AGENTS Est. 1990


PROPERTY    TYPE:   detached

VENDOR      ADDRESS              PRICE    BEDS    TENURE
Smith ,C    2  Liberal  Walk     44675    4       free
Bowyer, F   69  Church  View     44350    4       free
Sumner,S    3  Hope  street      43000    3       free


    •           •                   •        •       •


TOTAL  NUMBER  OF  PROPERTIES:  23


PROPERTY    TYPE:   semi-detached

VENDOR      ADDRESS              PRICE    BEDS    TENURE
Jones ,M    145  River  Walk     36750    3       free
Evans ,M    27  Ridge  Bank      35500    3       free
```

Algorithm to read the property file and write to a text report file.

open property file for reading
write heading to report
read record from property file
WHILE NOT EOF(property file) DO
    store type of property
    initialise property total to zero
    CASE property code OF
    'A' Write detached to sub-heading of report
    'B' Write semi-detached to sub-heading of report
    'C' Write terraced to sub-heading of report
    'D' Write bungalow to sub-heading of report
    'E' Write flat to sub-heading of report
    END
    write next sub-heading of report
    WHILE NOT EOF(property file) AND same property type DO
        Write vendor, address, price and number of bedrooms to report
        IF tenure = 'F' THEN
            Write 'free' to report
        ELSE
            Write 'lease' to report
        END
        increase property total by 1
        read record from property file

END
Write property total to report
END

[3]. Three files contain lists of English words and their meanings in alphabetical sequence. Each word (key) and its meaning occupies one fixed length record. Design and write a program to merge the three files into one output file.

4. Modify the worked example to update the staff file. Your modifications should include a run-time validation on the transaction file codes (A)mend,(D)elete and (I)nsert and the values of the transaction and master file keys. Consider the following situations that could arise.

The transaction file key is less than the master file key yet the transaction file codes are either (A)mend or (D)elete. Codes (A)mend and (D)elete implicitly define that the staff record already exists yet transaction and master keys are not equal.

The transaction file key is equal to the master file key yet the transaction code is (I)nsert. This implies that the record on the master file exists yet an attempt is being made to insert it again.

[5]. In a simplified weekly wages system factory employees are allocated one fixed-length record per employee on the wages master file. The format of a record on the file is:

employee number - 10 characters;
hourly rate of pay - real;
fixed allowance against pay - real;
total gross income to date - real;
total tax paid to date - real;
total pension contributions to date - real;
total National Insurance contributions to date - real.

For every employee the pension contribution is 6% of the gross income, the National Insurance is £10.50 and the tax is levied at 30% of taxable income. Taxable income is calculated as the difference between gross income and pension contributions and fixed allowances.

A transaction file contains fixed-length records with the format:

employee number - 10 characters;
hours worked per week - real.

Design and write a program to process the transaction file against the master file and produce both an updated master file and pay-slips for each employee on the transaction file. Assume that both files are sequential and ordered on employee number. The number of employees on the transaction file is less than those on the master file and only amendments to the master file are required (no insertions or deletions). The format of the payslip is:

```
Employee  Number:  X342567SMI

                              Gross   wage:  £307.69
                              Pension:       £18.46
                              Nat  Ins:      £10.50
                              Tax:           £77.77

Nett  wage:  £200.96
```

[6]. A small college keeps on file a description of all its rooms. the format of a record on the master room file is:

> room number (key) - integer;
> description of use - 20 characters.

The records on the master room file are stored in ascending order. Over the period of a year the use each room is put to may change. The records on the master file will, therefore, have to be updated. Such changes that exist will be:

> change of use of room (amendment to the description);
> room demolished (deletion);
> new room built (insertion).

These changes are described in a transaction file the format of which is:

> room number (key) - integer;
> transaction code - 1 character (A-amend, D-delete, I-insert);
> description of use - 20 characters.

Note: this last field is absent when a record on the master file is to be deleted.

The records on the transaction file are stored in ascending key order, and each record has a unique key.

Design and write a program to update the master file from the transaction file. Incorporate into your design error conditions that might exist between the keys on the two files.

17

Common Extensions

This chapter examines several extensions to the language that are not found in Standard Pascal, yet have become accepted as being necessary in dialects of the language.

17.1 String Data Type.

The only method used in this book, to define a variable that represented a string of characters, was through an ARRAY OF CHAR. In such cases it was necessary to define the size of the array at the time of coding the program. Arrays are static data structures, they do not grow or shrink according to the volume of data that they contain. A variable of type string is essentially a *packed array* of characters, but with a dynamically changing number of elements. A string variable in Sheffield Pascal is not compatible with either a variable declared as PACKED ARRAY[1..N] OF CHAR or a variable of type CHAR. However, this limitation is relaxed in Turbo Pascal.

The number of characters in a string defines the length of the string. In Sheffield Pascal a default maximum is 80 characters, but this can be overridden in the declaration to a maximum of 32767 characters. The maximum length of a string in Turbo Pascal is 255 characters, with no default. Turbo Pascal uses cell zero, in a string array, to store the length of the string. Should a programmer want to overwrite this value, the code would be *item[0]:=#80;* where item is the name of the string array; 80 is the size of the string and the # character signifies the character representation of, in this case, 80. String variables can be defined in both dialects as:

VAR   LineOfText : STRING[120];

where 120 represents the maximum length of the string LineOfText. The individual characters within a string are indexed from 1 through to the length of the string. In the following example the variable alphabet is declared as a string of maximum length 26 characters. The variable is initialised to the letters of the alphabet and its value displayed. Every other letter of the alphabet, starting with the letter A, is also displayed.

```
PROGRAM StringExample(OUTPUT);
CONST
      letters = 'ABCDEFGHIJKLMNOPQRSTUVWXYZ';
      MaxLength = 26;
VAR
      alphabet : string[MaxLength];
      index : INTEGER;
BEGIN
      alphabet := letters;
      WriteLn('the alphabet');
      WriteLn(alphabet);
      WriteLn;
      WriteLn('every other letter starting at A');
      index:=1;
      REPEAT
         Write(alphabet[index]);
         index:=index+2;
      UNTIL index > 25;
      WriteLn;
END.{StringExample}
```

Results from program being run

the alphabet
ABCDEFGHIJKLMNOPQRSTUVWXYZ

every other letter starting at A
ACEGIKMOQSUWY

Although a string variable must be defined as being of a finite length, the contents of the string can be any length up to this maximum value. A string variable may be compared to any other string variable or to a string constant, regardless of its current dynamic length.

17.2 String Procedures and Functions.
DELETE(S,I,N) - procedure changes the value of string S by deleting N characters starting at the Ith character of S.

e.g.   Name := 'What is your name?';
        DELETE(Name, 1, 8);
        WriteLn(Name);

output your name?

INSERT(S1,S2,I) - procedure changes the value of the string S2 by inserting the string S1 at the Ith position of S2.

e.g.   Name := 'Henry Smythe';
        INSERT('James ', Name, 7);
        WriteLn(Name);

output Henry James Smythe

STR(I,S) - procedure converts the integer variable I into a string variable S. Turbo Pascal extends this procedure to cover the conversion of real variables.

e.g.   Value := 31672;
        STR(Value, StringValue);
        WriteLn(StringValue[3]);

output 6

VAL(S,V,code) - this procedure is the reverse of STR. The string S is converted to a real or integer type and stored in V. If no errors are detected during execution of the procedure, code remains at zero. This function applies to Turbo Pascal only.

e.g.   StringValue := '25';
         VAL(StringValue, Value, ErrorCode);
         IF ErrorCode = 0 THEN WriteLn(4*Value : 3);

  output 100

COPY(S,I,N) - function that returns the substring of S which is the N characters starting at the Ith position.

e.g.   StringValue = 'ABCDEFG';
         WriteLn(COPY(StringValue,3,2));
         WriteLn(COPY(StringValue,1,6));
         WriteLn(COPY(StringValue,4,1));

output   CD
            ABCDEF
            D

CONCAT(S1,...,Sn) - function that returns the result of the concatenation (joining strings together) of the strings S1,...Sn. In Turbo Pascal the operator + is also used to concatenate strings (S1+S2+S3).

e.g.   S1 := 'ABCD';
        S2 := 'EFGHIJ';
        S3 := 'XYZ';
        S4 := CONCAT(S1,S2,S3);
        WriteLn(S4);

  output ABCDEFGHIJXYZ

LENGTH(S) - function that returns the length of string S.

e.g.   X := 'Strings in Pascal are fun!';
        WriteLn(LENGTH(X):3);

  output 26

POS(S1,S2) - function that scans through the string S2 to find the first occurrence of the substring S1 within S2. The value returned is the index within S2 of the first character of the matched substring. If the substring cannot be found the function returns the value of zero.

e.g.   MinorString := 'me';
        MajorString := 'can you find me?'
        WriteLn(POS(MinorString, MajorString):3);

  output 14

17.3 String Processing.

Problem. Write a program to read a message from a text file and convert the message into Morse code. The Morse code for each letter of the alphabet is stored in groups of four characters, comprising dot(s), dash(es) and space(s). The code is left justified in the four character field, and space filled where necessary. The Morse code has been given in figure 17.1. This code has been represented in the program as a series of constant strings that are concatenated together into one string called DotDash. This string is divided into groups of four characters, with each group being stored in a one-dimensional array. The array will be used as a look-up table. The Morse Code for 'A' will be stored in the first cell, 'B' in the second cell, and so on.

A	.-	H	....	O	---	V	...-
B	-...	I	..	P	.--.	W	.--
C	-.-.	J	.---	Q	--.-	X	-..-
D	-..	K	-.-	R	.-.	Y	-.--
E	.	L	.-..	S	...	Z	--..
F	..-.	M	--	T	-		
G	--.	N	-.	U	..-		

Figure 17.1 The Morse Code for the letters of the alphabet A to Z

```
PROGRAM MorseCode(message, OUTPUT);
{program to read a message from a text file and convert the message into Morse Code}
CONST
        MaxChar=80;
        space=CHR(32);
{constant substrings representing the Morse Code for the groups of letters A to H, I to P and
Q to Z respectively}
DotDash1= '.-  -...  -.-.  -..  .   ..-.  --.  ....';
DotDash2= '..  .---  -.-  .-..  --  -.   --  .--.';
DotDash3= '--.-.-.  ...  -   ..-  ...-  .--  -..-  -.--  --..';
TYPE
        code=STRING[4]; {data type of a single Morse Code}
VAR
        Line:STRING[MaxChar]; {single line of the message}
        message : TEXT;
        DotDash:STRING[104]; {concatenated substrings forming Morse code for A to Z}
        CodeStore:ARRAY[1..26] OF code; {An array of Morse codes for A to Z}
        character:CHAR; {single character read from message}
```

```pascal
PROCEDURE initialise;
{build a string of morse codes and divide the string up into individual codes that are stored in
an array}
VAR
      start, index:INTEGER;
BEGIN
      DotDash:=CONCAT(DotDash1,DotDash2,DotDash3);
      start:=1;
      FOR index:=1 TO 26 DO
      BEGIN
         CodeStore[index]:=COPY(DotDash,start,4);
         start:=start+4;
      END;
END; {initialise}

FUNCTION translate(character:CHAR):code;
{function to return the Morse code of a letter of the alphabet}
BEGIN
      translate:=CodeStore[ORD(character)-64];
END; {translate}

BEGIN
      ASSIGN(message,'A:message');
      RESET(message);
      initialise;
      WHILE NOT EOF(message) DO
      BEGIN
         WHILE NOT EOLN(message) DO
         BEGIN
            Read(message,character);
            IF character IN ['A'..'Z'] THEN
            BEGIN
               Write(translate(character));
               Write(space, space, space);
            END
            ELSE
               WriteLn;
            {end if}
         END;
         {end while}
         ReadLn(message);
         WriteLn;
      END;
      {end while}
END. {MorseCode}
```

Contents of message file

HELLO HELLO
HERR FLICK HAS LOST HIS SAUSAGE

Results from program being run

```
....  .        .-..  .-..  ---
....  .        .-..  .-..  ---
....  .        .-.   .-.
..-.  .-..  ..       -.-.  -.-
....  .-    ...
.-..  ---   ...      -
....  ..    ...
...   .-    ..-  ...  .-    --.  .
```

17.4 Direct Access Files.

With sequential file processing a key to a record does not give the position of that record in relation to the other records. It is impossible given a key to access a record directly without having first to inspect each key of each record before the record that is required can be found.

With direct access files the key to each record is translated by the computer system into a position on the disc surface where the record is stored. Thus knowing the key to a record means that access to that record is direct without having to search through the keys of other records in the file.

The only new activity associated with direct access files in Pascal is to position the record pointer against the record to be processed, having first specified the key to the record. A direct access record key is a positive integer that represents the relative position of a logical record with respect to the beginning of a file. For example, a record with a key value of 10 represents the record occupying the tenth logical record area in the file, irrespective of whether the relative record areas 1 through 9 have been filled. However, with record deletions, or the fact that the keys are numerically spaced apart, gaps of wasted space can soon occur in such a file organisation.

The Pascal statement used to position the record pointer is:

SEEK(filename, record key);

this can be used prior to reading from or writing to the file.

Direct access to files is non-standard in Pascal and, therefore, different compilers support different implementations of this method.

For example, Sheffield Pascal numbers its direct access records from 1, whereas Turbo Pascal is numbered from 0.

Sheffield Pascal requires that direct access files are opened with an OPEN procedure; Turbo Pascal can be opened with either RESET or REWRITE depending upon the mode of I/O.

Sheffield Pascal has a predefined function LASTREC, which returns the number of the last record in the file. Turbo Pascal has two predefined functions FILEPOS which returns the current position of the file pointer, and FILESIZE which returns the current size of the file.

Problem. A text file on the top selling musical tunes of the week, contains information on the chart rating (not in ascending order), title and artist. Write a program to read this file and store the contents in a direct access file, such that the file may be interrogated to find the title and artist, given the position of a tune in the top pop chart.

```
PROGRAM PopCharts(INPUT, DataFile, chart);
{program that reads the current top pop music information from a text file and stores each
line as a separate record in a direct access file. The title and performer of any artist in the top
pop file can then be found using the position of the music in the charts}

TYPE
     information =   RECORD
                         tune:STRING[30];
                         performer:STRING[30];
                     END;
     PopDetails = FILE OF information;
VAR
     DataFile:TEXT;
     chart:PopDetails;
     ChartEntry:information;
     position:LONGINT;
     title:STRING[30];
     artist:STRING[30];
BEGIN
     WriteLn('* * * T O P     P O P     C H A R T * * *'); WriteLn;
     ASSIGN(DataFile, 'A:DataFile');
     ASSIGN(chart,'A:chart');
     RESET(DataFile);
     REWRITE(chart);
     WHILE NOT EOF(DataFile) DO
     BEGIN
        ReadLn(DataFile, position, title, artist);
        ChartEntry.tune:=title;
        ChartEntry.performer:=artist;
        SEEK(chart, position);
        Write(chart, ChartEntry);
     END;
```

```
        RESET(chart);
        REPEAT
            Write('input chart position (zero to exit) = > '); ReadLn(position);
            IF (position > 0) AND (position < = FileSize(chart)-1) THEN
            BEGIN
                SEEK(chart, position);
                IF NOT EOF(chart) THEN Read(chart, ChartEntry);
                WriteLn; WriteLn;
                Write('This weeks chart entry at number ',position:2, ' is ');
                WriteLn(ChartEntry.tune);
                WriteLn(' by ',ChartEntry.performer); WriteLn;
            END;
        UNTIL position < = 0;
END. {PopCharts}
```

Contents of DataFile

6	Living Doll	Cliff Richard
8	Under the Boardwalk	Rolling Stones
3	Ferry across the Mersey	Gerry and the Pacemakers
1	Love me tender	Elvis Presley
2	Stranger on the Shore	Acker Bilk
4	Good Golly Miss Molly	Gerry Lee Lewis
5	She Loves you	The Beatles
7	Blowing in the Wind	Peter, Paul and Mary
9	The Urban Spaceman	Bonzo Dog Do Dah Band
10	Purple Haze	Jimmy Hendrix

Results from program being run

```
* * * T O P   P O P   C H A R T * * *

input chart position (zero to exit) = > 1

This weeks chart entry at number 1 is Love me tender
 by Elvis Presley

input chart position (zero to exit) = > 9

This weeks chart entry at number 9 is The Urban Spaceman
 by Bonzo Dog Do Dah Band

input chart position (zero to exit) = > 4

This weeks chart entry at number 4 is Good Golly Miss Molly
 by Gerry Lee Lewis

input chart position (zero to exit) = > 0
```

17.5 External Procedures.

It is sometimes convenient to compile one or more procedures and/or functions separately, so that they can subsequently be incorporated into other programs. When these routines are used by another program, they must be declared in the procedure part of the program in the usual way, except that the body of the routine is replaced by the directive EXTERN (which is not a reserved word). For example:

> PROCEDURE name(parameters); EXTERN;
> FUNCTION name(parameters):type; EXTERN;

Note that Turbo Pascal uses EXTERNAL and not EXTERN. One possible problem area when using external routines is that of the length compatibility between variables. Sheffield Pascal uses long reals and long integers (by default), therefore, this will cause problems with routines written in another language that only uses reals, integers and short integers. Other difficulties can arise when routines are written in a language where arrays are stored in column order, since in Pascal they are stored in row order.

When the same area of memory is to be accessed by different procedures then it is possible to declare this area as being COMMON. It is possible to make some global variables common by use of the compiler directive %COMMON in Sheffield Pascal. This directive may only appear in the global variable declaration part of the program and its effect is to put the first variable which is declared after the directive into a COMMON block. The name of the COMMON block is the same as that of the variable. A separate %COMMON directive is required for each variable which is to be made common.

The following example illustrates the use of external procedures and COMMON block declarations in Pascal programs. Two programs are written, the first (producer) allows a character to be input at the keyboard of a terminal and stored in a common area of memory. The second (consumer) accesses the character from the common memory and displays the character on the screen of a terminal. Each program is run from a separate terminal in a PRIME multi-user system. The effect is to input from one keyboard and display the value on the screen of a different terminal.

Both the processes of production and consumption of characters to and from the common memory are controlled by the use of two semaphores. Since the consumption of a character cannot take place until there is a character in common memory the program (consumer) is forced to wait (on a semaphore). As soon as a character is available for consumption the producer must release the waiting consumer, and temporarily suspend itself until the character is consumed. Once the character has been consumed, the consumer must release the producer, and suspend itself until there is another character to consume. The external routines to these programs are procedures to drain (initialise) wait and signal on the semaphores.

```
PROGRAM producer(INPUT);
CONST
    terminator = CHR(46);
VAR
    {begin common memory}
    %COMMON
    ch : CHAR;
    {end common memory}
    sem1, sem2, code : SHORTINT;

{declare external procedures}
PROCEDURE sem$nf(VAR sem, code : SHORTINT); EXTERN;
PROCEDURE sem$wt(VAR sem, code : SHORTINT); EXTERN;
PROCEDURE sem$dr(VAR sem, code : SHORTINT); EXTERN;
{end external declarations}

BEGIN
    {set numbered semaphores}
    sem1:=60; sem2:=61;
    {drain (initialise) semaphores}
    sem$dr(sem1, code); sem$dr(sem2, code);
    {input character from keyboard and store in buffer}
    Read(ch);
    WHILE ch < > terminator DO
    BEGIN
        {release consumer}
        sem$nf(sem1, code);
        {wait until buffer empty}
        sem$wt(sem2, code);
        {input character from keyboard and store in buffer}
        Read(ch);
    END;
END.{producer}

PROGRAM consumer(OUTPUT);
CONST
    terminator = CHR(46);
VAR
    {begin common memory}
    %COMMON
    ch : CHAR;
    {end common memory}
    sem1, sem2, code : SHORTINT;

{begin external declarations}
PROCEDURE sem$wt(VAR sem, code : SHORTINT); EXTERN;
PROCEDURE sem$nf(VAR sem, code : SHORTINT); EXTERN;
{end external declarations}
```

```
BEGIN
      {set numbered semaphores}
      sem1:=60;sem2:=61;
      WHILE ch < > terminator DO
      BEGIN
            {wait on first semaphore for buffer to be filled}
            sem$wt(sem1,code);
            {display contents of buffer on screen}
            Write(ch);
            {signal on second semaphore that buffer is empty}
            sem$nf(sem2,code);
      END;
END.{consumer}
```

17.6 Summary.

The data type STRING is probably the most common of the extensions to Standard Pascal. The maximum size of the string must be declared, however, strings of smaller sizes can be stored under this type. Strings of different sizes may also be declared.

The individual characters in a string can normally be accessed as though they were stored in a one-dimensional array.

In addition to the STRING type, Pascal dialects often support a range of string handling functions and procedures.

The ability to be able to manipulate the file position pointer, provides the user with the advantage of being able to gain direct access to records that have been ordered by numerical position.

The ability of the language is extended by using EXTERN to be able to incorporate externally written and compiled procedures and functions from other languages.

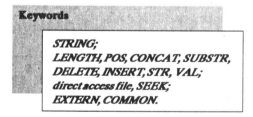

Keywords

STRING;
LENGTH, POS, CONCAT, SUBSTR,
DELETE, INSERT, STR, VAL;
direct access file, SEEK;
EXTERN, COMMON.

17.7 Questions.

1. Extend the program given in 17.3 to read from a text file a phrase in Morse code and translate and output the phrase in English.

[2]. Write a program using a direct access file to store a daily diary for each day in a year. The key to an entry in the diary is the day number, which is obtained from the date.

18

Turbo Units

Within this chapter the reader is introduced to a non-standard mechanism in Pascal known as a unit. This is the first of three chapters that points the reader towards modern methods of producing computer programs.

The technique of separating the procedures that are required in a program solution, from the detailed coding of these procedures, is known as procedural abstraction. The use of units serves to enhance the idea of procedural abstraction.

18.1 What is a Unit?

A unit is a collection of constants, data types, variables, procedures and functions that are normally related to a particular activity. A unit can be compiled separately from other units or programs and stored in a library of units for use by either other units or programs.

There is nothing new about the concept of a unit. Similar mechanisms can be found in Modula-2 under the name of *modules* and in Ada under the name of *packages*. However, in these languages the feature is standard and part of the language, whereas, a unit is a non-standard feature found in Turbo Pascal.

The structure of a unit is:

> UNIT *identifier;*
> INTERFACE
> USES {*list of other units used by this unit (optional)*}
> {*list of constants, data types, variables, procedures and functions that are public to the user*}
> IMPLEMENTATION
> USES {*list of other units used by this unit (optional)*}
> {*list of private declarations not seen by the user*}
> {*implementation of the procedures and functions that are described by the interface*}
> BEGIN
> > {*initialisation of the unit (if applicable)*}
> END.

From this description the reader will observe that a unit is specified in two parts, the interface section and the implementation section.

The interface section informs the user of the constants, data types, variables, procedures and functions that are available for use. The description of the procedures and functions is limited to only the heading line containing the formal parameter list. The actual code that is used in the procedures and functions is not made visible to the user. There may be identifiers visible in this section that are used in other units, in which case the units from which these identifiers are declared must be listed against the uses entry.

The implementation section contains the working code for all the procedures and functions listed in the interface. This code cannot be accessed for modification by the user. The code is said to be *private*. The implementation section can have further procedures and functions that have never been made visible in the interface section. Such routines would normally be used by the procedures and functions that were visible. Any identifiers that are used in this section and are declared in other units must have the names of the units listed in this section.

The code between the BEGIN..END. of a unit is known as the body of the unit. The body of a unit is always executed before the body of a main program that uses such a unit. This is known as the initialisation of a unit. A unit that uses other units with bodies, will be initialised in the order in which the units are listed.

For example in the following segment of code:

```
UNIT unit1;
INTERFACE

IMPLEMENTATION
USES unit2;
BEGIN
    {executable statements for unit1}
END. {unit1}
```

if unit2 had a body then the order of initialisation would be unit2, unit1 followed by the main body of the program that uses unit1.

18.2 Random Number Function Revisited.

In chapter 9 a random number generator function was descibed to the reader. This function had two drawbacks. Firstly, every time the function was needed it would have to be coded in a program. Secondly, the user had to be aware of initialising the value of the seed. By treating the random number function as a function within a unit it is possible to remove these drawbacks.

The random number function might appear in the following unit. The implementation section has been shaded to indicate that it is not visible to a user.

```
{$N+}
UNIT utility;
INTERFACE
FUNCTION RND:DOUBLE;

IMPLEMENTATION
VAR
     seed:LONGINT;
FUNCTION RND:DOUBLE;
CONST
     a=LONGINT(19);
     b=LONGINT(100000000);
VAR
     RN:DOUBLE;
     y:LONGINT;
BEGIN
     y:= (a*seed) MOD b;
     seed:=y;
     RN:=ABS(y);
     REPEAT
         RN:=RN/10.0;
     UNTIL RN < 1.0;
     RND:=RN;
END; {RND}
BEGIN
     seed:=19; {initialisation of unit utility}
END. {utility}
{$N-}
```

The only visible item in the unit utility is the function RND. There is no mention of the variable seed in the interface, therefore, the user is unaware of its existence. The variable seed has been delared in the implementation section and initialised in the body of the unit.

The unit is created, using an editor, in the same way as any other Pascal program. However, when the unit is compiled the system generates a .TPU (Turbo Pascal Unit) file.

A program can gain access to the random number generator function by specifying that it uses utility. The function can then be used as if it had been explicity coded into the program. For example:

```
{$N+}
PROGRAM random(INPUT, OUTPUT);
USES utility;
VAR
      trials:INTEGER;
      number:INTEGER;
BEGIN
      Write('input number of trials => ');
      ReadLn(trials);
      FOR number:=1 TO trials DO
      BEGIN
         IF (number-1) MOD 10 = 0 THEN
            WriteLn;
         {end if}
         Write(((TRUNC(1000.0*RND) MOD 6)+1):2);
      END;
END. {random}
{$N-}
```

The output from this program is identical to that found in chapter 9, section 4.

18.3 Modular (Unit) Programming.

Writing a program as a collection of units, rather than one single piece of code, is known as modular programming and offers the following advantages.

A large program can be designed as a collection of smaller units. This has the advantage that each unit can be designed, coded and tested independently of the remaining units. A clear interface between the units can be established through the interface section of each unit.

Members of a programming team can be assigned individual units to develop, hence the allocation of work in project management can be improved.

Program modification is easier, since the programmer can change the details of an implementation section, without affecting the rest of the program, provided the interface section remains the same.

Separate compilation of units is possible, hence changes to a unit does not result in the entire program having to be re-compiled.

Programmers can develop libraries of re-usable code. This not only saves time in the development of a system, but contributes towards the reliability of the system, since the units have already undergone testing for other programs.

18.4 Standard Units.
The following eight units are available in Turbo Pascal 5.5.

Crt Expoits the full power of a PC's display and keyboard, including screen mode control, extended keyboard codes, colour, windows and sound.

Dos Supports numerous DOS functions, including date-and-time control, directory search and program execution.

Graph A powerful graphics package with device-independent graphics with support for many graphics cards.

Graph3 Implements Turbo Pascal 3.0 Turtlegraphics.

Overlay Implements Turbo Pascal 5.0's overlay manager.

Printer Allows access to the system printer.

System Turbo Pascal's run-time library. This unit is automatically used by any unit or program.

Turbo3 Provides a degree of compatibility with Turbo Pascal 3.0.

These units, standard to Turbo Pascal, are used in exactly the same manner as programmer-defined units. The contents of the various units is quite extensive and the documentation fills a book in itself!

If you are a user of Turbo Pascal then you will have all the documentation available in a reference guide and a user guide. It is not the intention of the author to reproduce any of this material in this book since it is more than adequately covered by the Turbo Pascal manuals.

18.5 Morse-Code Revisited.
As a means of illustrating how the pre-defined units can be used, the Morse code example given in the last chapter can be modified to include the Morse code being generated at the system loudspeaker and printed on paper.

The two units that make this possible are *Printer* and *Crt*.

The *Printer* unit is a very small unit, designed to make life easier when using the printer from within a program. *Printer* declares a text file called *Lst,* and associates it with the *LPT1* device. Using *Printer* saves you the trouble of declaring, assigning, opening and closing a text file yourself.

The *Crt* unit provides three procedures, there are many more but not used here, for controlling the loudspeaker. These procedures are:

Sound(Hz:WORD) starts the internal speaker. Hz is the frequency of the emitted sound.
NoSound explicitly turns off the loudspeaker.
Delay(ms:WORD) provides a delay for a specified number of milliseconds.

The statements shown in bold typeface illustrate the use of Printer, Crt and their respective procedures and functions.

```
PROGRAM MorseCode(message, OUTPUT);
{program to read a message from a text file and convert the message into audible Morse Code
through the computer's loudspeaker and visible Morse code on the computer's printer}
USES Crt, Printer;
CONST
      MaxChar=80;
      space=CHR(32); dot=CHR(46); dash=CHR(45);
      {constant substrings representing the Morse Code for the groups of letters A to H, I to
      P and Q to Z}
      DotDash1='.-   -...  -.-. -..   .    ..-. --. ....';
      DotDash2='..    .--- -.- .-.. -- -.  --- .-.';
      DotDash3='--.- .-.  ...  -    ..- ...- .-- -..- -.---..';
TYPE
      code=STRING[4]; {data type of a single Morse Code}
VAR
      Line:STRING[MaxChar]; {single line of the message}
      message : TEXT;
      DotDash:STRING[104]; {concatenated substrings forming Morse code for A to Z}
      CodeStore:ARRAY[1..26] OF code; {An array of Morse codes for A to Z}
      character:CHAR; {single character read from message}
      MorseString:code; {a block of four characters dots, dashes or spaces}
      index:INTEGER;

PROCEDURE initialise;
{build a string of morse codes and divide the string up into individual codes that are stored in
an array}
VAR
      start,index:INTEGER;
BEGIN
      DotDash:=CONCAT(DotDash1,DotDash2,DotDash3);
      start:=1;
      FOR index:=1 TO 26 DO
      BEGIN
         CodeStore[index]:=COPY(DotDash,start,4);
         start:=start+4;
      END;
END; {initialise}

FUNCTION translate(character:CHAR):code;
{function to return the morse code of a letter of the alphabet}
BEGIN
      translate:=CodeStore[ORD(character)-64];
END; {translate}
```

```
BEGIN
ASSIGN(message,'A:message');
RESET(message);
     initialise;
     WHILE NOT EOF(message) DO
     BEGIN
        WHILE NOT EOLN(message) DO
        BEGIN
           Read(message, character);
           IF character IN ['A'..'Z'] THEN
           BEGIN
              MorseString:=translate(character);
              Write(Lst,MorseString);
              Write(Lst,space, space, space);

              {convert the Morse code into sound}
              FOR index:=1 TO 4 DO
              BEGIN
                 CASE MorseString[index] OF
                 dot :   BEGIN
                           Sound(800); {short sound}
                           Delay(50);
                           NoSound;
                         END;
                 dash : BEGIN
                           Sound(800); {long sound}
                           Delay(200);
                           NoSound;
                         END;
                 space: Delay(0);
                 END;
                 Delay(50); {short delay after dot or dash}
              END;
              {end for}
           Delay(200); {long delay after code for letter}
           END
           ELSE
              WriteLn(Lst);
           {end if}
        END;
        {end while}
     ReadLn(message);
     WriteLn(Lst);
     END;
     {end while}
END. {MorseCode}
```

The results from this program being run are best tried by the reader.

18.6 Programmer and Standard Units.

It is possible to use both programmer defined and pre-defined standard units in the same unit. In the last worked example of the chapter a program has been written to read from a text file the amount of monthly rainfall over the period of a year. These figures are to be converted into a bar chart showing the distribution of rainfall over a year.

A programmer defined unit has been written that will draw to scale a three-dimensional bar chart. The unit BarChart uses several procedures, functions and constants from the standard unit Graph.

These procedures, functions and constants are as follows.

Detect is a predefined constant to request autodetection of a graphics card.

InitGraph(VAR GraphDriver:INTEGER; VAR GraphMode:INTEGER; PathToDriver:STRING) initialises the graphics system and puts the hardware into graphics mode.

GraphResult is a function that returns an error code for the last graphics operation. If the value of GraphResult is not the graphics error constant *grOK* then the graphics unit cannot be opened and the program will terminate by executing Halt.

CloseGraph shuts down the graphics system. Since the same procedure name is used in the unit BarChart, it has been necessary to qualify CloseGraph from unit Graph with Graph.CloseGraph, otherwise, CloseGraph would appear to be set up as a recursive call, which was not the intention of the procedure.

The maximum size of a Hercules screen is shown in figure 18.1. Notice that the origin is in the top left-hand corner of the screen.

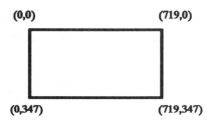

(0,0)   **(719,0)**

(0,347)   **(719,347)**

Figure 18.1 Coordinates of extremeties of a Hercules Graphics Screen

ClearDevice clears the graphics screen and prepares it for output.

Line(x1,y1,x2,y2:INTEGER) draws a line from (x1,y1) to (x2,y2).

OutTextXY(x,y:INTEGER; TextString:STRING) sends a string to the output device, with the first character being displayed at coordinates x,y.

Bar3D(x1,y1,x2,y2:INTEGER; Depth:WORD; Top:BOOLEAN) draws a single three-dimensional bar using the current fill style and colour. Depth is the number of pixels deep of the three-dimensional outline. A typical depth could be calculated by taking 25% of the width of the bar. The predefined constants *TopOn* and *TopOff* indicate whether a top is present on the bar.

The unit BarChart contains the following visible identifiers.

```
UNIT BarChart;
INTERFACE
CONST
        MaxBar=26;{maximum number of bars that can be output}
TYPE
        data=ARRAY[1..MaxBar] OF INTEGER; {frequencies to be displayed}

PROCEDURE OpenGraph;
{procedure to detect graphics card in use, if none available program halts, otherwise
initialises the graphics system and puts the hardware into the graphics mode}

PROCEDURE CloseGraph;
{procedure to shut down the graphics system}

PROCEDURE DrawChart(width, height, bars:INTEGER; VAR frequencies:data);
{procedure to draw a 3-D bar chart; width and height refer to the lengths of the x and y axes
repectively; bars refers to the number of bars to be drawn; the height of each bar is
proportional to the frequency it represents}

PROCEDURE TextDisplay(x,y:INTEGER; message:STRING);
{procedure to display information about the bar chart from position x,y}
{end interface}
```

From which the reader will deduce that it is possible to open and close the graphics mode, write messages to any part of the graphics screen and draw a three-dimensional bar-chart on the screen.

The procedure DrawChart(width, height, bars:INTEGER; VAR frequencies:data); takes as input parameters the approximate size of the bar-chart, where width and height are the lengths of the x and y axes respectively, and bars is the number of bars to draw on the chart. The height of each bar is proportional to each frequency found in the one-dimensional array frequencies.

The implementation of the unit BarChart follows. The section is shaded to indicate to the reader that the implementation section is not visible to the user.

```
IMPLEMENTATION
USES Graph;
CONST
        ScWidth=720; ScHeight=348; {screen width and screen height when using a Hercules
        Monochrome Graphics card}
```

```
PROCEDURE OpenGraph;
VAR
      GraphDriver, GraphMode : INTEGER;
BEGIN
      GraphDriver: = Detect;
      InitGraph(GraphDriver, GraphMode, ");
      IF GraphResult < > grOK THEN HALT;
END; {OpenGraph}

PROCEDURE CloseGraph;
BEGIN
      Graph.CloseGraph;
END; {CloseGraph}

PROCEDURE axes(width, height:INTEGER);
VAR
      x1,x2,y1,y2:integer;
BEGIN
      {calculate coordinates of x and y axes}
      x1: = (ScWidth-width) DIV 2;
      x2:=x1 +width;
      y1: = (ScHeight-height) DIV 2;
      y2: =y1 + height;

      {output heading and axes}
      ClearDevice;
      OutTextXY(300,1,'B A R    C H A R T');
      line(x1,y2,x2,y2);
      line(x1,y2,x1,y1);
END; {axes}

PROCEDURE DrawChart(width, height, bars:INTEGER; VAR frequencies:data);
VAR
      MaxValue:INTEGER; {maximum frequency in distribution}
      index:INTEGER;
      x1, y1, x2, y2:INTEGER;
      startX, startY : INTEGER; {initial coordinates of base of first bar}
      DisplayWidth, DisplayHeight:INTEGER; {size of screen area}
      BarWidth, BarHeight, BarThickness:INTEGER; {dimensions of a bar}
      BarHeightUnit:integer; {scaling factor to determine height of bar from frequency}
      VerticalScale:string;
BEGIN
      {find largest frequency to represent}
      MaxValue: = -MAXINT;
      FOR index: = 1 TO bars DO
         IF frequencies[index] > MaxValue THEN
            MaxValue: = frequencies[index];
         {end if}
      {end for}
```

```
      {draw axes}
      axes(width, height);

      {calculate value of coordinates for foot of first bar in relationship to the axes}
      startX:=((ScWidth-width) DIV 2)+10; {10 units to the right of y-axis}
      startY:=((ScHeight-height) DIV 2)+height-10; {10 units above the x-axis}

      {calculate amount of space available for displaying bar chart}
      DisplayWidth:=width-10;
      DisplayHeight:=height-10;

      {calculate size of bars in relationship to screen size and maximum frequency}
      BarWidth:=DisplayWidth DIV bars;
      BarThickness:=BarWidth DIV 4;
      BarHeightUnit:=DisplayHeight DIV maxvalue;

      {display bars of 3-D bar chart}
      x1:=startX; y1:=startY;
      FOR index:=1 TO bars DO
      BEGIN
          Bar3D(x1,y1,x1+BarWidth,y1-frequencies[index]*BarHeightUnit,BarThickness,
              TopOn);
          x1:=x1+BarWidth;
      END;

      {display class interval label, A, B, C ... }
      x1:=startX+(BarWidth DIV 2); y1:=startY+20;
      FOR index:=1 TO bars DO
      BEGIN
          OutTextXY(x1,y1,CHR(index+64));
          x1:=x1+BarWidth;
      END;

      {display each frequency on the vertical scale}
      x1:=startX-40;
      FOR index:=1 TO bars DO
      BEGIN
          STR(frequencies[index],VerticalScale);
          OutTextXY(x1,startY-BarHeightUnit*frequencies[index],VerticalScale);
      END;
END; {DrawChart}

PROCEDURE TextDisplay(x,y:INTEGER; message:STRING);
BEGIN
      OutTextXY(x,y,message);
END; {TextDisplay}

END. {BarChart}
```

Having compiled and saved the .TPU file, the unit BarChart can be incorporated into the following program.

```
PROGRAM rainfall(DataFile);
{program to demonstrate the use of the library unit BarChart in representing annual rainfall
figures}

USES BarChart;

VAR
        frequency:data;
        DataFile:TEXT;
        MonthNumber:INTEGER;
        bars:INTEGER;

BEGIN
        ASSIGN(DataFile,'A:DataFile');
        RESET(DataFile);
        MonthNumber:=1;

        WHILE NOT EOF(DataFile) DO
        BEGIN
            ReadLn(DataFile,frequency[MonthNumber]);
            MonthNumber:=MonthNumber+1;
        END;

        bars:=MonthNumber-1;
        OpenGraph;
        DrawChart(350,300,bars,frequency);
        TextDisplay(1,1,'Annual Rainfall');
        TextDisplay(1,10,'A - January');
        TextDisplay(1,20,'B - February');
        TextDisplay(1,30,'C - March');
        TextDisplay(1,40,'.');
        TextDisplay(1,50,'.');
        TextDisplay(1,60,'L - December');
        ReadLn; {pause to look at output}
        CloseGraph;
    END. {rainfall}
```

Results from program being run

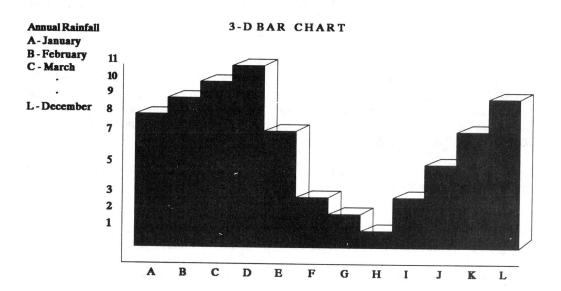

Annual Rainfall
A - January
B - February
C - March
.
.
L - December

3 - D B A R   C H A R T

18.7 Summary.

The technique of separating the procedures required in a program, from the detailed coding of the procedures, is known as procedural abstraction.

Procedural abstraction is possible in Turbo Pascal owing to the inclusion of units. A unit conveys the procedure/function headings in the interface section, keeping the details of the coding of these procedures/functions quite separate in the implementation section.

The interface section is the only part of a unit that is visible to a user. For this reason a user cannot tamper with the code included in the implementation section.

A unit may be initialised if it contains executable code within the body of the unit.

Units can be defined by a programmer, or bought in as part of the system. Turbo Pascal offers eight units as part of the system.

The method of including programmer defined units and pre-defined standard units is the same.

Keywords

*UNIT, USES, INTERFACE,
IMPLEMENTATION;
Unit Body, initialisation;
visible, private;
Standard Units.*

18.8 Questions.

1. Write a procedure RANDOMIZE to be incorporated into the unit utility. The RANDOMIZE procedure should be called before using RND whenever a different set of random numbers are required. RANDOMIZE changes the starting position of the first number to be generated. This starting position could be input as a parameter. For example RANDOMIZE(50), would start at the 50th random number in the series.

Write a separate program to use both RANDOMIZE and RND to generate different groups of random numbers.

[2]. Write a unit called TriCalc for calculating the properties of a triangle. Write a test program that uses TriCalc, and requests the user to enter different available data on the size of a triangle. Calculate and print comprehensive information about the triangle.

3. The results of school examinations are stored as lines in a text file as follows.

Pupil Number Maths English Geography History French Science

For example: 01003 36 21 40 45 39 20

Write a program to read the file and calculate the average mark in each of the six subjects. Use BarChart to display a three-dimensional chart showing the average marks over the six subjects.

[4]. Write a unit that contains the following procedures.

(i) A procedure to draw a circle with its centre at the centre of the screen and a radius in the range 1 to 150 pixels.

(ii) A procedure to erase the last circle that was drawn on the screen.

(iii) A procedure to make a noise according to the radius of the circle. Large circles should have a higher frequency than smaller circles. However, smaller circles appear on the screen for a longer period than larger circles.

You will need to use the procedures SOUND, DELAY and NOSOUND from the unit Crt and the function GetColor (gets the foreground colour), and procedures SetColor (sets the foreground colour), GetBkColor (gets the background colour) and Circle from the unit Graph. Hint - to erase a circle, change the foreground colour to the background colour and draw the circle again. Restore the foreground colour to its original value.

Write a program to generate circles of different radii, pulsating about the same centre, to the sound of a change in frequency on the loudspeaker.

19

Object-oriented Programming (OOP)

Object-oriented programming is a relatively new approach to implementing software systems. Its major goals are to improve programmer productivity by increasing software extensibility and reusability and to control the complexity and cost of software maintenance.

Borland has extended Turbo Pascal to include OOP. Within this chapter the reader will be exposed to those extensions together with an explanation of the fundamental concepts involved in this new programming technique.

19.1 Abstract Data Types.

Data abstraction is the technique of combining a data type with a set of operations on data of the same type. This concept is not new. Consider for a moment the data type INTEGER. Data of type integer can have the operations of addition(+), subtraction(-), multiplication(*) and division(DIV), as well as various standard functions and procedures applied to the data. The method of implementing the integer type is machine specific and hidden from the user. Similarly the implementation details for the various integer operators and functions are also hidden from the user.

A user is allowed to specify variables of type INTEGER, and perform operations on the variables of this type without needing to know how the type, operators, functions and procedures are implemented.

An abstract data type specification describes data structures not by their implementation, but by a list of operations available on the structure.

Consider for a moment the stack data structure introduced in 15.2. The type stack was defined as:

```
TYPE
      stack= ^ node;
      node=RECORD
               data:CHAR;
               link:stack;
            END;
```

with operations on the stack of:

```
PROCEDURE initialise(VAR s:stack);
FUNCTION empty(s:stack):BOOLEAN;
PROCEDURE push(VAR s:stack;character:CHAR);
PROCEDURE pop(VAR s:stack;VAR character:CHAR);
```

The information could be incorporated into a Turbo unit as:

UNIT StackUnit;

INTERFACE
TYPE
      stack= ^ node;
      node=RECORD
               data:CHAR;
               link:stack;
            END;

PROCEDURE initialise(VAR s:stack);
FUNCTION empty(s:stack):BOOLEAN;
PROCEDURE push(VAR s:stack;character:CHAR);
PROCEDURE pop(VAR s:stack;VAR character:CHAR);

IMPLEMENTATION

PROCEDURE initialise(VAR s:stack);
BEGIN
 s:=NIL;
END; {initialise}

FUNCTION empty(s:stack):BOOLEAN;
BEGIN
 IF s=NIL THEN
 empty:=TRUE
 ELSE
 empty:=FALSE;
 {end if}
END; {empty}

PROCEDURE push(VAR s:stack;character:CHAR);
VAR
 temp:stack;
BEGIN
 NEW(temp);
 temp^.data:=character;
 temp^.link:=s;
 s:=temp;
END; {push}

PROCEDURE pop(VAR s:stack;VAR character:CHAR);
VAR
 temp:stack;
BEGIN
 IF NOT empty(s) THEN
 BEGIN
 temp:=s;
 character:=s^.data;
 s:=s^.link;
 DISPOSE(temp);
 END;
END; {pop}
END. {StackUnit}

Any program that uses a stack of characters need only specify USES StackUnit to obtain all the operations on the data structure defined as a stack.

When the unit StackUnit is compiled, a .TPU file is produced. This file is not human-readable. If the corresponding .PAS file is withheld from any potential user of the unit, the only information that need be passed to the user are the operations on the data type stack.

The method of implementing the stack, in this case a linked list with entry and exit at one end only, can also be hidden from the interface section if it is stored in a separate unit, and the user is denied access to this unit. For example, the separate unit could be defined as:

```
UNIT StackDefn;
INTERFACE
TYPE
        stack= ^ node;
        node=RECORD
                data:CHAR;
                link:stack;
            END;
IMPLEMENTATION
END. {StackDefn}
```

The interface section for StackUnit can then be modified to include USES StackDefn, with the type description for stack being omitted. The user can now be supplied with a full listing of the INTERFACE only of StackUnit and not an edited version. The listings of the IMPLEMENTATION section and UNIT StackDefn can be denied to the user, hence they become implicity *private* and can only be modified by the programmer who has access to the .PAS files.

The advantage of keeping the type declaration and implementation private, is that the programmer may wish to change the data structure from a linked list to an array. Such a change to the type declaration and the implementation section code would not alter the interface section, and the user would be unaware of the change in the underlying structure of the stack.

The *public* information available to a user of the abstract data type stack would be displayed as:

```
UNIT StackUnit;
INTERFACE
USES StackDefn;

PROCEDURE initialise(VAR s:stack);
{identify a stack for subsequent use}

FUNCTION empty(s:stack):BOOLEAN;
{returns TRUE when stack s is empty, otherwise returns FALSE}

PROCEDURE push(VAR s:stack;character:CHAR);
{will insert one character at the top of the stack}

PROCEDURE pop(VAR s:stack;VAR character:CHAR);
{will remove one character from the top of the stack}
END. {StackUnit}
```

The program example given in 15.2 could be re-coded as follows to incorporate the use of the abstract data type stack. Notice that the function and procedures that operate on the stack are now supplied from the unit StackUnit. Since the format of the stack is not known to the user it is necessary to include StackDefn.

```
PROGRAM demo1(INPUT, OUTPUT);
USES StackUnit, StackDefn;
CONST
        terminator=CHR(32);
VAR
        character:CHAR;
        stack1, stack2: stack;
BEGIN
        initialise(stack1); initialise(stack2);
        WriteLn('enter single characters on to a stack SPACE RETURN to exit');
        Read(character);
        WHILE character < > terminator DO
        BEGIN
           push(stack1,character);
           Read(character);
        END;
        WriteLn('characters input at keyboard');
        WHILE NOT empty(stack1) DO
        BEGIN
           pop(stack1,character);
           push(stack2,character);
        END;
        WHILE NOT empty(stack2) DO
        BEGIN
           pop(stack2,character);
           WriteLn(character);
        END;
END. {demo1}
```

19.2 Classes and Objects.

A class is a term that is applied in object-oriented languages to describe a type. A class definition defines the interface to all the operations that can be performed on an underlying data type. The class definition also specifies the implementation details and data structure of the type.

In Turbo Pascal the class definition interface is defined using the word OBJECT. This can cause confusion, since a class definition is a TYPE definition. An object is a variable declared to be of a specific class.

The abstract data type given in the last section can be re-coded so that it describes a class definition for a stack. The unit StackDefn has been editted to indicate that stack is a type.

```
UNIT StackDefn;
INTERFACE
TYPE
        StackType= ^ node;
        node=RECORD
                data:CHAR;
                link:StackType;
             END;
```

IMPLEMENTATION
END. {StackDefn}

The procedures and function that operate on the stack are re-named as methods in object-oriented programming. The unit StackIO is an editted version of StackUnit to include in the class *stack*, the type *StackType* and the methods that operate on the stack.

UNIT StackIO;

INTERFACE
USES StackDefn;
TYPE
 stack=OBJECT
   s:StackType;
   PROCEDURE initialise;
   FUNCTION empty:BOOLEAN;
   PROCEDURE push(character:CHAR);
   PROCEDURE pop(VAR character:CHAR);
  END;

IMPLEMENTATION

PROCEDURE stack.initialise;
BEGIN
 s:=NIL;
END; {stack.initialise}

FUNCTION stack.empty:BOOLEAN;
BEGIN
 IF s=NIL THEN
  empty:=TRUE
 ELSE
  empty:=FALSE;
 {end if}
END; {stack.empty}

PROCEDURE stack.push(character:CHAR);
VAR
 temp:StackType;
BEGIN
 NEW(temp);
 temp^.data:=character;
 temp^.link:=s;
 s:=temp;
END; {stack.push}

```
PROCEDURE stack.pop(VAR character:CHAR);
VAR
      temp:StackType;
BEGIN
      IF NOT empty THEN
      BEGIN
         temp:=s;
         character:=s ^ .data;
         s:=s ^ .link;
         DISPOSE(temp);
      END;
END; {stack.pop}
END. {StackIO}
```

An object is an instance of a class type and is declared as a variable.

```
VAR
      stack1, stack2 : stack;
```

Notice that the methods used to define the operations on the stack no longer contain any reference in the formal parameter list to a variable of type stack.

An object is created by calling the appropriate method. In this example, stack1.initialise and stack2.initialise would create two objects stack1 and stack2.

A key concept in object-oriented programming is that objects, once created, have actions performed on the objects by calling the methods described in the class definition. For example, stack1.push(character), stack2.pop(character), stack1.empty, etc.

This is in contrast to procedural programming where the user must pass data to the appropriate procedure of function. From the unit StackUnit given in 19.1, the user must inform each procedure or function which stack to manipulate by supplying the name of the stack as the first parameter in the actual parameter list. For example push(stack1, character), pop(stack2, character), empty(stack1), etc.

The following program illustrates the object-oriented approach to the stack manipulation problem first encountered in 15.2, and re-stated using an abstract data type in 19.1.

```
PROGRAM demo2(INPUT, OUTPUT);
USES StackIO;
CONST
      terminator=CHR(32);
VAR
      character:CHAR;
      stack1, stack2: stack; {instances of stack}
BEGIN
      stack1.initialise; stack2.initialise;
      WriteLn('enter single characters on to a stack SPACE RETURN to exit');
      Read(character);
```

```
        WHILE character < > terminator DO
        BEGIN
            stack1.push(character);
            Read(character);
        END;
        WriteLn('characters input at keyboard');
        WHILE NOT stack1.empty DO
        BEGIN
            stack1.pop(character);
            stack2.push(character);
        END;
        WHILE NOT stack2.empty DO
        BEGIN
            stack2.pop(character);
            WriteLn(character);
        END;
END. {demo2}
```

19.3 Inheritance.
Consider the following class definition of a point.

```
TYPE
    point=OBJECT
            x,y:INTEGER;
            PROCEDURE initialise(NewX, NewY:INTEGER);
            PROCEDURE plot;
            PROCEDURE erase;
            PROCEDURE ShowXY;
            PROCEDURE ClearXY;
            PROCEDURE move(toX, toY:INTEGER);
        END;
```

The position of the point [x,y] has the following methods associated with it.

PROCEDURE initialise(NewX,NewY:INTEGER); defines a new point at the position [NewX, NewY].

PROCEDURE plot; displays an illuminated pixel at the position of the point.

PROCEDURE erase; removes the illuminated pixel by displaying the background colour at the position of the point.

PROCEDURE ShowXY; displays the coordinates of the point [NewX, NewY].

PROCEDURE ClearXY; removes the display of the coordinates of the point [NewX, NewY].

PROCEDURE move(toX, toY:INTEGER); erases the point at position [x,y] and plots a new point at the position [toX, toY].

The implementation of these procedures could be coded as follows.

```
PROCEDURE point.initialise(NewX, NewY:INTEGER);
BEGIN
      x:=NewX;
      y:=NewY;
END; {point.initialise}

PROCEDURE point.plot;
BEGIN
      PutPixel(x,y,GetColor);
END; {point.plot}

PROCEDURE point.erase;
BEGIN
      PutPixel(x,y,GetBkColor);
END; {point.erase}

PROCEDURE point.ShowXY;
VAR
      s,Xs,Ys:STRING[30];
BEGIN
      Str(x,Xs); Str(y,Ys);
      s:='['+Xs+','+Ys+']';
      OutTextXY(x,y,s);
END; {point.ShowXY}

PROCEDURE point.ClearXY;
VAR
      Colour:WORD;
BEGIN
      Colour:=GetColor;
      SetColor(GetBkColor);
      ShowXY;
      SetColor(Colour);
END; {point.ClearXY}

PROCEDURE point.move(toX, toY:INTEGER);
BEGIN
      erase;
      x:=toX;
      y:=toY;
      plot;
END; {point.move}
```

Now consider for a moment another class of object that has similar characteristics to a point, a *blob*, which is no more than a fat point! A blob will have a centre at [x,y] and in addition a size denoted as small, medium or large. A blob can be plotted, erased, have its coordinates shown or cleared and moved around the screen. These characteristics can be inherited from the class of point.

```
     BlobSize=(small, medium, large);
     blob= OBJECT(point)
             size:BlobSize;
         END;
```

By specifying blob=OBJECT(point), all the methods associated with point are now inherited by blob. Blob is a descendant of point, and point is the ancestor of blob.

Inheritance is the process by which one class inherits the characteristics of another class. A class becomes a descendant of one or more other classes when it is designed as an extension or specialization of these classes.

In this example the inherited methods initialise, plot and erase are of little use to blob, since they only apply to an object of class point. The methods themselves need to be redefined for a blob. The inherited methods are overridden by defining new methods with the same name. Using the same name for two different methods is known as *overloading* the name. Methods can be overloaded, for example the names initialise, plot and erase, can be the same for both classes. However, items of data such as x,y cannot be overloaded.

```
TYPE
     blob= OBJECT(point)
             size:BlobSize;
             PROCEDURE initialise(NewX, NewY:INTEGER; NewSize:BlobSize);
             PROCEDURE plot;
             PROCEDURE erase;
         END;
```

Procedures initialise, plot and erased are redefined as follows.

```
PROCEDURE blob.initialise(NewX, NewY:INTEGER; NewSize:BlobSize);
BEGIN
     point.initialise(NewX, NewY);
     size:=NewSize;
END; {blob.initialise}
```

```
PROCEDURE blob.plot;
VAR
     radius:WORD;
     Xasp, Yasp:WORD;
BEGIN
     {select the size of the blob}
     CASE size OF
         small:    radius:=2;
         medium:   radius:=5;
         large:    radius:=9;
     END;
     {the following procedures are found in Graph:
     GetAspectRatio -   returns the resolution of the screen in order that the aspect ratio
     can be calculated;
     Ellipse -   draws an ellipse;
```

FillEllipse - fills in an ellipse; Although a blob will be represented as a circle it has
been necessary to draw a circle using the ellipse procedure since there is
no procedure to fill in a circle }

```
GetAspectRatio(Xasp, Yasp);
Ellipse(x,y,0,360,radius, radius*LONGINT(Xasp) DIV Yasp);
FillEllipse(x,y,radius, radius*LONGINT(Xasp)DIV Yasp);
END; {blob.plot}

PROCEDURE blob.erase;
VAR
     Colour:WORD;
     radius:WORD;
     Xasp, Yasp:WORD;
BEGIN
     CASE size OF
         small:    radius:=2;
         medium:  radius:=5;
         large:    radius:=9;
     END;
     {the following procedures are found in Graph:
     SetFillStyle - sets the fill in pattern and colour 0 is black, 1 is white on a monochrome
                 screen;
     SetColor - sets the current drawing colour;
     GetBkColor - gets the current backgroud colour }

     SetFillStyle(EmptyFill, 0);
     blob.plot;
     Colour:=GetColor;
     SetColor(GetBkColor);
     GetAspectRatio(Xasp, Yasp);
     Ellipse(x,y,0,360,radius, radius*LONGINT(Xasp) DIV Yasp);
     SetColor(Colour);
     SetFillStyle(SolidFill, 1);
END; {blob.erase}
```

Notice that the inherited methods ShowXY, ClearXY and move have not been redefined
and can be used to display or clear the coordinates of the centre of blobs and move blobs about
the screen, respectively. However, more about this later.

Let us assume that the classes point and blob, and their associated methods have been
saved in a Turbo unit named *draw*. The following program defines two objects blob1 and blob2,
plots the blobs on the screen then several seconds later moves blob1 to a new position.

```
PROGRAM demo3(OUTPUT);
USES draw;
VAR
      blob1, blob2:blob;
BEGIN
      {create objects blob1 and blob2, both of medium size, with coordinates at [100,100] and
      [200,150] respectively}
      blob1.initialise(100,100,medium);
      blob2.initialise(200,150,medium);

      {display both blobs and their coordinates}
      blob1.plot; blob2.plot;
      blob1.ShowXY; blob2.ShowXY;
      crt.delay(5000);

      {clear the coordinates of blob1, and move blob1 to new a position, display the new
      coordinates [100,200] of blob1}
      blob1.ClearXY;
      blob1.move(100, 200);
      blob1.ShowXY;
      crt.delay(5000);
END. {demo3}
```

Results from program being run, before and after movement of blob

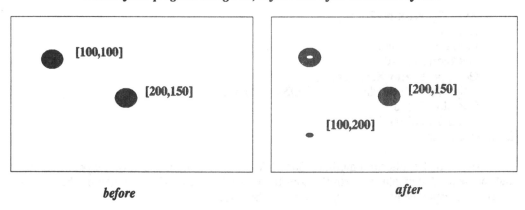

before   after

The results are not quite what was expected! It is true that both blobs have been plotted, but the inherited method move has moved a point to [100,200] and not blob1 as instructed by blob1.move(100,200). The blob at position [100,100] has only had a point within it erased. What has gone wrong? The answer to this question will be explained in the next section.

19.4 Static and Virtual Methods.
In the last example the method move, inherited by blob from point, needs to be implemented differently between point and blob, in order for it to function correctly. Upon examining the code for move and the last result:

```
PROCEDURE point.move(toX, toY:INTEGER);
BEGIN
      erase;
      x:=toX;
      y:=toY;
      plot;
END; {point.move}
```

it is clear that the compiler has used point.erase and point.plot and not blob.erase and blob.plot even though the instruction was blob1.move(100,200). One way of overcoming this problem would be to redefine point.move as blob.move for the class of object blob.

This would add further code to the class of object blob as shown in bold type face. For the sake of brevity, the code for the procedures in italics has not been repeated.

```
blob=OBJECT(point)
      size:BlobSize;
      PROCEDURE initialise(NewX, NewY:INTEGER; NewSize:BlobSize);
      PROCEDURE plot;
      PROCEDURE erase;
      PROCEDURE move(toX, toY:INTEGER);
      END;
```

PROCEDURE blob.initialise(NewX, NewY:INTEGER; NewSize:BlobSize);

PROCEDURE blob.plot;

PROCEDURE blob.erase;

```
PROCEDURE blob.move(toX, toY:INTEGER);
BEGIN
      erase;
      x:=toX;
      y:=toY;
      plot;
END;
```

Since move has been overridden the compiler would use erase from blob.erase and plot from blob.plot when compiling blob.move. This method is far from satisfactory since it requires coding the same procedure twice. Notice there is no difference between blob.move and point.move. In other examples the amount of extra coding might be excessive!

The class methods described so far are *static*. The compiler allocates them and resolves all references to them at compile time. This is known as *early-binding*. That is why blob1.move(100,200) in the last example was executed using point.move. In order to overcome the problems stated, class methods should be defined as being *virtual*. If point.erase, point.plot, blob.erase and blob.plot are defined as being virtual then the references to erase and plot in the method point.move will be resolved at run-time through the object being used (known as *late-binding*); blob1.move(100,200) will automatically use blob.erase and blob.plot in the inherited method point.move.

Every class of object that has virtual methods must have a *constructor*. Each individual instance of an object must be initialised by a separate constructor call.

Every class of object has only one *virtual method table* (VMT) in the data segment of memory. This table contains the size of the object and pointers to the code for each virtual method associated with the class of object. A constructor establishes a link between the instance of the object calling the constructor and the class of object's VMT.

Once an ancestor method is tagged as virtual all the descendant types that implement a method of the same name must tag that method as virtual.

Figure 19.1, on the next page, illustrates the internal representation of instances of objects (i) with static methods, (ii) with virtual methods and (iii) on instances of a single class.

19.5 Polymorphism.

Polymorphism is a way of giving an action one name that is shared up and down an object hierarchy, with each object in the hierarchy implementing the action in a way appropriate to itself. Therefore, in the last example the method move, inherited by blob from point needs to be implemented as a polymorphic method. It is then possible to inherit point.move in the class of object blob without having to redefine the method. Actions on an object, such as blob1.move(100,200), would then be executed correctly.

An object can only become polymorphic if it is defined as being virtual.

The Turbo Unit draw has been recoded to include erase and plot as virtual methods and replacing the procedures point.initialise and blob.initialise as constructors.

UNIT draw;

INTERFACE
USES Graph, Crt;

TYPE
    point=OBJECT
            x,y:INTEGER;
            CONSTRUCTOR initialise(NewX, NewY:INTEGER);
            PROCEDURE plot; VIRTUAL;
            PROCEDURE erase; VIRTUAL;
            PROCEDURE ShowXY;
            PROCEDURE ClearXY;
            PROCEDURE move(toX, toY:INTEGER);
      END;

unit draw is continued on page 332

(i) Static Methods

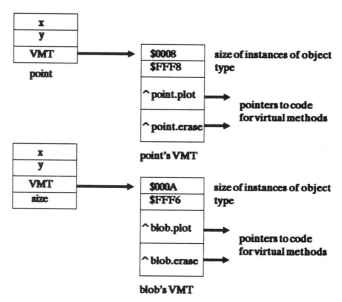

The fields of an object are stored in the order of declaration as a contiguous sequence of variables in the program's data segment.

(ii) Virtual methods

The link between the instance of the object's VMT field and the VMT is established by the constructor.

(iii) Instances of a single class (blob)

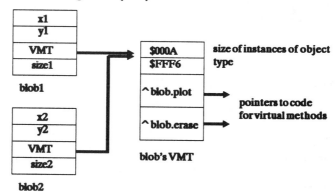

Every instance of an object must be initialised by a separate constructor call, otherwise the link between the VMT field entry and the VMT cannot be made.

Figure 19.1

```
        BlobSize = (small, medium, large);
        blob = OBJECT(point)
                size:BlobSize;
                CONSTRUCTOR initialise(NewX, NewY:INTEGER; NewSize:BlobSize);
                PROCEDURE plot; VIRTUAL;
                PROCEDURE erase; VIRTUAL;
            END;

IMPLEMENTATION
VAR
        Graphdriver, GraphMode : INTEGER;

CONSTRUCTOR point.initialise(NewX, NewY:INTEGER);
BEGIN
        x: = NewX;
        y: = NewY;
END; {point.initialise}

PROCEDURE point.plot;
BEGIN
        PutPixel(x,y,GetColor);
END; {point.plot}

PROCEDURE point.erase;
BEGIN
        PutPixel(x,y,GetBkColor);
END; {point.erase}

PROCEDURE point.ShowXY;
VAR
        s,Xs,Ys:STRING[30];
BEGIN
        Str(x,Xs); Str(y,Ys);
        s: = '['+Xs+','+Ys+']';
        OutTextXY(x,y,s);
END; {point.ShowXY}

PROCEDURE point.ClearXY;
VAR
        Colour:WORD;
BEGIN
        Colour: = GetColor;
        SetColor(GetBkColor);
        ShowXY;
        SetColor(Colour);
END; {point.ClearXY}
```

```
PROCEDURE point.move(toX, toY:INTEGER);
BEGIN
      erase;
      x:=toX;
      y:=toY;
      plot;
END; {point.move}


CONSTRUCTOR blob.initialise(NewX, NewY:INTEGER; NewSize:BlobSize);
BEGIN
      point.initialise(NewX, NewY);
      size:=NewSize;
END; {blob.initialise}


PROCEDURE blob.plot;
VAR
      radius:WORD;
      Xasp, Yasp:WORD;
BEGIN
      CASE size OF
          small:    radius:=2;
          medium:   radius:=5;
          large:    radius:=9;
      END;
      GetAspectRatio(Xasp, Yasp);
      Ellipse(x,y,0,360,radius, radius*LONGINT(Xasp) DIV Yasp);
      FillEllipse(x,y,radius, radius*LONGINT(Xasp)DIV Yasp);
END; {blob.plot}


PROCEDURE blob.erase;
VAR
      Colour:WORD;
      radius:WORD;
      Xasp, Yasp:WORD;
BEGIN
      CASE size OF
          small:    radius:=2;
          medium:   radius:=5;
          large:    radius:=9;
      END;
      SetFillStyle(EmptyFill, 0);
      blob.plot;
      Colour:=GetColor;
      SetColor(GetBkColor);
      GetAspectRatio(Xasp, Yasp);
      Ellipse(x,y,0,360,radius, radius*LONGINT(Xasp) DIV Yasp);
      SetColor(Colour);
      SetFillStyle(SolidFill, 1);
END; {blob.erase}
```

```
BEGIN
      GraphDriver:=Detect;
      InitGraph(GraphDriver, GraphMode, ");
      IF GraphResult < > grOK THEN
         HALT;
      {end if}
END. {draw}
```

The demonstration program demo3 given in 19.3 could be run again using the modified unit draw, and will run correctly.

19.6 Extensibility.

The Turbo Pascal OOP manual defines extensibility as "..a natural outgrowth of inheritance. You inherit everything that all your ancestor types have, and then you add what new capability you need".

Use can be made of a .TPU file that was created in the past by allowing new object classes to inherit from classes in the file. For example, in a program that uses the .TPU file draw, created in the last section, a new class can be created from point, called cross, having all the characteristics of point.

```
USES draw;
TYPE
      cross=OBJECT(point)
                PROCEDURE plot;VIRTUAL;
                PROCEDURE erase;VIRTUAL;
            END;

PROCEDURE cross.plot;
BEGIN
      Line(x-5,y,x+5,y);
      Line(x,y-5,x,y+5);
END; {cross.plot}

PROCEDURE cross.erase;
VAR
      colour:WORD;
BEGIN
      colour:=getColor;
      SetColor(GetBkColor);
      plot;
      SetColor(colour);
END; {cross.erase}
```

Since cross has all the characteristics of point, cross can utilise the constructor initialise and the procedures ShowXY, ClearXY and move. If an an object CrossHair is instantiated, then:

CrossHair.initialise(100,200) would create a cross, with its centre at the position [100,200].

CrossHair.plot would display the cross on the screen, and CrossHair.erase would delete the cross from the screen.

CrossHair.ShowXY would display the coordinates [100,200] of the centre of the cross and CrossHair.ClearXY would clear these coordinates from the screen.

CrossHair.move(300,150) would display the cross at the new position [300,150] on the screen. The old cross at [100,200] would be deleted from the screen.

19.7 Dynamic Objects.

Up to now the instances of objects have been defined as static objects. For example,

    VAR spot:blob;

However, there is no reason why instances of objects should not be dynamic, in the same way as other data types have been allocated to or deallocated from memory. Given

    TYPE   BlobPointer = ^blob;
    VAR   spot : BlobPointer;

memory allocation is possible using NEW(spot). If the dynamic object contains virtual methods then it must be initialised with a constructor before any of the methods are used. Turbo Pascal has combined both the memory allocation and constructor initialisation into an extension of the NEW statement. Thus

    NEW(spot, initialise(100,200)) is the same as:
    NEW(spot); spot^.initialise(100,200);

Similarly, when objects are no longer needed they must be disposed. There is more to disposing of a dynamic object than releasing memory. Therefore, the DISPOSE statement on its own is inadequate. Since an object can contain pointers to dynamic structures or objects that need to be disposed of in a particular order, Turbo Pascal provides a special type of method called a *destructor* for such purposes. A destructor combines the memory deallocation step with whatever other tasks are necessary for a given object type.

Destructors can be inherited and can be either static or virtual methods.

Destructors need only be used on dynamically allocated objects. To deallocate memory space the destructor must be called as a part of the extended syntax of the DISPOSE statement. For example the DESTRUCTOR finalise is called through DISPOSE(temp^.item, finalise). The amount of space to deallocate for an object is taken from the first entry in the VMT of the object.

A destructor method can be empty, see point.finalise below, in which case the code generated by the compiler in response to the word DESTRUCTOR, will carry out *behind the scenes* work providing an invisible service.

The Turbo unit draw has been modified to include an empty DESTRUCTOR for a point.

```
UNIT draw;

INTERFACE
USES Graph, Crt;
TYPE
      point=OBJECT
                  x,y:INTEGER;
                  CONSTRUCTOR initialise(NewX, NewY:INTEGER);
                  DESTRUCTOR finalise; VIRTUAL;
                  PROCEDURE plot; VIRTUAL;
                  PROCEDURE erase; VIRTUAL;
                  PROCEDURE ShowXY;
                  PROCEDURE ClearXY;
                  PROCEDURE move(toX, toY:INTEGER);
            END;

      BlobSize=(small, medium, large);
      blob=OBJECT(point)
                  size:BlobSize;
                  CONSTRUCTOR initialise(NewX, NewY:INTEGER; NewSize:BlobSize);
                  PROCEDURE plot; VIRTUAL;
                  PROCEDURE erase; VIRTUAL;
            END;

IMPLEMENTATION
VAR
      Graphdriver, GraphMode : INTEGER;

CONSTRUCTOR point.initialise(NewX, NewY:INTEGER);
BEGIN
      x:=NewX;
      y:=NewY;
END; {point.initialise}

DESTRUCTOR point.finalise;
BEGIN
END; {point.finalise}

{remainder of the code for draw is unchanged}

END. {draw}
```

In the final example of this chapter blobs of three different sizes are stored in a linked list. The contents of the linked list is then output and finally the memory space disposed.

In this example a linked list has been treated as a class. The data structure for the class is a record with the methods to initialise (allocate memory), finalise (deallocate memory), insert (items into the linked list) and display (the contents of the linked list).

The records that form the linked list contain two pointer fields. The first points at the dynamically allocated instances of a blob and the second points to the next record in the linked list. The method algorithms used in this program should be familiar to the reader from the work on pointers and dynamic structures found in chapters 14 and 15 respectively.

Figure 19.2 illustrates the data structures and VMT used in the solution to the problem.

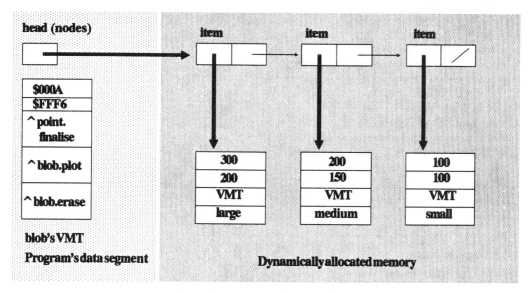

Figure 19.2 Dynamic Objects

```
PROGRAM demo4;
{program to store graphical objects in a linked list and display the contents of the linked list}
USES draw, crt;
TYPE
        BlobPointer = ^ blob;
        pointer = ^ node;
        node = RECORD
                    item:BlobPointer;
                    link:pointer;
                END;

        LinkedList = OBJECT
                        nodes: pointer;
                        CONSTRUCTOR initialise;
                        DESTRUCTOR finalise;VIRTUAL;
                        PROCEDURE insert(item:BlobPointer);
                        PROCEDURE ListOut;
                    END;
```

```
CONSTRUCTOR LinkedList.initialise;
BEGIN
      nodes:=NIL;
END; {LinkedList.initialise}

DESTRUCTOR LinkedList.finalise;
VAR
      temp:pointer;
BEGIN
      WHILE nodes < > NIL DO
      BEGIN
         temp:=nodes;
         DISPOSE(temp ^ .item, finalise);
         nodes:=temp ^ .link;
         DISPOSE(temp);
      END;
END; {LinkedList.finalise}

PROCEDURE LinkedList.insert(item:BlobPointer);
VAR
      temp:pointer;
BEGIN
      NEW(temp);
      temp ^ .item:=item;
      temp ^ .link:=nodes;
      nodes:=temp;
END; {LinkedList.insert}

PROCEDURE LinkedList.ListOut;
VAR
      current:pointer;
BEGIN
      current:=nodes;
      WHILE current < > NIL DO
      BEGIN
         current ^ .item ^ .plot;
         current ^ .item ^ .ShowXY;
         current:=current ^ .link;
      END;
      crt.delay(5000);
END;{LinkedList.ListOut}

VAR
      ObjectList:LinkedList;
BEGIN
      {create a linked list}
      Objectlist.initialise;
      {create three different sizes of blob and insert these in the linked list}
      ObjectList.insert(NEW(BlobPointer,initialise(100,100,small)));
      ObjectList.insert(NEW(BlobPointer,initialise(200,150,medium)));
      ObjectList.insert(NEW(BlobPointer,initialise(300,200,large)));
```

```
        {display the contents of the linked list on the screen}
        ObjectList.ListOut;
        {deallocate the contents of the linked list using a destructor}
        ObjectList.finalise;
  END. {demo4}
```

Results from program being run

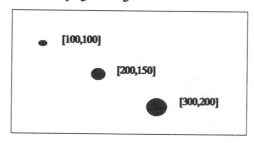

[100,100]
[200,150]
[300,200]

19.8 Summary.

The design of a system can be naturally separated from its implementation and can be limited to include up to the interface level of development.

OOP encourages the use of libraries of objects. Software can be reusible and can also be extended, which in turn should help to reduce development costs. The maintainability of software is improved in terms of better standards of documentation and changes to software can take place at a localised level.

Development time is shorter and development costs are lower. Reliability is improved. OOP is useful for the rapid prototyping of systems.

Data abstraction is a key feature of OOP. Classes contain data structures and methods that operate on the structures.

In Turbo Pascal data abstraction can be implemented by using Turbo units. Such units can allow for the implementation of data structures and methods to be kept private from a user. This has the advantage that the underlying structure and methods algorithms can be changed without any inconvenience to the user.

Classes are defined in Turbo Pascal units to allow for re-use and extensibility of classes. A class mey inherit all the characteristics, data structures and methods, from another class. Inherited methods can be overridden by overloading (using the same method name) the name of the inherited method and using a different method algorithm.

Methods that are overridden should be declared as virtual. Every object type that has virtual methods must have a constructor that is invoked before any call to a virtual method is possible. When overridden virtual methods are called from a single method, the appropriate overridden method for the class will be substituted at run-time. This is known as late-binding.

Polymorphism permits an inherited class method to be used with an object such that, the method calls other methods appropriate to the class of the object.

Classes defined in a Turbo Pascal unit can be imported from the unit such that new classes can be formed that inherit from the imported classes. This is the basis of class extensibility. A class must contain virtual methods if it is to be extended.

Instances of objects can be defined as having either static or dynamic memory allocation.

Only dynamic objects need to use destructors to 'clean-up' memory space when an object is no longer needed.

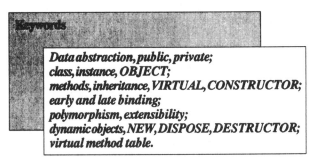

Keywords

*Data abstraction, public, private;
class, instance, OBJECT;
methods, inheritance, VIRTUAL, CONSTRUCTOR;
early and late binding;
polymorphism, extensibility;
dynamic objects, NEW, DISPOSE, DESTRUCTOR;
virtual method table.*

19.9 Questions.

1. Derive a Turbo Pascal unit that describes the class of object called a point, as used in this chapter. Using inheritance and polymorphism describe further classes for horizontal and vertical straight lines, a right-angled triangle, a square, a rectangle and a circle.

2. Using the Turbo Pascal unit created in question (1), write a program to create and display different figures made up from classes of objects described in the unit. Hint - a profile of a lorry can be made up from circles as wheels, a rectangle as a body, a triangle as a spoiler, a square as a bonnet, etc. The figure should be displayed and moved horizontally across the screen. A function to move a shape around the screen using the arrowed keys is given in the Turbo Pascal 5.5 OOP Guide.

[3]. Using OOP, draw a turtle, and in response to the arrowed keys, move it around the screen. Draw straight lines showing the path of the turtle.

[4]. Using OOP, invent your own space invaders game. Program a gun-sight to move around the screen in response to the arrowed keys being pressed. Invaders appear in random positions on the screen at random intervals. Only when an invader is within the gun-sight can it be zapped!

[5]. Derive a Turbo Pascal unit that fully describe the class of object *dictionary,* implemented as a binary tree. The dictionary will have methods to load and save a file of words, and to search for and insert words.

[6]. Using the Turbo unit created in question (5) write an interactive program to read a text file of statements written in English, and check the spelling of each word. When a mis-spelling is encountered the system will give the user the opportunity to correct the word. When the first text file is being read, a second text file is being created, as a duplicate of the first, so that any words that are mis-spelt can be corrected and stored on the second file. Confine all words to lower-case letters.

20

Case Studies in OOP

This final chapter brings together the work on Pascal programming and the use of data structures found in previous chapters. This information is combined with the object-oriented approach to building software systems. The two case studies are the most extensive that the reader will encounter in this book. Both systems have been fully tested and can be implemented on any PC compatible microcomputer that uses Borland's Turbo Pascal version 5.5.

20.1 Case Study One.

The first of two case studies shows how a music composing system can be implemented using OOP. The system is menu driven and enables simple tunes to be composed at the computer keyboard and played back to the composer at different tempos.

20.2 Mini-Composer Specification.

The human-computer interface for this case study is one screen of information and is shown below in figure 20.1.

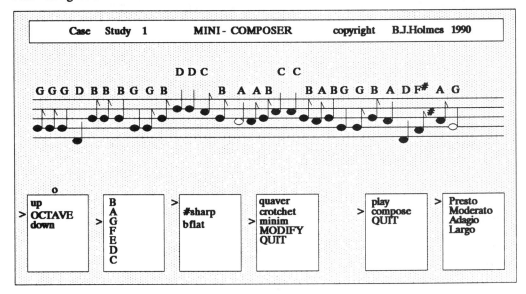

Figure 20.1 Human-computer Interface for the Mini-Composer Case Study One

The user is presented with a screen of menus, each with its own line cursor. The initial menu is given as

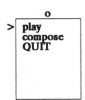

where the > symbol is the line cursor and is controlled by the up-arrow and down-arrow keys on the numeric pad of the keyboard. The circle o above the menu indicates that it is the current 'active' menu. From the initial menu, if **play** is selected (pointed at by the line cursor and selected by pressing the RETURN or ENTRY key), the next menu to become active is the speed or tempo at which the stored tune is to be played.

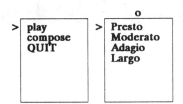

Here the user is given a choice of four tempos, although there more as depicted in figure 20.2. The choice of tempo equates to the number of beats per minute. This has been taken as the amount of time a note should be played for, or the delay factor of a note.

Tempo		Delay Factor
very slow	Larghissimo	
	Largo	27
	Larghetto	
	Grave	
	Lento	
	Adagio	16
slow	Adagietto	
	Andante	
medium	Andantino	
	Moderato	10
fast	Allegretto	
	Allegro	
	Vivace	
	Veloce	
	Presto	6
very fast	Prestissimo	

Figure 20.2 Selection of tempos and the corresponding Delay factors.

When the appropriate tempo has been selected the stored tune is played to the composer. If no tune had been composed the system would return to the initial menu.

Upon selecting compose from the initial menu, four further menus become respectively active, one at a time.

The first of these four menus allows a composer to select the octave. OCTAVE contains middle C; **up** is one octave above and **down** is one octave below the middle C octave. In other words this system only has a three octave range. After the appropriate octave has been selected the next menu allows the composer to choose a note.

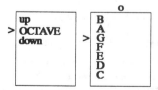

The frequency of notes in the octave of middle C is shown in figure 20.3 over the page. Corresponding notes in the next octave up are obtained by doubling the respective frequencies of the notes and those in the next octave down are obtained by halving the respective frequencies of the notes.

Note	Frequency Hz
C	261.63
D	293.66
E	329.63
F	349.23
G	392.00
A	440.00
B	493.88

**Figure 20.3 Frequency of notes
in octave containing middle C**

After a note has been chosen the next menu to become active allows the composer to choose a **pure note**, a **b flat** or a **# sharp**. The blank line above the **#** sharp, being pointed at by the line cursor, indicates a pure note.

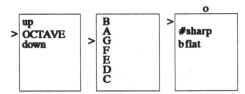

The final menu of this series enables a composer to choose the type of note, **quaver,
crotchet** or **minim**, **MODIFY** the previous selection of octave, note, pure/sharp/flat, or to
QUIT the composition. If the composer selects QUIT the last three selections of octave, note
and pure/sharp/flat are ignored.

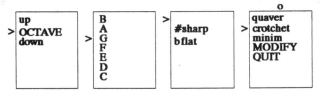

When a note of music is composed it will appear in the correct position on a stave, with the name of the note printed above the note, as depicted in figure 20.4. The sound of the note is also played, in fixed Largo tempo, at the time it is created.

Figure 20.4 Notes on a stave

The next menu to become active is the initial menu and the user is given a choice of playing the tune that has been composed, being allowed to continue with the composition or quiting from the system and thereby destroying the tune that was composed and stored in the memory of the computer.

There are no facilities for editting a note once it has been displayed on the stave and played. Similarly no facility exists for storing the tune on floppy disc and retrieving the tune during a session at the computer.

20.3 Unit Design.

The key to designing a simple yet effective implementation of the specification is to modularise the programming components. From the specification it should be evident that the following units need to be created.

Screens - a unit to draw rectangular windows on the screen and manipulate the information contained in the windows. This is the basis of the menu system.

Music - a unit to draw musical notes on the screen and play the musical notes.

MusicStore - a unit to store the musical notes as they are created at the keyboard and play the entire tune in the required tempo.

Figure 20.5 illustrates the order in which the units are to be developed and how they contribute towards the final program.

In designing an object oriented approach to program development it is only necessary at this stage to sort out what classes of objects are required and to fully document these classes at the INTERFACE level of each unit. The implementation details of the classes can be postponed until a later stage in the development of the system.

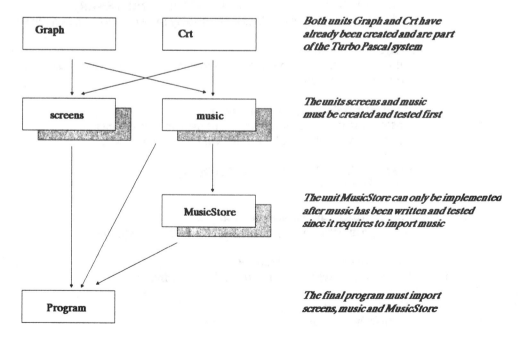

Graph   Crt

Both units Graph and Crt have already been created and are part of the Turbo Pascal system

screens   music

The units screens and music must be created and tested first

MusicStore

The unit MusicStore can only be implemented after music has been written and tested since it requires to import music

Program

The final program must import screens, music and MusicStore

Figure 20.5 Import diagram showing the units that need to be imported at the different levels
of program development.

The class of object known as a windo (excuse the spelling, only window is a pre-defined identifier in Turbo Pascal) is defined in the unit that follows.

```
UNIT screens;
INTERFACE
USES Graph,Crt;
TYPE
    windo = OBJECT
            X1,Y1,X2,Y2,X,Y,Ymin,Ymax : INTEGER;
            {X1,Y1 - coordinates of the top left-hand corner of the window;
            X2,Y2 - coordinates of the bottom right-hand corner of the window;
            X,Y - coordinates of the current marker for the active window;
            Ymin, Ymax - ordinate values of the top and bottom of the entries
            in the window}

            contents:ARRAY[1..25] OF MaxString;
            {the contents of every window is stored in an array of 25 lines (max) with
            each line containing 80 characters (max)}

            current, NextEntry: INTEGER;
            {current is the current ordinal position of the line cursor and
            NextEntry is the position of the next line of text to be inserted
            into the window}

            PROCEDURE create(newX1,newY1,newX2,newY2:INTEGER);
            {creates a new window but does NOT display the window on the screen}

            PROCEDURE show;
            {draws a rectangular window on the screen with the coordinates used
            to create the window}

            PROCEDURE insert(item:MaxString);
            {inserts a string of text into one line of the window and increases
            the NextEntry subscript by 1 if the window is not full of text}

            PROCEDURE select(VAR item:MaxString);
            {select a line of text from the window}

            PROCEDURE CurrentWindowOn;
            {display a marker (circle) above the current 'active' window}

            PROCEDURE CurrentWindowOff;
            {erase the marker above the current 'active' window}

            PROCEDURE showCursor;
            {display the line cursor in the correct position}

            PROCEDURE eraseCursor;
            {erase the line cursor}
```

PROCEDURE move;
{Move the position of the line cursor by pressing the up-arrow or
down-arrow keys on the numeric pad. The line cursor is a wrap-
around cursor so continuous depression of the down-arrow key
will cause the cursor to move down to the last item in the window,
then wrap-around to the item at the top of the window. A similar
feature happens when the up-arrow key is depressed, only the cursor
wraps around in the opposite direction}
END; {windo}

The class of object known as a MusicalNote is an ancestor of minim, crotchet and quaver.
These classes of objects are depicted in the next unit.

UNIT music;
INTERFACE
USES Graph, Crt;
TYPE
　　　ToneType = (flat, pure, sharp);
　　　MusicalNote = OBJECT
　　　　　　　octave : STRING [6];
　　　　　　　note : STRING [2];
　　　　　　　{The characteristics of a musical note are the octave
　　　　　　　it is played in - octave corresponds to the menu choice
　　　　　　　up, OCTAVE, down; and the type of note corresponding to
　　　　　　　the menu choices BAGFEDC and pure (blank line), #sharp
　　　　　　　or b flat}

　　　　　　　CONSTRUCTOR create(NewOctave:STRING; NewNote:STRING);
　　　　　　　{Musical notes must be dynamically created and destroyed
　　　　　　　since the number of notes is not known in advance. Notes
　　　　　　　are created at run-time by the composer}

　　　　　　　DESTRUCTOR finalise;
　　　　　　　{When the system is no longer required the data structures that
　　　　　　　contain the notes must relinquish memory space back to the heap}

　　　　　　　FUNCTION duration:INTEGER; VIRTUAL;
　　　　　　　{duration is the length of a note and is dependent upon the type of
　　　　　　　note: a minim will be played for 4x the normal duration of a quaver;
　　　　　　　a crotchet will be played for 2x the normal duration of a quaver}

　　　　　　　PROCEDURE display(x,y:INTEGER;tone:ToneType); VIRTUAL;
　　　　　　　{The procedure is dependent upon the type of note; the
　　　　　　　diagrammatic representation of a note is displayed in the
　　　　　　　correct position x,y on the stave}

　　　　　　　PROCEDURE ShowNote(x,y:INTEGER);
　　　　　　　{The procedure displays the value of the note on the stave}

```
            PROCEDURE play(tempo:STRING);
            {The procedure will play the note that has been composed using
            the tempo that has been chosen}

            PROCEDURE stave(x,y:INTEGER);
            {The procedure will plot the stave, show the value of the note,
            calculate the position of the diagrammatic representation of
            the note and display the note}
        END; {MusicalNote}
```

{Since minims, crotchets and quavers differ in their characteristics of duration
of sound and their diagrammatic representation, they inherit all the characteristics
of MusicalNote and have the function duration and the procedure display overwritten.
If both duration and display are virtual methods then the correct function and
procedure is allocated to the note at run-time}

```
minim=   OBJECT(MusicalNote)
            FUNCTION duration:INTEGER; VIRTUAL;
            PROCEDURE display(x,y:INTEGER;tone:ToneType); VIRTUAL;
         END;


crotchet=OBJECT(MusicalNote)
            FUNCTION duration:INTEGER; VIRTUAL;
            PROCEDURE display(x,y:INTEGER;tone:ToneType); VIRTUAL;
         END;


quaver=   OBJECT(MusicalNote)
            PROCEDURE display(x,y:INTEGER;tone:ToneType); VIRTUAL;
         END;
```

Finally the same technique used in chapter 19 for storing dynamic objects in a linked list is
used here to store notes in a linked list.

```
UNIT MusicStore;
INTERFACE
USES music;
TYPE
     pointer= ^ node;
     NotePointer= ^ MusicalNote;
     node=RECORD
             item:NotePointer;
             link:pointer;
          END;

LinkedList=OBJECT
             head, rear :pointer;
             CONSTRUCTOR initialise;
             {create a linked list to store the notes}
```

```
        DESTRUCTOR finalise;VIRTUAL;
        {relinquish memory space back to the system heap}

        PROCEDURE insert(item:NotePointer);
        {insert a new note into the linked list}

        PROCEDURE ListOut(tempo:STRING);
        {play every note, in the chosen tempo, in the correct order,
         from the linked list}
    END; {LinkedList}
```

20.4 Unit Implementation.

The IMPLEMENTATION sections of the units screens, music and MusicStore are given below. The TYPE definition of the classes and methods have been omitted from the INTERFACE section since it would only duplicate what was given in the last section.

```
UNIT screens;
INTERFACE
USES Graph,Crt;
```

(TYPE omitted since the information is found in section 20.3)

```
IMPLEMENTATION
VAR
        GraphDriver, GraphMode:INTEGER;

PROCEDURE windo.create(newX1,newY1,newX2,newY2:INTEGER);
BEGIN
        X1:=newX1;Y1:=newY1;X2:=newX2;Y2:=newY2;
        X:=(X1+X2) DIV 2;Y:=Y1-10; {coordinates of current marker for active window}
        Ymin:=Y1;Ymax:=Y1; {Ymin=Ymax since there are no entries in the window}
        NextEntry:=1;Current:=1; {since window is empty both subscripts are set at 1}
END; {windo.create}

PROCEDURE windo.insert(item:STRING);
BEGIN
        contents[NextEntry]:=item;
        {Test to see if the next entry can be accommodated within the window frame. Assume
         that one entry has a line width of 10 pixels}
        IF NextEntry < (Y2-Y1-10) DIV 10 THEN
        BEGIN
           NextEntry:=NextEntry+1;
           Ymax:=Ymax+10;
        END;
END; {windo.insert}

PROCEDURE windo.select(VAR item:STRING);
BEGIN
        item:=contents[current];
END; {windo.select}
```

```
PROCEDURE windo.show;
VAR
      index:INTEGER;
BEGIN
      Rectangle(X1,Y1,X2,Y2); {draw window frame}
      {output the contents of the array into the window frame}
      FOR index:=1 TO NextEntry-1 DO
          OutTextXY(X1+10,Y1+(10*index),contents[index]);
      {end for}
END; {windo.show}

PROCEDURE windo.CurrentWindowOn;
BEGIN
      circle(X,Y,3); {draw a circle to show the active window}
END; {windo.CurrentWindowOn}

PROCEDURE windo.CurrentWindowOff;
VAR
      colour:WORD;
BEGIN
      {erase the circle above the active window}
      colour:=GetColor;
      SetColor(GetBkColor);
      circle(X,Y,3);
      SetColor(colour);
END; {windo.CurrentWindowOff}

PROCEDURE windo.ShowCursor;
BEGIN
      OutTextXY(X1-10,Y1+10,'>');
END; {cursor.Show}

PROCEDURE windo.eraseCursor;
VAR
      colour:WORD;
BEGIN
      colour:=GetColor;
      SetColor(GetBkColor);
      windo.ShowCursor;
      SetColor(colour);
END; {windo.eraseCursor}

FUNCTION direction(VAR Yinc:INTEGER):BOOLEAN;
```

{This is an adaptation of the method used in Borland's Turbo Pascal Version 5.5 OOP
Guide, to move an object about the screen. The purpose of the function in the context
of this unit is to detect whether the line cursor is to be moved up or down the menu.

The up-arrow and down-arrow keys use extended two byte codes, therefore, it is necessary
to read a first character and if the code is zero to read a second character. If the second

character is code 72 then the line cursor is to be moved upwards, if the code is 80 then the line cursor is to be moved downwards. The variable Yinc is set to -1 for upward movement, 0 for no movement and +1 for downward movement. Only when the RETURN or ENTRY key is pressed (code 13), will this signal that a selection has been made from the menu.}

```
VAR
      KeyChar:CHAR;
      quit:BOOLEAN;
BEGIN
      Yinc:=0;
      direction:=TRUE;
      REPEAT
         KeyChar:=ReadKey;
         quit:=TRUE;
         CASE ORD(KeyChar) OF
             0: BEGIN
                   KeyChar:=ReadKey;
                   CASE ORD(KeyChar) OF
                      72:Yinc:=-1;
                      80:Yinc:=+1;
                   ELSE
                      quit:=FALSE;
                   END;
                END;
             13:direction:=FALSE;
         ELSE
             quit:=FALSE;
         END;
      UNTIL quit;
END; {direction}


PROCEDURE windo.move;
VAR
      Yinc:INTEGER;
BEGIN
      ShowCursor;
      WHILE direction(Yinc) DO
      BEGIN
         eraseCursor;
         {calculate the new position of the cursor, if this position is beyond the top of
          the window then wrap around to the last entry in the window}
         Y1:=Y1+(10*Yinc);
         IF Y1 < Ymin THEN
         BEGIN
             Y1:=Ymax-10;
             current:=NextEntry-1;
         END
         {if the calculated position of the line cursor is beyond the last entry in the window
          then wrap around to the first entry in the window}
```

```
        ELSE IF Y1 > Ymax-10 THEN
        BEGIN
            Y1:= Ymin;
            current:=1;
        END
        {line cursor movement is within the limits of the entries in the window}
        ELSE
            current:=current+Yinc;
        {end if}
        ShowCursor;
    END;
END; {windo.move}


BEGIN
    {initialisation of screen graphics}
    GraphDriver:=Detect;
    InitGraph(GraphDriver, GraphMode,");
    IF GraphResult < > grOK THEN
        HALT;
    {end if}
END. {screens}



UNIT music;
INTERFACE
USES Graph, Crt;
```

(TYPE omitted since the information is found in section 20.3)

```
IMPLEMENTATION
CONST
    radius=4; {used to depict the size of the note on the screen}
    time=10; {used in the duration of a note}
    displacement=55; {vertical distance above the graphical representation of a note}
TYPE
    NoteType=(C,D,E,F,G,A,B);
VAR
    GraphDriver, GraphMode:INTEGER;
    frequency:ARRAY[C..B] OF INTEGER; {array used to store frequency of the notes}
    index:NoteType;
    NoteValue:NoteType;
    tone:ToneType;
    x,y:INTEGER; {position on the stave where the note is to be drawn}

CONSTRUCTORMusicalNote.create(NewOctave:STRING; NewNote:STRING);
BEGIN
    octave:=NewOctave;
    note:=NewNote;
END; {MusicalNote.create}
```

```
DESTRUCTOR MusicalNote.finalise;
BEGIN
END; {MusicalNote.finalise}

FUNCTION MusicalNote.duration:INTEGER;
BEGIN
      duration:=time;
END;

PROCEDURE MusicalNote.display(x,y:INTEGER;tone:ToneType);
BEGIN
END; {MusicalNote.display}

PROCEDURE MusicalNote.ShowNote(x,y:INTEGER);
BEGIN
      OutTextXY(x,y-displacement,note[1]);
      OutTextXY(x+5,y-displacement-5, note[2]);
END; {MusicalNote.ShowNote}

PROCEDURE MusicalNote.play(tempo:STRING);
VAR
      DelayFactor:INTEGER; {period of time note sounds for, corresponding to tempo}
      FrequencyFactor:REAL; {used to select the frequency of a note in an octave}
      NoteFrequency:INTEGER;
      SemiTone:INTEGER;
BEGIN
      CASE note[1] OF
      'A':NoteValue:=A;
      'B':NoteValue:=B;
      'C':NoteValue:=C;
      'D':NoteValue:=D;
      'E':NoteValue:=E;
      'F':NoteValue:=F;
      'G':NoteValue:=G;
      END;

      CASE note[2] OF
      '#':tone:=sharp;
      'b':tone:=flat;
      '':tone:=pure;
      END;

      CASE tempo[1] OF
      'L':DelayFactor:=27; {Largo}
      'A':DelayFactor:=16; {Adagio}
      'M':DelayFactor:=10; {Moderato}
      'P':DelayFactor:=6; {Presto}
      END;
```

```
CASE octave[1] OF
'd': FrequencyFactor:=0.5; {down}
'O': FrequencyFactor:=1; {OCTAVE}
'u': FrequencyFactor:=2; {up}
END;

{calculate the frequency of a note from the information selected from the menus}

NoteFrequency:=ROUND(FrequencyFactor*frequency[NoteValue]);
IF (tone=sharp) AND (NoteValue < > B) THEN
    SemiTone:=(frequency[SUCC(NoteValue)]-frequency[NoteValue]) DIV 2
ELSE IF (tone=flat) AND (NoteValue < > C) THEN
    SemiTone:=(frequency[PRED(NoteValue)]-frequency[NoteValue]) DIV 2
ELSE
    SemiTone:=0;
{end if}
NoteFrequency:=NoteFrequency+ROUND(FrequencyFactor*SemiTone);
SOUND(NoteFrequency);
Delay(duration*DelayFactor); {play note for period according to selected tempo}
NoSound;
END; {MusicalNote.play}

PROCEDURE MusicalNote.stave;
VAR
    index:INTEGER;
BEGIN
    {draw stave}
    FOR index:=1 TO 5 DO
    BEGIN
        Line(0,y-10*(index-1),690,y-10*(index-1));
    END;

    {calculate ordinal position of note with respect to the octave}
    CASE octave[1] OF
    'u': y:=y-35;
    'O': {do not adjust};
    'd': y:=y+35;
    END;

    ShowNote(x,y); {display the value of the note}
    {calculate the ordinal position of the note within the chosen octave}
    CASE note[1] OF
    'B':y:=y-20;
    'A':y:=y-15;
    'G':y:=y-10;
    'F':y:=y-5;
    'E':{base line};
    'D':y:=y+5;
    'C':y:=y+10;
    END;
```

```
      CASE note[2] OF
      '#':tone:=sharp;
      'b':tone:=flat;
      '':tone:=pure;
      END;

      display(x,y,tone); {display graphical representataion of note on the stave}
END; {MusicalNote.stave}

FUNCTION minim.duration:INTEGER;
BEGIN
      duration:=4*time;
END; {minim.duration}

PROCEDURE minim.display(x,y:INTEGER;tone:ToneType);
BEGIN
      Ellipse(x,y,0,360,radius,radius DIV 2);
      Line(x+radius,y,x+radius,y-20);
      IF tone=sharp THEN
          OutTextXY(x+radius+5,y-15,'#')
      ELSE IF tone=flat THEN
          OutTextXY(x+radius+5,y-15,'b');
      {end if}
END; {minim.display}

FUNCTION crotchet.duration:INTEGER;
BEGIN
      duration:=2*time;
END; {crotchet.duration}

PROCEDURE crotchet.display(x,y:INTEGER;tone:ToneType);
BEGIN
      Ellipse(x,y,0,360,radius,radius DIV 2);
      Line(x+radius,y,x+radius,y-20);
      FillEllipse(x,y,radius, radius DIV 2);
      IF tone=sharp THEN
          OutTextXY(x+radius+5,y-15,'#')
      ELSE IF tone=flat THEN
          OutTextXY(x+radius+5,y-15,'b');
      {end if}
END; {crotchet.display}

PROCEDURE quaver.display(x,y:INTEGER;tone:ToneType);
BEGIN
      Ellipse(x,y,0,360,radius,radius DIV 2);
      Line(x+radius,y,x+radius,y-20);
      FillEllipse(x,y,radius, radius DIV 2);
      Line(x+radius,y-20, x+radius+5,y-10);
```

```
        IF tone=sharp THEN
            OutTextXY(x+radius+5,y-15,'#')
        ELSE IF tone=flat THEN
            OutTextXY(x+radius+5,y-15,'b');
        {end if}
END; {quaver.display}


BEGIN
        {initialise screen graphics}
        GraphDriver:=Detect;
        InitGraph(GraphDriver, GraphMode,'');
        IF GraphResult < > grOK THEN
            HALT;
        {end if}

        {initialise frequency of notes in Middle C octave}
        frequency[C]:=262; frequency[D]:=294; frequency[E]:=330;
        frequency[F]:=349; frequency[G]:=392; frequency[A]:=440;
        frequency[B]:=494;
END. {music}




UNIT MusicStore;
INTERFACE
USES music;
```

(TYPE omitted since information found in section 20.3)

```
IMPLEMENTATION
CONSTRUCTOR LinkedList.initialise;
BEGIN
        head:=NIL;
        rear:=head;
END; {LinkedList.initialise}

DESTRUCTOR LinkedList.finalise;
VAR
        temp:pointer;
BEGIN
        WHILE head < > NIL DO
        BEGIN
            temp:=head;
            DISPOSE(temp^.item, finalise);
            head:=temp^.link;
            DISPOSE(temp);
        END;
END; {LinkedList.finalise}
```

```
PROCEDURE LinkedList.insert(item:NotePointer);
VAR
     temp:pointer;
BEGIN
     NEW(temp);
     temp^.item:=item;
     temp^.link:=NIL;
     IF head = NIL THEN
        head:=temp
     ELSE
        rear^.link:=temp;
     {end if}
     rear:=temp;
END; {LinkedList.insert}


PROCEDURE LinkedList.ListOut(tempo:STRING);
VAR
     current:pointer;
BEGIN
     current:=head;
     WHILE current < > NIL DO
     BEGIN
        current^.item^.play(tempo);
        current:=current^.link;
     END;
END; {LinkedList.ListOut}
END. {MusicStore}
```

20.5 Program Design.

The hard work in coding a solution to this problem is almost over. Once the units have been implemented and fully tested the program to compose and play a tune is straightforward.

The first level of program design is:

```
display menus
get data from initial menu
WHILE menu item < > QUIT DO
   IF menu item = play THEN
       play music
   ELSE
       compose music
   {end if}
   get data from initial menu
{end while}
close system
```

Display menus involves creating different windows on the screen, inserting the appropriate text into each window and displaying the menus.

A function should be developed for capturing a selected item from any specified menu. This will take the form:

> *FUNCTION CaptureData(VAR CurrentWindow:windo):STRING;*
>   *show which window is current;*
>   *move the cursor to the requested item;*
>   *select item;*
>   *window is deselected and no longer current;*
> *END;*

Having defined a function to capture data it can be used to obtain information on the octave, frequency, tone and beat, from the menus, about a note

To compose a tune the algorithm should be of the form:

> *PROCEDURE compose;*
>   *REPEAT*
>   *get details of note;*
>   *WHILE beat menu = MODIFY DO*
>   *get details of note*
>   *{end while}*
>   *IF beat menu < > QUIT THEN*
>   *play note;*
>   *{end if}*
>   *UNTIL beat menu = QUIT;*
> *END;*

Where *play note* is a procedure to select, display, play and store the note as part of the tune.

20.6 Program Implementation.

PROGRAM CaseStudyOne;
{program to allow a user to compose and play simple tunes}

USES music, MusicStore, screens;
CONST
        forever = FALSE;
TYPE
        quaverPoint = ^ quaver;
        crotchetPoint = ^ crotchet;
        minimPoint = ^ minim;
VAR
        banner, menu, beat, frequency, octavo, tempo, tone :windo; {menu objects}
        note1:quaver; note2:crotchet; note3:minim; {note objects}
        store:LinkedList; {data store object}
        NoteBeat, NoteOctave, NoteFrequency, NoteTone, NoteValue:STRING;
        MenuItem, TempItem:STRING;
        x,y:INTEGER; {coordinates of a note on the stave}

```
PROCEDURE CreateWindows;
{build and display screen menus}

BEGIN
     store.initialise;
     x:=10; y:=150;
     WITH banner DO
     BEGIN
        create(10,1,690,31);
        insert(' Case Study 1    MINI-COMPOSER    copyright B.J.Holmes 1990');
        show;
     END;

     WITH menu DO
     BEGIN
        create(500,240,580,330);
        insert('play'); insert('compose'); insert('QUIT');
        show;
     END;

     WITH tempo DO
     BEGIN
        create(600,240,680,330);
        insert('Presto'); insert('Moderato'); insert('Adagio'); insert('Largo');
        show;
     END;

     WITH beat DO
     BEGIN
        create(320,240,400,330);
        insert('quaver'); insert('crotchet'); insert('minim');
        insert('MODIFY'); insert('QUIT');
        show;
     END;

     WITH frequency DO
     BEGIN
        create(120,240,200,330);
        insert(' B'); insert(' A'); insert(' G'); insert(' F'); insert(' E');
        insert(' D'); insert(' C');
        show;
     END;

     WITH octavo DO
     BEGIN
        create(10,240,100,330);
        insert('up' ); insert('OCTAVE'); insert('down');
        show;
     END;
```

```
        WITH tone DO
        BEGIN
           create(220,240,300,330);
           insert(' '); insert('# sharp'); insert('b flat');
           show;
        END;
END; {CreateWindows}


FUNCTION CaptureData(VAR CurrentWindow:windo):STRING;
{extract a selected item from a menu}
VAR
        item:MaxString;
BEGIN
        WITH CurrentWindow DO
        BEGIN
           CurrentWindowON;
           move;
           select(item);
           CurrentWindowOFF;
           CaptureData:=item;
        END;
END; {CaptureData}


PROCEDURE CaptureNote;
{select from the menus information on a particular note}
BEGIN
        NoteOctave:=CaptureData(octavo);
        NoteFrequency:=CaptureData(frequency);
        NoteTone:=CaptureData(tone);
        NoteBeat:=CaptureData(beat);
        NoteValue:=NoteFrequency[3]+NoteTone[1];
END; {CaptureNote}


PROCEDURE PlayNote;
{create a note, display it on the stave, play the note and store it as part of the tune}
CONST
        PlayTempo='Largo';
BEGIN
        IF NoteBeat='quaver' THEN
        BEGIN
           note1.create(NoteOctave, NoteValue);
           note1.stave(x,y);
           note1.play(PlayTempo);
           store.insert(NEW(quaverPoint, create(NoteOctave, NoteValue)));
        END;
        IF NoteBeat='crotchet' THEN
        BEGIN
           note2.create(NoteOctave, NoteValue);
           note2.stave(x,y);
```

```
            note2.play(PlayTempo);
            store.insert(NEW(crotchetPoint, create(NoteOctave, NoteValue)));
        END;
        IF NoteBeat='minim' THEN
        BEGIN
            note3.create(NoteOctave, NoteValue);
            note3.stave(x,y);
            note3.play(PlayTempo);
            store.insert(NEW(minimPoint, create(NoteOctave, NoteValue)));
        END;
        x:=x+15;
END; {PlayNote}


PROCEDURE compose;
BEGIN
        REPEAT
            CaptureNote;
            WHILE NoteBeat = 'MODIFY' DO
                CaptureNote;
            {end while}
            IF NoteBeat < > 'QUIT' THEN PlayNote;
        UNTIL NoteBeat='QUIT';
END; {compose}



BEGIN
        CreateWindows;
        MenuItem:=CaptureData(menu);
        WHILE MenuItem < > 'QUIT' DO
        BEGIN
            IF MenuItem='play' THEN
                store.ListOut(CaptureData(tempo))
            ELSE
                compose;
            {end if}
            MenuItem:=CaptureData(Menu);
        END;
        {end while}
        Graph.RestoreCrtMode;
        store.finalise;
END. {CaseStudyOne}
```

20.7 Extensions.

The reader might be interested in extending this case study in the following ways.

When a tune has been composed store the contents of the linked list in a secondary storage file. Give the composer the option to load the contents of this file from the initial menu.

Offer a facility to edit a piece of music. This will require the insertion, amendment or deletion of notes on the stave.

Implement a note pointer (bouncing ball!) to show which note is being played from the stave during the playback of a tune.

As this is the last chapter of the book the reader should have gained sufficient confidence in programming to be able to complete these extensions without a need to look at the answers! There are sufficient examples in the latter part of the book to aid the reader in the implementation of these extensions. For these reasons the answers to the extensions are not available in this text or in the Answer Supplement.

20.8 Case Study Two.

The second case study shows how a small database package can be implemented using OOP. The system is menu driven and enables records to be created, amended, deleted, displayed on the screen of a VDU and output to a printer. The system has been built to store the details of companies who participate in taking students on an industrial placement scheme.

20.9 Database Package Specification.

The human-computer interface for this package is more complex than for the last case study, owing to the fact that many more screen menus are involved. Upon loading and running the system the initial screen, figure 20.6, is displayed to a user.

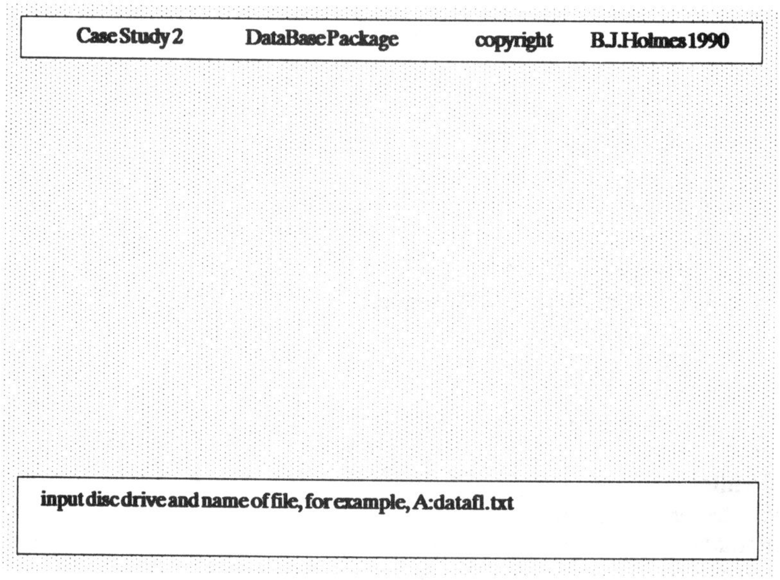

Case Study 2	DataBase Package	copyright	B.J.Holmes 1990

input disc drive and name of file, for example, A:datafl.txt

Figure 20.6

The name of the database file should already exist in the disc directory, even if the database is empty. Depending upon the user's response the system will respond with the appropriate messages given in figure 20.7. If there is a fatal error then the system will be abandoned and revert back to MSDOS (or Turbo Pascal), depending upon the version of the system being used.

System messages are displayed in a lower window for several seconds. If the message is a warning or an error the terminal will beep, otherwise no sound is emitted.

verify file opened

fatal error file not found

building tree data file from disc

Figure 20.7

If the database file is correctly loaded into memory from disc, the user will be presented with a menu as depicted in figure 20.8.

| Case Study 2 | DataBase Package | copyright | B.J.Holmes 1990 |

> input
modify
delete
inspect
display
print
QUIT

Figure 20.8

The access to information in a menu is via the line cursor and the *enter* or *return* key. This is the same technique that was used in the first case study. If the user selects input, the screen is cleared and a new menu appears as depicted in figure 20.9.

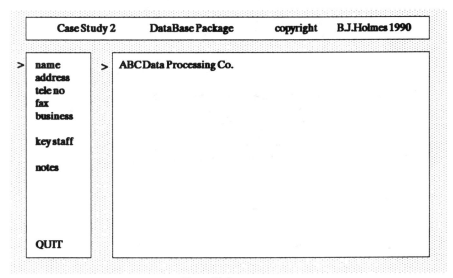

Figure 20.9

The left-hand menu of this screen contains the choice of fields for the records to be created. The right-hand window is used for inputting information about the record fields. For example, in figure 20.9, the user has selected the name field (this is the primary key field of the record), and input the name of the company *ABC Data Processing Co.* The data is accepted by pressing the *enter* or *return* key. The user is then free to select a new item from the left-hand menu and then input information about the selected field. Upon quiting from this screen the user will see one of two messages depicted in figure 20.10.

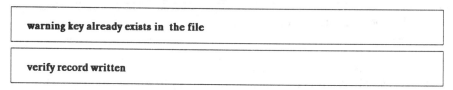

> **warning key already exists in the file**

> **verify record written**

Figure 20.10

If the key (information in the name field) already exists in the file the user will have lost the screenful of information and must reselect a new item from the menu depicted in figure 20.8.

When the user chooses the modify option from the menu, the key of the record to modify, must be input to the system. If this value is not known then the message *record does not exist with given key* is displayed, as shown in figure 20.12. If the value of the key is accepted then the information held in this record is displayed on the screen. The user is then at liberty to change any of the information, including the key field, in the record. The method of modification is the same as explained for inputting new information to a record. The user is presented with a screen of information similar to that shown in figure 20.11. When this screen is quit the message *verify record modified* will appear in a window at the bottom of the screen. Remember message windows only appear on the screen for a few seconds. There is no requirement for a user to press any keys to clear such windows unless specifically instructed to do so. The next menu to show is depicted in figure 20.8 and will allow the user to make another selection.

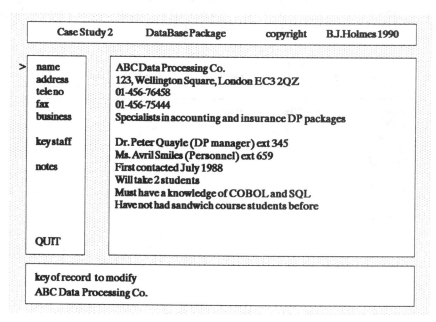

Figure 20.11

```
verify record modified
```

```
record does not exist with given key
```

Figure 20.12

If the option chosen is to delete a record, the system will respond by asking for the value of the key for the record to be deleted, figure 20.13.

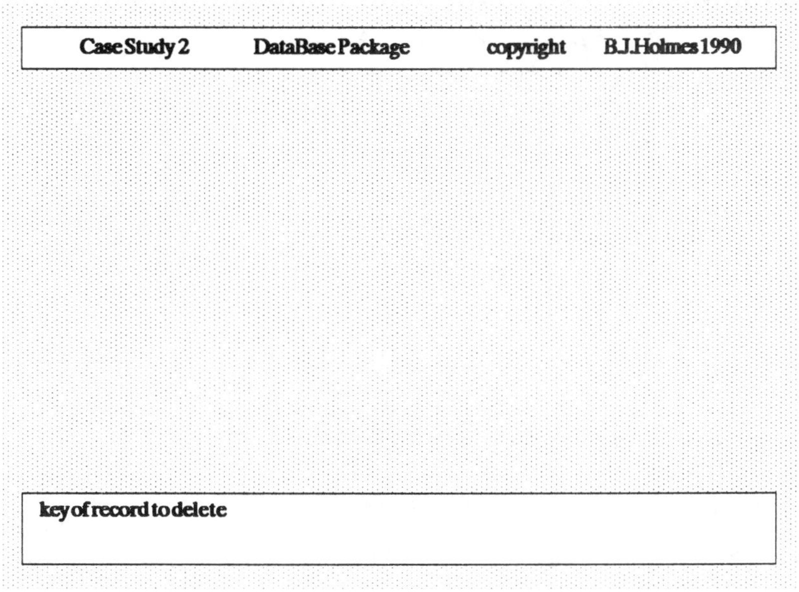

Case Study 2	DataBase Package	copyright	B.J.Holmes 1990

```
key of record to delete
```

Figure 20.13

The appropriate message, shown in figure 20.14, will depend upon the information the user inputs to the system.

```
verify record deleted
```

```
record does not exist with key given
```

Figure 20.14

Again returning to the menu depicted in figure 20.8 if the user selects to inspect a record, the system requests a value for the key of the record to be input. Depending upon this value the appropriate message from figure 20.16 will be displayed. If the key to the record exists the information is displayed on the screen in the format shown in figure 20.15. The user can browse through this screen at leisure since the signal to return to the menu depicted in figure 20.8, is the depression of any key to clear the screen.

Case Study 2	DataBase Package	copyright	B.J.Holmes 1990

name	ABC Data Processing Co.
address	123, Wellington Square, London EC3 2QZ
tele no	01-456-76458
fax	01-456-75444
business	Specialists in accounting and insurance DP packages
key staff	Dr. Peter Quayle (DP manager) ext 345
	Ms. Avril Smiles (Personnel) ext 659
notes	First contacted July 1988
	Will take 2 students
	Must have a knowledge of COBOL and SQL
	Have not had sandwich course students before
QUIT	

key of record
ABC Data Processing Co.

Figure 20.15

press any key to clear

record does not exist with key given

Figure 20.16

If the user requests to display every record in the file, the format of each record will be similar to that shown in figure 20.17. Progression from one record to the next is by pressing any key. The messages that accompany this part of the system are given in figure 20.18. The records are displayed in alphabetical key sequence. When the end of the file has been reached the *end of file* message will be displayed.

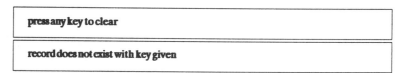

ABC Data Processing Co.
123, Wellington Square, London EC3 2QZ
01-456-76458
01-456-75444
Specialists in accounting and insurance DP packages

Dr. Peter Quayle (DP manager) ext 345
Ms. Avril Smiles (Personnel) ext 659
First contacted July 1988
Will take 2 students
Must have a knowledge of COBOL and SQL
Have not had sandwich course students before

Figure 20.17

contents of data file

press any key to change record

end of file

Figure 20.18

Should the user require a hard copy of the contents of the file, then the print option is chosen from the menu depicted in figure 20.8. A list of messages are then displayed to the user, these are shown in figure 20.19. Output will be directed to a printer that is on-line to the computer. Each record is printed on a new page until the entire contents of the file has been output.

PRINTER POWER ON AND SWITCHED ON-LINE?

press any key to confirm

output directed to printer

Figure 20.19

When the printed output is complete the system returns to the menu depicted in figure 20.8. If the user chooses to QUIT the system the contents of the file that is stored in memory must first be copied back to disc for future use. The message shown in figure 20.20 explains this to the user.

writing contents of tree file to disc

Figure 20.20

20.10 Unit Design.
This case study demonstrates the reusibility of a class of object and shows how such a class can also be extended to produce a new class of object. From the specification of what the system is required to do, it is very obvious that the unit screens developed in case study one, will be of use here. However, the class of object *windo* must be extended to cater for information to be input and output at a window at run-time, to turn the line-cursor on and off and to erase a particular screen.

A unit *NewScreens* should be created that contains a class of object known as *screen*. *Screen* inherits from *windo* defined in the unit screens.

The disc-based file is to be organised as a text file containing fixed-length records. The contents of this file is read into a binary tree structure at the time of opening the file. Provided the first record in the file has a key that is approximately half-way through the alphabet, the binary tree that is formed should be reasonably balanced. This will ensure that the time taken to search for a particular record will be reasonably fast. When the disc-based file is to be closed the contents of the binary tree must be copied back to the file. The tree must be traversed using a *preorder* tree traversal. A preorder traversal starts at the root node and writes the contents of the next node to the text file before traversing either of the subtrees. This algorithm ensures that the balanced structure of the tree is preserved on disc. All the user operations on the file, input, modify and delete will be with respect to the binary tree. Such operations have already been explained in chapter 15 on dynamic structures and should be familiar to the reader. A new unit, called *FileUnit*, is required that defines methods to open and close the file, read, write, delete and display records from the file. Figure 20.21 illustrates the development and importation of the units required to build the database system.

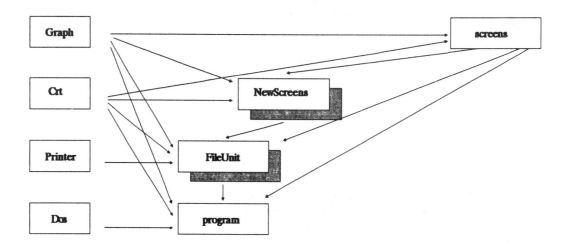

Figure 20.21 Import diagram showing the units that need to be imported at the different levels of program development

The class of object known as *screen* is defined in the unit that follows.

```
UNIT NewScreens;
INTERFACE
USES Graph, Crt, screens;

TYPE
      screen=OBJECT(windo)

      PROCEDURE ScreenInput(NewCurrent:INTEGER; VAR SelectedItem:MaxString);
      {input text into a window at the position NewCurrent}

      PROCEDURE ScreenOutput(NewCurrent:INTEGER; SelectedItem:MaxString);
      {output text in a window at the position NewCurrent}
```

PROCEDURE CursorON(NewCurrent:INTEGER);
{show the line-cursor at the position NewCurrent}

PROCEDURE CursorOFF(NewCurrent:INTEGER);
{erase the line-cursor from the position NewCurrent}

PROCEDURE Erase;
{erase an entire window}
END; {screen}

The classes of object known as *TreeRecord* and *TreeFile* are defined in the unit that follows.

UNIT FileUnit;
INTERFACE
USES Graph, Printer, Crt, screens, NewScreens;
CONST
  MaxFields=15;
TYPE
  OutputMode=(vdu, print);
  RecordType=ARRAY[1..MaxFields] OF MaxString;

  TreeRecord= OBJECT
     RecordArray:RecordType;

     PROCEDURE InitialiseFields;
     {set each field to a null character}

     PROCEDURE BuildField(FieldNumber:INTEGER;
               field:MaxString);
     {store information in a single field of a record}
    END; {TreeRecord}

tree= ^ node;
node=RECORD
  left:tree;
  contents:RecordType;
  right:tree;
  END;

  TreeFile=OBJECT(TreeRecord)
    NameOfFile:TEXT;
    BinaryTree:tree;
    PROCEDURE OpenFile(name:MaxString; VAR success:BOOLEAN;
             VAR message:MaxString);
    {attempt to open the file specified and store the contents in a binary
    tree}
    PROCEDURE CloseFile;
    {store the contents of the binary tree back in the original data file}

```
          PROCEDURE WriteRecord(VAR success:BOOLEAN; VAR
                                     message:MaxString);
          {attempt to write a record, both success and message report on the
          outcome}

          PROCEDURE ReadRecord(key:MaxString; VAR success:BOOLEAN;
                                     VAR message:MaxString);
          {attempt to read a record using the supplied key}

          PROCEDURE DeleteRecord(key:MaxString; VAR success:BOOLEAN;
                                     VAR message:MaxString);
          {attempt to delete a record with the supplied key}

          PROCEDURE Display(mode:OutputMode);
          {output the contents of the file either on the screen (vdu) or at a
          printer (print)}
END; {TreeFile}
```

20.11 Unit Implementation.

The IMPLEMENTATION sections of the units NewScreens and FileUnit are given below.
The TYPE definition of the classes and methods have been omitted from the INTERFACE
section since this would only duplicate what was given in the last section.

```
UNIT NewScreens;
INTERFACE
USES Graph, Crt, screens;
```

(TYPE omitted since the information is found in section 20.10)

```
IMPLEMENTATION
PROCEDURE screen.ScreenInput(NewCurrent:INTEGER;VAR SelectedItem:MaxString);
CONST
        EnterKey=13;    DelKey=83;
        Xinc=8; {number of pixels assigned to plot each character}
        null=CHR(0);    MaxChar=80;
VAR
        KeyChar:CHAR;
        index, TempIndex, NewX,NewY:INTEGER;
        colour:WORD;
        item:MaxString;
        ExtendedCode:BOOLEAN;
BEGIN
        Rectangle(X1,Y1,X2,Y2); {draw window}
        NewX:=X1+10; NewY:=Y1+(10*NewCurrent); {position of first character}
        index:=0; {subscript to array item}
        REPEAT
           KeyChar:=ReadKey;
        UNTIL ORD(KeyChar)< >EnterKey;
```

```
      WHILE ORD(KeyChar) < > EnterKey DO
      BEGIN
         ExtendedCode: = FALSE;
         index: = index + 1;
         item[index]: = KeyChar; {store character in cell of array}
         OutTextXY(NewX,NewY,item[index]); {output character in window}
         KeyChar: = ReadKey;
         CASE ORD(KeyChar) OF
         0:  BEGIN {test for Del key being pressed}
                 ExtendedCode: = TRUE;
                 KeyChar: = ReadKey;
                 CASE ORD(KeyChar) OF
                 DelKey:   BEGIN {delete line of input text, clear window and array}
                              REPEAT
                                 colour: = GetColor;
                                 SetColor(GetBkColor);
                                 OutTextXY(NewX,NewY,item[index]);
                                 SetColor(colour);
                                 NewX: = NewX-Xinc;
                                 index: = index-1;
                              UNTIL index = 0;
                           END;
             END;
           END;
         END;
         IF (ORD(KeyChar) = DelKey) AND (ExtendedCode) THEN
            REPEAT
               KeyChar: = ReadKey;
            UNTIL ORD(KeyChar) < > EnterKey;
         {end if}
         NewX: = NewX + Xinc;
      END;

      FOR TempIndex: = index + 1 TO MaxChar DO
         item[TempIndex]: = null; {fill remainder of array with null characters}
      {end for}
      item[0]: = #80; {set the string length to maximum}
      SelectedItem: = item;
END; {screen.ScreenInput}

PROCEDURE screen.ScreenOutput(NewCurrent:INTEGER; SelectedItem:MaxString);
VAR
      NewX, NewY:INTEGER;
BEGIN
      NewX: = X1 + 10; NewY: = Y1 + (10*NewCurrent);
      OutTextXY(NewX,NewY,SelectedItem);
END; {screen.ScreenOutput}
```

```
PROCEDURE screen.CursorON(NewCurrent:INTEGER);
VAR
      NewX, NewY:INTEGER;
BEGIN
      NewX:=X1-10; NewY:=Y1+(10*NewCurrent);
      OutTextXY(NewX,NewY,'>');
END; {screen.CursorON}

PROCEDURE screen.CursorOFF(NewCurrent:INTEGER);
VAR
      colour:WORD;
BEGIN
      colour:=GetColor;
      SetColor(GetBkColor);
      screen.CursorON(NewCurrent);
      SetColor(colour);
END; {screen.CursorOFF}

PROCEDURE screen.Erase;
VAR
      colour:WORD;
BEGIN
      colour:=GetColor;
      SetColor(GetBkColor);
      Show;
      SetColor(colour);
END; {screen.Erase}
END.{NewScreens}


UNIT FileUnit;
INTERFACE
USES Graph, Printer, Crt, screens, NewScreens;

(TYPE omitted since the information is found in section 20.10)

IMPLEMENTATION
CONST
      null=CHR(0);
      FormFeed=CHR(12);

PROCEDURE TreeRecord.InitialiseFields;
VAR
      index:INTEGER;
BEGIN
      FOR index:=1 TO MaxFields DO
          RecordArray[index]:=null;
      {end for}
END; {TreeRecord.InitialiseFields}
```

```
PROCEDURE TreeRecord.BuildField(FieldNumber:INTEGER; field:MaxString);
BEGIN
      RecordArray[FieldNumber]:=field;
END; {TreeRecord.BuildField}

PROCEDURE initialise(VAR parent:tree);
BEGIN
      parent:=NIL;
END; {initialise}

PROCEDURE attach(VAR parent:tree; NewContents:RecordType; VAR
                       success:BOOLEAN; VAR message:MaxString);
BEGIN
     IF parent=NIL THEN
     BEGIN
        NEW(parent);
        parent ^ .left:=NIL;
        parent ^ .contents:=NewContents;
        parent ^ .right:=NIL;
        success:=TRUE;
        message:='transaction ok';
     END
     ELSE IF NewContents[1] < parent ^ .contents[1] THEN
        attach(parent ^ .left, NewContents, success, message)
     ELSE IF NewContents[1] > parent ^ .contents[1] THEN
        attach(parent ^ .right, NewContents, success, message)
     ELSE
     BEGIN
        success:=FALSE;
        message:='warning key already exists in the file';
     END;
END; {attach}

PROCEDURE search(VAR parent:tree; key:MaxString;   VAR NewContents:RecordType;
                     VAR success:BOOLEAN; VAR message:MaxString);
BEGIN
     IF parent = NIL THEN
     BEGIN
        success:=FALSE;
        message:='record does not exist with key given';
     END
     ELSE IF key < parent ^ .contents[1] THEN
        search(parent ^ .left, key, NewContents, success, message)
     ELSE IF key > parent ^ .contents[1] THEN
        search(parent ^ .right, key, NewContents, success, message)
     ELSE
     BEGIN
        success:=TRUE;
        message:='transaction ok';
```

```
                  NewContents:=parent ^ .contents;
           END;
           {end if}
END; {search}


PROCEDURE successor(VAR parent:tree; VAR NewContents:RecordType);
VAR
        temp:tree;
BEGIN
      IF parent < > NIL THEN
          IF parent ^ .left=NIL THEN
          BEGIN
              NewContents:=parent ^ .contents;
              temp:=parent;
              parent:=parent ^ .right;
              DISPOSE(temp);
          END
          ELSE
              successor(parent ^ .left, NewContents);
          {end if}
      {end if}
END; {successor}


PROCEDURE remove(VAR parent:tree; key:MaxString; VAR success:BOOLEAN;
                       VAR message:MaxString);
VAR
        temp:tree;
        NewContents:RecordType;
BEGIN
      IF parent < > NIL THEN
      BEGIN
          IF key=parent ^ .contents[1] THEN
          BEGIN
              success:=TRUE;
              IF (parent ^ .left=NIL) AND (parent ^ .right=NIL) THEN
              BEGIN
                  temp:=parent;
                  parent:=NIL;
                  DISPOSE(temp);
              END
              ELSE IF parent ^ .left = NIL THEN
              BEGIN
                  temp:=parent;
                  parent:=parent ^ .right;
                  DISPOSE(temp);
              END
              ELSE IF parent ^ .right = NIL THEN
              BEGIN
                  temp:=parent;
```

```
                    parent:=parent ^ .left;
                    DISPOSE(temp);
                END
                ELSE
                BEGIN
                    successor(parent ^ .right, NewContents);
                    parent ^ .contents:=NewContents;
                END
            END
            ELSE IF key < parent ^ .contents[1] THEN
                remove(parent ^ .left, key, success, message)
            ELSE
                remove(parent ^ .right, key, success, message);
            {end if}
        END
        ELSE
        BEGIN
            success:=FALSE;
            message:='warning supplied key not found in file';
        END;
        {end if}
END; {remove}


PROCEDURE FindAndWrite(VAR NameOfFile:TEXT; VAR parent:tree);
{preorder tree traversal for copying contents of tree to a text file}
VAR
        index:INTEGER;
BEGIN
        IF parent < > NIL THEN
        BEGIN
            FOR index:=1 TO MaxFields DO
                WriteLn(NameOfFile, parent ^ .contents[index]);
            {end if}
            FindAndWrite(NameOfFile, parent ^ .left);
            FindAndWrite(NameOfFile, parent ^ .right);
        END;
END; {FindAndWrite}


PROCEDURE TreeFile.OpenFile(    name:MaxString; VAR success:BOOLEAN;
                                VAR message:MaxString);
LABEL 1;
VAR
        index:INTEGER;
BEGIN
        ASSIGN(NameOfFile, name);
        {$I-}
        RESET(NameOfFile);
        {$I+}
        IF IOResult < > 0 THEN
```

```
        BEGIN
            success:=FALSE;
            message:='fatal error file not found';
            GOTO 1;
        END;
        initialise(BinaryTree);
        WHILE NOT EOF(NameOfFile) DO
        BEGIN
            FOR index:=1 TO MaxFields DO
                ReadLn(NameOfFile, RecordArray[index]);
            {end for}
            attach(BinaryTree, RecordArray, success, message);
        END;
        success:=TRUE;
1: {exit}
END; {TreeFile.OpenFile}


PROCEDURE TreeFile.CloseFile;
BEGIN
        REWRITE(NameOfFile);
        FindAndWrite(NameOfFile,BinaryTree);
        Close(NameOfFile);
END; {TreeFile.CloseFile}


PROCEDURE TreeFile.WriteRecord(VAR success:BOOLEAN;VAR message:MaxString);
BEGIN
        attach(BinaryTree, RecordArray, success, message);
END; {TreeFile.WriteRecord}


PROCEDURE TreeFile.ReadRecord(    key:MaxString; VAR success:BOOLEAN;
                                  VAR message:MaxString);
BEGIN
        search(BinaryTree, key, RecordArray, success, message);
END; {TreeFile.ReadRecord}


PROCEDURE TreeFile.DeleteRecord(key:MaxString; VAR success:BOOLEAN;
                                  VAR message:MaxString);
BEGIN
        remove(BinaryTree, key, success, message);
END; {TreeFile.DeleteRecord}


PROCEDURE TreeFile.Display(mode:CutputMode);
        PROCEDURE FindAndDisplay(VAR parent:tree);
        CONST
            X=10;
        VAR
            KeyPressed:CHAR;
            index, CharIndex:INTEGER;
        BEGIN
            IF parent < > NIL THEN
```

```
        BEGIN
            FindAndDisplay(parent ^ .left);
            IF mode=vdu THEN
            BEGIN
                FOR index:=1 TO MaxFields DO
                    OutTextXY(X, (10*index), parent ^ .contents [index]);
                {end for}
                KeyPressed:=Crt.ReadKey;
                ClearDevice;
            END
            ELSE
            BEGIN
                FOR index:=1 TO MaxFields DO
                BEGIN
                    CharIndex:=1;
                    WHILE parent ^ .contents[index, CharIndex] < > null DO
                    BEGIN
                        Write(LST, parent ^ .contents[index, CharIndex]);
                        CharIndex:=CharIndex+1;
                    END;
                    WriteLn(LST);
                END;
                Write(LST,FormFeed);
            END;
            {end if}
            FindAndDisplay(parent ^ .right);
        END;
    END;
BEGIN
    ClearDevice;
    FindAndDisplay(BinaryTree);
END; {TreeFile.Display}
END. {FileUnit}
```

20.12 Program Design.

The first level of program design follows. Much of the detail has been omitted from this design since its purpose is to give an overview of the solution.

```
define procedures that create the menus
define procedures that capture data from the menus
define a procedure to output the system messages
open data file
display main menu and select item
WHILE menu item < > QUIT DO
    CASE menu item OF
    input :    input data for fields of a record
               write the record to the file
    modify:    input key of record to modify
               read record details into temporary store
```

                         delete record from file
                         modify fields of record
                         write the modified record to the file
           delete: *input key of record to delete*
                         delete record
           inspect: *input key of record to inspect*
                         read record
                         display contents of record
           display: *display contents of file, one record at a time, on the screen of a vdu*
           print :   *output the contents of the file to the printer*
      END
      display main menu and select item
END
close data file

Since the main menu items are not ordinal values they cannot be used in a CASE statement in the following Pascal implementation of the program. However, the positions of these items in the main menu can be used. Therefore, *inspect* corresponds with menu position 1, *modify* with position 2, *delete* with position 3 and so on.

20.13 Program Implementation.

```
{$M 65520,0,655360}
PROGRAM CaseStudyTwo;
USES Crt, Dos, Graph, NewScreens, FileUnit, screens;
CONST
      {ON/OFF signals whether a message is to be accompanied by a warning beep}
      ON=TRUE;  OFF=FALSE;
VAR
      info, message, key, MenuItem, item:MaxString;
      success:BOOLEAN;
      banner, menu, data, fields, KeyData, information:screen;
      NewFile:TreeFile;
      index:INTEGER;
      RecordArray:RecordType;
      colour:WORD;
      KeyChar:CHAR;


PROCEDURE Screen1;
{case study logo with copyright notice}
BEGIN
      ClearDevice;
      WITH banner DO
      BEGIN
         create(10,1,690,31);
         insert(' Case Study 2 DataBase Package copyright B.J.Holmes 1990');
         show;
      END;
END; {Screen1}
```

```
PROCEDURE Screen2;
{main menu}
BEGIN
     WITH menu DO
     BEGIN
        create(300,100,400,190);
        insert('input');
        insert('modify');
        insert('delete');
        insert('inspect');
        insert('display');
        insert('print');
        insert('QUIT');
        show;
     END;
END; {Screen2}

PROCEDURE Screen3;
BEGIN
     With fields DO
     BEGIN
        create(10,40,110,220);
        insert('name');
        insert('address');
        insert('tele no');
        insert('fax');
        insert('business');
        insert('');
        insert('key staff');
        insert('');
        insert('notes'); insert(''); insert(''); insert('');
        insert(''); insert(''); insert('');
        insert('QUIT');
        show;
     END;
END; {Screen3}

PROCEDURE Screen4;
{screen used to capture data for fields of record}
BEGIN
     data.create(140,40,690,220);
END; {Screen4}

PROCEDURE Screen5(prompt:MaxString; VAR info:MaxString);
{screen used to capture general information}
BEGIN
     WITH KeyData DO
     BEGIN
        create(10,250,690,290);
```

```
            ScreenOutput(1,prompt);
            ScreenInput(2,info);
        END;
END; {Screen5}


PROCEDURE Screen6(item:MaxString;beep:BOOLEAN);
{screen used to output messages}
VAR
      colour:WORD;
BEGIN
      WITH information DO
      BEGIN
          create(10,300,690,330);
          insert(item);
          show;
          IF beep THEN
          BEGIN
              Crt.SOUND(1000); Crt.DELAY(500);
              Crt.NOSOUND;
              Crt.DELAY(1000);
          END
          ELSE
              Crt.DELAY(1500);
          {end if}
          Erase;
      END;
END; {Screen6}


FUNCTION CaptureData(VAR CurrentWindow:windo):MaxString;
VAR
      item:MaxString;
BEGIN
      WITH CurrentWindow DO
      BEGIN
          move;
          select(item);
          CaptureData:=item;
      END;
END; {CaptureData}


BEGIN
      Screen1; {display banner}
      Screen5('input disc drive and name of file, for example, A:datafl.txt', info);
      NewFile.OpenFile(info, success, message);
      If NOT success THEN
      BEGIN
          Screen6(message,ON);
          RestoreCrtMode;
          HALT;
      END
```

```
ELSE
    Screen6('verify file opened',OFF);
{end if}
Screen6('building tree data file from disc',OFF);
ClearDevice;
Screen1;
Screen2; {display main menu}
MenuItem:=CaptureData(menu);
WHILE MenuItem < > 'QUIT' DO
BEGIN
    CASE menu.current OF
    1:  BEGIN {input}
            Screen1; Screen3; Screen4;
            NewFile.InitialiseFields;
            MenuItem:=CaptureData(fields);
            WHILE MenuItem < > 'QUIT' DO
            BEGIN
                data.CursorON(fields.current);
                data.ScreenInput(fields.current,item);
                data.CursorOFF(fields.current);
                NewFile.BuildField(fields.current, item);
                MenuItem:=CaptureData(fields);
            END;
            NewFile.WriteRecord(success, message);
            IF NOT success THEN
                Screen6(message,ON)
            ELSE
                Screen6('verify record written',OFF);
            {end if}
        END;
    2:  BEGIN {modify}
            Screen1;
            Screen5('key of record to modify', key);
            NewFile.ReadRecord(key, success, message);
            IF NOT success THEN
            BEGIN
                Screen6(message,ON);
            END
            ELSE
            BEGIN
                NewFile.DeleteRecord(key, success, message);
                Screen3; Screen4;
                FOR index:=1 TO MaxFields DO
                    data.ScreenOutput(index, NewFile.RecordArray[index]);
                {end for}
                data.show;
                MenuItem:=CaptureData(fields);
                WHILE MenuItem < > 'QUIT' DO
                BEGIN
```

```
                    data.CursorON(fields.current);
                    colour:=GetColor;
                    SetColor(GetBkColor);
                    data.ScreenOutput(fields.current,
                                  NewFile.RecordArray[fields.current]);
                    SetColor(colour);
                    data.ScreenInput(fields.current,item);
                    data.CursorOFF(fields.current);
                    NewFile.BuildField(fields.current, item);
                    MenuItem:=CaptureData(fields);
                END;
                NewFile.WriteRecord(success, message);
                IF NOT success THEN
                    Screen6(message,ON)
                ELSE
                    Screen6('verify record modified',OFF);
                {end if}
            END;
            {end if}
        END;
    3:  BEGIN {delete}
            Screen1;
            Screen5('key of record to delete', key);
            NewFile.ReadRecord(key,success,message);
            IF NOT success THEN
                Screen6(message,ON)
            ELSE
            BEGIN
                NewFile.DeleteRecord(key, success, message);
                IF NOT success THEN
                    Screen6(message,ON)
                ELSE
                    Screen6('verify record deleted',OFF);
                {end if}
            END;
            {end if}
        END;
    4:  BEGIN {inspect}
            Screen1;
            Screen5('key of record to inspect', key);
            NewFile.ReadRecord(key, success, message);
            IF NOT success THEN
                Screen6(message,ON)
            ELSE
            BEGIN
                screen3; Screen4;
                FOR index:=1 TO MaxFields DO
                    data.ScreenOutput(index, NewFile.RecordArray[index]);
                {end for}
```

```
                  data.show;
                  Screen6('press any key to clear',OFF);
                  KeyChar:=ReadKey;
               END;
            END;
        5: BEGIN {display}
               ClearDevice;
               Screen1;
               Screen6('contents of data file',OFF);
               Screen6('press any key to change record',OFF);
               NewFile.Display(vdu);
               ClearDevice;
               Screen6('end of file',OFF);
            END;
        6: BEGIN {print}
               ClearDevice;
               Screen1;
               Screen6('PRINTER POWER ON AND SWITCHED TO ON-LINE ?',ON);
               Screen6('press any key to confirm',OFF);
               KeyChar:=ReadKey;
               Screen6('output directed to printer',OFF);
               NewFile.Display(print);
               ClearDevice;
            END;
        END;
        Screen1; Screen2;
        MenuItem:=CaptureData(menu);
      END;
      {end while}
      Screen1;
      Screen6('writing contents of tree file to disc',OFF);
      NewFile.CloseFile;
      RestoreCrtMode;
END. {CaseStudyTwo}
```

20.14 Extensions.

Case study two forms the basis of any file-based information retrieval system. The menus can be changed to cater for different scenarios that the reader may wish to use.

The reader might be interested in extending the case study in the following ways.

Allow a user to exit at any time, by pressing the ESC key, from the routine that displays the contents of the file on the screen.

Modify the display method to include the field names in addition to the contents of the fields.

Introduce a second (and maybe third or fourth) object file(s) and be able to search through each file cross-referencing data and obtaining relevant information across all the file objects.

For the reasons given in case study one, answers to these extensions will not be available in this text or in the Answer Supplement.

20.15 Summary.

The approach to developing both case studies was to provide a brief specification for each system, giving information about data, results and the human-computer interface. From the respective specifications it was possible to deduce the nature of the units required to contribute towards the overall solution of the problems. The interaction between units and the order in which units were developed was decided at this stage.

Thought was then given to the parts of each system that could be modelled as objects and the necessary methods that would be required to manipulate these objects. Still at the design level, it was possible to document the interface section of each unit, without getting bogged down in intricate details of coding. Only when the design and interaction of the units, classes and methods was understood could work begin on the implementation of the methods for each unit.

At this stage decisions were made about appropriate data structures and file organisations to use.

Since the amount of Pascal coding required for each method was small, no more than between one and two sides of A4 paper, the design and implementation of such code was relatively straightforward.

Although not documented, each method was tested with a desk-check and a live run using a suitable test program. These tests formed the basis of *white-box* testing, since it was at this stage that a comprehensive check on each control path (if possible) that the computer could take through the code was examined. Remember methods are essentially small procedures, so a great deal of effort should go into testing these basic system components at this stage.

When all the methods in a unit had been checked, the unit itself under went a form of *black-box* testing. A separate test program was written that tested the input and output from each method. At this stage a simple form of integrative testing took place since the input to one method may be dependant upon the output from another method. When all the units had been tested the design of the main application program could begin.

The design of the program could use the step-wise refinement method, described in chapter 8, that eventually lead to Pascal code. However, it was more appropriate to produce a first level outline of the design, and implement detailed Pascal code directly from it. This was possible since the coding required to manipulate the objects was fairly simple. The hard work had been done in implementing the objects' methods.

Finally a strategy for a comprehensive integrative testing campaign was formulated and carried out.

Appendices

Computer Environment - section 1.11

1. Central processing unit, main memory, secondary storage units, input unit, output unit.

3. Pascal is a high-level language, therefore, the instructions are not in a machine recognisable form (machine code). A Pascal program must be translated into machine code using a compiler.

4.   Phase 1 - creation of a Pascal program in text mode using the editor.
       Phase 2 - translation of the program using a Pascal compiler.
       Phase 3 - link/loading.
       Phase 4 - program execution.

Data - section 2.10.

3. | character | ASCII code |
       |-----------|------------|
       | A | 65 |
       | M | 77 |
       | * | 42 |
       | a | 97 |
       | m | 109 |
       | / | 47 |
       | ? | 63 |
       | BEL | 7 |
       | NUL | 0 |
       | 9 | 57 |

5.   b) net-pay hyphen illegal
       d) cost of paper embedded spaces are illegal
       e) ReadLn reserved word
       f) ?X?Y ? character illegal
       g) 1856AD first character must be a letter of the alphabet.

6.
```
PROGRAM IncomeTax(INPUT, OUTPUT);
CONST
       SingleAllowance = 1200;
       MarriedAllowance = 2300;
       ChildAllowance = 100;
       Band1 = 1000;
       Band2 = 2000;
       Band3 = 4000;
       Rate1 = 0;
       Rate2 = 0.2;
       Rate3 = 0.3;
       Rate4 = 0.4;
VAR
       GrossSalary : REAL;
```

```
PersonalStatus : CHAR;
NumberOfChildren : INTEGER;
TaxableIncome : REAL;
tax : REAL;
```

Instruction Sequence - section 3.10

1.   a) A B C D
         36 36 36 36

      b) A B C D
         10 14 29 89

      c) A B
         48 50

      d) X Y
         19 -13

      e) X Y Z
         18 3 54

      f) A   B
         12.5 2.0

      g) A B X
         16 3 5

      h) C D Y
         18 5 3

      i) K   H
         -37   -36.54

      j) D   E
         -16   -16.9

5. a)
```
PROGRAM C3Q5a(INPUT, OUTPUT);
CONST
      numbers=3;
VAR
      x,y,z : INTEGER;
      mean:REAL;
BEGIN
      Write('input three integers separated by spaces e.g. 2 5 7');
      WriteLn('then press the RETURN key');
      ReadLn(x,y,z);
      mean:=(x+y+z)/numbers;
      WriteLn('arithmetic mean of integers = ', mean:10:2);
END.{C3Q5a}
```

5. b)
```
PROGRAM C3Q5b(INPUT, OUTPUT);
CONST
      pi=3.14159;
VAR
      radius:INTEGER;
      SurfaceArea, volume:REAL;
BEGIN
      Write('input integer value for the radius of the sphere =>');
      ReadLn(radius);
      SurfaceArea:=4*pi*radius*radius;
      volume:=SurfaceArea*radius/3;
      WriteLn('surface area of sphere =',SurfaceArea:10:2);
      WriteLn('volume of sphere =',volume:10:2);
END.{C3Q5b}
```

5. c)
```
PROGRAM C3Q5c(INPUT, OUTPUT);
CONST
      VAT=0.15;
VAR
      item1, item2, item3:REAL;
      SubTotal, Tax, Total:REAL;
BEGIN
      WriteLn('SALES INVOICE'); WriteLn; WriteLn;
      Write('input cost of item 1');ReadLn(item1);
      Write('input cost of item 2');ReadLn(item2);
      Write('input cost of item 3');ReadLn(item3);
      SubTotal:=item1+item2+item3;
      Tax:=SubTotal*VAT;
      total:=SubTotal+Tax;
      WriteLn('Sub Total', SubTotal:10:2);
      WriteLn('VAT @ 15%', Tax:10:2);
      WriteLn('Total ', Total:10:2);
END.{C3Q5c}
```

6.
```
PROGRAM C3Q6(INPUT, OUTPUT);
CONST
      InchConv=2.54;
      StoneConv=6.364;
VAR
      Initial1, Initial2:CHAR;
      height, weight:REAL;
      NewHeight, NewWeight:REAL;
BEGIN
      Write('input two initials of your name => ');
      ReadLn(Initial1, Initial2);
      Write('input your height in inches => ');
      ReadLn(height);
      Write('input your weight in Stones => ');
      ReadLn(weight);
      NewHeight:=height*InchConv;
      NewWeight:=weight*StoneConv;
      WriteLn('PERSONAL DETAILS');
```

```
        WriteLn('IDENTIFICATION:',Initial1, Initial2);
        WriteLn('HEIGHT (cm): ',NewHeight:4:1);
        WriteLn('WEIGHT (Kg): ',NewWeight:5:2);
END. {C3Q6}
```

7.
```
PROGRAM C3Q7(INPUT, OUTPUT);
VAR
        Fahrenheit, Centigrade:REAL;
BEGIN
        Write('input temperature in degrees Fahrenheit = > ');
        ReadLn(Fahrenheit);
        Centigrade:=(Fahrenheit-32.0)*(5.0/9.0);
        WriteLn('equivalent temperature in degrees Centigrade = > ', Centigrade:4:1);
END. {C3Q7}
```

Data Types - section 4.6

2.   **a)** DecimalDigit = 0..9;
         b) week = 1..52;
         c) compass = 1..360;
         d) IdCode = 100..999;
         e) alphabet = 'A'..'Z';

3.   **a)** operator = (+,-,*,/);
         b) CardSuits = (clubs, diamonds, hearts, spades);
         c) CardValue = (deuce, three, four, five, six, seven, eight, nine, ten,
                          Jack, Queen, King, Ace);
         d) points = (North, South, East, West);

4.   **a)** >   **b)**]   **c)** 58   **d)** Q

5.
```
PROGRAM C4Q5(INPUT, OUTPUT);
TYPE
        ascii=0..127;
VAR
        character:CHAR;
        code:ascii;
BEGIN
        Write('input single character = > ');  ReadLn(character);
        WriteLn('ASCII code = > ', ORD(character):3);
        Write('input ASCII code = > ');   ReadLn(code);
        WriteLn('equivalent character = >',CHR(code));
END. {C4Q5}
```

Selection - section 5.8

1. **a)** FALSE   **b)** TRUE **c)** TRUE   **d)** FALSE   **e)** TRUE
    f) TRUE   **g)** TRUE

2. **a)** X=Y   **b)** XY   **c)** A>=B   **d)** Q<=T   **e)** X>=Y
    f) (X<=Y) AND (AB)
    g) (A>18) AND (H>68) AND (W>75)
    h) (G<100) AND (G>50)   **i)** (H<50) OR (H>100)

3.
A	B	C	output
16	16	32	y
16	-18	32	x
-2	-4	16	z

4.
```
PROGRAM C5Q4(INPUT, OUTPUT);
CONST
    Band1=999.0; Band2=9999.0; Band3=99999.0;
    Comm1=0.01; Comm2=0.05; Comm3=0.1;
VAR
    sales, commission:REAL;
BEGIN
    Write('input sales figure => ');
    ReadLn(sales);
    IF (sales > Band2) AND (sales <=Band3) THEN
        commission:=sales*Comm3
    ELSE
        IF (sales > Band1) AND (Sales <= Band2) THEN
            commission:=sales*Comm2
        ELSE
            commission:=sales*Comm1;
        {end if}
    {end if}
    WriteLn('commission on sales => ',commission:6:2);
END. {C5Q4}
```

5.
```
PROGRAM C5Q5(INPUT, OUTPUT);
CONST
    FlatRate=8; Rate1=12; Rate2=16;
    Normalhours=35; threshold=60;
VAR
    HoursWorked : INTEGER;
    OvertimePay : REAL;
BEGIN
    Write('input hours worked => ');
    ReadLn(HoursWorked);
    IF HoursWorked > threshold THEN
        OvertimePay:=(threshold-NormalHours)*Rate1+(HoursWorked-threshold)*Rate2
    ELSE
        IF HoursWorked > NormalHours THEN
            OvertimePay:=(HoursWorked - NormalHours)*Rate1
```

```
          ELSE
              OvertimePay:=0;
          {end if}
      {end if}
      WriteLn('overtime pay = > ', OvertimePay:6:2);
END. {C5Q5}
```

Repetition - section 6.8

1.

```
PROGRAM C6Q1(INPUT, OUTPUT);
CONST
      OvertimeRate=12;
      NormalHours=40;
      MaxEmployee=10;
VAR
      HoursWorked, OvertimePay, employee:INTEGER;
BEGIN
      FOR employee:=1 TO MaxEmployee DO
      BEGIN
          Write('input hours worked for employee ', employee:2,' = > ');
          ReadLn(HoursWorked);
          IF HoursWorked > NormalHours THEN
              OvertimePay:=(HoursWorked-NormalHours)*OvertimeRate
          ELSE
              OvertimePay:=0;
          {end if}
          WriteLn('overtime pay due = > ', OvertimePay:4);
      END;
      {end for}
END. {C6Q1}
```

2.

```
PROGRAM C6Q2(OUTPUT);
VAR
      counter:INTEGER;
      result:REAL;
      index:CHAR;
BEGIN
      {a} counter:=1;
      REPEAT
          Write(counter:3);
          counter:=counter+2;
      UNTIL counter > 29;
      WriteLn;

      {b} counter:=2;
      REPEAT
          result:=counter*counter;
          Write(result:6:1);
```

```
            counter:=counter+2;
        UNTIL counter > 20;
        WriteLn;

        {c} result:=0;
        counter:=1;
        REPEAT
            result:=result+(counter*counter);
            counter:=counter+2;
        UNTIL counter > 13;
        WriteLn('sum of squares = > ', result:6:1);

        {d} WriteLn('UPPER CASE');
        FOR index:='A' TO 'Z' DO
            Write(index);
        {end for}
        WriteLn;
        WriteLn('lower case');
        FOR index:='a' TO 'z' DO
            write(index);
        {end for}
        WriteLn;
END. {C6Q2}
```

3.
```
PROGRAM C6Q3(OUTPUT);
VAR
        a,b,index:INTEGER;
BEGIN
        a:=1; b:=1;
        FOR index:=1 TO 10 DO
        BEGIN
            WriteLn(a:5,b:5);
            a:=a+b;
            b:=b+a;
        END;
        {end for}
END. {C6Q3}
```

5.
```
PROGRAM C6Q5(INPUT, OUTPUT);
VAR
        index:INTEGER;   MaxNumber, number:REAL;
BEGIN
        Write('input number = > ');
        ReadLn(number);
        MaxNumber:=number;
        FOR index:=2 TO 10 DO
        BEGIN
            Write('input number = > ');   ReadLn(number);
            IF number > MaxNumber THEN
                MaxNumber:=number;
            {end if}
        END;
        {end for}
```

```
        WriteLn('largest number in list = > ', MaxNumber:6:1);
END. {C6Q5}
```

6.
```
PROGRAM C6Q6(OUTPUT);
CONST
        conversion = 1.6093;
VAR
        miles:INTEGER;
        kilometres:REAL;
BEGIN
        WriteLn('miles kilometres');
        FOR miles:=1 TO 20 DO
        BEGIN
            kilometres:=conversion*miles;
            WriteLn(miles:5, kilometres:12:4);
        END;
        {end for}
END. {C6Q6}
```

9.
```
PROGRAM C6Q9(INPUT, OUTPUT);
VAR
        NextChar:CHAR;
BEGIN
        WHILE NOT EOLN DO
        BEGIN
            Read(NextChar);
            WriteLn('ASCII code for ',NextChar,' = > ',ORD(NextChar));
        END;
        {end while}
        ReadLn;
END. {C6Q9}
```

Procedures - section 7.7

1.
a) The actual parameter list is missing in the call to procedure alpha.
b) The formal parameter list of procedure beta is missing.
c) The corresponding variable C between the actual and formal parameter lists is not consistent. C has been defined as a variable yet appears as a constant 18.
d) There is a data type mis-match between the actual and formal parameter lists. X and Y are of type CHAR, yet i,j, and k are of type INTEGER. Furthermore, the number of parameters in both lists is not the same.

2.
a) 122 (not 90 since z is lower case).

b) The pattern that is output forms a right-angled triangle, made up from 10 rows of dots, where the number of dots in each row is equal to the row number.

```
.
..
...
....
.....
......
.......
........
.........
..........
```

4.
```
PROGRAM C7Q4(INPUT, OUTPUT);
VAR
        radius, diameter, circumference, area:REAL;

PROCEDURE DataIn(VAR radius:REAL);
BEGIN
        WriteLn('terminate with zero');
        REPEAT
            Write('input radius => ');
            ReadLn(radius);
        UNTIL radius >=0.0;
END; {DataIn}

PROCEDURE calculate(radius:REAL; VAR diameter, circumference, area:REAL);
CONST
        pi=3.14159;
BEGIN
        diameter:=2*radius;
        circumference:=2*pi*radius;
        area:=pi*radius*radius;
END; {calculate}

PROCEDURE results(diameter, circumference, area:REAL);
BEGIN
        WriteLn('diameter => ',diameter:10:2);
        WriteLn('circumference => ',circumference:10:2);
        WriteLn('area => ',area:10:2);
END; {results}

BEGIN
        DataIn(radius);
        WHILE radius <> 0 DO
        BEGIN
            calculate(radius, diameter, circumference, area);
            results(diameter, circumference, area);
            DataIn(radius);
        END;
        {end while}
END. {C7Q4}
```

5.

```
PROGRAM C7Q5(INPUT, OUTPUT);
VAR
      mark, distinction, merit, pass, fail, candidates:INTEGER;

PROCEDURE initialise;
BEGIN
      distinction:=0; merit:=0; pass:=0; fail:=0; candidates:=0;
END; {initialise}

PROCEDURE DataIn;
BEGIN
      WriteLn('terminate with 999');
      REPEAT
         Write('input examination mark (0..100) => ');
         ReadLn(mark);
      UNTIL ((mark>=0) AND (mark<=100)) OR (mark=999);
END; {DataIn}

PROCEDURE grade;
BEGIN
      candidates:=candidates+1;
      IF mark>=85 THEN
         distinction:=distinction+1
      ELSE IF mark >=65 THEN
         merit:=merit+1
      ELSE IF mark >=40 THEN
         pass:=pass+1
      ELSE
         fail:=fail+1;
      {end if}
END; {grade}

PROCEDURE results;
BEGIN
      WriteLn('grade frequency');
      WriteLn('distinction',distinction:9);
      WriteLn('merit ',merit:9);
      WriteLn('pass ',pass:9);
      WriteLn('fail ',fail:9);
      WriteLn;
      WriteLn('number of valid examination marks was => ',candidates:3);
END; {results}

BEGIN
      initialise;
      DataIn;
      WHILE mark <> 999 DO
      BEGIN
         grade;
         DataIn;
      END;
      {end while}
      results;
END. {C7Q5}
```

Mathematics - section 9.8

3.
```
PROGRAM C9Q3(OUTPUT);
CONST
      scale=30;
      centre=40;
      increment=0.1;
      pi=3.14159;
      space=CHR(32);
VAR
      index:INTEGER;
      angle:REAL;

FUNCTION trace:INTEGER;
BEGIN
      trace:=TRUNC(centre-scale*EXP(-angle)*SIN(2*pi*angle));
END; {trace}

BEGIN
      angle:=0;
      WHILE angle >=0 DO
      BEGIN
         FOR index:=1 TO trace DO
            Write(space);
         {end for}
         WriteLn('+');
         angle:=angle+increment;
      END;
      {end while}
END. {C9Q3}
```

5.
```
PROGRAM C9Q5(INPUT, OUTPUT);
VAR
      trials, Die1, Die2, count:INTEGER;
      one, two, three, four, five, six:INTEGER;

FUNCTION RollOfDice:INTEGER;
{function uses the Turbo Pascal random number generator}
BEGIN
      RollOfDice:=TRUNC(6*random+1);
END; {RollOfDice}

PROCEDURE initialise;
BEGIN
      Randomize;
      one:=0; two:=0; three:=0; four:=0; five:=0; six:=0;
END; {initialise}
```

```
PROCEDURE NumberOfTrials(VAR trials:INTEGER);
BEGIN
     WriteLn('type zero (0) to exit');
     REPEAT
         Write('input number of trials => ');
         ReadLn(trials);
     UNTIL trials >= 0;
END; {NumberOfTrials}

PROCEDURE results;
BEGIN
     WriteLn;
     WriteLn('frequency of doubles in ',trials:4,' trials');
     WriteLn('face 1 2 3 4 5 6');
     WriteLn('freq',one:5,two:5,three:5,four:5,five:5,six:5);
END; {results}

BEGIN
     NumberOfTrials(trials);
     WHILE trials <> 0 DO
     BEGIN
         initialise;
         FOR count:=1 TO trials DO
         BEGIN
             Die1:=RollOfDice;
             Die2:=RollOfDice;
             IF Die1=Die2 THEN
                 CASE Die1 OF
                 1:one:=one+1;
                 2:two:=two+1;
                 3:three:=three+1;
                 4:four:=four+1;
                 5:five:=five+1;
                 6:six:=six+1;
                 END;
                 {end case}
             {end if}
         END;
         {end for}
         results;
         NumberOfTrials(trials);
     END;
     {end while}
END. {C9Q5}
```

6 and 7 combined. The extensions required in question 7 are shown in italics. The answer to question 6 is all of the non-italicised type.

```
PROGRAM C9Q67(INPUT, OUTPUT);
CONST
     HandOfCards=13;
VAR
     card, total:INTEGER;
     suit,value:CHAR;
```

```pascal
BEGIN
     total:=0;
     FOR card:=1 TO HandOfCards DO
     BEGIN
        Write('input card number ',card:2,' suit and value => ');
        ReadLn(suit,value);
        IF (suit IN ['C','D','H','S']) AND
        (value IN ['2','3','4','5','6','7','8','9','T','J','Q','K','A']) THEN
        BEGIN
           CASE value OF
           '2':Write('duce');
           '3':Write('three');
           '4':Write('four');
           '5':Write('five');
           '6':Write('six');
           '7':Write('seven');
           '8':Write('eight');
           '9':Write('nine');
           'T':Write('ten');
           'J':BEGIN Write('jack'); total:=total+1; END;
           'Q':BEGIN Write('queen'); total:=total+2; END;
           'K':BEGIN Write('king'); total:=total+3; END;
           'A':BEGIN Write('ace'); total:=total+4; END;
           END;
           {end case}

           CASE suit OF
           'C':Write(' of Clubs');
           'D':Write(' of Diamonds');
           'H':Write(' of Hearts');
           'S':Write(' of Spades');
           END;
           {end case}

           WriteLn;
        END
        ELSE
           WriteLn('ERROR - DATA NOT IN CORRECT FORMAT');
        {end if}
     END;
     {end for}
     WriteLn('number of points in hand => ', total);
END. {C9Q67}
```

Arrays - section 10.8

1.
```
PROGRAM C10Q1(OUTPUT);
CONST
     alphabet='ABCDEFGHIJKLMNOPQRSTUVWXYZ';
     MaxColumn=26;
VAR
     AlphaString:PACKED ARRAY[1..MaxColumn] OF CHAR;
     index:INTEGER;
BEGIN
     AlphaString:=alphabet;
     {(a) display alphabet}
     WriteLn(AlphaString);

     {(b) display first six characters}
     FOR index:=1 TO 6 DO
         Write(AlphaString[index]);
     {end for}
     WriteLn;

     {(c) display the last ten characters}
     FOR index:=17 TO 26 DO
         Write(AlphaString[index]);
     {end for}
     WriteLn;

     {(d) display the tenth character}
     WriteLn(AlphaString[10]);
END. {C10Q1}
```

2.
```
PROGRAM C10Q2(INPUT, OUTPUT);
CONST
     MaxColumn=8;
TYPE
     numbers=ARRAY[1..MaxColumn] OF INTEGER;
VAR
     X, Y :numbers;
     index:INTEGER;
BEGIN
     WriteLn('input eight integers in ascending order');
     FOR index:=1 TO MaxColumn DO
         Read(X[index]);
     {end for}

     {store numbers in array Y in reverse order}
     FOR index:=MaxColumn DOWNTO 1 DO
         Y[MaxColumn-index+1]:=X[index];
     {end for}

     {display the contents of array Y}
     WriteLn('numbers in descending order');
```

```
        FOR index:=1 TO MaxColumn DO
            Write(Y[index]:5);
        {end for}
        WriteLn;
END. {C10Q2}
```

3.
```
PROGRAM C10Q3(INPUT, OUTPUT);
CONST
     nought='O';
     cross='X';
     space=CHR(32);
     no='n';
     range=3; {upper limit of random number range}
TYPE
     player=(computer,you);
VAR
     board:PACKED ARRAY[1..3,1..3] OF CHAR;
     who:player;
     success:BOOLEAN;
     reply:CHAR;
     moves:INTEGER;

PROCEDURE initialise;
VAR
     row, column :INTEGER;
BEGIN
     FOR row:=1 TO 3 DO
        FOR column:=1 TO 3 DO
            board[row, column]:=space;
        {end for}
     {end row}
     Randomize;
     moves:=0;
END; {initialise}

PROCEDURE CheckPosition(row, column:INTEGER; VAR success:BOOLEAN);
BEGIN
     IF board[row,column] = space THEN
        success:=TRUE
     ELSE
        success:=FALSE;
     {end if}
END; {CheckPosition}

PROCEDURE CheckWinner(who:player; VAR success:BOOLEAN);
VAR
     character:CHAR;
     row, column:INTEGER;
BEGIN
     success:=FALSE;
     IF who=you THEN
        character:=nought
     ELSE
        character:=cross;
```

```
    {check for rows}
    FOR row:=1 TO 3 DO
        IF (board[row,1]=character) AND (board[row,2]=character)
        AND (board[row,3]=character) THEN
            success:=TRUE;
        {end if}
    {end for}

    {check for columns}
    IF NOT success THEN
    BEGIN
        FOR column:=1 TO 3 DO
            IF (board[1,column]=character) AND (board[2,column]=character)
            AND (board[3,column]=character) THEN
                success:=TRUE;
            {end if}
        {end for}
    END;
    {end if}

    {check diagonals}
    IF NOT success THEN
    BEGIN
        IF (board[1,1]=character) AND (board[2,2]=character)
        AND (board[3,3]=character) THEN
            success:=TRUE;
        {end if}
    END;
    {end if}
    IF NOT success THEN
    BEGIN
        IF (board[1,3]=character) AND (board[2,2]=character)
        AND (board[3,1]=character) THEN
            success:=TRUE;
        {end if}
    END;
    {end if}
END; {CheckWinner}

PROCEDURE display;
VAR
    row, column:INTEGER;
BEGIN
    WriteLn; WriteLn;
    FOR row:=1 TO 3 DO
    BEGIN
        FOR column:=1 TO 3 DO
        BEGIN
            Write(board[row,column]);
            IF column < > 3 THEN Write(space,'|',space);
        END;
        WriteLn;
        IF row < > 3 THEN WriteLn('---------');
    END;
    WriteLn; WriteLn;
END; {display}
```

```
PROCEDURE play(who:player);
VAR
      row, column:INTEGER;
      success:BOOLEAN;
BEGIN
      IF who=you THEN
      BEGIN
         REPEAT
            REPEAT
               Write('input position of play => ');
               ReadLn(row, column);
            UNTIL ((row >=1) AND (row <=3)
            AND (column >=1) AND (column <=3));
            CheckPosition(row, column, success);
         UNTIL success;
         board[row, column]:=nought;
      END
      ELSE
      BEGIN
         REPEAT
            row:=Random(range)+1;
            column:=Random(range)+1;
            CheckPosition(row, column, success);
         UNTIL success;
         board[row, column]:=cross;
      END;
      {end if}
END; {play}

BEGIN
      REPEAT
         initialise;
         REPEAT
            who:=computer;
            play(who); display; moves:=moves+1;
            CheckWinner(who, success);
            IF success THEN WriteLn('computer wins - ha, ha!');
            IF (NOT success) AND (moves<9) THEN
            BEGIN
               who:=you;
               play(who); display; moves:=moves+1;
               CheckWinner(who, success);
               IF success THEN WriteLn('you win - smarty pants!!');
            END;
         UNTIL (success) OR (moves=9);
         IF (NOT success) AND (moves=9) THEN WriteLn('stale mate');
         WriteLn('another game sucker? - answer y(es) or n(o) ');
         ReadLn(reply);
      UNTIL reply=no;
END. {C10Q3}
```

4.
```
PROGRAM C10Q4(INPUT, OUTPUT);
CONST
      MaxColumn=80;
```

```
            space=CHR(32);
VAR
            buffer:ARRAY[1..MaxColumn] OF CHAR;
            index1, index2:INTEGER;
            palindrome:BOOLEAN;
BEGIN
            Write('input a single word => ');
            FOR index1:=1 TO MaxColumn DO
                IF EOLN THEN
                    buffer[index1]:=space
                ELSE
                BEGIN
                    index2:=index1;
                    Read(buffer[index1]);
                END;
                {end if}
            {end for}
            ReadLn;
            {test if word is a palindrome}
            index1:=1;
            palindrome:=TRUE;
            WHILE (index1 <= index2) AND palindrome DO
            BEGIN
                IF buffer[index1] = buffer[index2] THEN
                BEGIN
                    index1:=index1+1;
                    index2:=index2-1;
                END
                ELSE
                    palindrome:=FALSE;
                {end if}
            END;
            {end while}
            IF palindrome THEN
                WriteLn('this word is a palindrome')
            ELSE
                WriteLn('this word is NOT a palindrome');
            {end if}
END. {C10Q4}


5.
PROGRAM C10Q5(INPUT, OUTPUT);
CONST
            space=CHR(32);
            mined='M';
VAR
            field:PACKED ARRAY[0..9,0..9] OF CHAR;
            mines:INTEGER;
            row, column:INTEGER;
            MineCount:INTEGER;
            boom:BOOLEAN;
            LastRow, LastColumn:INTEGER;

PROCEDURE initialise;
VAR
            row, column:INTEGER;
```

```
BEGIN
      FOR row:=0 TO 9 DO
          FOR column:=0 TO 9 DO
              field[row,column]:=space;
          {end for}
      {end for}
      {start position}
      Randomize;
      LastRow:=9; LastColumn:=Random(10);
      field[LastRow,LastColumn]:='^';
      {generate number of mines}
      REPEAT
          mines:=Random(11);
      UNTIL mines>0;
      MineCount:=0;
      boom:=FALSE;
      {generate position of mines}
      REPEAT
          row:=Random(10);
          column:=Random(10);
          IF field[row,column] = space THEN
          BEGIN
              field[row,column]:=mined;
              MineCount:=MineCount+1;
          END;
      UNTIL MineCount=mines;
END; {initialise}

PROCEDURE search(row,column:INTEGER; VAR boom:BOOLEAN);
BEGIN
      IF field[row,column]=mined THEN
      BEGIN
          WriteLn; WriteLn;
          WriteLn('B O O M B O O M !!');
          WriteLn; WriteLn;
          boom:=TRUE;
      END
      ELSE
      BEGIN
          boom:=FALSE;
          field[row,column]:='^';
      END;
      {end if}
END; {search}

PROCEDURE display(reveal:BOOLEAN);
VAR
      row,column:INTEGER;
BEGIN
      WriteLn; WriteLn;
      WriteLn('          NORTH');
      WriteLn('0 1 2 3 4 5 6 7 8 9');
      FOR row:=0 TO 9 DO
      BEGIN
          Write(row:2);
```

```
            FOR column:=0 TO 9 DO
            BEGIN
                IF (field[row,column] = mined) AND reveal THEN
                    Write(space, mined)
                ELSE IF (field[row, column] = mined) THEN
                    Write(space, space)
                ELSE
                    Write(space, field[row, column]);
                {end if}
            END;
            {end for}
            WriteLn;
        END;
        WriteLn; WriteLn;
END; {display}

BEGIN
    initialise;
    display(FALSE);
    REPEAT
        REPEAT
            Write('input coordinates of next step = > ');
            ReadLn(row, column);
        UNTIL ((row>=0) AND (row<=9)) AND ((column>=0) AND (column<=9))
        AND ((row=LastRow) OR (row=LastRow-1) OR (row=LastRow+1))
        AND ((column=LastColumn) OR (column=LastColumn-1) OR
        (column=LastColumn+1));
        LastRow:=row; LastColumn:=column;
        search(row, column, boom);
        IF boom THEN
            display(TRUE)
        ELSE
            display(FALSE);
        {end if}
    UNTIL (boom) OR (row=0);
    IF NOT boom THEN
    BEGIN
        WriteLn('Congratulations!! You made it to the');
        WriteLn('North through the following minefield');
        display(TRUE);
    END;
    WriteLn('press return to finish');
    ReadLn;
END. {C10Q5}
```

Sorting and Searching - section 11.7

1.
```
PROGRAM C11Q1(INPUT, OUTPUT);
VAR
    table:ARRAY[1..100] OF INTEGER;
```

```
PROCEDURE initialise;
VAR
     index:INTEGER;
BEGIN
     FOR index:=1 TO 100 DO
         table[index]:=0;
     {end if}
END; {initialise}

PROCEDURE DataIn;
VAR
     index,datum:INTEGER;
BEGIN
     WriteLn('input ten different numbers, unsorted, in the range 1..100');
     WriteLn;
     FOR index:=1 TO 10 DO
     BEGIN
        REPEAT
           Write(' = > ');
           ReadLn(datum);
        UNTIL datum < > table[datum];
        table[datum]:=datum;
     END;
     {end for}
END; {DataIn}

PROCEDURE display;
VAR
     index:INTEGER;
BEGIN
     FOR index:=1 TO 100 DO
        IF table[index] < > 0 THEN
           WriteLn(table[index]:4);
        {end if}
     {end for}
END; {display}

BEGIN
     initialise;
     DataIn;
     display;
END. {C11Q1}
```

2.
```
PROGRAM C11Q2(INPUT, OUTPUT);
CONST
     MaxNumber=40; {cater for a maximum of 40 numbers in the set}
TYPE
     data=ARRAY[0..MaxNumber-1] OF INTEGER;
VAR
     table:data;
     NumbersStored:INTEGER;
```

```
PROCEDURE DataIn(VAR NumbersStored:INTEGER);
VAR
      index, datum:INTEGER;
BEGIN
      WriteLn('input a set of numbers - one per line - terminate with 0');
      WriteLn;
      index:=0;
      ReadLn(datum);
      WHILE datum < > 0 DO
      BEGIN
          table[index]:=datum;
          index:=index+1;
          ReadLn(datum);
      END;
      {end while}
      NumbersStored:=index;
END; {DataIn}

FUNCTION median(NumbersStored:INTEGER):REAL;
VAR
      MidPoint:INTEGER;
BEGIN
      MidPoint:=TRUNC((NumbersStored-1)/2.0);
      IF ODD(NumbersStored) THEN
          median:=table[MidPoint]
      ELSE
          median:=(table[MidPoint]+table[MidPoint+1])/2.0;
      {end if}
END; {median}

PROCEDURE sort(VAR A:data; size:INTEGER);
VAR
      current, location, index:INTEGER;
BEGIN
      FOR index:=1 TO size-1 DO
      BEGIN
          current:=A[index];
          location:=index;
          WHILE (location > 0) AND (A[location-1] > current) DO
          BEGIN
              A[location]:=A[location-1];
              location:=location-1;
          END;
          {end while}
          A[location]:=current;
      END;
      {end for}
END; {sort}

BEGIN
      DataIn(NumbersStored);
      sort(table, NumbersStored);
      WriteLn('median of the set of numbers is ', median(NumbersStored):5:1);
END. {C11Q2}
```

Recursion - section 12.6

1.
```
PROGRAM C12Q1(INPUT, OUTPUT);
CONST
      MaxNumber=10;
TYPE
      data=ARRAY[0..MaxNumber-1] OF INTEGER;
VAR
      table:data;

PROCEDURE DataIn;
VAR
      index:INTEGER;
BEGIN
      WriteLn('input ten positive integers');
      FOR index:=0 TO MaxNumber-1 DO
          ReadLn(table[index]);
      {end for}
END; {DataIn}

FUNCTION sum(table:data; size:INTEGER):INTEGER;
BEGIN
      IF size < 0 THEN
          sum:=0
      ELSE
          sum:=table[size]+sum(table, size-1);
      {end if}
END; {sum}

BEGIN
      DataIn;
      WriteLn('sum of numbers in array is ', sum(table, MaxNumber-1));
END. {C12Q1}
```

2.
```
PROGRAM C12Q2(INPUT, OUTPUT);
VAR
      X,n:INTEGER;

FUNCTION power(X,n:INTEGER):INTEGER;
BEGIN
      IF n=0 THEN
          power:=1
      ELSE
          power:=X*power(X,n-1);
      {end if}
END; {power}

BEGIN
      Write('input a value for X => '); ReadLn(X);
      Write('input a value for n => '); ReadLn(n);
      WriteLn('X raised to the power of n is => ', power(X,n):6);
END. {C12Q2}
```

4.
```
PROGRAM C12Q4(INPUT, OUTPUT);
CONST
      MaxNumber=10;
TYPE
      data=ARRAY[0..MaxNumber-1] OF INTEGER;
VAR
      table:data;
      big:INTEGER;

PROCEDURE DataIn;
VAR
      index:INTEGER;
BEGIN
      WriteLn('input ten positive integers');
      FOR index:=0 TO MaxNumber-1 DO
          ReadLn(table[index]);
      {end for}
END; {DataIn}

PROCEDURE largest(table:data; size:INTEGER);
LABEL 1;
BEGIN
      IF size=0 THEN
          GOTO 1
      ELSE
      BEGIN
          IF table[size] > big THEN
              big:=table[size];
          {end if}
          largest(table, size-1);
      END;
      {end if}
1:END; {largest}

BEGIN
      DataIn;
      big:=table[0];
      largest(table, MaxNumber-1);
      WriteLn('largest number in the list is ', big:5);
END. {C12Q4}
```

Text Files - section 13.8

1. Example of Stock File

67451	Master Brew Mild	Brls	150	20.00
14562	Best Bitter	Brls	200	25.00
23478	Stock Ale	Brls	100	15.50
61234	Lager	Crates	55	5.00

34789	Cider	Hogs	20	14.50
54870	Apple Perry	Bottles	35	1.00
42567	Sherry - sweet	Cask	5	50.00
23897	Sherry - dry	Cask	3	45.00
23696	Wine - dry white	Bottles	26	2.00
56348	Wine - sweet red	Bottles	34	2.50

File sorted using MSDOS SORT utility: SORT < Stock.txt > StkSort.txt

14562	Best Bitter	Brls	200	25.00
23478	Stock Ale	Brls	100	15.50
23696	Wine - dry white	Bottles	26	2.00
23897	Sherry - dry	Cask	3	45.00
34789	Cider	Hogs	20	14.50
42567	Sherry - sweet	Cask	5	50.00
54870	Apple Perry	Bottles	35	1.00
56348	Wine - sweet red	Bottles	34	2.50
61234	Lager	Crates	55	25.00
67451	Master Brew Mild	Brls	150	20.00

2.
```
PROGRAM C13Q2(data, report);
CONST
      StockChar = 5;
      DescChar = 25;
TYPE
      StockString = PACKED ARRAY[0..StockChar-1] OF CHAR;
      DescString = PACKED ARRAY[0..DescChar-1] OF CHAR;
VAR
      StockNumber:StockString;
      description:DescString;
      quantity:INTEGER;
      price:REAL;
      data, report:TEXT;
      value, TotalValue:REAL;

PROCEDURE ReadLine(    VAR FileName:TEXT;
                       VAR StockNumber:StockString;
                       VAR description:DescString;
                       VAR quantity:INTEGER;
                       VAR price:REAL);
CONST
      space = CHR(32);
VAR
      index:INTEGER;
BEGIN
      FOR index:=0 TO StockChar-1 DO
         Read(FileName, StockNumber[index]);
      {end for}
      FOR index:=0 TO DescChar-1 DO
         Read(FileName, description[index]);
      {end for}
      Read(FileName, quantity, price);
      ReadLn(FileName);
END; {ReadLine}
```

```
BEGIN
    ASSIGN(data,'a:StkSort.txt');
    ASSIGN(report,'a:report.txt');
    RESET(data); REWRITE(report);
    WriteLn(report,'            STOCK REPORT');
    WriteLn(report);
    WriteLn(report,'STOCK        DESCRIPTION UNIT LEVEL VALUE');
    WriteLn(report,'NUMBER                          COST');
    WriteLn(report);
    TotalValue:=0;
    WHILE NOT EOF(data) DO
    BEGIN
        ReadLine(data,StockNumber,description,quantity,price);
        value:=price*quantity;
        TotalValue:=TotalValue+value;
        WriteLn(report,StockNumber,'',description,'',price:5:2,quantity:8,value:8:2);
    END;
    {end while}
    WriteLn(report);
    WriteLn(report,'                              TOTAL VALUE',TotalValue:10:2);
    RESET(report);
END. {C13Q2}
```

Pointers - section 14.6

1.

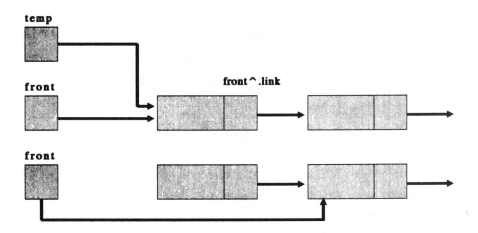

Deletion of a node from the front of a linked list

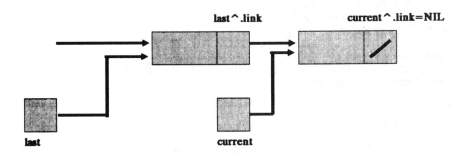

Deletion of a node at the end of a linked list

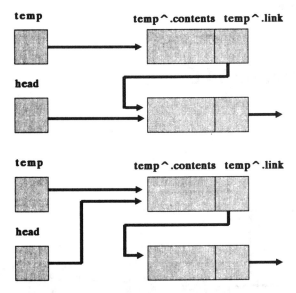

Insertion of a node at the head of a linked list

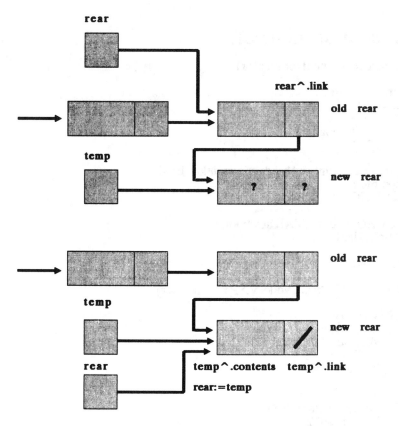

Insertion of a node at the end of a linked list

2.
{insertion of a node at the head of a linked list}
NEW(temp);
temp^.contents:=item;
temp^.link:=head;
head:=temp;

{insertion of a node at the end of a linked list}
NEW(temp);
rear^.link:=temp;
temp^.contents:=data;
temp^.link:=NIL;
rear:=temp;

{deletion of a node from the front of a linked list}
temp:=front;
front:=front^.link;
DISPOSE(temp);

{deletion of a node from the rear of a linked list}
last^.link:=current^.link;
DISPOSE(current);

3.

```
PROGRAM C14Q3(INPUT, OUTPUT);
CONST
      terminator=0; {input terminator}
TYPE
      pointer= ^ node;
      node=RECORD
                  number:INTEGER;
                  link:pointer;
               END;
VAR
      head1, head2:pointer; {heads of two linked lists}
      last:pointer;
      max:INTEGER;

PROCEDURE CreateList(VAR head:pointer);
{build first linked list}
VAR
      last:pointer;

      PROCEDURE CreateNode(VAR next:pointer);
      BEGIN
         NEW(next);
         Write('input integer = > ');
         ReadLn(next ^ .number);
         next ^ .link:=NIL;
      END; {CreateNode}

BEGIN
      WriteLn('terminate with 0');
      CreateNode(head1);
      last:=head1;
      WHILE last ^ .number < > terminator DO
      BEGIN
         CreateNode(last ^ .link);
         last:=last ^ .link;
      END;
      {end while}
END; {CreateList}

PROCEDURE ListOut(head:pointer);
{display the contents of a linked list}
VAR
      current:pointer;
BEGIN
      current:=head;
      WHILE current < > NIL DO
      BEGIN
         WriteLn(current ^ .number:4);
         current:=current ^ .link;
      END;
      {end while}
END; {ListOut}
```

```
PROCEDURE DeleteNode(VAR head:pointer; max:INTEGER);
{search for the largest item in the list and delete the node containing this item}
VAR
      temp, last, current:pointer;
BEGIN
      current:=head;
      last:=head;
      WHILE current ^ .number < > max DO
      BEGIN
         last:=current;
         current:=current ^ .link;
      END;
      {end while}
      IF head=current THEN
      BEGIN
         head:=head ^ .link;
         DISPOSE(current);
      END
      ELSE
      BEGIN
         last ^ .link:=current ^ .link;
         DISPOSE(current);
      END;
      {end if}
END; {DeleteNode}


FUNCTION largest(VAR head:pointer):INTEGER;
{function that returns the largest integer in the linked list}
VAR
      max:INTEGER;
      current:pointer;
BEGIN
      current:=head;
      max:=-MAXINT;
      WHILE current < > NIL DO
      BEGIN
         IF current ^ .number > max THEN
            max:=current ^ .number;
         {end if}
         current:=current ^ .link;
      END;
      {end while}
      largest:=max;
END; {largest}


PROCEDURE build(VAR next:pointer; value:INTEGER);
{procedure to build a second linked list containing integers sorted into descending order}
BEGIN
      NEW(next);
      next ^ .number:=value;
      next ^ .link:=NIL;
END; {build}
```

```
BEGIN
      CreateList(head1);
      max:=largest(head1);
      build(head2,max);
      last:=head2;
      DeleteNode(head1,max);
      WHILE head1 < > NIL DO
      BEGIN
         max:=largest(head1);
         build(last ^ .link,max);
         last:=last ^ .link;
         DeleteNode(head1,max);
      END;
      ListOut(head2);
END. {C14Q3}
```

Dynamic Structures - section 15.7

1.
```
FUNCTION StackSize(s:stack):INTEGER;
VAR
      temp:stack;
      counter:INTEGER;
BEGIN
      counter:=0;
      temp:=s;
      WHILE temp < > NIL DO
      BEGIN
         temp:=temp ^ .link;
         counter:=counter+1;
      END;
      {end while}
      StackSize:=counter;
END; {StackSize}
```

```
PROCEDURE push(VAR s:stack; character:CHAR);
VAR
      temp:stack;
BEGIN
      {MaxStack is a predefined limit on the maximum size of the stack}
      IF StackSize(s)=MaxStack THEN
         WriteLn('ERROR - STACK OVERFLOW')
      ELSE
      BEGIN
         NEW(temp);
         temp ^ .data:=character;
         temp ^ .link:=s;
         s:=temp;
      END;
      {end if}
END; {push}
```

4.

```
PROGRAM C15Q4(INPUT, OUTPUT);
CONST
      SetSize=20;
TYPE
      tree= ^ node;
      node=RECORD
                  left:tree;
                  number:INTEGER;
                  right:tree;
              END;
VAR
      structure:tree;
      value:INTEGER;
      success:BOOLEAN;
      count:INTEGER;

PROCEDURE initialise(VAR parent:tree);
BEGIN
      parent:=NIL;
END; {initialise}

PROCEDURE attach(VAR parent:tree; NewNumber:INTEGER; VAR BOOLEAN);
BEGIN
      IF parent=NIL THEN
      BEGIN
         NEW(parent);
         parent ^ .left:=NIL;
         parent ^ .number:=NewNumber;
         parent ^ .right:=NIL;
         success:=TRUE;
      END
      ELSE IF NewNumber < parent ^ .number THEN
         attach(parent ^ .left, NewNumber, success)
      ELSE IF NewNumber > parent ^ .number THEN
         attach(parent ^ .right, NewNumber, success)
      ELSE
      BEGIN
         WriteLn('WARNING ',NewNumber:5,' ALREADY EXISTS IN TREE');
         success:=FALSE;
      END;
      {end if}
END; {attach}

PROCEDURE display(VAR parent:tree);
BEGIN
      IF parent < > NIL THEN
      BEGIN
         display(parent ^ .left);
         WriteLn(parent ^ .number:5);
         display(parent ^ .right);
      END;
      {end if}
END; {display}
```

```
BEGIN
     Randomize;
     count:=0;
     initialise(structure);
     WriteLn('generated random numbers');
     REPEAT
     {generate random numbers in the range 1-100}
         value:=TRUNC(100*Random+1);
         WriteLn(value:5);
         attach(structure,value,success);
         IF success THEN count:=count+1;
     UNTIL count=SetSize;
     WriteLn;
     WriteLn('contents of tree - sorted into ascending order');
     display(structure);
     WriteLn;
END. {C15Q4}
```

5.
```
PROGRAM C15Q5(DataFile, OUTPUT);
CONST
     MaxString=80;
     space=CHR(32);
TYPE
     list=^node;
     node=RECORD
               operand:CHAR;
               value:REAL;
               link:list;
            END;

     stack=^StackNode;
     StackNode= RECORD
                     data:REAL;
                     link:stack;
                  END;
     TextString=PACKED ARRAY[0..MaxString-1] OF CHAR;
VAR
     expression:TextString;
     head, current, last:list;
     DataFile:TEXT;
     OK:BOOLEAN;
     size:INTEGER; {length of reverse Polish string}

PROCEDURE search(VAR head, last, current:list; NextOperand:CHAR;
                     VAR OperandValue:REAL;
                     VAR NotFound:BOOLEAN);
LABEL 1;
BEGIN
     NotFound:=TRUE;
     current:=head;
     last:=current;
     WHILE (current <> NIL) AND NotFound DO
     BEGIN
         IF NextOperand < current^.operand THEN
```

```
            GOTO 1
         ELSE IF NextOperand = current ^ .operand THEN
         BEGIN
            NotFound:=FALSE;
            OperandValue:=current ^ .value;
            GOTO 1;
         END
         ELSE
         BEGIN
            last:=current;
            current:=current ^ .link;
         END;
         {end if}
      END;
      {end while}
1:END;{search}

PROCEDURE insert(VAR head, last, current:list; NextOperand:CHAR; value:REAL);
VAR
      temp:list;
BEGIN
      NEW(temp);
      temp ^ .operand:=NextOperand;
      temp ^ .value:=value;
      temp ^ .link:=current;
      IF last=current THEN
         head:=temp
      ELSE
         last ^ .link:=temp;
      {end if}
END; {insert}

PROCEDURE NewList(VAR head:list);
BEGIN
      head:=NIL;
END; {NewList}

PROCEDURE initialise(VAR s:stack);
BEGIN
      s:=NIL;
END; {initialise}

FUNCTION empty(s:stack):BOOLEAN;
BEGIN
      IF s=NIL THEN
         empty:=TRUE
      ELSE
         empty:=FALSE;
      {end if}
END; {empty}

PROCEDURE push(VAR s:stack; number:REAL);
VAR
      temp:stack;
BEGIN
```

```
            NEW(temp);
            temp^.data:=number;
            temp^.link:=s;
            s:=temp;
END; {push}


PROCEDURE pop(VAR s:stack; VAR number:REAL);
VAR
        temp:stack;
BEGIN
        IF NOT empty(s) THEN
        BEGIN
            temp:=s;
            number:=s^.data;
            s:=s^.link;
            DISPOSE(temp);
        END;
        {end if}
END; {pop}


PROCEDURE evaluate(expression:TextString;size:INTEGER);
{routine to traverse the reverse Polish string and evaluate the
string according to the algorithm given in the question}
VAR
        index:INTEGER;
        answer:REAL;
        s:stack;
        first, second:REAL;
        symbol:CHAR;
        OperandValue:REAL;
BEGIN
        initialise(s);
        index:=0;
        FOR index:=0 TO size-1 DO
        BEGIN
            symbol:=expression[index];
            IF  (symbol='+') OR
                (symbol='-') OR
                (symbol='*') OR
                (symbol='/') THEN
            BEGIN
                pop(s,first);
                pop(s,second);
                CASE symbol OF
                '+':answer:=second+first;
                '-':answer:=second-first;
                '*':answer:=second*first;
                '/': IF first <> 0 THEN
                        answer:=second/first
                     ELSE
                        answer:=MAXINT;
                    {end if}
                END;
                {end case}
                push(s,answer);
            END
```

```
      ELSE
      BEGIN
          search(head, last, current, symbol, OperandValue, OK);
          push(s,OperandValue);
      END;
      {end if}
   END;
   {end for}
   pop(s,answer);
   WriteLn('evaluation of reverse polish string using the operands');
   WriteLn('given is ', answer:8:2);
END; {evaluate}

PROCEDURE AssignOperands(VAR expression:TextString; VAR size:INTEGER);
{procedure to build a linked list containing the names of the operands and their values}
VAR
      NextOperand:CHAR;
      index:INTEGER;
      OperandValue:REAL;
BEGIN
      WriteLn('reverse Polish string is ',expression);
      Newlist(head);
      index:=0;
      WHILE expression[index] < > space DO
      BEGIN
         NextOperand:=expression[index];
         IF  (NextOperand '+') AND (NextOperand '-') AND
             (NextOperand '*') AND (NextOperand '/') THEN
         BEGIN
            search(head, last, current, NextOperand, OperandValue, OK);
            IF OK THEN
            BEGIN
               Write('input value of operand ', NextOperand, ' = > ');
               ReadLn(OperandValue);
               insert(head, last, current, NextOperand, OperandValue);
            END;
            {end if}
         END;
         {end if}
         index:=index+1;
      END;
      {end while}
      size:=index;
END; {AssignOperands}

PROCEDURE ReadString(VAR FileName:TEXT; VAR buffer:TextString);
VAR
      index:INTEGER;
BEGIN
      FOR index:=0 TO MaxString-1 DO
         IF EOLN(FileName) THEN
            buffer[index]:=space
         ELSE
            Read(FileName, buffer[index]);
         {end if}
```

```
        {end for}
        ReadLn(FileName);
END; {ReadString}

BEGIN
        ASSIGN(DataFile,'a:datafl.txt');
        RESET(DataFile);
        WHILE NOT EOF(DataFile) DO
        BEGIN
            ReadString(DataFile, expression);
            AssignOperands(expression,size);
            evaluate(expression,size);
        END;
        {end while}
        RESET(DataFile);
END. {C15Q5}
```

Record Files - section 16.10

1. Program to build file of records.
```
PROGRAM C16Q1A(INPUT,OUTPUT,account);
CONST
        MaxString=6;
        no='n';
TYPE
        TextString=PACKED ARRAY[1..MaxString] OF CHAR;
        AccountDetails=RECORD
                            BranchCode:TextString;
                            AccountNo:TextString;
                            shares:INTEGER;
                        END;
        AccountFile=FILE OF AccountDetails;
VAR
        AccountRecord:AccountDetails;
        account:AccountFile;
        reply:CHAR;

PROCEDURE BuildRecord;
VAR
        index:INTEGER;
BEGIN
        WITH AccountRecord DO
        BEGIN
            WriteLn('input branch code => ');
            FOR index:=1 TO MaxString DO
                Read(BranchCode[index]);
            {end for}
            ReadLn;
            WriteLn('input account number => ');
            FOR index:=1 TO Maxstring DO
                Read(Accountno[index]);
```

```
            {end for}
            ReadLn;
            WriteLn('input number of £1 shares = > ');
            ReadLn(shares);
         END;
         Write(account, AccountRecord);
    END; {BuildRecord}

BEGIN
     ASSIGN(account,'a:account.txt');
     REWRITE(account);
     REPEAT
        BuildRecord;
        Write('more data - y(es) n(o)? ');
        ReadLn(reply);
     UNTIL reply=no;
     RESET(account);
END. {C16Q1A}
```

Program to create report.

```
PROGRAM C16Q1B(OUTPUT,account);
CONST
     MaxString=6;
     no='n';
TYPE
     TextString=PACKED ARRAY[1..MaxString] OF CHAR;
     AccountDetails=RECORD
                         BranchCode:TextString;
                         AccountNo:TextString;
                         shares:INTEGER;
                       END;
     AccountFile=FILE OF AccountDetails;
VAR
     AccountRecord:AccountDetails;
     account:AccountFile;
     code:TextString;
     TotalShares:INTEGER;
     EndOfFile:BOOLEAN;

PROCEDURE ReadFile(VAR FileName:AccountFile;
                        VAR RecordName:AccountDetails;
                        VAR EndOfFile:BOOLEAN);
BEGIN
     EndOfFile:=FALSE;
     IF EOF(FileName) THEN
        EndOfFile:=TRUE
     ELSE
        Read(FileName, RecordName);
     {end if}
END;{ReadFile}

BEGIN
     ASSIGN(account,'a:account.txt');
     RESET(account);
```

```
        WriteLn(' THE HAPPY HOMES BUILDING SOCIETY');
        WriteLn('DETAILS OF ORDINARY SHARE ACCOUNT CUSTOMERS');
        WriteLn;
        ReadFile(account, AccountRecord, EndOfFile);
        WHILE NOT EndOfFile DO
        BEGIN
            code:=AccountRecord.BranchCode;
            WriteLn('BRANCH CODE: ',code); WriteLn;
            WriteLn('ACCOUNT NUMBER £1 SHARES');
            TotalShares:=0;
            WHILE NOT EndOfFile AND (code=AccountRecord.BranchCode) DO
            BEGIN
                WITH AccountRecord DO
                BEGIN
                    WriteLn(AccountNo,shares:36);
                    TotalShares:=TotalShares+shares;
                END;
                ReadFile(account, AccountRecord, EndOfFile);
            END;
            {end while}
            WriteLn(' TOTAL ', TotalShares:10);
        END;
        {end while}
END. {C16Q1B}
```

4.
```
WHILE (NOT EndofTrans) OR (NOT EndOfMaster) DO
BEGIN
        IF (TransRecord.name < StaffRecord.name) AND
        (TransRecord.TransCode=Insert) THEN
        BEGIN
            WriteRecord(NewMaster,TransRecord,staffRecord);
            ReadTrans(transaction, TransRecord, EndOfTrans);
        END
        ELSE IF (TransRecord.name < StaffRecord.name) AND
        ((TransRecord.TransCode=Amend) OR (TransRecord.TransCode=Delete)) THEN
        BEGIN
            WriteLn('ERROR IN TRANSACTION RECORD - IGNORE
                    TRANSACTION');
            ReadTrans(transaction, TransRecord, EndOfTrans);
        END
        ELSE IF (TransRecord.name = StaffRecord.name) THEN
        IF TransRecord.TransCode = Amend THEN
        BEGIN
            WriteRecord(NewMaster, TransRecord, StaffRecord);
            ReadTrans(transaction,TransRecord,EndOfTrans);
            ReadMaster(master,StaffRecord,EndOfMaster);
        END
        ELSE IF TransRecord.TransCode = Delete THEN
        BEGIN
            ReadTrans(transaction,TransRecord,EndOfTrans);
            ReadMaster(master,StaffRecord,EndOfMaster);
        END
        ELSE
            WriteLn('ERROR IN TRANSACTION RECORD - IGNORE
                    TRANSACTION');
```

```
            ReadTrans(transaction,TransRecord,EndOfTrans);
            Write(NewMaster, StaffRecord);
            ReadMaster(master,StaffRecord,EndOfMaster);
        END
        ELSE
        BEGIN
            Write(NewMaster, StaffRecord);
            ReadMaster(master,StaffRecord,EndOfMaster);
        END;
          {end if}
      END;
      {end while}
      RESET(NewMaster);
END. {update}
```

Common Extensions - section 17.7

1.
Example of data file - note the use of delimiters between codes.
```
..../.    /.-../.-../--- /
..../.    /.-../.-../--- /
..../.    /.-. /.-. /
..-/.-.. /.. /.-./.-. /
..../.-  /.... /
.-../--- /.... /- /
..../.. /.... /
... /.- /..- /.... /.- /--./. /
```

```
PROGRAM C17Q1(morse, OUTPUT);
LABEL 1;
CONST
      DotDash1='.-    -... -.-. -.. .   ..-. --. ....';
      DotDash2='..    .--- -.- -.. -- -.   --- .--.';
      DotDash3='--.- -.  ... - ..- ...- .-- -..- -.-- --..';
TYPE
      code=STRING[4];
VAR
      morse:TEXT;
      DotDash:STRING[104];
      CodeStore:ARRAY['A'..'Z'] OF code;
      separator:CHAR;
      MorseCode:code;
      index:CHAR;

PROCEDURE initialise;
VAR
      start:INTEGER;
      index:CHAR;
BEGIN
      DotDash:=CONCAT(DotDash1, DotDash2, DotDash3);
```

```
        start:=1;
        FOR index:='A' TO 'Z' DO
        BEGIN
           CodeStore[index]:=COPY(DotDash,start, 4);
           start:=start+4;
        END;
END; {initialise}

BEGIN
        ASSIGN(morse,'a:morse.txt');
        RESET(morse);
        initialise;
        WHILE NOT EOF(morse) DO
        BEGIN
           WHILE NOT EOLN(morse) DO
           BEGIN
              Read(morse, MorseCode);
              FOR index:='A' TO 'Z' DO
                 IF MorseCode=CodeStore[index] THEN
                 BEGIN
                    Write(index);
                    GOTO 1;
                 END;
                 {end if}
              {end for}
           1:  Read(morse,separator);
           END;
           {end while}
           ReadLn(morse);
           WriteLn;
        END;
        {end while}
END. {C17q1}
```

Turbo Units - section 18.8

1.
```
{$N+}
UNIT utility;
INTERFACE
FUNCTION RND:DOUBLE;
PROCEDURE RANDOMIZE(StartPosition:INTEGER);

IMPLEMENTATION
VAR
        seed:LONGINT;

FUNCTION RND:DOUBLE;
CONST
        a=LONGINT(19);
        b=LONGINT(100000000);
```

```
VAR
      RN:DOUBLE;
      y:LONGINT;
BEGIN
      y:=(a*seed) MOD b;
      seed:=y;
      RN:=ABS(y);
      REPEAT
          RN:=RN/10.0;
      UNTIL RN < 1.0;
      RND:=RN;
END; {RND}

PROCEDURE RANDOMIZE(StartPosition:INTEGER);
VAR
      index:INTEGER;
      FlushNumber:REAL;
BEGIN
      IF StartPosition < > 0 THEN
          FOR index:=1 TO StartPosition-1 DO
              FlushNumber:=RND;
          {end for}
END; {RANDOMIZE}

BEGIN
      seed:=19;
END. {utility}
```

Test program.

```
{$N+}
PROGRAM C18Q1(INPUT, OUTPUT);
USES utility;
VAR
      trials, number, RandomNumber, StartPosition:INTEGER;
BEGIN
      Write('input start position in list of random numbers = > ');
      ReadLn(StartPosition);
      RANDOMIZE(StartPosition);
      Write('input number of trials = > ');
      ReadLn(trials);
      FOR number:=1 TO trials DO
      BEGIN
          IF (number-1) MOD 10 = 0 THEN WriteLn;
          RandomNumber:=(TRUNC(1000.0*RND)MOD6)+1;
          Write(RandomNumber:2);
      END;
      {end for}
END. {C18Q1}
```

3.
```
PROGRAM C18Q3(results, OUTPUT);
USES BarChart;
CONST
      subjects=6;
```

```
VAR
     bars:INTEGER;
     means:data;

PROCEDURE CollectData(VAR means:data);
VAR
     index:INTEGER;
     PupilCount, PupilNumber:INTEGER;
     table:data;
     results:TEXT;
BEGIN
     ASSIGN(results,'a:results.txt');
     RESET(results);
     PupilCount:=0;
     FOR index:=1 TO subjects DO
         means[index]:=0;
     {end for}
     WHILE NOT EOF(results) DO
     BEGIN
         Read(results, PupilNumber);
         PupilCount:=PupilCount+1;
         FOR index:=1 TO subjects DO
         BEGIN
             Read(results, table[index]);
             means[index]:=means[index]+table[index];
         END;
         {end for}
         ReadLn(results);
     END;
     {end while}
     FOR index:=1 TO subjects DO
         means[index]:=means[index] DIV PupilCount;
     {end for}
END; {CollectData}

BEGIN
     CollectData(means);
     bars:=subjects;
     OpenGraph;
     DrawChart(350,300,bars,means);
     TextDisplay(1,1,'% mark');
     TextDisplay(1,10,'A-Maths');
     TextDisplay(1,20,'B-English');
     TextDisplay(1,30,'C-Geography');
     TextDisplay(1,40,'D-History');
     TextDisplay(1,50,'E-French');
     TextDisplay(1,60,'F-Science');
     ReadLn;
     CloseGraph;
END. {C18Q3}
```

Object-oriented Programming - section 19.9

1.
```
UNIT shapes;
INTERFACE
USES Graph, Crt;
TYPE
     point=OBJECT
              x,y:INTEGER;
              CONSTRUCTOR initialise(NewX, NewY:INTEGER);
              DESTRUCTOR finalise; VIRTUAL;
              PROCEDURE plot; VIRTUAL;
              PROCEDURE erase; VIRTUAL;
              FUNCTION GetX:INTEGER; VIRTUAL;
              FUNCTION GetY:INTEGER; VIRTUAL;
              PROCEDURE move(toX, toY:INTEGER);
          END;

     VertLine=OBJECT(point)
              X1,Y1,X2,Y2:INTEGER;
              CONSTRUCTOR initialise(NewX1,NewY1,NewX2,NewY2:INTEGER);
              PROCEDURE plot;VIRTUAL;
              PROCEDURE erase; VIRTUAL;
          END;

     HorizLine=OBJECT(VertLine)
              CONSTRUCTOR initialise(NewX1,NewY1,NewX2,NewY2:INTEGER);
              PROCEDURE plot;VIRTUAL;
              PROCEDURE erase;VIRTUAL;
          END;

     triangle=OBJECT(point)
              side:INTEGER;
              CONSTRUCTOR initialise(NewX, NewY, NewSide :INTEGER);
              PROCEDURE plot;VIRTUAL;
              PROCEDURE erase;VIRTUAL;
          END;

     square=OBJECT(point)
              side:INTEGER;
              CONSTRUCTOR initialise(NewX, NewY, NewSide :INTEGER);
              PROCEDURE plot;VIRTUAL;
              PROCEDURE erase;VIRTUAL;
          END;

     rect=OBJECT(point)
          side1, side2:INTEGER;
          CONSTRUCTOR initialise(NewX, NewY, NewSide1, NewSide2 :INTEGER);
          PROCEDURE plot;VIRTUAL;
          PROCEDURE erase;VIRTUAL;
        END;
```

```
        circ=OBJECT(point)
              radius:INTEGER;
              CONSTRUCTOR initialise(NewX, NewY, NewRadius :INTEGER);
              PROCEDURE plot; VIRTUAL;
              PROCEDURE erase; VIRTUAL;
        END;

IMPLEMENTATION
VAR
      GraphDriver, GraphMode : INTEGER;

CONSTRUCTOR point.initialise(NewX, NewY:INTEGER);
BEGIN
      x:=NewX;
      y:=NewY;
END; {point.initialise}

DESTRUCTOR point.finalise;
BEGIN
END; {point.finalise}

PROCEDURE point.plot;
BEGIN
      PutPixel(x,y,GetColor);
END; {point.plot}

PROCEDURE point.erase;
BEGIN
      PutPixel(x,y,GetBkColor);
END; {point.erase}

FUNCTION point.GetX:INTEGER;
BEGIN
      GetX:=x;
END; {point.GetX}

FUNCTION point.GetY:INTEGER;
BEGIN
      GetY:=y;
END; {point.GetY}

PROCEDURE point.move(toX, toY:INTEGER);
BEGIN
      erase;
      x:=toX;
      y:=toY;
      plot;
END; {point.move}

CONSTRUCTOR VertLine.initialise(NewX1,NewY1,NewX2,NewY2:INTEGER);
BEGIN
      X1:=NewX1; Y1:=NewY1; X2:=NewX2; Y2:=NewY2;
      x:=(X1+X2) DIV 2;
      y:=(Y1+Y2) DIV 2;
END; {VertLine.initialise}
```

```
PROCEDURE VertLine.plot;
VAR
      length:INTEGER;
BEGIN
      length:=ABS(Y2-Y1);
      Line(x,y,x,y-length DIV 2); Line(x,y,x,y+length DIV 2);
END; {VertLine.plot}

PROCEDURE VertLine.erase;
VAR
      Colour:WORD;
BEGIN
      Colour:=GetColor;
      SetColor(GetBkColor);
      VertLine.plot;
      SetColor(Colour);
END; {VertLine.erase}

CONSTRUCTOR HorizLine.initialise(NewX1,NewY1,NewX2,NewY2:INTEGER);
BEGIN
      VertLine.initialise(NewX1,NewY1,NewX2,NewY2);
END; {HorizLine.initialise}

PROCEDURE HorizLine.Plot;
VAR
      length:INTEGER;
BEGIN
      length:=ABS(X2-X1);
      Line(x,y,x-length DIV 2,y); Line(x,y,x+length DIV 2,y);
END; {HorizLine.Plot}

PROCEDURE HorizLine.erase;
VAR
      Colour:WORD;
BEGIN
      Colour:=GetColor;
      SetColor(GetBkColor);
      HorizLine.plot;
      SetColor(Colour);
END; {HorizLine.erase}

CONSTRUCTOR triangle.initialise(NewX, NewY, NewSide:INTEGER);
BEGIN
      point.initialise(NewX, NewY);
      side:=NewSide;
END; {triangle.initialise}

PROCEDURE triangle.plot;
VAR
      Ax,Ay,Bx,By:INTEGER;
BEGIN
      Ax:=TRUNC(x-side/SQRT(2)); Ay:=TRUNC(y+side/SQRT(2));
      Bx:=TRUNC(x+side/SQRT(2)); By:=TRUNC(y+side/SQRT(2));
      Line(x,y,Ax,Ay);
```

```
        Line(x,y,Bx,By);
        Line(Ax,Ay,Bx,By);
END; {triangle.plot}

PROCEDURE triangle.erase;
VAR
      Colour:WORD;
BEGIN
      Colour:=GetColor;
      SetColor(GetBkColor);
      triangle.plot;
      SetColor(Colour);
END; {triangle.erase}

CONSTRUCTOR square.initialise(NewX, NewY, NewSide:INTEGER);
BEGIN
      point.initialise(NewX, NewY);
      side:=NewSide;
END; {square.initialise}

PROCEDURE square.plot;
VAR
      Ax,Ay,Bx,By:INTEGER;
BEGIN
      Ax:=x; Ay:=y-side;
      Bx:=x+side; By:=y;
      Rectangle(Ax,Ay,Bx,By);
END; {square.plot}

PROCEDURE square.erase;
VAR
      Colour:WORD;
BEGIN
      Colour:=GetColor;
      SetColor(GetBkColor);
      square.plot;
      SetColor(Colour);
END; {square.erase}

CONSTRUCTOR rect.initialise(NewX, NewY, NewSide1, NewSide2:INTEGER);
BEGIN
      point.initialise(NewX, NewY);
      side1:=NewSide1;
      side2:=NewSide2;
END; {rect.initialise}

PROCEDURE rect.plot;
VAR
      Ax,Ay,Bx,By:INTEGER;
BEGIN
      Ax:=x; Ay:=y-side1;
      Bx:=x+side2; By:=y;
      Rectangle(Ax,Ay,Bx,By);
END; {rect.plot}
```

```pascal
PROCEDURE rect.erase;
VAR
      Colour:WORD;
BEGIN
      Colour:=GetColor;
      SetColor(GetBkColor);
      rect.plot;
      SetColor(Colour);
END; {rect.erase}

CONSTRUCTOR circ.initialise(NewX, NewY, NewRadius:INTEGER);
BEGIN
      point.initialise(NewX, NewY);
      radius:=NewRadius;
END; {circ.initialise}

PROCEDURE circ.plot;
BEGIN
      Circle(x,y,radius)
END; {circ.plot}

PROCEDURE circ.erase;
VAR
      Colour:WORD;
BEGIN
      Colour:=GetColor;
      SetColor(GetBkColor);
      circ.plot;
      SetColor(Colour);
END; {circ.erase}

BEGIN
      GraphDriver:=Detect;
      InitGraph(GraphDriver, GraphMode, ");
      IF GraphResult < > grOK THEN
         HALT;
      {end if}
END. {shapes}
```

2.
```pascal
PROGRAM C19Q2;
USES shapes, Crt;
VAR
      stripe1, stripe2:HorizLine;
      bonnet:square;
      body:rect;
      spoiler:triangle;
      FrontWheel, RearWheel:circ;

FUNCTION direction(VAR Xinc:INTEGER):BOOLEAN;
VAR
      KeyChar:CHAR;
      quit:BOOLEAN;
BEGIN
      Xinc:=0;
```

```
        direction:=TRUE;
        REPEAT
           KeyChar:=ReadKey;
           quit:=TRUE;
           CASE ORD(KeyChar) OF
           0:  BEGIN
                  KeyChar:=ReadKey;
                  CASE ORD(KeyChar) OF
                  75:Xinc:=-1;
                  77:Xinc:=+1;
                  ELSE
                     quit:=FALSE;
                  END;
              END;
           13:direction:=FALSE;
           ELSE
               quit:=FALSE;
           END;
        UNTIL quit;
END; {direction}

PROCEDURE MoveFigure;
VAR
        Xinc,displacement:INTEGER;
        stripe1X,stripe1Y,stripe2X,stripe2Y:INTEGER;
        bonnetX,bonnetY,bodyX,bodyY,FrontWheelX,FrontWheelY:INTEGER;
        spoilerX,spoilerY:INTEGER;
        RearWheelX,RearWheelY:INTEGER;
BEGIN
        stripe1X:=stripe1.GetX;stripe1Y:=stripe1.GetY;
        stripe2X:=stripe2.GetX;stripe2Y:=stripe2.GetY;
        bonnetX:=bonnet.GetX;bonnetY:=bonnet.GetY;
        bodyX:=body.GetX;bodyY:=body.GetY;
        spoilerX:=spoiler.GetX;spoilerY:=spoiler.GetY;
        FrontWheelX:=FrontWheel.GetX;FrontWheelY:=FrontWheel.GetY;
        RearWheelX:=RearWheel.GetX;RearWheelY:=RearWheel.GetY;
        WHILE direction(Xinc) DO
        BEGIN
           displacement:=Xinc*5;
           stripe1X:=stripe1X+displacement;
           stripe2X:=stripe2X+displacement;
           bonnetX:=bonnetX+displacement;
           bodyX:=bodyX+displacement;
           spoilerX:=spoilerX+displacement;
           FrontWheelX:=FrontWheelX+displacement;
           RearWheelX:=RearWheelX+displacement;
           stripe1.move(stripe1X,stripe1Y);
           stripe2.move(stripe2X,stripe2Y);
           bonnet.move(bonnetX,bonnetY);
           body.move(bodyX,bodyY);
           spoiler.move(spoilerX,spoilerY);
           FrontWheel.move(FrontWheelX,FrontWheelY);
           RearWheel.move(RearWheelX,RearWheelY);
        END;
END; {MoveFigure}
```

```
BEGIN
      bonnet.initialise(100,200,50);
      bonnet.plot;
      body.initialise(150,200,100,200);
      body.plot;
      stripe1.initialise(175,175,325,175);
      stripe1.plot;
      stripe2.initialise(175,170,325,170);
      stripe2.plot;
      spoiler.initialise(165,86,20);
      spoiler.plot;
      FrontWheel.initialise(120,220,20);
      RearWheel.initialise(300,220,20);
      FrontWheel.plot; RearWheel.plot;
      MoveFigure;
END. {C19Q2}
```

program

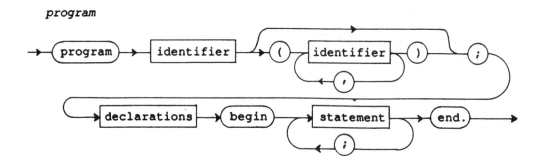

declarations

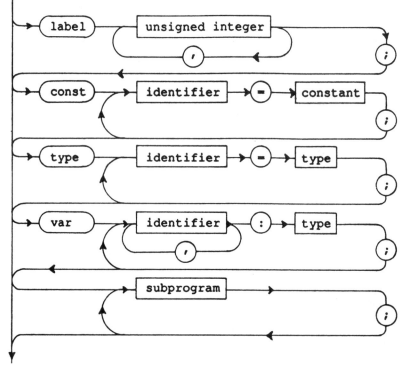

subprogram

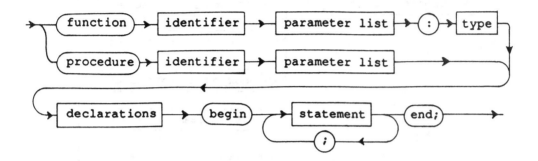

parameter list

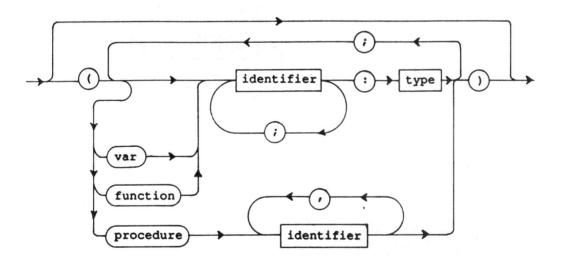

statement

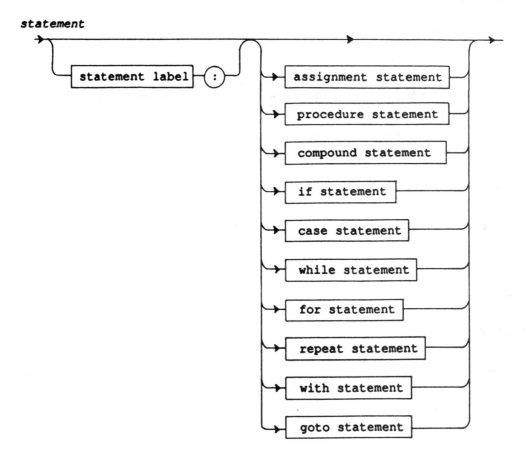

assignment statement

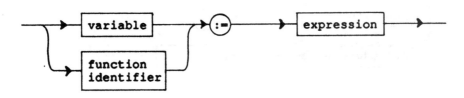

procedure statement

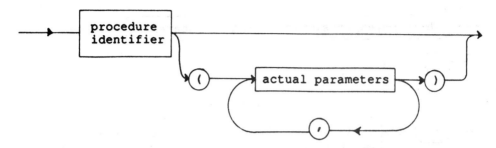

compound statement

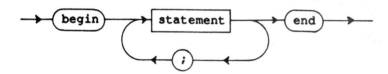

if statement

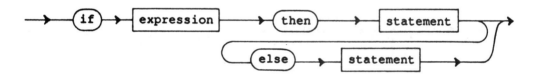

case statement

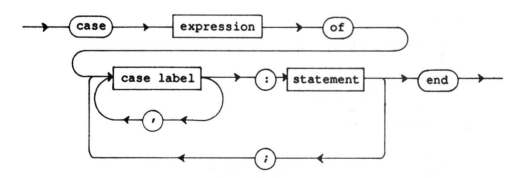

while statement

for statement

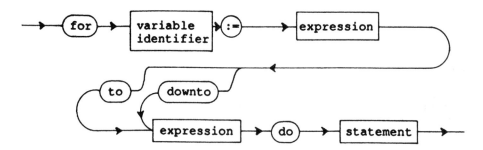

repeat statement

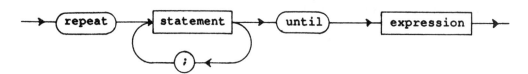

with statement

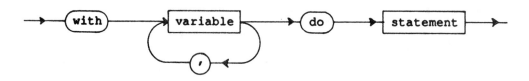

goto statement

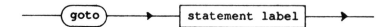

actual parameter

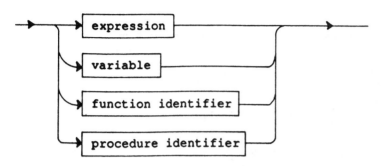

expression

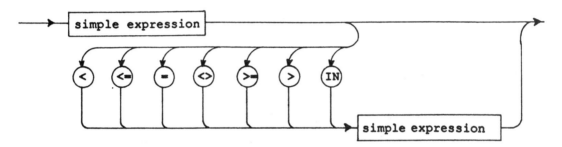

simple expression

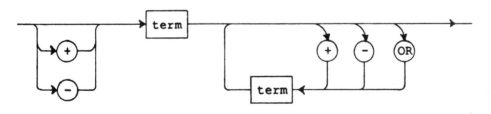

term

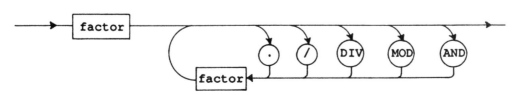

factor

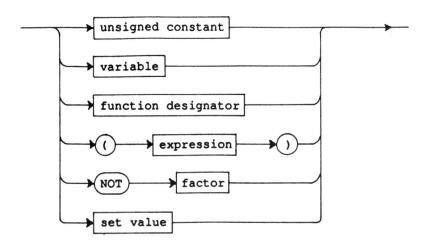

function designator

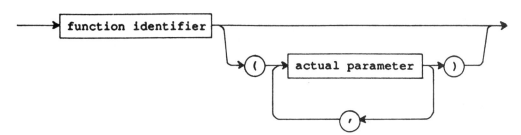

set value

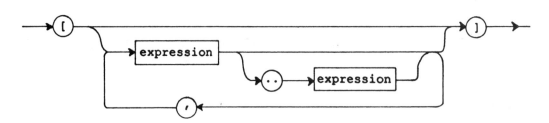

variable

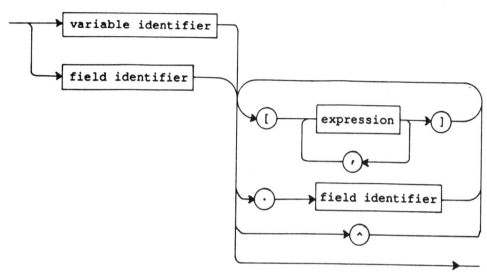

unsigned constant

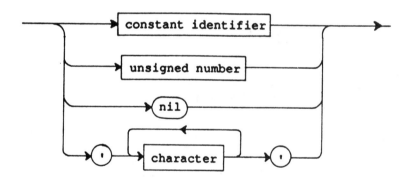

constant

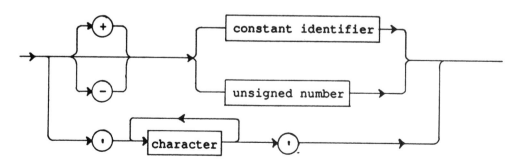

simple type

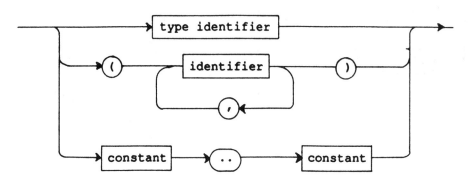

type

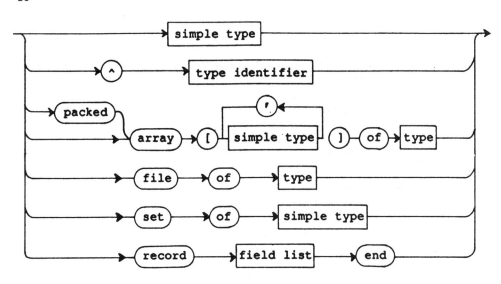

field list

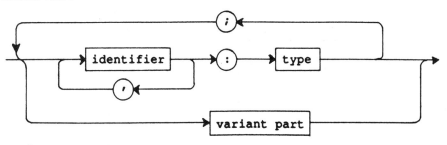

variant part

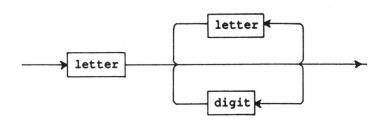

identifier

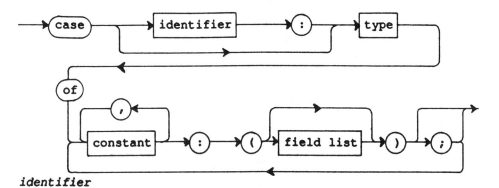

unsigned integer

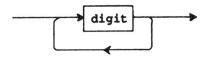

unsigned number

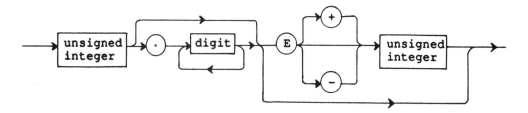

letter

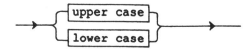

upper case

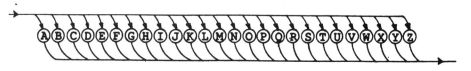

lower case

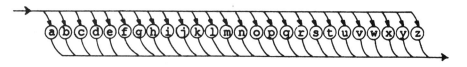

digits

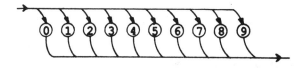

Bibliography

Borland International Inc. Turbo Pascal version 5.0 Reference Guide, 1989

Borland International Inc. Turbo Pascal version 5.0 User's Guide, 1989

Borland International Inc. Turbo Pascal version 5.5 Object-oriented Programming Guide, 1988

Cooper, D. Standard Pascal User Reference Manual, 1983, WW Norton & Co.

Findlay, W. & Watt, D. Pascal - An introduction to Methodical Programming, 1982, Pitman

Forsyth, R.S. Pascal at Work and Play, 1982, Chapman Hall

French, C.S. Computer Science, 1980, DP Publiactions Ltd

Gilbert, R.J. The University of Sheffield Pascal System for PRIME computers, 1986.

Helman, P. & Veroff, R. Intermediate Problem Solving and Data Structures, 1986, Benjamin Cummings

Holmes, B.J. Modula-2 Programming, 1989, DP Publications Ltd

Holmes, B.J. Pascal Programming - First Edition, 1987, DP Publications Ltd

Jensen, K. & Wirth, N. Pascal - User Manual and Report - second edition, 1975, Springer-Verlag

Koffman, E.B. Problem Solving and Structured Programming in Pascal, 1981, Addison Wesley

Meyer, B. Object-oriented Software Construction, 1988, Prentice-Hall

Plews, C. Pascal Programming, Oxford Polytechnic Computer Centre, 1984

Skvarcius, R. Problem Solving using Pascal, 1984, PWS Publications

Stubbs, D.F. & Webre, N.W. Data Structures and Abstract Data Types and Pascal, 1985, Brooks/Cole

Wiener, R.S. & Pinson, L.J. An Introduction to Object-oriented Programming and C++, 1988, Addison Wesley

Index